Keywords for Children's Literature, Second Edition

Keywords

Collaborative in design and execution, the books in the Keywords series bring together scholars across a wide range of disciplines in the humanities and social sciences. These books speak to today's most dynamic and vexed discussions of political and social life, both inside and outside of the academy.

For additional online resources, visit:
keywords.nyupress.org

Keywords for African American Studies
Edited by Erica R. Edwards, Roderick A. Ferguson, and Jeffrey O. G. Ogbar

Keywords for American Cultural Studies, Third Edition
Edited by Bruce Burgett and Glenn Hendler

Keywords for Asian American Studies
Edited by Cathy J. Schlund-Vials, Linda Trinh Võ, and K. Scott Wong

Keywords for Children's Literature, Second Edition
Edited by Philip Nel, Lissa Paul, and Nina Christensen

Keywords for Disability Studies
Edited by Rachel Adams, Benjamin Reiss, and David Serlin

Keywords for Environmental Studies
Edited by Joni Adamson, William A. Gleason, and David N. Pellow

Keywords for Latina/o Studies
Edited by Deborah R. Vargas, Nancy Raquel Mirabal, and Lawrence La Fountain-Stokes

Keywords for Media Studies
Edited by Laurie Ouellette and Jonathan Gray

Keywords for Children's Literature

Second Edition

Edited by

Philip Nel, Lissa Paul, and Nina Christensen

NEW YORK UNIVERSITY PRESS New York

NEW YORK UNIVERSITY PRESS
New York
www.nyupress.org

References to internet websites (URLs) were accurate at the time of writing. Neither the author nor New York University Press is responsible for URLs that may have expired or changed since the manuscript was prepared.

Library of Congress Cataloging-in-Publication Data

Names: Nel, Philip, 1969- editor. | Paul, Lissa, editor. | Christensen, Nina, 1968- editor.
Title: Keywords for children's literature / edited by Philip Nel, Lissa Paul, and Nina Christensen.
Description: Second edition. | New York: New York University Press, [2021] | Series: Keywords | Includes bibliographical references and index.
Identifiers: LCCN 2020015860 (print) | LCCN 2020015861 (ebook) | ISBN 9781479843695 (hardback) | ISBN 9781479899678 (paperback) | ISBN 9781479885435 (ebook) | ISBN 9781479843664 (ebook)
Subjects: LCSH: Children's literature—History and criticism—Terminology.
Classification: LCC PN1009.A1 K48 2021 (print) | LCC PN1009.A1 (ebook) | DDC 809/.89282014—dc22
LC record available at https://lccn.loc.gov/2020015860
LC ebook record available at https://lccn.loc.gov/2020015861

New York University Press books are printed on acid-free paper, and their binding materials are chosen for strength and durability. We strive to use environmentally responsible suppliers and materials to the greatest extent possible in publishing our books.

Manufactured in the United States of America

10 9 8 7 6 5 4 3 2 1

Also available as an ebook

Contents

The following essays are available online at
keywords.nyupress.org

Expanding the Map

An Introduction to the Second Edition

Philip Nel, Lissa Paul, and Nina Christensen

We organize information on maps in order to see our knowledge in a new way. As a result, maps suggest explanations; and while explanations reassure us, they also inspire us to ask more questions, consider other possibilities.

To ask for a map is to say, "Tell me a story."

—Peter Turchi, *Maps of the Imagination: The Writer as Cartographer*

Depending on their field, readers and scholars of children's literature may see the word *keyword* as a search term, or a designation for the limited-vocabulary words of a British reading primer from the 1960s, or perhaps an entry in a scholarly dictionary. The word *keyword* is itself a keyword in Raymond Williams's sense: a commonly used term that people assume has a shared meaning but in fact lacks this shared meaning. Because they are words about which there is some debate, keywords reveal conflicts. They are words that, in Williams's phrase, "involve ideas and values" (1983b, 17).

The essays in *Keywords for Children's Literature* offer a cartography of fissures in meaning and the etymological and ideological tensions they produce. Each keywords essay explains where a critical idea came from, what it means, and why its meanings shift. It offers expository theory, charting a constellation of connotations, and striving for a balance between several elements: an account of the word's origins, the different and conflicting ways that the word figures in discussions of children's literature and culture, and diverse examples from creative work and criticism. All of this needs to fit in an essay of roughly 1,500 words.

The keywords essay's intricate structure can make it feel more like writing a poem or assembling a puzzle. It is not a typical thesis-driven critical essay, and yet it does have an implied thesis communicated through its structure and the particular critical debates illuminated therein. Though it is compact like the encyclopedia entry, it is not within that informational genre because its emphasis is on the tensions in the term rather than on information. Indeed, though this book's alphabetical organization might suggest a reference work, *Keywords for Children's Literature* is not a reference work. As Williams said of his project, we say of ours: It is "not a dictionary or glossary," nor is it "a series of footnotes to dictionary histories." Instead, it is "the record of an inquiry into a vocabulary" (1983b, 15)—in this case, a vocabulary related to children and children's literature. These essays offer speculative, particular, subjective mappings of key questions that circle around a term. They provide not a definition but the beginning of a conversation. In this sense, our book strives to be not definitive but rather generative, launching scholars (whether beginning or advanced) on to new fields of inquiry.

This second edition of *Keywords for Children's Literature* expands its own field of inquiry. Unlike the first edition, the second is explicitly international. When, in his *Keywords*, Williams gestures toward and ultimately defers the possibility of internationalizing his own book, we sympathize. As he writes,

> I have had enough experience of trying to discuss two key English Marxist terms—*base* and *superstructure*—not only in relation to their German originals, but in discussions with French, Italian, Spanish, Russian and Swedish friends, in relation to their forms in these other languages, to know not only that the results are fascinating and difficult, but that such comparative analysis is crucially important, not just as philology, but as a central matter of intellectual clarity. It is greatly to be hoped that ways will be found of encouraging and supporting these comparative inquiries, but meanwhile it should be recorded that while some key developments, now of international importance, occurred first in English, many did not and in the end can only be understood when other languages are brought consistently into comparison. (1983b, 20)

We understand why he settled on the aspirational "It is greatly to be hoped that" and an affirmation of cross-cultural, transnational, multilingual work. Such "comparative work" is, as he says, "crucially important," "fascinating and difficult." More difficult than we at first realized. We thank our Keywords 2.0 International Advisory Board for helping each essay meet this edition's international mandate. The advisory board was an invaluable resource, guiding us to literary works and scholarship beyond our own narrowly national knowledges.

Our own efforts toward internationalizing these essays often reminded us of how deeply children's literature and its scholarship are rooted in national traditions. For most of us, knowledge of children's books begins growing within the national context of our own childhoods, and then we graft on shoots from foreign plants. During the process of editing these essays, the contours of an unofficial transnational canon of children's literature has emerged, including authors such as Astrid Lindgren, Tove Jansson, Erich Kästner, Charles Perrault, J. K. Rowling, Hans Christian Andersen, and Lewis Carroll. Each essay references some works in this widely translated Western canon and introduces works that are indispensable and well known in specific national, geographical, or cultural contexts. In this way, the essays can expand our knowledge of children's literature that originates outside of our own linguistic context.

Keywords for Children's Literature does not mark the first time that a book in NYU Press's Keywords series has a chapter title in more than one language. (Vargas, Mirabal, and La Fountain-Stokes's *Keywords for Latina/o Studies* [2017] may hold that distinction.) But the essays do explore how linguistic variation creates variant understandings. Vanessa Joosen's "Fairy Tale / Märchen" indicates how different etymologies gesture toward different histories. The English *fairy tale* and French *conte de fées* denote "stories about fairies," evoking the tales' emergence from eighteenth-century French salon culture and offering a description of the genre. As Joosen says, "Many of the most popular fairy tales today—think of 'Snow White,' 'Little Red Riding Hood' or 'The Ugly Duckling'—do not contain any fairies." In contrast, both *Märchen* and its Dutch counterpart, *sprookje*, are diminutives (perhaps, she says, "an indication of the belittlement of fairy tales by the literary establishment") and refer to the contested issue of whether these tales originate in oral narratives. In its venture into divergent etymologies, Charles Hatfield's "Graphic Novel / Comics" essay points out that *comics* abbreviates *comic weeklies* and thus "highlights the medium's links to jokes." However, the "term for comics in Danish and Swedish are, respectively, *tegneserie* and *tecknade serier*, which literally mean 'drawn serial,' emphasizing the seriality of the medium." In writing about *Boyhood*, Eric Tribunella notes that "Scandinavian languages—Danish, Norwegian, and Swedish—share the word *barndom*, a term for childhood that can apply to both boys and girls, but lack an exact term for *boyhood* and *girlhood*." Differences in languages not only point to distinctions between (and similarities among) national traditions but—in showing how words' histories establish the parameters of inquiry—suggest how etymology shapes ontology. Even the best translation cannot fully convey the nuances of the translated term.

Ebony Elizabeth Thomas's "Diversity," Debra Dudek's "Multicultural," and Katharine Capshaw's "Race" illuminate the variance in conversations surrounding difference. If Canada and the US conceive of national identity as inherently multicultural, European countries traditionally imagine national identity as more monocultural: as a result, in North America, diversity discourse emphasizes respecting differences between people within national borders; in Europe, imagology discourse advocates respecting different people beyond national borders. However, as indicated by that *if*, the previous sentence's apparently tidy distinction bumps into a messier history. In North America, citizenship has typically depended on one's proximity to the shifting boundaries of Whiteness,[1] an

elision of the colonizer's theft of Indigenous land. In a comparable effacement of its own racialized past, the European tendency to consider multiculturalism (when acknowledged) as a relatively recent (post–World War II) phenomenon ignores both the legacy of colonialism and the long history of Black Africans and other non-White populations in Europe. Many laborers arriving in Europe after the Second World War were citizens or ex-citizens of a colonizing European power (Chin 2017).

One of the most important global problems today is the mistreatment of children of different ethnic groups, cultures, religions, and nationalities. In both literature and the world, children are refugees, migrants, and members of diasporic communities. In the English-speaking world, attempts to understand their experiences are reflected in terms like *authenticity*, *diaspora*, *Indigenous*, and *race*. In a European context, the word *race* had all but disappeared from serious or scientific contexts, since during World War II, Germany's Nazi government (and its allies) used the term to justify the murder of six million Jews, up to half a million Gypsies, and many others it deemed "genetically" inferior. Recently, it has begun to return as a way of naming and diagnosing the surge in legal, social, and physical violence directed at racial and ethnic minorities. While we were editing this book, the European immigration crisis that began in 2015 and the rise of right-wing movements in many countries have underscored the necessity of a transnational language for addressing these issues and for children's books that promote multicultural democracy and international understanding.

The second edition of *Keywords for Children's Literature* began in international conversation. Invited by

1   In our introduction and in some essays, the *B* in *Black* and the *W* in *White* receive capital letters when they refer to races. Capitalization distinguishes race from color (since race is not color) and echoes the US Census, which capitalizes all racial and ethnic categories, including White. In recognition

of the fact that this is an international volume (and that capitalizing is not yet standard), we have respected authors' preferences, allowing for variance in capitalizing these (and variants of these) words.

Nina Christensen and Kristin Ørjasæter, Phil and Lissa gave a talk on the first edition at the conference Nordic Children's Literature—a New Research Question? (Nordisk barnelitteratur—et nytt kunstforskningsspørsmål?) in Oslo, Norway, in August 2012. Nordic scholars of children's literature asked Lissa and Phil to explain why our map of keywords in the field did not include more examples beyond Anglo-Saxon traditions. The simple answer is that we had deliberately planned it that way. As the first edition's introduction notes, we anchored it in "traditions in English" in order to keep the volume manageable and increase the likelihood of particular works of children's literature cropping up repeatedly. However, like two-dimensional Mercator projection maps, Anglocentrism in children's literature criticism distorts the global picture. While access to nonanglophone primary works of literature may impede those of us who do not speak the language, the fact that significant critical terms vary from culture to culture and from language to language requires that we make the effort. A term such as *African American*, though completely intelligible and even expected in North American contexts, reads as obliquely insulting in its neglect of African diasporic literatures and cultures. And though *Indigenous* is understood as an essential term in the "settler" cultures of Australia and the Americas, its relevance is not always clear to people from other parts of the world.

Inspired by their conversations in Norway, Lissa and Phil assembled an international roundtable discussion on *Keywords for Children's Literature* at the International Research Society for Children's Literature conference in Maastricht in August 2013. They invited a critique from panelists based in four different countries—Nina Alonso (Luxembourg), Nina Christensen (Denmark), Francesca Orestano (Italy), and Emer O'Sullivan (Germany)—and from an audience composed of people from many more countries. Phil and Lissa invited all to respond to these two questions:

1. Are there well-known texts in your language or country that ought to be included in *Keywords for Children's Literature*? Which keywords do these texts speak to? Offer an example of how a specific keyword might be applied to this text.
2. Are there missing keywords specific to your language, culture, or country? As per the book, we are interested in words that are crucial to the discussion of children's literature but also that are contested or conflicted.

Lissa and Phil noted that they had already identified *poetry, fairy tale, family,* and *genre* as keywords to include in a second edition. They spent the rest of the session listening and taking notes. Those suggestions provided valuable insights and areas to consider pursuing, should sales of the first edition justify a second. When in October 2015 Eric Zinner told Lissa and Phil that sales did warrant a second edition, they invited Nina Christensen to join the editorial team.

Having editors from three different countries (US, Canada, Denmark) broadens our international range of knowledge, and one editor from a non-Anglo country helps make the book less Anglo-centric. We have contributors who are natives of twelve different countries: Australia, Belgium, Canada, Denmark, England, France, Germany, Ireland, Netherlands, Norway, Scotland, Sweden, and the US. We established an international advisory board to help internationalize both the words revised for and the words new to the second print edition. The international advisory board includes scholars who either are based in or were born in Australia, Belgium, Brazil, Canada, England, France, Germany, Italy, Luxembourg, Netherlands, Norway, the Philippines, Poland, Spain, Sweden, and the US. In addition, we have included contributors for whom English is not their first language and who specialize in non-English children's literature and culture.

Yet we are also aware that covering a term's history and use in the children's literature of all 196 countries on this planet is well beyond the scope of what any of these essays can accomplish. Since our contributors could not be expected to internationalize to that extent, we encouraged them to seek interesting national or linguistic differences in use and to include examples from children's literatures in different countries. Like Alice after her fall through the rabbit hole to Wonderland, we knew that there were undiscovered countries lying just out of sight. The second edition of *Keywords for Children's Literature* does not claim to offer a complete map of the field. We have instead had as our goal a map with fewer blank spaces—a map that will, like all maps, need to be redrawn as the landscape changes. That said, our efforts to internationalize have made us more acutely aware of our omissions. We acknowledge the absence—both on our advisory board and among contributors—of Bangladesh, China, Cuba, Egypt, Haiti, India, Indonesia, Japan, Nigeria, Pakistan, and Russia, among many others. We hope that colleagues—especially the emerging young scholars from Asia, Africa, and Latin America—will write the scholarship that fills these gaps, hold us accountable for our inadvertent elisions, and help the next edition of this book and our scholarly community become more truly international.

Since they necessarily omit, maps always raise questions of inclusion. Fortunately, NYU Press's Keywords website allows the expansion of our map without losing any of the first edition's cartography. All words omitted from the codex version of the second edition are available for free on the Keywords website in perpetuity. Reasons vary for their relocation from print to web. Some were too narrowly American and so did not fit our

international emphasis. Reflecting the temporality of any such endeavor, other words seemed less central to the conversation than they were ten years ago. Finally, we wanted all returning essays to be updated for the second edition, but not everyone could commit to a revised version for various reasons, including other demands on their time, retirement, ill health, and death. Though June Cummins (1963–2018), David Booth (1938–2018), and Margaret Meek Spencer (1925–2020) have left the map, their intellect continues to illuminate: on the Keywords website, their essays on "Marketing," "Censorship," and "Reading" still guide us through three tricky areas of the field.

The second edition of *Keywords for Children's Literature* arrives in what feels like a different world than the one in which the first edition appeared. As the postwar world order comes unraveled, so too has the post–Cold War hope in the historical inevitability of democracy and the consequent decline of totalitarianism. As the rise of the nativist right and xenophobia threaten democracies, a pandemic has killed 400,000 people (as of June 2020), and the pace of climate change endangers life on planet earth. Our impression is that this new edition emerges in a more perilous time for the planet and all who inhabit it. We realize that proximity to perilousness is not randomly distributed across age, race, gender, class, sexuality, gender identity, or region of the globe but is rather intersectional and concentrated in particular communities.

As an academic discipline, the landscape for studies in children's literature has also changed dramatically from the one into which our first edition was published in 2011. At the time, some of the authors felt the need to remark on the "lower-class" status of the discipline and the struggle for acknowledged standing as a scholarly field. The need for that kind of statement has all but evaporated in this second edition, published just ten years after the first. One reason is that there is now a second generation of scholars, many of whom hold PhDs in children's literature. That is a new phenomenon. In the 1970s, when the scholarly apparatus for the field was just beginning to be established, the academic homes of the people teaching the courses and publishing in newly established journals (*Barnboken*, *Children's Literature*, *Lion and the Unicorn*, *Signal*) had slipped into the field via a range of disparate disciplines: English literature, comparative literature, library and information studies, and education. The multidisciplinary origin of studies in children's literature has proven to be one of its lasting strengths.

Another substantial change within the field is the increasing intersection among children's literature studies, childhood studies, and media studies. In many countries, children's literature studies emerged in departments of languages and literature, where literary history and textual analysis were at the core of research interests. Today, we see a shift from an interest in children primarily as implied readers toward interest in children as producers and users of texts. This development can be linked to the fact that childhood sociologists have underscored children's right to having an influence on their own lives, including their texts and media. This attention toward children's *agency* has been supported by the rapid development of media and platforms—smartphones, tablets, YouTube, and forums for fan fiction—which facilitate children's access to transnational means of production. A Harry Potter fan of the twenty-first century will meet this narrative in transmedial contexts: through books, movies, computer games, internet sites, clothes, illustrated books, and drama. The story's circulation in multiple media highlights the need for terms such as *book*, *play*, *adaptation*, *media*, and *intermedial*, all of which are included in this volume. All speak to the increasingly diversified ways in which young people access texts.

Within children's literature studies, neither the current inclusion of visual texts, audiobooks, and transmedia narratives nor an interest in important aspects of their content has diminished a commitment to form. For as long as scholars trained in languages and literature have studied children's literature, the field has paid close attention to how a text's formal elements make meaning. Studying the literariness of children's literature reminds readers that words not only impart information but evoke emotion, inspire reflection, and invite experimentation. Navigating the nonsense of Wonderland, Alice and the reader learn that language can be unstable, beautiful, powerful, and humorous. In the first edition of *Keywords to Children's Literature*, explorations of formal elements emerged in essays on "Aesthetics," "Nonsense," "Story," and "Voice" and in the current edition in the essays on "Poetry" and "Irony," among others.

In the 1970s, in the early days of modern children's literature studies, discussions on quests for (presumably) stable physical, national, or racial identities were standard subjects of scholarly interest. Today, in the age of LGBTQIA (lesbian, gay, bi, trans, queer, intersex, and asexual [or allied]), even the idea of stable identities seems quaint. At least twenty keywords essays, including Karen Coates's "Identity," speak to the ways that old identity categories have been dismantled and reassembled into a wide array of variations. Kelly Hager's "Body" essay brings into its orbit the essays on "Animal," "Posthuman," "Disability," "Gender," "Boyhood," "Girlhood," "Queer" and "Trans." Karen Sánchez-Eppler's essay on "Childhood" resonates through discussions of "Innocence," "Size," "Liminality," "Crossover," and "Voice." In this already crowded network of related ideas, Debra Dudek's "Multicultural" essay engages others on "Race," "Transnational," "Diaspora," and "Indigenous" in conversations about how children develop within (and in spite of) racially embodied structures of power.

Misuse of power has also shifted the book's emphasis away from Sherman Alexie's *The Absolutely True Diary of a Part-Time Indian* (2007). Although one of the most-cited works in the first edition, the novel appears less frequently in the second. One reason is that in meeting our international mandate, the second edition has less space for anglophone works. The other reason is that Alexie's sexual harassment of many women—which became public news in March 2018—has substantially altered his esteem among scholars of children's and young adult literature. The American Indian Library Association rescinded its 2008 Best Young Adult Book Award for *The Absolutely True Diary of a Part-Time Indian*, and the American Library Association, which had just announced Alexie's *You Don't Have to Say You Love Me: A Memoir* (2017) as the winner of its Carnegie Medal, gave no medal in 2018. Teachers are either changing their syllabi or changing the way they teach Alexie's work. Instead of only discussing his writing, scholars now also ask whether it is ethical to teach a writer who used his success to harm others.

When such an author writes for young readers, reckoning with the ugly facts of his or her biography collides with many assumptions about childhood and its literatures, notably the specter that an adult's moral corruption will—via a literary work—harm vulnerable young readers. After being convicted of eleven counts of assault against young girl fans, British fantasist William Mayne went to prison, and his works were removed from shelves and curricula. A member of the Danish Nazi Party and contributor to a Nazi newspaper during the occupation (1940–45), Harald Bergstedt spent two years in prison after the war, and his children's songs (and other work) were banned from Danish national radio until 1963. Belgian artist Hergé's characters remain beloved despite the fact that he published *Tintin* in fascist newspapers both before and during the Nazi occupation. There is an array of possible responses to artists who abuse their power or otherwise build their careers on the victimization of others, and in the spirit of the Keywords endeavor, our book catalogs the tension rather than insisting on a single answer. Some contributors separate art from artist, believing that a writer's personal failings have no bearing the greatness of their art. Others feel that there is no legacy so important that we can look the other way. As the American author Roxane Gay writes in her essay "Can I Enjoy the Art but Denounce the Artist?" (2018), "I no longer struggle with artistic legacies. It is not difficult to dismiss the work of predators and angry men because agonizing over a predator's legacy would mean there is some price I am willing to let victims pay for the sake of good art." The decision to retain, revise, or replace an Alexie reference maps a moral debate.

We think of these essays as *mapping meanings* because the goal of *Keywords for Children's Literature* is not to fix meanings in place but rather to delineate tentative boundaries of a shifting conversation. In this second edition, we have a more capacious sense of that conversation than we did in the first edition. Our book's aims still depart from those of Göte Klingberg, who in 1970 began an ultimately unfinished "Nomenklatur-Project" in order to develop a common vocabulary for children's literature scholars of different languages (Müller 2009). Where Klingberg hoped to "introduce genre concepts which can be strictly defined" (2008, 9), we strive not for strict definitions but cartographies of contested borders. However, we now include some "genre concepts" that we wrongly excluded from the first edition: "Fairy Tale / Märchen" and "Poetry." These have fostered the necessary degree of critical debate and thus are included, as has "Didactic," another term that can describe a genre.

Indeed, genre itself is the subject of a Keywords essay, in which its author, Karin Westman, notes, "Genre is an amorphous category whose definition shifts over time and context." Or, as Betty Fussell (2016) writes in a different context, "our minds and imaginations shape geographical facts, and our differing expectations create different landscapes" (44).

In resisting the totalizing impulse, *Keywords for Children's Literature* offers not a unified field theory but what Paul Saint Amour calls "weak theory." As Saint Amour (2018) writes, "there are specific, non-totalizing ways in which weak theory can get to grips with bad totalities. The challenge here, of course, would be keeping one's own theory weak rather than permitting it to drift toward doctrine, coherentism, triumphalism, and sovereign self-understanding." Weakness, in this sense, creates spaces for questions, dialogue, and collaboration. In describing rather than defining, this approach renders ambiguity with clarity, inviting critical engagement without proscribing the terms of that engagement: "A field's strength (in the normative sense)—its vitality, generativity, and populousness—may increase as the immanent theory of its central term weakens (in the descriptive sense). What I mean is that the less sovereign a hold the central term has upon the field it frames, the more ferment and recombination can occur within that field, and among more elements" (Saint Amour 2018).

Though Saint Amour makes these claims about modernism, their logics reverberate in the capacious and expanding world of children's literature. In delineating the topographical contours of our weak-boundaried field, *Keywords for Children's Literature* welcomes scholars—at any level—across its open borders. Ignore its alphabetical ordering and read the essays in any order you like, guided only by your particular interests. Bring ideas from your areas of expertise into this one, and carry ideas from here into your fields of inquiry. Pursue the connections that emerge when you find yourself interdisciplinarily intertwined. Listen to your doubts. Ask questions. Resist the comfort of easy answers. Challenge *our* map of the field. Shape the critical conversation. We look forward to seeing how you use this book and to learning from you, our readers.

A Note on Classroom Use

Philip Nel, Lissa Paul, and Nina Christensen

As we note at the end of our introduction, this book aspires to provoke questions, create dialogue, and invite collaboration. In that spirit, here are some suggestions for using the book in the classroom.

While editing this second, more international edition of *Keywords for Children's Literature*, we applied the lessons we were learning to our classroom practice. With the parameters outlined for the book's contributors so clearly in our minds, both Lissa Paul and Phil Nel set "keywords assignments" for their students in their respective master's level classes. Lissa's assignment was for students in the winter 2017 session of "Introduction to Social and Cultural Contexts of Education: Developing a Critical Language"; Phil's for the course "Critical Approaches to Children's Literature" in spring 2017. In pedagogical terms, we both decided to give our students "problem-based learning assignments"—that is, the tasks we assigned to our students closely resembled the ones we gave to established scholars. Phil and Lissa gave similar assignments to their students, though Lissa designated hers as keywords "for education" and Phil "for children's literature." To avoid repetition, we have reproduced an edited version of Phil's assignment here and are granting permission to use with appropriate credit.

Assignment

Write an essay for *Keywords for Children's Literature*. Your essay cannot be about a word that is already in the book.

It needs to be about a keyword that the book has failed to include.

Choosing a Word

Choose a word that is not only crucial to the discussion of children's literature but also contested or conflicted. As Raymond Williams wrote in his *Keywords* (1976, 1983b), keywords "involve ideas and values" and get used in "interesting or difficult ways"—and in different ways by different people. If you find that in critical conversations, a particular word is getting used in different ways by different people, then that is a candidate for your keyword. If you are stuck, take a second look at the introduction to *Keywords for Children's Literature*.

Writing the Essay

Adopting, modifying, and expanding criteria from Bennett, Grossberg and Morris's *New Keywords* and Burgett and Hendler's *Keywords for American Cultural Studies*, we have developed the following guidelines:

- Your definition should offer a scholarly account of the word's origins in your mother tongue and in any other language you are familiar with. You should focus on a particular interpretation of the word's significance for the study of children's literature, media, and culture. Please look at the relevant entry or entries from the *Oxford English*

Dictionary, the *Oxford Encyclopedia of Children's Literature,* or other relevant reference works that you might be able to access online via the databases at the library.

- In your very first paragraph, begin with a history of the keyword itself. From there, move on to the critical controversies in which this keyword is enmeshed.

- To quote the *New Keywords* editors, your essay "should offer concrete examples of usage." Those examples should come from children's literature (primarily) but can certainly include children's culture and media. You are encouraged to include examples from at least two countries in order to add an international dimension to your essay. These might be from English-speaking countries across the world or other transnational contexts.

- Include a bibliography of works cited at the end of your essay.

Though the instructions resemble those given to contributors to the first edition of *Keywords for Children's Literature,* we did of course recognize that the students were at the beginnings of their academic careers, and we judged their work accordingly. In addition, we want to note that since Lissa's students were encouraged to "think locally," her students made specific references to school boards in the Niagara region, to provincial (Ontario) guidelines, and to Canadian contexts.

Because Lissa asked her students to identify keywords associated with pedagogical discourse and the "social and cultural" contexts of the course, students addressed issues related to class, gender, age, ability, religion, and race. Words under discussion in class included *innocence, multicultural, race,* and *liminality,* among others from *Keywords for Children's Literature,* though the conversations expanded to include other critical terms such as

hegemony and *ideology.* All the theoretical discussions were set in conversation with works of children's literature in order to demonstrate the relationships between theory and practice. Throughout the term, Lissa was very pleased to find that the students used the experience of working with the essays they were reading to inform the essays they were writing.

Neither Phil nor Lissa was strict about essay length, but we aimed for around 1,500 words because that was the word count we set for contributors to the second edition. Lissa's students initially thought that they would be able to manage the relatively short format with ease. That was before Lissa kept turning the drafts back for revision and insisting that the students bring the same professionalism to their essays that we expect from the authors writing for the book. As students began critiquing one another's work, they also began to develop higher expectations for one another than they would typically have been accustomed to in a classroom context.

Throughout their courses, Phil and Lissa invited students to be receptive to potential keywords. When class discussions began to circulate around a particular idea, we (in our respective classes) would ask if that idea qualified as a keyword. In what different ways was the word being used? What ideas or values were at stake? Which literary texts might we discuss in such an essay? In Phil's course, all eighteen students were required to choose their keywords in the seventh week (Lissa's students had to choose sooner, by about the third week of their twelve-week course). In the twelfth week, Phil devoted one class day to workshopping the keywords papers: each student brought in multiple copies of a draft, and using a rubric, their fellow students evaluated the draft. (Having written a draft, several students also met with Phil to discuss the challenges they were facing.) Students then turned in and discussed their essays in class during the final week. As there were only six students in Lissa's graduate class, some class time was given most weeks to discussions on the progress of the essays. Lissa also met with each student for individual tutorials.

Lissa and Phil used the first edition of *Keywords for Children's Literature* as a core text in our respective classes and made donations to charity to offset the royalties (about a dollar) we receive for each book, Lissa to the Canadian Children's Book Centre and Phil to Reading Is Fundamental.

Nina has used single essays from the first edition in optional courses on children's literature and media at the graduate and undergraduate levels. For instance, Debra Dudek's essay "Multicultural" proved very useful and thought provoking when informing Danish students (and teachers) on the history and use of the concept in an Anglo-Saxon context and in discussions of Scandinavian examples and national discussions of the term. It is a challenge to transfer the uses of contested terms to new geographical and cultural settings, since terms naturally have very different histories, meanings, values, and uses, and knowledge of fictional and scholarly examples differs across the globe.

For instance, Danish students were surprised to learn that in Sweden, the picture book *Mustafas kiosk* (1999) by Jakob Martin Strid, a well-known and award-winning Danish children's poet and illustrator, was criticized for its depictions of the character named Mustafa. Danish readers would recognize Strid's style of drawing and be familiar with his critical and satirical attitude toward most aspects of life and society. However, in 2013, some Swedish readers called out Strid's illustrations for being offensive to minority groups. Such differences in the reception of specific words and images show us how cultural literacies emerge in dialogue among local, national, and international readers. Among the Danish students were teachers who had used Strid's book with a diverse group of children, and their arguments for and against

using the book put discussions of *Keywords* essays into perspective. Using the second edition, conversations about similar examples could be informed by essays such as "Authenticity," "Identity," "Taboo," "Irony," and "Nonsense" and thereby help students move beyond their own national knowledges.

During the editing process, we have been aware of the challenge of speaking across linguistic and cultural differences. As we have done while assembling this second edition, we encourage readers to pursue discussions of the interaction among local, national, and international aspects of children's literature. In adapting the keyword assignments to a particular national context, additional questions for students' production of their own keywords might include the following: How do your own linguistic or national contexts complicate or encourage a rethinking of a particular keyword essay? What would this information add to discussions of the term? Which local, cultural, or national parts of the etymology of the word, the history of use, and the discussions around the term are most relevant to include? How would examples of critical work and fiction from your local or national context enrich the discussions of the term?

Whether a person is an established scholar or a student, writing a keywords essay is one of the most challenging and intellectually rewarding assignments she or he can undertake. By compelling us to look closely at a single term's many and conflicting permutations, writing one of these essays shows us how words can obscure what they purport to reveal. In teaching us how language can conceal complexity, the keywords essay can create a richer, more nuanced relationship not just with education and children's literature but with discourse more generally. The process gives us what Williams calls "that extra edge of consciousness" (1983b, 24), enabling us to better examine our own acculturation and to develop our and our students' critical literacies.

1

Adult

Victoria Ford Smith

Adult derives from the Latin *adultus*: "full-grown, mature, firmly established." To be an adult, the root implies, is to reach the endpoint of a developmental arc—to attain the physical, behavioral, and social norms of maturity—but this fantasy of fulfillment is tenuous. *Adult*'s first *OED* definitions are adjectives, unmoored from a stable subject. *Adult* might make *any* person full grown; it also makes an attitude sophisticated or a movie erotic. *Adult*'s noun form—"a person who is fully developed; one who has reached maturity"—is similarly volatile, its boundaries porous enough to let in its supposed opposite, the child. Half the quotations the *OED* provides in support of this definition reference children, many aligning adult and child experiences. (Herbert Spencer, for example, wonders "what rights are common to children and adults.") Compounds yoke adults to ideas associated with young people: *adult student, adult illiteracy*. The word's desultory travel between subject and descriptor emphasizes the contradictions at its heart, inviting us to explore the fraught relationships between adult and child.

Scholars frequently cast adult-child relationships as oppositional and mutually constitutive. In *Centuries of Childhood* (1960), French historian Philippe Ariès claims societies invented childhood when they acknowledged what "distinguishes the child from the adult" (128). Subsequent studies insist on the importance but fragility of

the boundary between adult and child; in the 1980s, Neil Postman lamented the erosion of "the dividing line between childhood and adulthood" (1982, xii). Despite such anxieties, the adult remains a flexible and remarkably resilient antonym for the child, reinforced by legal norms such as ages of consent and political participation that mark (arbitrarily) a young person's acquisition of the rights and responsibilities associated with maturity. Spaces such as the school or nursery allow adults to both isolate and regulate children's bodies but are, in turn, often featured as home base in texts that playfully exclude adults, as in the work of E. Nesbit.

The adult-child binary leads scholars to parse the characteristics we assign each: innocence versus knowingness, vulnerability versus power. These oppositions form the bedrock of the most persistent notions of childhood, including the Romanticism epitomized in Wordsworth's cloud-bedecked infant, a creature alien to the experience-imprisoned adult, or the nostalgic moppets championed by some Golden Age authors who exile children to Wonderlands inaccessible to adults. The opposition between adult and child also lurks in the intergenerational enmity often at the center of children's books: Roald Dahl's Matilda battles the Trunchbull; Pan terrorizes Hook. According to Jacqueline Rose, Perry Nodelman, James Kincaid, and Karín Lesnik-Oberstein, our insistence on imagining adult and child as contraries reveals that childhood is a construction that responds to adult desires from the nostalgic to the sexual.

Critical accounts of children's literature posit that the stark divide between adult and child continues to shape the genre in profound ways. In *The Pleasures of Children's Literature*, Nodelman and Mavis Reimer argue that children's literature could not exist "until adults came to believe that children were different from adults in ways that made them need a literature of their own" (2003, 81). In turn, adults—whose social and economic power exceeds that of children—create and purchase books that produce docile or desirable children inside and outside the text. One of the most fertile lines of inquiry in children's literature scholarship since the field's origins has been the interrogation of children's culture as a vehicle for adult ideologies. In *The Hidden Adult*, Nodelman argues children's literature is "an adult practice with intentions toward child readers" (2008, 4), while others examine the particular historical circumstances that drive adults to use children's literature as a mouthpiece. In *Learning from the Left*, for example, Julia Mickenberg identifies children's texts as "a key outlet for leftists in the mid-twentieth century"; radical writers turned to young audiences because "other avenues were closed to them" or because they sought to "influence the future through the younger generation" (2005, 5). Such studies assume, to varying degrees, models of adult authority and child receptivity figured as author-audience, teacher-student, parent-child, or colonizer-colonized.

In response, some consider the ways children's literature militates against adult authority, destabilizing the adult-child binary that assumes the former's power. While Maria Nikolajeva acknowledges the "aetonormativity" of children's literature—the "asymmetry between children and adults" that "governs the way children's literature has been patterned from its emergence until the present day" (2010, 8)—she argues that children's literature can "subvert its own oppressive function" (9), pointing to Astrid Lindgren's *Pippi Långstrump* (1945; trans. *Pippi Longstocking*, 1950) and its heroine's strength and social capital. Similar reversals motivate F. Anstey's *Vice Versa* (1882), Janusz Korczak's *Król Maciuś Pierwszy* (*King Matt the First*; 1986), and Mary Rodgers's *Freaky Friday* (1972). Cross-writing—defined variously as the simultaneous address of adults and children, the "dialogic mix of older and younger voices," or the movement of texts across audiences—disrupts hierarchies of adult author and child receiver (Knoepflmacher and Myers 1997; Falconer 2009). Sandra Beckett notes that this blurring of audiences has generated cross-linguistic terms—Norway's *allalderslitteratur* (literature for all ages) and Germany's *Bruckenliteratur* (bridge literature)—and has led to presses like Spain's Las Tres Edades (The Three Ages). Cross-writing reminds us that the divide between adults' and children's literature has always shifted and sometimes disappeared. Consider H. Rider Haggard's *King Solomon's Mines* (1885), dedicated to "all the big and little boys," and nineteenth-century American children's poetry, which Angela Sorby and Karen Kilcup argue was both connected to and distinct from adult verse.

In tension with the adult-child opposition is the assumption that children follow a linear trajectory of growth into adulthood. This model emerges in developmental theories by Piaget, Freud, Erikson, and Froebel as well as in contemporary theories in psychology and sociology that outline norms in mental, biological, and social development (Hockney and James 2003; Mintz 2015). In children's literature, familiar plot patterns and genres—the didactic text, the home-away-home narrative, the bildungsroman—reiterate growth from child to adult (Trites 1998; Tribunella 2010), while texts such as E. B. White's *Charlotte's Web* (1952) or Natalie Babbitt's *Tuck Everlasting* (1975) feature protagonists who learn the proper progression of childhood, maturation, and death. Roberta Seelinger Trites (2014) attributes the recurrence of metaphors of growth in adolescent literature and its scholarship to the fact that growth is an embodied, cognitive concept that structures our understanding of both adolescence and its narratives.

Yet we often accuse adults of acting like children—an insult that registers adulthood's precariousness. Truly, any number of contingencies might preclude a subject from claiming adulthood at all, force a subject into adulthood prematurely, or leave them stranded in between. In *The Queer Child, or Growing Sideways in the Twentieth Century* (2009), Kathryn Bond Stockton examines the "sidelong movements" of not only queer adults and children, who cannot embody linear development because they have "simply nowhere to grow," but also children as a category, whose "slow unfolding" belies maturation's vertical movement (3, 4). Stockton raises fundamental questions about how we define adulthood. Who gets to be an adult? If we imagine adulthood requires, for example, economic independence, self-sufficiency, marriage, and reproduction, who is included in and excluded from its status?

Considering adulthood through race, class, gender, and their intersections raises similar questions. Anthropologist Alcinda Honwana explores how high unemployment rates in Mozambique, Senegal, South Africa, and Tunisia force young people into "waithood," or "a prolonged period of suspension between childhood and adulthood" (2012, 4) in which they cannot participate in economic and heteronormative familial institutions—a state that resembles the "boomerang generation" or "adultolescents" in the US or *parasito shinguru* (parasite singles) in Japan, similarly stranded by hostile economies (24). Women, queer people, and people of color in the US and beyond have been oppressed as perpetual children (Field 2014; Halberstam 2011), while black children have been misread as adults in a racist narrative that stretches from at least the nineteenth century to the present, evidenced by systems of structural racism and acts of police violence against black youth (Bernstein 2011b; Epstein, Blake, and González 2017). Children's literature reflects the violence of designating a child as an adult or vice versa through texts that participate in this practice, such as Defoe's *Robinson Crusoe* (1719) and its childlike Friday, or that critique it, such as Angie Thomas's *The Hate U Give* (2017) and its depiction of the consequences of misreading black teens as violent adults.

Emerging critical conversations surrounding child agency provide avenues to further interrogate adulthood's ideological freight by refusing to presume adult power and examining the ways children adopt, negotiate, or resist adult discourse. Richard Flynn's study of June Jordan's partnerships with children, Rachel Conrad's research on child writers, Robin Bernstein's theory of scripted and scripting children, and Katharine Capshaw's exploration of children's participation in the civil rights movement all reimagine adult-child relationships to consider connections and collaborations, rather than differences and enmities, between generations. These approaches require revising naturalized narratives of development. Marah Gubar, for example, proposes an alternative "kinship model," which holds "that children and adults are fundamentally akin to one another, even if certain differences or deficiencies routinely attend certain parts of the aging process" (2016b, 299). This model accounts for growth as "a messy continuum, an ongoing process that involves losses as well as gains" (294). Detaching adulthood from a developmental narrative is a generative rebellion, opening multiple directions for our field to grow.

2

Aesthetics

Joseph T. Thomas Jr.

The neglect of sustained, theoretical inquiry into the aesthetics of children's literature is a symptom of our discipline's history. As it developed in North America, the academic discipline of children's literature emerged in the context of the canon-busting and -expanding cultural studies movements of the 1960s and '70s, a theoretical milieu newly suspicious of objective claims of aesthetic value. In recent years, however, the global field has seen renewed interest in aesthetics as "sensuous knowledge," a mode of apprehension inextricably bound to both history and ideology.

The word *aesthetics* has ancient roots, its earliest forms the Greek *aisthanomai* and *aisthetikos* (both summoning the idea of perception). In his seminal study *Aesthetica* (1750–58), Alexander Baumgarten reworked these ancient terms—including *aisthēsis* (sensation)—into our more contemporary understanding of *aesthetics*. The term has oscillated between apparent opposites: aesthetic value as both subjective and universal, as perceived sensually but primarily understood via intellectual contemplation, and as inhering in objects themselves yet requiring cultivated judgment to be experienced. As Raymond Williams reminds us, Baumgarten uses the term to describe "beauty as phenomenal perfection" (1983a, 31). Lars-Olof Åhlberg argues that since Baumgarten, aesthetics "has mostly been conceived of as the philosophy of art, or, as the theory of the arts" (2003, 149), whereas "Baumgarten's idea of aesthetics as the theory of sensuous knowledge has been all but ignored" (151).

In *Critique of Judgment*, Immanuel Kant complicates and extends Baumgarten's insights. Whereas Baumgarten maintains that the aesthetic affects us solely through the senses, Kant argues that the beautiful encourages *intellectual* contemplation, famously linking beauty to taste. He writes, "*Taste* is the ability to judge an object, or a way of presenting it, by means of a liking or disliking *devoid of all interest*. The object of such a liking is called *beautiful*" ([1790] 1987, 53). He continues, "[If] someone likes something and is conscious that he himself does so without any interest, then he cannot help judging that it must contain a basis for being liked [that holds] for everyone" (53–54). Taste, then, is the ability to distinguish between what is "agreeable to *me*" (55) and what is *beautiful*, and taste rests, for Kant, on *sensus communis*, "common sense" (160), a sense that is counterintuitively anything but common. Common sense in the Kantian formulation is reserved for the educated elite, for there is a correct and incorrect apprehension of beauty—a quality that, Kant maintains, inheres in objects themselves. Some artifacts are beautiful and some are not. By linking beauty to taste, Kant marks the aesthetic as both subjective *and* universal.

The idea of "common sense" aesthetics becomes immediately tangled once children enter into the discussion of aesthetic value. Kant's logic is seductive, and it no doubt informs ideological commonplaces like the teleological notion that children have not yet developed *taste*. This lack of developed taste explains why their tastes are often not in concert with those of cultured adults. Adults *know* that Chris Van Allsburg's intricate pencil drawings are beautiful, whereas children may similarly (but wrongly) apprehend the new Dora the Explorer sticker book as beautiful (in Kantian terms, we might grant that the former is beautiful, whereas the latter would simply be agreeable to some; i.e., children).

The construction of such aesthetic hierarchies generally runs contrary to the study of children's literature, which, as a discipline, tends to focus on the ideological, social, and thematic implications of childhood texts rather than their aesthetic value. As a (usually) commercial medium, children's literature also collides with the notion that mass-produced objects cannot also be art. In *Aesthetic Theory*, Theodor Adorno imagines an aesthetic continuum on which any given artwork's placement depends on how autonomous it is of distortion "by exchange, profit, and the false needs of a degraded humanity" ([1970] 2004, 298). For Adorno, autonomous art is not the product of "socially useful labor," and as a result, it resists "bourgeois functionalization" (298). In opposition to autonomous art, we have what Adorno calls "heteronomous" art. As Lambert Zuidervaart explains, heteronomous art is not adequately "independent from other institutions of bourgeois society" (1991, 227). That is, heteronomous art describes artworks "produced and received to accomplish purposes that are directly served by other institutions." As examples, he includes "everything from liturgical dance to tribal masks, from advertising jingles to commercial movies." (To this list we might add "children's literature," with its history of didacticism.) Since aesthetics has conventionally focused on fine autonomous art, ignoring popular heteronomous art, the gap between aesthetics and the discipline of children's literature widens on both ends: the latter tends toward cultural studies and a postmodern aesthetic, whereas the former focuses on "fine art" to the exclusion of popular, agreeable art designed to entertain.

However, even within the discipline of children's literature, we find scholars privileging work that suggests autonomous "fine art"—work that references canonical painting or literature, such as Laurent de Brunhoff and Phyllis Rose's exploration of fine art in *Babar's Museum*

of Art (2003). Perry Nodelman, however, argues that children's literature's aesthetic appeal resides in its simplicity rather than its perceived complexity. He writes, "[Children's texts] seem so simple and yet allow for so much thought. There's something magical," he continues, "about texts so apparently straightforward being so non-straightforward" (2000a, 2). Striking a blow against our tendency to canonize a priori texts of a more evident complexity, Nodelman explains, "I find more obviously complex texts much less magical" (2).

However, complex aesthetic questions haunt even seemingly straightforward texts. The retellings of Helen Bannerman's *The Story of Little Black Sambo* (1899) occasion consideration of whether aesthetic taste can be decoupled from ideology or whether the two are inextricably bound. Although composed by a Scottish woman living in India, Bannerman's illustrations, as Nina Mikkelsen writes, are "harsh caricatures" of Sambo and his family, all of whom appear "to be African rather than Indian" (2001, 260). Frequently amplifying that caricature, *Sambo*'s many unauthorized versions—which flourished in the US from the early to mid-twentieth century—featured new illustrations with increasingly egregious "pickaninny" imagery. Beyond its racist caricature, Bannerman's art, as Michelle H. Martin writes, is "amateur," consisting of "crude, somewhat surreal, and perhaps even child-like sketches" (2004, 3). Hardly what most aestheticians would label "high art." If the book's aesthetic and racist history seem to banish it from the category of the beautiful, many artists and scholars of taste (in the Kantian sense) claim to apprehend the beauty of *Sambo*, suggesting an inherent aesthetic beauty that—via new art—might be liberated from the story's racist history. Julius Lester views the book as worth "saving": with illustrator Jerry Pinkney, he reimages the story as *Sam and the Tigers* (1996). Similarly, Fred Marcellino reclaims Bannerman's tale by situating it in India, beautifully reillustrating Bannerman's only slightly revised text to produce *The Story of Little Babaji* (1996); likewise, Anne Isaacs and Mark Teague's *Pancakes for Supper* (2006) changes the setting to New England and replaces Sambo with a white girl named Toby Littlewood. Yet in a Borgesian paradox, the traces of Bannerman's text always inform its revisions. The story's persistence suggests that the original is both aesthetically pleasurable *and* ideologically irredeemable.

Adult ideology, then, inflects our experience of the aesthetic, even as it leads us to police the children's literature canon. Karen L. Kilcup and Angela Sorby's anthology of nineteenth-century children's poetry, *Over the River and through the Wood*, revises the historical record by omitting popular racist poetry for failing to conform to the editors' "contemporary tastes and biases" (2013, xxi), providing readers with, as Katherine Wakely-Mulroney and Louise Joy note in their *Aesthetics of Children's Poetry*, "a somewhat skewed vision of the poetry to which nineteenth century children were exposed" (2017, 14). Likewise, we rarely study Eugenio Cherubini's *Pinocchio in Africa* (1911), accepting as apparent aesthetic failings the racist caricatures found therein. However, Cherubini's decision to send Pinocchio to Africa differs little from J. M. Barrie's decision to send the Darling children to an island filled with "Indians" in 1905 (*Peter Pan*) and again in 1911 (*Peter and Wendy*). Barrie's deployment of "Indians" hardly differs from Charles Dodgson's choice to have little Alice meet a hookah-smoking caterpillar: all emerge from a colonialist relationship with the world outside Europe, one that encourages aesthetic flourishes steeped in Orientalism. Jean de Brunhoff's ([1931] 1961) *Babar the Elephant* also participates in the ideological suppositions found in Cherubini's *Pinocchio in Africa*, implying that the world exists to be robbed, colonized, or—in Babar's case—improved by interaction with the West (educated in Paris, Babar returns to Africa to be coronated). Indeed, ideology and aesthetics are so enmeshed that it has been—until recent years—all but impossible to perceive the racist caricatures that inform Dr. Seuss's *The Cat in the Hat* (see Philip Nel's *Was the Cat in the Hat Black?* [2017]).

As these cases illustrate, aesthetic debates haunt the periphery of our discipline, but those debates are rarely put in *terms* of aesthetics. This hesitance to summon aesthetics—to treat, as Gianni Vattimo puts it in *Art's Claim to Truth*, the "ontological weight of art" ([1985] 2008, 44)—is tied to the politics and history of the discipline itself, one that is still negotiating a place in academia. Kenneth Kidd suggests these complexities when he avers, "For so long children's literature wasn't taken seriously, and just as it's being granted greater respect, the academy is turning to cultural and area studies, theory and 'everyday life'" (2002, 146). Kidd asks, "Will our emergent interest in children's culture be indulged at the expense of the literary tradition we have worked so hard to champion?" His answer is an excited maybe, but he quickly insists upon his "enthusiasm about the shift away from a narrow vision of literature, criticism, and academic life"—and, we should add, a narrow view of what is aesthetically successful in children's literature. Kidd's response points to the productive tensions between literature and cultural studies. Any future conversations about aesthetics in children's literature must be mindful of such productive tensions.

3

Affect

Louise Joy

Current research in the arts and humanities operates in the wake of what has been termed the "affective turn" (Clough and Halley 2007). Since feminist and queer theory turned our gaze on the body, the emotions have become a major site of interest across the disciplines. The term *affect*, which derives from the Latin *affectus*, meaning "mental or emotional state or reaction," is today used both generically as an umbrella term to indicate the emotions and more technically to designate a particular subset of this domain. Attempts to encapsulate the meaning of *affect* in shorthand are impeded by the fact that theorists of affect have taken pains precisely to distinguish *affect* from rather than as "feeling" or "emotion" and because *affect* acquires its significance as that which eludes conscious definition or straightforward articulation. Nevertheless, the *OED* ventures a definition of *affect* as a "feeling or subjective experience accompanying a thought or action or occurring in response to a stimulus; an emotion, a mood."

This encapsulates something of the meaning that the early Christian thinker Augustine reserves for *affectus* as opposed to *passio*, two distinct motions of the soul. The Enlightenment tendency to refer to "passions and affections of the mind" (Cogan 1813) carries traces of this earlier discrepancy. In the nineteenth century, it was common to subsume such variegated terms within the overarching category of "emotion," and the term *affect* and its variants dropped out of common usage. In literary criticism, the ensuing mid-twentieth-century lack of interest in affective terminology went in tandem with a suspiciousness toward emotion per se, a suspiciousness that is emblematized by W. K. Wimsatt and Monroe C. Beardsley's essay "The Affective Fallacy" ([1954] 1970), which helped promote the sorts of disinterested attention to the formal properties of the words on the page that came to be associated with New Criticism. With the publication of *Affect Imagery Consciousness* (1962), however, psychologist Silvan Tomkins resuscitated the importance of affect, originating "affect theory" (1984). Since the 1990s, especially after the publication of Sedgwick and Frank (1995) and Massumi (1995), affect theory has opened up lines of inquiry in fields as diverse as history, politics, visual culture, literature, film, and more recently, children's literature studies.

So what is affect? In the Anglo-European tradition, discussions of affect frequently reference Baruch Spinoza's claim that affect relates to capacity: it is the power "to affect and be affected" ([1667] 1992). The greater our power to be affected, the greater our power to affect. Brian Massumi, capturing something of this Spinozan idea, refers to affect as "the experiencing of experiencing" (2015, 4)—as distinct from emotion, "the capture of affect in the interiority of a subject" (210). Affect is thus the body thinking or, put another way, the mental aspect of a bodily event—a sign that the body has recognized what it is undergoing. Massumi insists that affect is relational; it is produced by interactions between the subject and the world, or the subject and another subject. Affect, then, is not individual but transindividual; it is fundamentally social, shaped as much by what it interacts with as by the subject itself. In this, affect is fundamentally political or at least "proto-political"; it "concerns the first stirrings of the political, flush with the felt intensities of life" (ix). If children's literature is also produced precisely to assist the child in navigating the intersection between subject and world and is necessarily concerned with the first felt intensities of life, then we might venture that the central preoccupation of children's literature—indeed its currency, perhaps even its form—is, or at least relates to, affect. Certainly, the collective nostalgia evoked by totemic characters such as Winnie-the-Pooh, Anne of Green Gables, the Little Prince, and Pippi Longstocking indicates the extent to which children's texts hold sway over the reader's affects, often well beyond childhood.

Broadly, scholars agree that affect has certain attributes. For one, it is mobile: it is the expression of the body constantly in motion, triggered by both innate and acquired stimuli. Evolutionary biologists have suggested that affect differs from emotion because it involves "little or no cognitive evaluation" (Stein, Hernandez, and Trabasso 2008, 578). Affect, then, is an urgent, general, abstract amplifier. It resists stasis: it is ever-moving and hence intangible. We are therefore only ever dimly aware of it. In this, affect cuts across our usual taxonomical categories such as subjective and objective, mind and body, passion and reason. As a result, there is significant disagreement among scholars even on essential questions: How does affect differ from emotion, feeling, or mood? How does affect relate to thought or cognition? Is affect conscious or unconscious? Where does affect originate and where is it located? Can we control it? As Michelle Yik (2010) asks, is Chinese emotion unique or is affect universal across time and place? Is it influenced by gender, sexuality, or ethnicity? Do animals have affects? Could machines have affects? These are some of the questions that children's texts have most urgently and imaginatively posed over the centuries: the evocation of animal sensibilities in Sarah Trimmer's *Fabulous Histories* (1786) and Anna Sewell's *Black Beauty* (1877) have altered readers' capacities to appreciate the parallels between human and animal subjectivity; our ideas about the emotions of mechanical nonhumans have been shaped by the depiction of characters such as Tik-Tok in L. Frank Baum's *Land of Oz* books. Indeed, emotional education is always implicitly at work in children's literature, even—indeed especially—in picture books designed for the very young. Each of Stian Hole's *Garmann* books, like Max Velthuijs's *Frog* books, inducts its small readers into the philosophical, social, and psychological complexities of particular emotions (fear, guilt, love). It is in large part through children's literature that we first learn about affect.

The importance of literature for our understanding of affect, and vice versa, has been much discussed in recent decades, since if "cognitive events and affective states are interdependent" (Antrobus 1970), then every act of language involves an expression of affect (Massumi 2015). Literary texts, as linguistic utterances, are performances of affect. To read a literary text is thus to uncover affect. To whom, though, do the affects contained in literary texts belong? Does the author generate them, or the reader, or the text itself? Do we catch affect through the process of reading, following Teresa Brennan's (2004) argument that affect is contagious, or do we "incarnate" it, as Margaret Mackey (2011) has proposed of young consumers of literature, film, and video games? Is our subjectivity porous, susceptible to contamination by alien affects, our bodies taking "the shape of the very contact they have with objects and others" (Ahmed [2004] 2014, 2), or is the formation of subjectivity "dialogical," as Robyn McCallum (1999a) has argued is the case in adolescent fiction? Certainly, the belief that literature is affectively dangerous—that it *infects* us—is at least as old as Plato's *Republic* (1966). But if literature operates on our emotions and can prompt what Theodor Adorno describes as "the subject's capacity to shudder" ([1970] 2004) and what John Steen identifies as the "pleasure of mood" (2018), so too can music, dance, and visual art. Is there anything peculiar about literary affect?

Marco Abel has identified affects as "asignifying intensities" (2007, x). But language, unlike music, and unlike affect itself, is representational; it signifies something outside of itself. This introduces a distinctive complication: it prompts us to wonder whether literary texts are transmissions of affect or *signs* of the transmission of affect. Are the affects that we experience through reading literature real or artificial, firsthand or secondhand, particular or general? The recent growth of interest in literary cognition has sought to address precisely these questions by analyzing the interrelations between affect and narrative (Burke and Troscianko 2017), examining how emotion can help explain recurrent story patterns (Hogan 2011), and tracing the processes that occur in the embodied minds of readers (Burke 2011). Believing that affect structures and coordinates what we perceive by arranging and prioritizing relevant information, cognitive critics such as Zunshine (2001) and Oatley (2002) probe how readers navigate literary texts by drawing on their knowledge of real-life emotions to facilitate inference and experience empathy (Keen 2007). For some, this process is ethically neutral; for others, it carries morally virtuous possibilities (Nussbaum 2003). The role, both virtuous and potentially vicious, played by children's literature in the acquisition of cognition has been central to recent work by Mike Cadden (2011), Roberta Trites (2014), and Maria Nikolajeva (2014). Where Cadden and Nikolajeva trace the ways in which narrative generates emotional identification in texts for young readers, Trites analyzes how it facilitates "growth" in older readers. Narrative, though, is not the only medium through which children's literary texts transmit affect. The recent collection of essays edited by Katherine Wakely-Mulroney and Louise Joy (2017) has showcased some of the ways in which children's poetry, through its reproduction of musical features and its workings on the child's inner ear, stimulates affective pleasure that rests as much on the aesthetic as the semantic properties of words.

Since the "affective turn," literary scholars have found affect lurking everywhere: in deconstruction (Terada 2001), abolitionist literature (Ahern 2016), contemporary literature (Vermeulen 2015), and literary depictions of torture (Richardson 2016). But its express pursuit into children's literature has only more recently been opened up with a spate of publications in this field in the last decade. Bettina Kümmerling-Meibauer's essay "Emotional Connection" (2012) sets out some important starting points for thinking about the representation of emotions in adolescent literature. Kerry Mallan (2013a) takes head-on the oft-asserted claim that children's literature fosters empathy and questions the legitimacy of this belief through discussion of a range of multicultural picture books. David Rudd (2013) has examined the affective currents lurking in the Lacanian symbolism that he sees at work in children's literature. Placing the focus more directly on the *purpose* of literary affect, John Stephens (2015) has championed it as a means by which young readers develop new "scripts" that enable them to understand literary works. In addition to these interventions to children's literature theory that seek to better understand the role of affect at a general level, a number of works have also charted the significance of particular affects in given cultural contexts. Lydia Kokkola (2013a) has analyzed children's literature's negotiation of the affects associated with the Holocaust. Minjie Chen has reflected on the ways in which affects associated with the Sino-Japanese War were passed into the consciousness of the postwar generation through literature for young people (2016). Ute Frevert's collection *Learning How to Feel* examines how children's literature refracts shifts in our understanding of emotional experience through a discussion of the representation of individual emotions (anxiety, shame, homesickness, boredom) in their historical contexts (2014). More recently, a 2017 collection analyzes how texts for children are tools for "emotional socialisation, enculturation, and political persuasion" (Moruzi, Smith, and Bullen 2017, 2), showing how children's literature shapes children's cognitive and affective development and acknowledging the cultural specificity of literary affects: Doris Wolf's essay, for example, reflects on the affective experience of collective trauma and reconciliation in Canada through a reading of Nicola Campbell's *Shinchi's Canoe* (2008); Jon M. Wargo probes the queer Latin young adult experience of "feeling brown" in Rigoberto Gonzalez's *The Mariposa Club* (2009).

As such studies have shown, children's literature provides important understanding about how emotions work across place and time. Furthermore, if even a preverbal person is "infra-linguistic" (Massumi 2015, 213), and if we acquire affect through "events that occur during infancy, especially transactions with social environment" (Schore 1994), then children's literature plays a foundational role in affect formation. A book such as *Ini Abasi and the Sacred Ram* (1966) by Nigerian author Ntieyong Udo Akpan shows how the act of reading can bind together a community through shared emotions and rituals; the series *Guri and Gura* (2002) by Japanese author Rieko Nakagawa habituates its readers toward certain quotidian affects, instilling social norms.

As J. A. Appleyard (1990) has shown, we are not born readers; we become them. As we learn to be affected by literary texts, so we learn affect, and so (for the more optimistic of critics, at least) we learn, in turn, to affect.

4

Agency
Nina Christensen

"But he doesn't have anything on!" (Andersen 2004, 94). With these words, a child opposes adults' hypocritical admiration of the naked sovereign proudly parading in Hans Christian Andersen's fairy tale "Kejserens nye Klæder" ("The Emperor's New Clothes"; 1837). Enacting agency, this child character makes an independent statement in opposition to the established adult order. Though the term can be traced back to the seventeenth century, its use within children's literature studies is a recent phenomenon.

Agency derives from the Latin verb *agere*, "to act," an origin reflected in a contemporary definition: "Ability or capacity to act or exert power" (*OED*). More specifically, sociologists describe agency as "the power of actors to operate independently of the determining constraints of social structure" and "the volitional, purposive nature of human activity as opposed to its constrained, determined aspects" (Jary and Jary 1995, 10). During the last decade of the twentieth century, central figures in the new sociology of childhood—Allison James, Adrian James, Chris Jenks, and Alan Prout—draw attention to children as active participants in negotiating, shaping, and creating identity. As the "capacity of individuals to act independently," the term *agency* "underscores children and young people's capacities to make choices about the things they do and to express their own ideas" (James and James 2008, 9). This approach has led historians of childhood to investigate how children were "active in determining their own lives and the lives of those around them" (Heywood 2001, 4). When children are not primarily perceived as inferior or subject to the power of adults, descriptions of children's relationships both with their peers and with adults become important in historical accounts of children's lives (Heywood 2001; Mintz 2004; Appel and de Coninck-Smith 2013–15).

Attempts to counter a tendency to generalize about childhood agency have been ongoing at least since Jacqueline Rose famously declared that "there is no child behind the category 'children's fiction,' other than the one which the category itself sets in place" (1984, 10). Rose's work led to a critique of a transcultural, transnational, transhistorical concept of the "universal" child within the field (O'Sullivan 2004). Representing a constructivist position, Karín Lesnik-Oberstein views "'the child' as an identity which is created and constructed differently within various cultures, historical periods, and political ideologies" (1998, 2). In Germany and the Scandinavian countries, the French history of mentality offered another path to analyses of childhood and the relationship between adults and children in children's literature, especially through historical perspectives (Ariès 1960; Ewers et. al 1989; Ewers 2001).

Recently, scholars' focus on agency has challenged the adult-child binary opposition. In a special issue of *Jeunesse* (2016) on the term, Richard Flynn critiques "an overemphasis on children's alterity, in a model of children as helpless or even as victims, implying that children exercise little to no agency in participating in and creating their culture" (2016, 255), a tendency he finds in Perry Nodelman's work. Marah Gubar has proposed instead a "kinship-model," focusing on the likeness and relatedness of children and adults as well as the heterogeneity within both categories. According to Gubar, growth must be regarded "a messy continuum" and not a fixed, general, and inevitable process

(2016b, 294). Both Flynn and Gubar subscribe to the idea that even though children are born into societies where a certain discourse and specific social conditions determine aspects of their lives and identity formation, "that discourse is also shaped by the comportment, doings, and utterances of young people" (Gubar 2016b, 295). In the same issue of *Jeunesse*, Sara L. Schwebel (2016) questions the authenticity of children's voices and children's agency when, for instance, they are told to write letters to authors in school, and she addresses the difficulties of finding historical examples of children's agency. However, such difficulties might also be an encouragement to increase and refine searches and develop new methods of critical analysis.

Three key areas highlight children's agency in relation to fiction: the degree of agency granted to fictional child characters, the attribution of agency to the implied child reader, and how the conditions of a book's production and distribution grant or deny children agency. First, children and young people are often main characters in narratives aimed at children and young people, and very often, relationships to peers and adults play an important part in these stories. In this context, key questions could be, How agential are main characters? and What characterizes the relationship between children and peers, children and adults, and the individual and society? The relationship between children and adults plays an important part in Erich Kästner's *Emil und die Detektive* (*Emil and the Detectives*; [1929] 1931). On a train trip to Berlin, Emil is robbed of the money he was supposed to give to his grandmother. In Berlin, a group of boys gathers to help Emil, and they are soon able to find the thief and get him arrested. The boys' inventiveness, their ability to act independently, and their lack of trust in adult superiority are at the core of the narrative. Adult authority is described as comic, thickheaded, and unjust:

when Emil's uncle thinks he should decide what Emil can do with his reward, first Emil and then his outspoken girl cousin speak up and question the uncle's authority, and Emil gets to influence the way his money is spent.

Second, when adult authors write for an audience of children, this relationship is reflected in the implied author and the implied reader of specific texts (Wall [1991] 1994; Weinreich 2000). Which strategies in the text may grant the implied reader aspects of agency—for example, an active role in the construction of the text's meaning? Socratic dialogues in many eighteenth-century texts for children engage a child reader in making up his or her own mind, but only within a limited range of possible choices. From the nineteenth century onward, the child reader is more often addressed as an individual who can and should have an influence on his or her own interpretation of a text. In "The Emperor's New Clothes," the reader must decide what to think of the emperor, and the nonsensical wordplay of Lewis Carroll's *Alice's Adventures in Wonderland* (1865; see Carroll 1990) offers a wide variety of interpretative strategies to a reader attempting to make sense of the text. While it is generally quite clear in Astrid Lindgren's *Pippi Långstrump* (1945) that the agentic, free, antiauthoritarian child is celebrated, the end of the story makes it possible also to perceive her independence as connected to loneliness and isolation.

Third, in children's literature's production, dissemination, and reception, are actual child readers granted agency and addressed as agentic individuals? Which roles do adults inhabit in these processes—for example, as individuals who must protect or challenge children or who should "set children free"? What would each of these roles imply in specific cases? Which possibilities or which limitations of children's agency are inherent in a new digital book market and digital media such as YouTube and Instagram?

Placing actual children's agency in a historical perspective, Matthew O. Grenby (2011) traces the ways in which children had an influence on what and how they read in England between 1700 and 1850. Marah Gubar (2009) has drawn attention to the fact that children were also producers and coproducers of texts for children in nineteenth-century England. In a contemporary perspective, quite a few books are now being published with and by young people with high numbers of followers on Instagram and YouTube. In 2014, two fourteen- and fifteen-year-old girls, Laura Arnesen and Marie Wivel, made it to the best-seller list with a book based on their Instagram account. Subsequently, the book was sold to fourteen countries in numbers most authors of children's literature can only dream of. In fora for fan fiction, children and young people can influence their favorite narratives and have the possibility of getting feedback from readers of all ages.

Discussions of agency are linked to race and gender. Angie Thomas's *The Hate U Give* describes the young black protagonist, Starr, and her development after having witnessed her black friend Khalil being shot by the police. Starr and other characters discuss the degree to which a person is, respectively, shaped by given conditions and structures or has an influence on his or her own life and can change such structures. Toward the end of the novel, Starr asks, "What's the point of having a voice if you're gonna be silent in those moments you shouldn't be?" (2017, 248), and when she gains courage to speak at a protest against police violence, she describes her voice as her "biggest weapon" (405). Focusing more on gender, Victoria Flanagan finds girls gaining greater agentic possibilities via digital technology in three contemporary novels that "showcase an incipient trend in YA fiction: the ideological construction of social media as a pro-feminist space that has the capacity to promote and produce agentic forms of feminine identity" (2017, 38).

A focus on agency provides an alternative to viewing the child as vulnerable and dependent on adult power and protection. At one end of the spectrum, the term recalls the romantic child: free, independent, divine. At another end, the child figure finds herself restricted, defined, denied by her structural predicament. Between the two positions, a range of variations coexist. Literature for young people, and the discussions related to this field, revolve around such ambivalences.

5

Animal
Colleen Glenney Boggs

The chief ambassador for the magic kingdom of childhood is an oversized mouse. One of a few cultural figures recognized by his first name alone, Mickey is such an icon that his ubiquitous smile and welcoming gloved hands have erased much of the strangeness and the history by which a cheerful rodent became a symbol for dreams beyond the Freudian variety of wolf-man nightmares. Insistently invoking imagination as the antidote to reality, the mouse subsumes culturally distinct renditions of animals and children under a generic rubric, the Disney fairy tale, which has all but erased its diverse cultural traces and origins. But the mouse inadvertently tells us something about the history of children and animals—namely, that they are fungible as categories and in their relation to one another. If Mickey defines childhood, he also reminds us of the fact that children and animals define one another as creatures similarly exempt from adult subjectivity, as pairs that contrast "the human" and "the animal," as companions or as adversaries. For that matter, the further we enter into the Magic Kingdom's invention of an animal kingdom, the more this strangeness becomes evident: If Mickey is a mouse, and Donald is a duck, and Goofy is a dog, then how can they have Pluto the pet? And for that matter, why do the mouse, the duck, and the dog wear white gloves, leaving only Pluto with paws? *Animal* is an unstable term, one that simultaneously differs from children and defines them. At the core of that contestation is the key question of how, whether, and when beings enter into the forms of subjectivity generally reserved for adulthood and what rights and responsibilities they carry at that threshold.

Etymologically speaking, *animal* already comprises these tensions. According to the *OED*, the term goes back to Latin roots that were widely incorporated into the word's Anglo-Norman, French, Catalan, Spanish, Portuguese, and English variants. The word generically describes a living organism, but it can be used to encompass all living creatures or to distinguish between human beings and all others. In short, the term can be a marker of universal inclusion or of human exception. At the same time, it can also designate versions of human beings—often denigrated as "brutes"—or aspects of human nature, such as "brutality." In that sense, *animal* refers to the self, an aspect of the self, and a version of the other when it comes to human beings' relation to the word in its etymological and cultural forms. *Animal* functions as both a noun and an adjective. As a noun, it designates ontological and epistemological categories. As an adjective, it unsettles those very categories. Scholars have attempted to coin new terms to specify these differences—for instance, arguing that we separate *animality* (i.e., traits shared between human beings and animals) from *animal* as a biological designation (Lundblad 2009), thereby reviving discussions energized by Jean-Jacques Rousseau's insistence on an "originary animality" that lies at the "foundation of natural right" (Billing 2013, 2).

Any definition of *animal* thus intervenes into the fraught question of how children map into nature and onto subjectivity. Animals relate to children in scientific ways as objects of study that became increasingly viewed with a scientific as opposed to a religious or spiritual gaze in the early modern period. René Descartes argued that animals were essentially machines whose cries were not reflections of any ethically recognizable

pain and who could therefore be vivisected—that is, cut up alive without anesthetics—at the scientist's will. Subject to the scientific gaze of the Enlightenment, animals became objects of scientific study and classification, being fitted into orderly systems by naturalists such as the Comte de Buffon, Thomas Jefferson, and the Darwins (Erasmus and Charles). Yet in *We Have Never Been Modern* (1993), Bruno Latour argues that the distinction between science and other modes of inquiry was always incomplete and that our current investment in interdisciplinarity masks the long-term entanglements of modern thought. That might be one way of making sense of the fact that animals populated the Shakespearean stage and early modern entertainment culture (Boehrer 2010), that animal breeding (Davidson 2009) and pet keeping (Ritvo 1986) emerged alongside scientific inquiry. Moreover, it is important to remember that scientific engagements with animals always ran parallel to narrative and cultural accounts, extending from Aesop to the medieval beast fable but also occurring in Ovid's account of metamorphoses and the fairy tales' portrayal of talking animals who engage in particular with children, such as "Little Red Riding Hood" and other tales that subvert and assert social coming-of-age expectations. These cultural forms are not only Western; as Henry Louis Gates Jr. (1988) demonstrates, the "Signifyin' Monkey" of Yoruba traditions significantly impacted African American trickster narratives, which in Joel Chandler Harris's appropriation cast Br'er Rabbit at the center of children's literature and popular entertainment culture, with Mickey Mouse as a not-so-distant cousin.

Even before Charles Darwin's account of evolution posited an evolutionary as well as emotional relationship to animals, children could be likened developmentally to animals, whose nominal limitations they surpassed as they grew up. In his *Some Thoughts concerning Education*, John Locke responded to a friend's query regarding the proper rearing of his son. Locke lamented that there were no books fit for children aside from *Aesop's Fables*. Making fables the basis for children's introduction to literature became a vogue in response to his writing—which was more widely circulated in the American colonies than his *Two Treatises of Government*. Inaugurating the field of children's literature, animals took on a primary role for the education of children into citizens. Arguing that children who were cruel to animals learned to be despots, Locke reasoned that kindness to animals inculcated the characteristics and virtues necessary for good citizenship. This call for good citizenship resonated in subsequent portrayals of animals, ranging from the rejection of cruelty in Victorian novels (Kreilkamp 2005) to the outright activism of books such as Anna Sewell's *Black Beauty* (1877) that insisted animal welfare needed to be part of civic society.

The project of *Black Beauty* should give us pause: modeled after Harriet Beecher Stowe's abolitionist work *Uncle Tom's Cabin* (1852) as well as the early nineteenth-century didactic tales F. J. Harvey Darton ([1932, 1958] 1970) identifies, Sewell's novel aspired to work toward animal liberation in the way that Stowe had worked for abolition. The facile parallel between animals and slaves reminds us of the ways in which the denigration of human beings has often taken the form of likening racialized others to animals and of infantilizing them in the process. Strangely, such animalized human beings inhabit a childlike position that often relies on children for its amelioration while, in the process, affirming those children's civic engagement and ability to enter into the requirements of citizenship. The characters with which we began are a reminder of that history as well: black faces and white gloves were the hallmarks of minstrel shows, which portrayed nonwhites as childlike and animalistic. In Mickey Mouse and the performance culture from which early cartoons sprang (Sammond

2015), we see echoes of this racial, animal, children's history carried into our own present moment.

The current scholarly field of so-called animal studies originated with Jacques Derrida's late writings and his proposition that we engage with *animaux*, the French plural for animals, which he punningly refashioned as "ani-mots"—that is, animal words that gain significance in their relation to one another (2008, 415). That sense of relation has been at the core of much work in the larger field of animal—or, we might say, human-animal—studies. A key figure, Donna Haraway, emphasizes that relationship when she talks about "companion species" (2003, 6). The term for her indicates not only that human beings and animals have a relation to one another but that—like Lyra and her dæmon in Philip Pullman's *His Dark Materials* trilogy (1995–2000)—we cannot think about the one without acknowledging the imbrications of the other.

How those connections are worked out, what formative elements they carry, and how they shape senses of being are questions that Kathryn Bond Stockton usefully takes up in relationship to children. Arguing that both children and animals are categorized as "other," she asserts that for queer children in particular, the relationship to animals offers a form of "growing sideways" instead of growing up (2009, 53). By that, she means that animals offer an alternative form of being for queer children than that of normative, gendered adulthood and that the relationships children develop with animals make it possible to conceptualize modes of relating other than those of the heteronormative family and the society that takes such heteronormativity for its premise.

Even within the framework of the heteronormative family, however, there is room for growing sideways into animals instead of adults. Kenneth Kidd reads Maurice Sendak's *Where the Wild Things Are* (1963) as a "bedtime-story version of Freud's Wolf Man case history of 1918, an updated and upbeat dream of the wolf boy" (Kidd 2011c, 106). Though "a queer interpretation of Sendak's work has yet to emerge," Max "may well be . . . queer to some degree—hard to manage, independent, animal-identified" (125). Sendak's "feral tale" (106) also participates in a long and still-growing lineage of publications: feral children in general and wolf-boys in particular captured Daniel Defoe's imagination when "Peter the Wild Boy" became a cause célèbre in the early eighteenth century (Newton 2002), one that Defoe examined in his pamphlet *Mere Nature Delineated* (1726). More recently, Marina Warner's *Managing Monsters* (1994) as well as Emily Hughes's *Wild* (2013) continue to explore the intersection between children and animals as children navigate their relation to nature, including their own.

The fluidity between children and animals is particularly pronounced in narratives that imagine forms of blended embodiment and of metamorphosis, such as the many versions of the *Little Mermaid*, ranging from Hans Christian Andersen's tale, to the Disney movie, to the story's cross-cultural adaptations. Anna Katrina Gutierrez traces the tale through its "glocal" reinterpretations to the films of Hayao Miyazaki. In *Ponyo on the Cliff by the Sea* (2008), Miyazaki blends Hans Christian Andersen's tale with "Urashima Taro" (a story first recorded in the eighth century CE). Miyazaki weaves an "interspecies romance" that signifies "the desire of nature and humanity to be united" (Gutierrez 2017, 169) but also reverses the trajectory from the natural to the human and emphasizes children's needs for communion with the animal and natural realm.

As Akira Lippit (2000) has indicated, animation in particular and the technologization of animals in general confront us with an increasingly difficult way of relating to animals—and, I might add, to children. As John Berger (1980) has cautioned, the loss of our direct gaze distorts both the animal and the sense of subject formation, or, as Steve Baker claims more polemically, "the basic procedure of disnification is to render it [the animal] stupid by rendering it visual" (1993, 141). For better and for worse, children's relationship to animals—and vice versa—is a cultural construct that is as fungible as it is essential to the social formations it reflects and creates.

ANIMAL   COLLEEN GLENNEY BOGGS

6

Archive

Lissa Paul

A curiously slippery word, *archive* is both singular and plural, noun and verb (*OED*). It can refer to the place where material is stored (such as a rare books library) and to the material itself (*OED*). The etymological evolution of *archive* through its Greek roots—*arkheia* (public records) and *arkhe* (government)—provides a map of the word's lexical tensions. In the seventeenth century, when *archive* first came into use, it was a place where (public) records were kept. As other forms of the root mean "beginnings"—as in *archeology* and *architecture*—the idea of a foundation also lingers. By way of contrast, the *OED* defines *library* as "a place set apart to contain books for reading, study, or reference." Although a library may house an archive, it is only in an archive that it is possible to search for origin stories. The verb form, *to archive*, does not appear until the twentieth-century.

Because archives are as secure and well protected as bank vaults, analogous questions about the value of content and access arise: What is worth saving? What material is secured to ensure its protection? And what is stored in order to hide and keep from circulation? Once access to an archive is gained, how is relevant material retrieved and how is it interpreted? As material archives—books, typed and handwritten drafts, annotated manuscripts, and the like—move to digital formats, what are the consequences for storage if the need diminishes for climate-controlled buildings? Do shifts to digital formats also fundamentally alter the kinds of research traditionally done in material archives? Will "archival research" morph into "data mining"?

To indicate how *archive* illuminates tensions that circulate around access, preservation, and interpretation of sources and the curious position of children and their literatures, consider a hypothetical scholar going online to the British Library "Archives and Manuscripts" catalog to search for items in the Edward James (Ted) Hughes Archive from among the "465 folders, 11 oversize items (5 in melinex enclosures), 4 oversize volumes, 2 boxes and 1 envelope" listed on the website (Edward James Hughes Papers). Melinex, by the way, is a kind of nonreactive polyester film used to protect fragile manuscripts and works on paper from disintegrating. The reader would have to turn up, in person, with the required authorization and identification to collect selected items—one at a time—from the Manuscripts Reading Room on the second floor of the British Library and view them at a designated desk under close surveillance by the librarians. No photographs allowed. And no pens.

Hughes—poet laureate of the UK between 1984 and his death in 1998—wrote by hand, with a fountain pen, on paper. Drafting his own works in progress, he used the blank backs of typed poems and stories by children submitted to the W. H. Smith Young Writers' Competition (formerly the *Daily Mirror* Children's Literary Competition); he served as a judge for over thirty years. There is something shockingly intimate about reading a Ted Hughes poem on one side of a page and a child's poem on the other—the latter surviving only because of its association with Hughes. Texts both for and by children are usually not so lucky.

Materials related to children's literature and culture are ephemeral almost by definition. Books, toys, and games used by real children quickly become torn, worn, and damaged. Once outgrown, childhood playthings are typically discarded. Yet as Kenneth Kidd suggests, the impulse to preserve materials persists, motivated perhaps by "a desire to return to childhood experience as much as by the desire to discover something new" (Kidd 2011a, 17). And sometimes miracles happen.

In 1986, Justin Schiller, a New York–based specialist dealing in antiquarian children's books, was asked to evaluate the estate of Elisabeth Ball of Muncie, Indiana. There, stored in a shoebox, he found what is now the Jane Johnson Manuscript Nursery Library: 438 pieces of instructional materials—alphabet cards, lesson cards, and story cards—handmade by Johnson, probably between 1738 and 1748, to teach her own young children to read. The cards are historically important, as their mid-eighteenth-century creation date provides tangible evidence of a mother crafting her own pedagogical tools. Though John Locke is typically credited with explaining, in *Some Thoughts concerning Education*, that children should be "cozened into a Knowledge of the Letters" ([1693] 1989, 224), Julia Briggs (2005) suggests that the credit is misplaced: mothers were already making those materials, and Locke was just reporting on established maternal practices. The Jane Johnson Manuscript Nursery Library, now protected in the Lilly Library in Indiana, stands as testimony to those maternal cultural practices. The survival of the material also testifies to the fact that for 250 years, there were people who thought that those tiny cards—all 438, remember, fit in one shoebox—were valuable enough to keep.

Children's literature and material culture potentially provide a window into social, cultural and literary histories in that they stand as something of a universal common ground: all adults have been children. But what survives depends on what is deemed important enough to preserve. The Hans Christian Andersen House and Museum, established in 1908 in Odense, Denmark, has a dedicated mandate to honor one of the country's most internationally famous authors, and the museum stands as iconic testimony to the cultural importance of a national hero. By way of contrast, the library that serves the Institut für Jugendbuchforschung (Department for Children's and Young Adult Literature Research), housed in Goethe University in Frankfurt, Germany, and founded in 1963, has a broader cultural mandate: the study of German children's literature and culture in their international context. The personal children's book collection of philosopher Walter Benjamin (1892-1940) is there. As Ian Grosvenor explains, Benjamin (who wrote movingly about the cultural value of his own children's books) speaks directly to the value of archives by capturing "the performative nature of 'remembering' and the relationship with traces of the past that remain in the present" (Grosvenor 2002, 111). The fact that scholars have access at all to archives containing historical collections of children's books, games, and toys is a kind of miracle. Because the material was intended for use, not posterity, it was not usually regarded as valuable or collectable. That's why research in studies in children's literature is largely thanks to the prescience of mid-twentieth-century collectors. Among the most well known are Fernand Renier (1905-1988) and Anne Renier (1911?-1988), who donated their collection to the Victoria and Albert Museum; Iona Opie (1923-2017) and Peter Opie (1918-1982), who sold their library to the Bodleian in Oxford; Lloyd Cotsen (1929-2017), who gave his collection to Princeton; Edgar Osborne (d. 1978), who donated his to the Toronto Public Library; and Ruth Baldwin (1918-1990), who gave hers to the University of Florida. And with the increasing recognition of the value of children's material culture in the context of cultural heritage (unmarked as being for children), institutions such as Seven Stories: The National Centre for Children's Books, in Newcastle, England, established in 1996 by Elizabeth Hammill and Mary Briggs, have started to take an active role in preserving material that would otherwise have disappeared. As Seven Stories states on its website, the center sees itself as the "protector" of the British "literary heritage for children." To that end, it has become home to the archives of some of Britain's most important authors and illustrators, including John Agard, David Almond, Aidan Chambers, Grace Nichols, and Michael Morpurgo.

Archives, however, are not just places that protect our cultural histories. They are also hiding places for materials we would rather forget. Because access is restricted, it is possible to remove material from public circulation and bury it. A case in point is "Ten Little Niggers" (1875), which began as a hugely popular song and flourished in many versions, including stand-alone picture books and as the original title for Agatha Christie's *And Then There Were None* (1939). The enduring popularity of the song now reads as emblematic of racist tropes we would rather forget. Yet only through the work of scholars—such as Wulf Schmidt-Wullfen's *Ten Little Niggers: Racial Discrimination in Children's Books* (2012)—is it possible to expose the dark corners of the archives in which those books have been hidden and to demonstrate the damage caused when they were in circulation.

Once materials—books, toys, games, manuscripts—make their way into protected archives, the people who manage to access them try to make those carefully stored things speak. That requires the skill of a good detective: finely tuned instincts, dogged determination to pay close attention to all clues, and openness to occasional moments of chance illumination. In anglophone children's literature, the most well-known story about archival research is E. L. Konigsburg's *From the Mixed-Up Files of Mrs. Basil E. Frankweiler* (1967), about two children who decide to run away from home to the Metropolitan Museum of Art in New York. The story is partly about proving the authenticity of one of the museum's recent acquisitions, a statue said to be by Michelangelo. The proof is hidden in one of the "mixed-up" files stored in a wall of Mrs. Basil E. Frankweiler's filing cabinets (soon to need a footnote of their own). The children are tasked with discovering the "search term" to find the file that will resolve the mystery. Only when one uses the dismissive term *boloney* does the other remember that their earlier research had informed them that the statue had been purchased in Bologna. The answer to the mystery was in the *B* files: a single sheet with Michelangelo's handwriting on one side (they'd seen examples) and his drawing of the statue on the other. As Kenneth Kidd, Lucy Pearson, and Sarah Pyke (2016) point out in their essay on archives, the "serendipity" of the baloney-Bologna connection provided the key. Archival scholarship requires the two elements foregrounded in the book: active research and chance.

Historically, material archives—books, toys, and games—have required designated storage space. As the production of texts change, so do the storage requirements, especially of papers by children's authors successful enough to be saved for posterity. From the late 1980s, authors began migrating from paper to digital formats, diminishing the chance of ever again seeing multiple drafts or drafts on the blank backs of poems written by children. Changing technologies may also curtail access even to saved material. Manuscripts composed on, say, an Apple II and stored on floppy disks are no longer readable unless the machine on which they were composed is preserved and maintained. Digitally connected archives also suddenly make it possible to make previously impossible links. The Study Platform on Interlocking Nationalisms (SPIN), for example, established in 2008 as a collaborative enterprise between the University of Amsterdam and the Huizinga Institute under the leadership of Joep Leerssen, is designed, as explained on the website, to "chart the cultural and historical root systems of European nationalisms" (http://spinnet.eu). What the site suddenly opens is the possibility of mapping the transmission of political and cultural trends across time and place.

Recent innovations such as "born-digital" texts and "cloud storage" present new problems. If the material has no physical presence, it no longer needs a physical storage space. But then who owns the material? Who manages the copyright? As we move into the future, we recalibrate our readings of the past.

7

Audience
Beverly Lyon Clark

The dominant modern meaning of *audience* refers to the viewers of an entertainment or readers of a book. According to the *OED*, such usages date to before 1387 (for a performance) and to 1760 (for a book or writer). Other early meanings including "the range or sphere of hearing," or being within a person's hearing, date to before 1393. Derived from the Latin *audīre*, "to hear," the term has a special resonance for children's literature because the youngest children are not readers but auditors of literature, truly an audience. Indeed, the broad term *audience* better captures the many ways in which children consume literature—and other aspects of culture—than does *reader*, the term generally preferred in literary criticism.

Raymond Williams (1976, 1983b) did not include *audience* in his *Keywords*. The term does receive an entry in *New Keywords*, edited by Tony Bennett, Lawrence Grossberg, and Meaghan Morris (2005): David Morley's account focuses almost entirely on the audience for mass media, especially addressing the extent to which such an audience is passively susceptible to or actively shapes the messages received. A popular approach in cultural criticism has been to assume that children lack agency and to castigate the media, arguing that our children must be protected from its effects. Since at least 1965, when the librarian Frances Clarke Sayers fired a salvo (Sayers and Weisenberg 1965)—and perhaps even from 1938, when Anne Carroll Moore expressed her concern—critics have deplored how reductive and saccharine Disney products are. Yet some cultural critics, such as Ellen Seiter (1993) and Gerard Jones (2002), highlight ways in which children respond actively, in an ongoing process of negotiation, perhaps reshaping what they see on television or using comic books to mitigate anxieties. Indeed, an increasing literature attends to media and material culture (Tobin 2004), such as dolls (Bernstein 2011b), including the numerous uses of Barbie—even if the most radical uses (Barbie as dildo) are often associated with adults (Rand 1995).

As for children's literature, the concept of audience has a special salience, for this literature is not by children, as the possessive might imply, but rather read by or to them: it is defined by its audience. Yet how exactly audience delimits children's literature is subject to debate. Scholars disagree as to whether it is defined by being intended for children (Nodelman 2008) or is simply literature that they read (Lerer 2008). Does a book appropriated by children, such as *Robinson Crusoe* (Defoe 1719), count? Do books that a publisher markets for children count, even if an author didn't have such an audience in mind while writing? Scholars also disagree about whether to focus more on the book or the child in their judgments, but even the book people can't altogether forget the target audience: "Naturally a knowledge of and sympathy with children is . . . vital," notes Brian Alderson in "The Irrelevance of Children to the Children's Book Reviewer" (quoted in Hunt 1991).

More broadly, the study of children's literature raises intriguing theoretical questions that are too often missed by mainstream literary theorists, who generally ignore children's literature. However well Stanley Fish's (1980) concept of an "interpretive community" might work for adult readers, for instance, how does one define such a community for children? How do they find meaning in a text? Can they find it without adult mentoring? Does their interpretive community necessarily include adults? Children's literature also points to the multiplicity of address of literature, given that no other literature so thoroughly excludes the intended audience from the various aspects of formal production and distribution. Very few young people have written, edited, published, or sold books. And relatively few children directly buy them; even if a smaller proportion of children's book sales are now to libraries than was the case in the 1960s, librarians, teachers, and other adults have continued to be the primary buyers (Stevenson 1997). The result, as Zohar Shavit (1986) and others have noted, is that children's literature has at least a double address: the children who are the ostensible audience and the adults whose decisions make it available.

Given that the decision-makers are not part of the ostensible audience, the nature of children's literature very much depends on how adults construct childhood and children. Indeed, Jacqueline Rose (1984) argues that it is impossible for adults truly to know children; rather, they are always constructing them. If adults construct children as beings to be molded for the future, then children's literature may be conceived as an important part of this molding—and therefore as necessarily didactic and needing to be monitored or censored, as Sarah Trimmer was systematically doing as long ago as 1802 (*The Guardian of Education* [1802–6]). Others, following a Romantic construction of childhood, feel that children's literature should provide wings for the imagination—a kind of projection onto the child that may also be freeing. Indeed, we should not lose sight of the fact that children are not just passive; they can be active agents too, constructing what they read—and themselves. For children are also real. A focus on the duality of the audience may, in fact, occlude its multiplicities, masking the heterogeneity of children. Children differ, for one thing, by age. Indeed, when does childhood end? Does one exclude humans over the age of perhaps twelve, or does one include young adults, a group whose upper age limit keeps rising? Does one include a new category of new adults who are primarily in their twenties? Children also differ by gender, race, class, abledness, religion, and nationality. Focus on "the child" as audience too often misses the real differences among children.

Some scholars observe the reading or viewing processes of actual children or examine their self-reports or perhaps how they deface books (Arizpe, Colomer, and Martínez-Roldán 2014; Benton [1995] 2005; Blackford 2004; Gubar 2011; Sánchez-Eppler 2011b; Schwebel 2016). The internet has enabled significant access to responses by the young, who can create fan fiction, art, videos, blogs, reviews, and more—no longer just "passively swallow[ing] the narratives adult institutions allow them" but "talk[ing] back" and even "developing aesthetic forms . . . to suit themselves" (Tosenberger 2014). Scholars such as Catherine Tosenberger have sampled fan responses to the Harry Potter series (more than eighty thousand items of fan fiction on fanfiction.net alone) and the Twilight series (more than thirty thousand), perhaps noting shifts in romantic pairings and eroticism (Morey 2012; Day 2014).

Other scholars study the kinds of address created within a work, the narratee or the implied reader (Wall [1991] 1994). Some look at the implied reader cross-culturally, noting, for instance, how differently various cultures tolerate showing depictions of nudity to children (Nikolajeva 2011) or how translators of *Pinocchio* (Collodi [1883] 1996) have adapted it to varying norms regarding what children should and can read or view, if indeed children are the target audience (O'Sullivan 2005). Even picture books may target adults more than children—but differently in different cultures. The parodic American picture book *Go the Fuck to Sleep*

(Mansbach 2011), which has been translated into more than thirty languages, would seem to target adults across cultures. But works that more ambiguously target both adults and children are less likely to translate across cultures and languages. These include books by the Danish writer Oskar K (Ole Dalgaard) about aborted fetuses or a children's undertaker and the Norwegian Gro Dahle's picture books on problems with divorce (see Ommundsen 2015) or on a child watching pornography. It's suggestive that only about half of the picture books by the eminent German illustrator Wolf Erlbruch have been translated into English. One book that includes cannibalism of a child has, significantly, not (Paul 2011).

In some cultures, the implied reader may be a child who is strongly in need of protection and instruction, whether moral or civic, directly or allegorically (e.g., Farquhar 1999; Ho 1997; Douglas and Malti-Douglas 1999). In postwar France, protectionist concerns about lying and disrespect for authority led to a reluctance to publish foreign imports and the drastic cutting of Astrid Lindgren's Pippi Longstocking trilogy (1945–48; Heywood 2015). In many countries in the postwar era, adults responded to the spread of American superhero and crime comic books with negative sanctions or countervailing initiatives (Jensen 2017; Lent 1999, 2009). More recently, in China, scholars may debate the need for mere enjoyment (Nelson and Morris [2014] 2016) or perhaps associate the Harry Potter books with the increasing childhood agency of a new generation, even as the books mediate between such individualism and the communal values of older generations (Gupta and Xiao 2009).

In any case, what we now consider to be children's literature arose through market segmentation. Early literature in the West—mystery plays, ballads, folk tales, sermons—embraced children as part of its audience.

Even later, literature for children long overlapped with that for the laboring and, later, working classes: children read chapbooks, evangelical tracts, and dime novels. What is often considered children's literature per se—an imaginative literature directly targeting the young—is generally seen as arising in the eighteenth century, along with the middle class, whether or not one dates the first anglophone work precisely to 1744 with *A Little Pretty Pocket-Book*, published by John Newbery. For most of the nineteenth century, nevertheless, cultural gatekeepers often assumed they should publish nothing "that could not be read aloud in the family circle," to quote an editor of *Harper's Monthly* in the 1890s (Mott 1938): they assumed that the young would be part of a general readership. And works that ostensibly targeted children, which subsequent readers have classified as children's literature, were often read by adults as well—not just in the company of children, as now with a bedtime story, but independently (Clark 2003).

About the turn of the twentieth century, the anglophone canons of taste changed. As the cultural gatekeepers shifted in the US from the likes of magazine editors to the professoriate, and Herman Melville's star, for one, ascended, only works (especially those by white men) seen as targeting an adult audience came to be seen as worthy of the highest approbation. Children's literature was thus inferior. If in 1893 "The Best American Books," published in the literary journal *The Critic*, included *Little Women* (Alcott [1868–69] 2004) and *Little Lord Fauntleroy* (Burnett [1886] 2009) among its top forty, twentieth-century lists of important books rarely included works we now classify as for children.

Nor did the academy provide a friendly audience for children's literature. Now, however, as academic departments devote courses and programs to this literature, as some books such as the Harry Potter series have reached a crossover audience, as publishers seem to welcome such crossovers (Beckett 2009a; Falconer 2009), and indeed, as *Keywords for Children's Literature* goes into a second edition, change is afoot.

8

Authenticity

Sarah Park Dahlen

According to the *OED*, the first instance of the word *authenticity* was in 1716, in letters to Dr. Richard Bentley regarding a translation of the New Testament (cited in McDonald 2016, 226). Variations of the word *authenticity*, however, appear earlier: "*autenticitat* (probably 1343)" and "French *authenticité* (1557)." Definitions of *authenticity* include "the fact or quality of being true or in accordance with fact; veracity; correctness"; "of undisputed origin and not a copy; genuine"; "made or done in the traditional or original way, or in a way that faithfully resembles an original"; and "based on facts; accurate or reliable" (*OED*).

Moving from religious to philosophical meanings, Kernis and Goldman claim that two aspects of "authentic functioning" are "people's (1) self-understanding" and "(2) openness to objectively recognizing their ontological realities (e.g., evaluating their desirable and undesirable self-aspects)" (2006, 284). Sartre agrees: "Man is nothing else but that which he makes of himself" ([1946] 2004, 282). In contrast, Heidegger defines *inauthenticity* as "a state in which life, stripped of purpose and responsibility, is depersonalized and dehumanized" (*Oxford Dictionary of Philosophy*).

Being authentic to oneself can collide with one's writing being authentic to a culture. The tension between the two derives from the fact that, though one's own story may be authentic to oneself, cultures are not monolithic. As a result, one's own story may be perceived as inauthentic to some members of that culture. Claims to authenticity—and accusations of inauthenticity—in children's literature emerge from the intimate entanglements of personal, cultural, and political histories. For example, in Europe, shifting responses to immigration patterns produce evolving definitions of who can be "European," particularly in relation to those perceived as ethnic "others" (Chin 2017, 2); White Europeans' perceptions of immigrants' assimilability impact the provision of and barriers to social services, acceptance, mobility, and so on, which then alter the materials conditions in which immigrants live. In a Chinese context, Minjie Chen evaluates how youth literature might represent—and misrepresent—certain aspects of Sino-Japanese histories, especially as they relate to war, violence, and power. While reading what we now call *diverse literature* may offer "the opportunity to experience the world through the written word," these delights may be eclipsed by "opposition, backlash, and debates," even raising questions as to diverse literature's "continued existence" (Harris 2006a, 108).

Readers assume that insiders write authentic stories, thus being faithful to themselves and to the expressions of themselves through text. One marker of "cultural authenticity" is that it is evident the writer "knows what's going on" (Bishop 2003, 29). Similarly, Jacqueline Woodson writes that "as a black person, it is easy to tell who has and who has not been inside 'my house'" (2003, 45). Others contend that "anybody can write about anything—if they're good enough . . . defining authenticity on some exclusionary basis won't change a thing" (Rochman 2003, 108). Non-Black writers such as Ezra Jack Keats have made what Michelle H. Martin calls "substantial contributions" to the body of Black children's literature; Keats's depiction of an "ordinary black boy . . . played such an instrumental part in the normalization of blackness in children's literature" that it merits inclusion in her book, *Brown Gold: Milestones* of *African-American Children's Picture Books, 1845–2002* (2004). These essays and books remain relevant as debates continue about the creation, marketing, and use of diverse literature, particularly but not only regarding the ways in which this literature is authentic.

Multicultural publishing data from the Cooperative Children's Book Center (CCBC, School of Education, University of Wisconsin–Madison) relay the diversity but not the authenticity or quality of American children's literature. The statistics include all books, regardless of quality, authorship, and authenticity, so long as a primary or secondary character is Indigenous or a person of color. Therefore, it is likely that the actual number of high-quality authentic texts is smaller than the reported 23 percent diverse total of all children's books published in 2018, 25 percent of all in 2017, 22 percent of all in 2016, and 15 percent of all in 2015. The American publishing industry's data make up the bulk of the CCBC's data; breaking down the numbers by countries of origin hardly changes the statistics. In the UK, the "Reflecting Realities" survey revealed that only 4 percent of children's books published in 2017 contained BAME (Black and minority ethnic) characters; only 1 percent had BAME main characters (Centre for Literacy in Primary Education 2018). While this report addressed genres, topics, and reading levels, it did not define what would make "authentic" children's literature but did comment that more "meaningful and accurate" portrayals are needed.

The shelves of libraries and bookstores remain full of children's books that present themselves as culturally authentic and yet distort, misrepresent, or caricature their subjects. *The Story of Little Black Sambo* (Bannerman 1899) and *Five Chinese Brothers* (Bishop 1938), both written and illustrated by white people, remain popular even as they contain egregious stereotypes; multiple authors and illustrators have created retellings

with new art (Lester 1996; Mahy 1990; Tucker 2003). Similarly, the inauthenticity of the picture book *Tikki Tikki Tembo* (Mosel 1968) can be traced directly to the creator's confusion about the story's country of origin. In "Rethinking Tikki Tikki Tembo," Grace Lin describes how, though the story originated in Japan, Arlene Mosel claimed that the story was based on a Chinese folktale. Despite claims to Chineseness, illustrator Blair Lent drew the characters as wearing kimonos and getas, both traditionally Japanese. In a related blog post, "The Problem with Celebrating Rikki Tikki Tembo," Lin also writes, "It took a non-Chinese story and pretended that it was old and authentic, added bogus traditions and words; and, in doing so, misrepresents Chinese culture." The danger of such sloppy "authenticity" is that it perpetuates the idea that two distinct Asian cultures and stories may be collapsed as one and the same. Although, as Junko Yokota writes, "eliminating books that are not culturally authentic from library collections and classroom use is paramount" (2009, 16), *Tikki Tikki Tembo* remains popular. It is a number-one best seller on Amazon with 4.7 out of 5.0 stars, and in early 2017, Hennepin County Library—Minnesota's largest public library system—reported that it was the highest-circulating picture book, suggesting that readers either are not aware of or may not care about its many inauthenticities.

Language is a frequent site of struggle between what is authentic and what is creative license. The popular picture book series *Skippyjon Jones* (Schachner 2003) employs what some critics have described as "Splanglish" or "Mock Spanish" (Slapin 2013; Martínez-Roldán 2013). Drawing on popular and negative Mexican stereotypes such as Speedy Gonzalez, the Taco Bell Chihuahua, and Frito Bandito, the protagonist adds *-ito* to the ends of words to make them "sound" Spanish. In 2016, advance praise for E. E. Charlton-Trujillo's young adult novel *When We Was Fierce* raised red flags regarding dialect among some readers. As K. T. Horning (2016) writes, "African-American Vernacular English is not 'broken English' . . . you can't just 'make it up.'" The novel's "constructed Ebonics" was "inconsistent," according to Jennifer Baker (2016), and Edith Campbell (2016) asked, "Who makes up language when portraying real people living in a contemporary society?" Horning, Baker, and Campbell—as insiders in particular ways (Horning, who is white, has a background in linguistics, and Baker and Campbell are both Black)—had the "reader's sense of truth" that Dana L. Fox and Kathy G. Short claim, "particularly when the reader is an insider" (2003, 5). However, some reviewers (who are mostly white women; see Low 2016) had given the book starred reviews, with Kirkus (2016) claiming that the book employed "Shakespearean word usage."

False claims to authenticity highlight the risk of essentializing a cultural identity (by defining it too narrowly) and the problem of an outsider misrepresenting a particular community. In addressing whether one has to be of a particular background in order to write an authentic text, *The Education of Little Tree* (1976) is an example of a text that was accepted—and widely celebrated—as an authentic memoir of a Cherokee man, but it was soon revealed that the author was a white supremacist who lied about his origins (Gates 2003). Forty years later, John Smelcer's claims to Native identity were similarly challenged after his book *Stealing Indians* (2016) was announced as a finalist for PEN Center USA's Literary Award in the young adult category. The *Huffington Post* reported, "For years, Smelcer's been an object of suspicion within Native circles, where authors including Sherman Alexie and Terese Mailhot, as well as scholar Debbie Reese, have raised questions about his Native heritage and his credentials, and critiqued his books as misrepresentations of history and Native cultures" (Fallon 2017). The revelation caused PEN Center

USA to withdraw *Stealing Indians* as a finalist (Reese 2017).

Questions regarding the relationships between literary merit and authenticity are worth asking. Gates contends that "our literary judgments . . . remain hostage to the ideology of authenticity" (2003, 135), concluding that while our social identities do matter, who we are and what we wish to or are able to write is not a relation "of fixed determinism" (142). The fear is that this kind of "policing the boundaries" (138) serves only to "[lock] us into smaller and tighter boxes" (Rochman 2003, 107). However, one must also remember the context: Native American stories have been appropriated (and people and land stolen) for centuries, and the majority of youth literature depicting Native people is not written by Native people. As Reese (2018) observes, because the majority of 2016 and 2017 publications by "Big Five" publishers were not written by Native people, "in one explicit or subtle way or another, they fail to provide Native children with mirrors." On the *American Indians in Children's Literature* blog, Reese has carefully vetted hundreds of books that demonstrate that many of the non-Native-authored and -illustrated texts remain deeply problematic. Can such a body of literature be "authentic"? Perhaps not if "an inside perspective is more likely to give an authentic view of what members of the cultural group believe to be true about themselves, whereas an outside perspective gives the view of how others see the particular group's beliefs and behaviors" (Yokota 1993, 158–59).

What one believes or perceives to be authentic and what is actually authentic is at odds and raises the question of who decides. In her "Danger of a Single Story" (2009) TED Talk, Nigerian novelist Chimamanda Ngozi Adichie shares that an American professor once told her that her story was not "authentically African," as if there exists something that is essentially African and that he could be the judge. Similarly, Cynthia Leitich Smith's editors initially refused her *Jingle Dancer* (2000) manuscript because they said no one would believe that a Native woman could be a lawyer (Smith was a lawyer before she started writing for youth). The industry continues to rely on "single stories," thus painting cultures and experiences as though they are monolithic and unvaried. Collectively, children's books tend to tell the same kind of story—for example, when black people are most often depicted in slave narratives or when Jewish narratives are set during and in the immediate aftermath of the Holocaust, and anything outside those narrow parameters may be deemed both unbelievable and inauthentic.

The hashtag #OwnVoices has been used to identify "kidlit about diverse characters written by authors from that same diverse group" (Duyvis 2015). Created by author and blogger Corinne Duyvis in 2015, #OwnVoices has taken on a life of its own, becoming "shorthand for a necessary concept." In 2017, Duyvis tweeted about how #OwnVoices had gotten "complicated and messy" (2017), similar to how authors of the essays in *Stories Matter* wrote about the complexities around texts such as the fabricated memoir *The Education of Little Tree*. In "Continuing Dilemmas, Debates, and Delights in Multicultural Literature," Violet Harris writes, "Questions about authenticity, insider/outsider views, and authorial freedom remain unresolved" (2006a, 116). Indeed, they do.

9

Body
Kelly Hager

Body is a noun, though it was a verb: "To give form, shape, or physical presence to; to embody. Now chiefly literary or poet" (*OED*). The *OED* gives five definitions for the noun: the "physical form of a person, animal, or plant"; the "main portion, the trunk"; "a person"; "a collective mass"; and "substance, matter, a portion of matter." Then the *OED* traces the etymology of the word back to "Old High German *botah*: body, corpse, trunk (of the body)." Additionally, the *OED* finds that "the sense development has been influenced by association with classical Latin corpus," which leads to *body* in the sense of a body of literature, or "a compendium of writings on a subject, textbook (e.g. *corpus iūris* law textbook)." The *OED*'s five core definitions all emphasize physicality and dominance, the concrete and the aggregate, the literal and the central or prevailing. These definitions highlight two key debates in the field of children's literature and culture: the way children's literature represents the physical body of the child and how we understand the body of texts we call children's literature. Both debates have to do with the normative, an association that can be traced back to the *OED*'s emphasis on "the main portion" and "the collective mass," and both debates, accordingly, swirl around questions of inclusion and exclusion.

Arguably, the two most explicit sites of children's literature's engagement with the physical body are fairy tales, with their emphasis on sex and violence, and YA fiction, with its focus on sexual maturation, orientation, body size, and physical abuse. Fairy tales and YA also have particular relevance to the canon debate, with some critics going so far as to exclude YA from the canon of children's literature explicitly (Seibert 2007), while others, in their equation of the canonical with classics and with Golden Age children's literature, do so implicitly (Lundin 2004; Kidd 2011b). Similarly, the body of tales the editors of *The Norton Anthology of Children's Literature* (2005) refer to as "the classic or conventional fairy tales of Perrault, the Grimms, and [Hans Christian] Andersen" (180) is, literally and figuratively, a textbook example of the canonical. As Maria Tatar (2017) reminds us, "print cultures enshrined standard tale versions that made variants deviations from the norm rather than unique reinventions. [But] those canonical versions of a story are nothing more than a fiction propping up our faith in defunct archetypes." What is more, the fairy tale's status as children's literature, as part of that body of literature, is itself highly contested. Tatar credits Bruno Bettelheim's *The Uses of Enchantment* (1976) with "put[ting] fairy tales squarely back into the canon of children's literature," while the editors of the *Norton Anthology* point to the fairy tale's "incorporation into children's formal education" at the end of the nineteenth century, a "trend . . . reinforced in the twentieth century." "With the help of teachers and librarians," they report, "the fairy tale became a staple of education throughout the West, and naturally a canon for children was established." Both Tatar's implication that fairy tales had been removed from the canon of children's literature at one time and the Norton editors' suggestion that canons are formed "naturally" bespeak this genre's complicated status within the larger body of children's literature.

Fairy tales and YA novels bookend the history of children's literature, but what comes in between is also marked by its attention to the corporeal and by worries over its status and stature. Eva Cherniavsky (2007) reminds us that it was not until the rise of "feminism, race and ethnic studies, and postcolonial studies" that "critical attention" was paid to "forms of material and abstract embodiment" and that "body thus has a relatively brief [career] as a focus of critical engagement in the study of culture." Studies of race and gender made possible, she argues, "a turn to those human subjects historically associated with the discredited life of the material body and so constituted as marginal to the arenas of cultural production and political representation: women, Africans and their New World descendants, Indigenous peoples, mestizos, and Asians, among other categories of 'overembodied' ethnic, sexual, and classed identity." To that list of marginalized bodies we might add the body of the child, and indeed, the history of children's literature and culture seems to follow the pattern Cherniavsky lays out: the inclusive aspirations of *Sesame Street* (first broadcast in 1969) and the rise of the YA novel in the 1960s and 1970s suggest that an interest in the "corporealized identity" of the child was also made possible by theories of race, class, gender, and orientation.

It is actually quite difficult to keep the sex out of the fairy tale, as Bill Willingham's *Fables* (2002–15) makes graphically clear. As Adam Zolkover emphasizes, "The characters in *Fables* are emotionally complex, sexually explicit, and physically present. In their transition to the comic book page, they are fleshed out, corporealized. . . . And further, as part of that same transition, they are eroticized" (2008, 42). That eroticization, he finds, "brings to the fore a great deal of the sexuality that is implicitly pervasive in the fairy-tale genre as a whole" (46). Similarly, in her exploration of three fairy tales that employ "the motif of cross-dressing" ("The Counterfeit Marquise," "Starlight," and "Belle-Belle ou le Chevalier Fortuné"), Lisa Brocklebank emphasizes the "potent critique of the status quo that begins with an examination of gender norms" and connects the tales' emphasis on "the performativity of gender and gender relations" with "the dynamics behind canon formation" (2000, 127). She asks, "Why have these tales come to be regarded as only for the nursery, when their original audience was highly sophisticated members of the French court?"

Just as indicative of children's literature and culture's fascination with gender and sexuality is the teacher's "'mysterious' copy of 'Professor somebody's Anatomy'" in *The Adventures of Tom Sawyer* (1876), "about which the children's curiosity is at a fever pitch," as Claudia Nelson (2004) reminds us. Ruth Saxton (1998) finds that "contemporary literary investigations into the Girl continue to envision girlhood according to tropes and plots familiar since the dawn of novelistic fiction" and that "physicality—the Girl's experience of her body, engagement in or denial of sex, her cultural 'value' as young female body—remains crucial." An especially clear example of the body's significance in literature for (and about) children can be found in the cross-dressing fictions of the nineteenth century, including Horatio Alger's *Tattered Tom* (1871), Eliza Leslie's "The Boy Girl" (1831) and "Billy Bedlow; Or, The Girl Boy" (1832), and Mark Twain's unfinished 1897 story "Hellfire Hotchkiss" (Taketani 1999; Norton 1999). Particularly interesting in this regard is *Tvillingsystrarna: Berättelse för unga flicko* (*The Twin Sisters: A Story for Young Girls*; 1893), a Swedish novel by Ellen Idström that "describes the creation of a new woman through an educational regime patterned on the upbringing of boys. By contrasting the progress of two twin sisters, one of which is brought up as a boy and the other as a girl, the novel explores gendered aspects of education, embodiment, and experience" (Andersson 2016). *Tvillingsystrarna* is not an anomaly either, as Andersson makes plain when she situates it

among "Swedish books for girls around the turn of the twentieth century" that "exemplify the wide range of behaviors that were explicitly coded as masculine."

Those books and their open exploration of gender and sexuality stand in marked contrast to their US counterparts half a century earlier, which are dedicated to disciplining the tomboy—in extremely corporeal fashion, usually by breaking her back—out of her nonnormative behavior. Susan Coolidge's *What Katy Did* (1872), Louisa May Alcott's *Jack and Jill* (1880), and Eleanor Porter's *Pollyanna* (1913) share with a host of other nineteenth-century fictions a focus on the transgressive body in need of discipline and punishment. The "repeated images of corporal punishment" in Catherine Sinclair's *Holiday House* (1839) are, as Jackie Horne (2001) argues, "deeply intertwined with the 'new' aspects of the novel, in particular its construction of the Romantic child."

"Historically, Finnish girls' literature generally follows the same themes, styles, and sub-genres as its Anglo-American counterpart," Myry Voipio (2013) asserts, but in the last ten years, in what she calls "the new wave" of Finnish girls' literature, "sexuality is the most prominent theme," something the protagonists "consider their own business" and, like "real contemporary Finnish girls [they] value their own decision making when it comes to their sexuality." "The novels," she finds, "bluntly describe different aspects of sexuality" and "openly represent a girl's sexual desire that generates pure pleasure instead of feelings of fear, shame or anxiety." In the UK and the US, Aidan Chambers's (1978–2005) six-novel "dance sequence" treats "issues of touch, desire, [and] masturbation," while Alice McKinley's examination of her vagina with a hand mirror in Phyllis Reynolds Naylor's *The Grooming of Alice* (2000) and the "play-by-play description of how to have intercourse" in Judy Blume's *Forever* (1975) bespeak twentieth- and twenty-first-century culture's desire to instruct (and delight) the child by explaining, and celebrating, her bodily nature (Trites 2000).

But to note those examples is not to deny a powerful strain of censorship with respect to the body of the child still at work in the culture. James Kincaid's (1992) argument that post-Victorian Western culture in general ignores the existence of children's sexuality is still applicable, and arguably those texts that depict an asexual, normative child are most likely to be included in the canon of children's literature. As Bettina Kümmerling-Meibauer and Anja Müller argue, twenty-first-century "approaches to canon issues in children's literature . . . retain an approach to the canon as an authoritative structure that makes statements about the intrinsic values of texts" (2017, 4).

The debate over the canon is of particular relevance to the field of children's literature, for not only was children's literature long excluded from the canon—an exclusion that is part of the institutional history of the field—but the debate also, paradoxically, makes us consider the fact that, as Beverly Lyon Clark (2003) puts it, "canonical works are always, in some sense, literature for children." Similarly, Jerry Griswold's (1996) assertion that "the American schoolroom was . . . the place where canons were made" (returning us to the link between curriculum and canon the *Norton Anthology* editors make about fairy tales) indicates that children's literature is both what is excluded and what is included. "Canonical works are precisely those that a culture wishes to preserve by passing them on to its young," Clark (2003) asserts. Or, as Guillory insists, "an individual's judgment that a work is great does nothing in itself to preserve that work, unless that judgment is made in a certain institutional context, a setting in which it is possible to insure the reproduction of the work, its continual reintroduction to generations of readers" (1993, 28).

According to Guillory, "the canon is never other than an imaginary list," but "what does have a concrete location as a list . . . is the syllabus, the list of works one reads in a given class, or the curriculum, the list of works one reads in a program of study." In that regard, then, this essay on "Body," which contains within it a list of works about the body, might be considered a body of children's literature about the body—a syllabus of sorts that is canonical in its aims.

10

Book

Patricia Crain

Rooted in old Germanic languages, *book* is a near relative of *beech* because of "the practice among Germanic peoples of scratching runes onto strips of wood" or, as others speculate, because of "the use of wooden writing tablets" (*OED*). Romance languages' *liber*, which English calls on for *library*, derives similarly from a word for *bark* (*OED*) or *leaf* (Partridge 1979), while *biblio* (for *Bible* and *-graphy*, *-phile*, and *-mania*) draws from a word for *papyrus*. As with many ancient words, especially words about words, the woodsy etymology of *book* evokes myth and ritual, investing materiality with magic. Many children's books may seem to distill the essence of bookness, opening—like fairy tales or Max's leafy bedroom in Maurice Sendak's *Where the Wild Things Are* (1963)—onto woods and forests. But the long-lived allure of the children's book, as of the book itself, has many roots and branches owing to the book's many ways of making meaning: as a format, as a trope, as a material artifact, as a commodity.

Book has largely come to mean the book-like thing you may or may not be holding now, that boxy container called a *codex*. This format, with pages bound between covers, overtook at least two previous technologies used for writing and reading: the clay or wax tablet (Roemer 2007) and the papyrus scroll or book roll (Johnson 2013). We might hesitate to anachronistically call these earlier inscription formats "books." Yet with the same sleight of hand that turns computer screens into "desktops," we are inclined to say we're reading "books"

digitally on our tablets, Nooks, and Kindles. The *OED* allows that "*book* may refer to a literary work in portable form written on a wide variety of other materials (as vellum, parchment, papyrus, cotton, silk, palm leaves, bark, tablets of wood, ivory, slate, metal, etc.), and put together in any of a number of forms (as a scroll, or as separate leaves which may be hinged, strung, stitched, or glued together)."

When we talk about reading or writing books, we tend to conflate container (whatever shape it takes) and contents. With the understanding that such a significant cultural artifact will always exceed categorization, in exploring *book* as a keyword, this essay leans toward materiality, container over content. For many people, an attachment to books in general as well as to particular ones derives from their tangible, haptic qualities—that they can, for example, when the size is right, be held in the hand (Piper 2012, 1–12). But while the codex book form and letterpress printing have had a long reign in the West, books have always come in other shapes using other inscription technologies. Media scholars distinguish between "media and formats"; the book, in this view, is a *format* and "a category of material goods . . . as well as a powerful metonym" (Gitelman 2014, 3, 6).

As a material format that can hide and reveal its contents, the book has been a reliquary-like vessel of religious and esoteric writing: Hindu Vedas, Buddhist sutras, the Torah, the Bible, the Koran. Due perhaps to these sacred resonances, as a trope the book offers to make vast swathes of experience legible: the book of life, of nature, of memory, of fate, of judgment. While colloquially the book stands metonymically for its contents (I've read that book), at the level of state, school, or religious authority, the book operates like an effigy (they've banned or burned that book). Where reading is widely valued as a good in itself, books in general, and books for children especially, have accrued symbolic social and cultural capital, as if the book form had an intrinsic value and an inherent power distinct from its content.

Books, in whatever shape or form, have always been in the hands of children, who learned to read and write on cuneiform tablets in the second-millennium BC Sumer (Robson 2007, 70–73), were schooled in Homer in ancient Greece and Rome (Lerer 2008, 24), recited from the first grammars off the Mainz and Venetian presses in the fifteenth and sixteenth centuries (Grendler 1989, 418), and learned their catechism in primers and read chapbook versions of old romances and ballads in the sixteenth and seventeenth centuries (Spufford 1985, 211; St. Clair 2007, 340). Generations of European children learned Latin and vernacular languages with Johann Amos Comenius's *Orbis Sensualium Pictus* (*The Visible World in Pictures*; 1658; see also Hürlimann 1968, 127–32).

But it took eighteenth-century print entrepreneurs to invent the *category* of the children's book when, circa 1750, the English bookseller Matthew Allison advertised "children's books of all sorts" amid the glimmering of a modern publishing industry (*OED*; Grenby 2011, 5). In the Anglo-American tradition, though others had sold books to children, the printer John Newbery was the first to market "a quality brand of children's books" (Immel 2010, 740–41). His *Little Pretty Pocket-Book* (1744) remains a handy touchstone, modeling long-standing aspects of the modern children's book, designed to entertain and prizing littleness, cuteness, pictures, and a warm relation between books and toys (it was sold with a ball or a pincushion; Darton [1932, 1958] 1970, 1–3). Widely reprinted in early America, Newbery's many steady sellers included *The Renowned History of Giles Gingerbread, a Little Boy, Who Lived upon Learning* (London, 1764; Boston, ca. 1776) and *The History of Little Goody Two-Shoes* (London, 1765; New York, 1775). Such books' small size, fetching woodcuts, and often avuncular direct address to child readers promoted what

was widely viewed as a desirable bond between book and child, which a famous and long-lived *New England Primer* rhyme captured as "My Book and Heart / Shall never part."

The openly commercial origin of the genre exposes tensions about the very category of the book for children. In contrast to literary genres differentiated by their formal qualities (prose, poetry, drama), "children's book" initiated a classification by readership, followed in the nineteenth century by "boys' books" and "girls' books" and in the mid-twentieth century by "young adult" books (Talley 2011; Kidd 2011b, 167). Such rubrics serve to make shopping easy, library cataloging rational, school committees pacified, authors and publishers profitable. And yet they may also bind the books they tag to putatively stable but actually quite fluid age and gender categories, uneasily interpellating a child, girl, boy, or young adult reader.

The book-as-commodity also raises the question of just how much the publishing industry has profited over time from children and their books. Contemporary best sellers (think Harry Potter) underscore what economic engines children's books can be (Marcus 2008, 312–15). Historically, too, children's books have always buoyed publishers' bottom lines, from the earliest grammars, to *Aesop's Fables*, to McGuffey readers, to fairy tales, to textbooks in constant and ever-updated demand. But we lack crucial metrics for an economic history of children's books, since historical statistics and figures have been notoriously difficult to come by (Suarez 2009, 48–49).

If books make money, still their status as commodities is occluded by a widespread "anti-commercial insistence that books are not ordinary products, but rather 'symbolic goods'" (Sánchez-Eppler 2008, 202). Like many other objects of intimate identification and fetishization, books are also fundamentally material artifacts and, as such, are explored by the interdisciplinary field of book history. Such an approach to the book object analyzes its size and form, the labor that went into its manufacture, the economics of its production and circulation, and even what anthropologists would call its "social life" (Appadurai 1986, 13)—that is, its journey from its commodity form to its stint as a particular child's book to, sometimes, its afterlife as a family heirloom or an artifact in the archive (as Lissa Paul's keywords essay observes).

For example, children's "gift books" and blank "friendship albums" in the nineteenth century included spaces for signing and inscribing, and many other books retain affectionate tributes to children by family members and friends. Children themselves would often sign their books with protective rhymes: "Steal not this book my honest friend for fear the gallows will be your end" (Crain 2016, 116). Whether "stories of possession" or of subversion (Lerer 2012, 131, 135), children's marginalia mark their engagement with and even, in a way, co-authorship of their books. The scribble-driven plot of Chris Van Allsburg's *Bad Day at Riverbend* (1995) depends entirely on a child's mediation as Old West townsfolk struggle to solve the alarming mystery of the "shiny, greasy slime" that her crayons have scrawled across the horses, cattle, and landscape of her coloring book.

In even more material ways, children have long been bookmakers themselves. The Brontë children (Anne, Charlotte, Emily, and Branwell) famously created manuscript books (Ezell 2014, 96), preserved because they are regarded as the juvenilia of notable authors. For centuries, young people have written in makeshift or purchased diary volumes, none more venerated—for both its vivid writerly contents and the poignance of what it represents—than Anne Frank's red plaid journal. Other children became published authors, like Palle Huld, the

Danish boy who wrote *A Boy Scout around the World* at fifteen, or Daisy Ashford, who wrote her wonderful comic Victorian novel *The Young Visiters or, Mr. Salteena's Plan* at nine, though it was published years later. Less celebrated children, too, have creatively "self-published": two generations of the New England Hale family's children produced 183 tiny manuscript volumes "in a wide array of genres" (Sánchez-Eppler 2008, 189). Children's handmade books speak of the entry of children into the system of books, with a ludic and satiric awareness of protocols and genres. And yet while elite children were making their own parlor books, working children had been involved in the book trade since the beginning—in print shops, in type foundries, and in paper mills and as compositors, inkers, and hand-colorists of illustrations (Abbott 1855; Grundy 2009, 148).

Books make meaning, then, not only by being read but also by being sold, given, owned, written in, or made. Even as a signifier in text or image, a book can speak of social or economic status, race, ethnicity, religion, or level of education. A child portrayed with a book might convey his docility or piety or aspiration but might also suggest that he has the leisure to read and the money to own a book. In much children's literature and visual imagery, children who are associated with books are thought to be inside the social order, while those lacking them, through choice or chance, are marked as racial or class others or outsiders. To bring *children* together with *book* can efface a thoughtful critique of either term; a nostalgic or sacralized sense of children or books can lead to inadvertent accepting and inculcating of race, class, gender, and other stereotypes under the cover of the innocence of a "children's book" (Nel 2017b; Bernstein 2011b).

Across the sociopolitical spectrum, adults have long anxiously strived to monitor children's contact with books. The digital-medial shift of recent decades calls up long-held feelings and concerns about children *in relation* to books, provoking debates about e-books and screen reading versus print (Kleckner, Martens, and Stoltz 2014). If it is true that books are now widely multimodal, with audio books and e-books now commonplace, alternative book formats have long been available to "print disabled readers" (Mills 2012). Taking the side of the codex form, Lane Smith's gently satiric *It's a Book* (2010) pictures a monkey reading a book and patiently fielding the questions of a digital-native jackass: "How do you scroll down?" and "Does it need a password?" *Treasure Island*, it turns out, is the text, and the book ends up captivating the jackass. And yet, mightn't he be just as engrossed reading Stevenson on a tablet? If we worry about children's relation to "cyberspace" (James and James 2008, 123), we might recall the extent to which books too have always been not only objects but spaces through which children have long roamed.

11

Boyhood

Eric L. Tribunella

Along with childhood and girlhood, boyhood is central to the definition of children's literature. John Newbery's *A Little Pretty Pocket-Book* (1744), frequently credited with igniting the English children's literature industry along with works by Thomas Boreman and Mary Cooper, addressed boys and girls separately as distinct audiences: the book was available for purchase with a toy described as a ball for boys and pincushion for girls. Historian Philippe Ariès identifies boys as "the first specialized children" (1962, 58). For much of the modern era in the West, boys were not differentiated from girls by their clothing until age seven or so, when a boy celebrated his growth out of childhood by exchanging gender-neutral gowns and smocks for breeches or pants. Girls lacked a similar ritual to mark the transition from early childhood to girlhood (Mintz 2004). However, anthropologists of childhood note that specific expectations of boys differ by time and place. In some cultures, such as the Igbo in Nigeria and the Inuit of North America, girls were traditionally required to give up play earlier than boys, but David Lancy observes that in a number of cultures, "gender differences" among young children "are of relatively little importance" until maturity, often at puberty, when initiation rituals both mark and exaggerate gender differences (2015, 202).

The linguistic record confirms the earlier specification of boyhood in English. The term *boyhood* is about 170 years older than *girlhood* and dates to the 1570s, while the word *boy* is even older (*OED*). Although first used in the mid-fifteenth century to refer to a male child, *boy* had also been used 150 years earlier, in a pejorative sense, to refer to a male servant or slave of any age or a male person of low or nonwhite status. Now archaic, the word *knave*, a cognate of the German *Knabe*, has a similarly dual meaning, while the French *garçon* can likewise refer to either a male youth or a man considered socially inferior. The common use of *boy* in this latter sense persisted well into the twentieth century as an offensive way to refer to men of color, irrespective of age. Manhood is often defined by the ability to dominate, care for, or exercise power over others, but these can be difficult or impossible for young men, poor men, or men of color.

The *OED* notes that the term *boyhood* rarely appears before the late eighteenth century, when children's literature began to crystallize as an established enterprise. This usage suggests that a more elaborate vocabulary and practice of childhood, including increased sex/gender specificity, went hand in hand with the expansion of children's culture. However, Scandinavian languages—Danish, Norwegian, and Swedish—share the word *barndom*, a term for childhood that can apply to both boys and girls, but lack an exact term for *boyhood*. Other approximations include *guttealder* (boy age) and *guttedager* (boy days) in Norwegian and *drengetid* (boy time) in Danish, which emphasize the temporality of youth more distinctly than the English *boyhood* does.

Boyhood has always constituted a kind of problem. To be a boy means to be a flawed, inchoate, or incomplete man, and boyhood involves the fundamental paradox between the privileges of maleness and the subaltern status of youth, class, or race. We find in children's literature the morally and socially subversive high jinks of boyhood, the sense of boyhood as a time of constraint and confinement, and the themes of escape and empowerment. Boys in children's literature frequently chafe against their inferior status, and the qualities and scenarios of boyhood are symptomatic of either resistance to that status or attempts to transcend it. The conflict between bucking the system and banking on future payoffs leaves the book about boyhood rife with conflict and contradiction.

The tension between sex/gender privilege and youthful subordination underlies themes of escape in the literature of boyhood. In their child-rearing guide *Practical Education* (1798), Maria and Richard Lovell Edgeworth warn parents *not* to permit young boys to read adventure stories, arguing that such tales would enflame the natural proclivities of boys to wander and explore and would ruin them for the duller, sedentary work of middle-class life. Adventure nevertheless remained popular with boys, and adventure novels such as R. M. Ballantyne's *The Coral Island* (1857) feature boy protagonists escaping home and parents and traveling the world. Along with adventure novels, the boys' school story, such as Thomas Hughes's *Tom Brown's Schooldays* (1857), and books about the quintessential bad boy, like Thomas Bailey Aldrich's *The Story of a Bad Boy* (1869), helped constitute what became known as the "boy book," a critical site for the construction of boyhood. In these works, the behavior of boy protagonists is considered both a problem in need of correction and a source of adult amusement or pride, and the different genres of boy books suggest diverse boyhood possibilities.

In addition to re-creating their own homes away from home or participating in colonial exploits, one way that boys can access a sense of authority, despite their youth, is by exercising dominion over animals and nature. Kipling's *The Jungle Books* (1894, 1895) depict Mowgli as superior to animals because he can wield fire, though he feels caged during his time in a human village and seeks to return to nature. *The Jungle Books* helped inspire the organizational structure of the Boy

Scouts developed by Robert Baden-Powell, whose *Scouting for Boys* (1908) explicitly cites Kim, the eponymous boy protagonist of Kipling's 1901 adventure novel, as a model for scouts. By the early twentieth century, the fear that boys "might be feminized by the transformed home, school, and church now dominated by women" (Jordan 2016, 7) fueled the development of organizations to give boys experiences predicated on the exclusion of female influences. John Stephens and Rolf Romøren still find instances in contemporary YA fiction of characters using nature to shore up boyhood or adult male masculinity, as in Arne Berggren's Norwegian novel *Fisken* (The fish; 1997), in which a father-son fishing trip tragically backfires.

Texts about boyhood trace the tension between one version of boyhood masculinity defined by physical prowess and another defined by moral virtue. Robert Richardson, who helped pioneer Australian children's literature, depicts ideal boyhood as defined more by moral character than physical strength (Mills 2007). In books like *The Boys of Springdale* (1875), he features sickly or sensitive boys who nonetheless possess or earn the esteem of their schoolfellows for their honesty and rectitude. In the iconic story of Pinocchio (1883) by Italian writer Carlo Collodi, the animated puppet only becomes a real boy after giving up his selfish ways, learning discipline and good behavior, and demonstrating his commitment to care for his father. Pinocchio's story centers directly on the problem of his out-of-control body, and he is rewarded for his good behavior with a stable human form.

Children's literature demonstrates the ways in which the boyhood body can be experienced or perceived as fundamentally problematic. While boys possess male privilege by virtue of their bodies, their youth interferes with their ability to exert physical or symbolic authority and points to endemic anxieties about the limitations of the male body in general. In South African writer Robin Malan's *The Sound of New Wings* (1998), a Pakistani boy named Shahraiz refuses to shower with other boys and eventually leaves school because of the bullying he suffers at the hands of bigger classmates, reflecting a long tradition of boys who must contend with social hierarchies based on size and strength.

The intersection of youth and race presents a double bind for boys of color, who lack the legal advantages of adulthood but from whom the privileges of childhood are often withheld. A group of researchers studying perceptions of Black youth found that "Black boys are seen as older and less innocent and that they prompt a less essential conception of childhood than do their White same-age peers" (Goff et al. 2014, 526). Jason Reynolds and Brendan Kiely's *All American Boys* (2015) and Angie Thomas's *The Hate U Give* (2017), two YA novels, depict police violence against Black boys who are wrongly seen as criminals. These works suggest that the broad freedoms afforded to "bad boys" require the racial privileges of whiteness.

Given the importance placed on sexual ignorance and inexperience as defining features of childhood "innocence," the line between boyhood and manhood is often drawn in terms of romantic desire or sexual experience. The conceptual dependence of manhood on "proper" sexual desire or activity further conspires to make romantic and sexual relations important concerns or milestones of boyhood maturation. In a cultural context that valorized romantic friendships between boys, Philip is made manlier by his love for and protection of a younger youth in Edward Prime-Stevenson's *Left to Themselves* (1891), described by its author as a homosexual novel for children. In contrast, Lutz van Dijk's German-language novella *Verdammt Starke Liebe* (*Damned Strong Love*; 1995), based on a true story about a romance between a Polish youth and German soldier during

World War II, depicts Stefan's emergent awareness of his same-sex desires as causing him to doubt his manhood. Japanese writer and illustrator Yun Kouga, following the tradition of *kemonomimi* (animal ears) manga, depicts boys in her Loveless series (2002–14) with cat ears and tails that are lost after sexual initiation, suggesting that sexually inexperienced boys are practically another species.

To assume that boys are the only consumers of boyhood in children's literature would be a mistake. The Edgeworths' assertion that adventure stories are safe for girls, who would supposedly be immune to the seduction of exploration, implies that girls might indeed read books about boys and boyhood. Beverly Lyon Clark (2003) finds evidence in reviews of *Tom Sawyer* (1876) that critics imagined both boys *and* girls as consumers of boyhood fiction. Sally Mitchell (1995) notes that such works were relished by girls who entertained fantasies of boyhood freedom, indicating that boyhood is by no means only for boys. While girls could enjoy the possibilities of boyhood by reading, Catherine Robson (2001) has argued that the real boyhood of the Victorian gentleman was actually more akin to girlhood in its feminine dependency and vulnerability and that male authors invented girl protagonists to recapture their lost girlhoods. A book like Cris Beam's *I Am J* (2011), which features a character who was assigned the female sex at birth but identifies as a boy, represents boyhood as a status or identity that can be asserted even when others fail to recognize that status and one's body does not conform to gendered expectations. Boyhood might be elusive even for boys who, like girls, might read boy books to experience the boyhoods they are perceived as lacking. Anchored mainly to the fictional worlds of children's literature, an empowered or successful boyhood appears to be an ideal that no boy or girl ever fully experiences. Though boyhood might be defined by subordination and subjection, at least boys can be represented in boy books as striking out on their own or claiming power that is unavailable to living children. This fantasy might partially explain the popular appeal of the boy book's depiction of boyhood and why girls read boy books more frequently than boys read books about girls.

Cohoon (2006), Kidd (2004), and Wannamaker (2008) each call attention to the contemporary "boy crisis," the broad cultural concern with the state of boys and boyhood and with how contemporary culture might harm or fail boys. The boy crisis has now gone global, with concerns about boyhood effeminacy prompting a Shanghai publisher to release a textbook for fourth- and fifth-grade boys in China titled *Little Man*, which includes lessons on how to be a proper boy (Wang 2016). That these concerns emerged as early as the nineteenth century indicates the perpetual uncertainty about what it means to be a boy. Boys are supposed to possess male privilege, yet their youth complicates their ability to claim the rewards of maleness or manhood. The multiple and fragmentary nature of identity and status along the lines of race, class, nation, or region can further intensify the subordination of boys and undermine their claims to sex/gender privilege. Some boys simply fail or refuse to enact the expectations or ideals of boyhood and face punishment for not seizing or embodying the benefits of maleness or masculinity. Being a boy and enacting boyhood can be difficult and even traumatic. Children's literature can provide sources of comfort and pleasure, models for behavior and identity, reflections of self and reality, and visions of better or less painful possibilities.

12

Childhood

Karen Sánchez-Eppler

Childhood is an ancient word in English. The *OED* takes as its earliest example for *cildhad* a tenth-century gloss between the lines of the Lindisfarne Gospels: "soð he cuoeð from cildhad" (Mark 9:21). A father explains to Jesus that fits had wracked his son's body since the earliest years of his life. The miraculous cure Jesus performs stands as a test of prayer. The gathered crowd, the disciples, and generations of interpreters since have voiced many questions about the meaning of this scene, but no one questions the meaning of childhood. This confident unanimity over the meaning of childhood is perhaps the most potent, and indeed dangerous, thing about this keyword. We have, it seems, a miraculous faith in childhood itself.

Young children everywhere must be fed, carried, taught to speak, and prepared to function appropriately within their particular social worlds (Stearns 2009). Conceptions of childhood all harken back to this trajectory from dependency toward autonomy, but there the consensus ends: Is the mewling infant darling or bestial, the roaming youth a crusader or a scamp, the laboring child valued or abused, the child reader virtuous, imaginative, or indolent? Childhood may be widely recognized as a life stage that stretches from birth until the taking on of adult competence and responsibility, but its meanings are formed by the particulars of each historical and social situation and the stories we tell about them. Perhaps it is because childhood simultaneously roots itself in both biological and ideological ground that it proves so effective at naturalizing cultural formations.

Ever since Philippe Ariès's provocative assertion that "in medieval society the idea of childhood did not exist" (1962, 128), scholars have striven to dismantle the essentialism of childhood, highlighting the frequent contradictions between any society's idea of childhood and the lived experiences of actual children. Ideas about childhood frequently articulate differences of status: modes of schooling and play mark national and class identity, differences between boys and girls, the transition from an agricultural to an urban/industrial economy, and racial inequality. Childhood manifests the processes of acculturation and assimilation that accompany global patterns of migration and colonial expansion. Changes in children's literature not only reflect these various biases but in many ways serve to create and disseminate them.

Books written for children provide a good gauge of a particular society's views of childhood and a measure we know children themselves engage with directly. Virtually all literate societies produce literacy primers in which learning to recognize scribal characters comes enmeshed in distinct values: compare, for example, the first couplet of *The New England Primer*, "In Adam's fall / We sinned all" (Ford [1777] 1889), with the opening lines of the *Three Character Classic* (*San Zi Jing*; 三字经), "People at birth / are naturally good / their natures similar / their habits different" (Wang 2011; Bai 2005). What disparate ideas of childhood and education are expressed in just those lines! If *The Story of Babar* (de Brunhoff 1931) or *The Jungle Books* (Kipling 1894) celebrate colonialism's feat of turning animals into children, this literary trope also prompts Sukumar Ray's Bengali rejoinder: a child's dream of talking animals in *HaJaBaRaLa* (1921; Goswami 2012).

Ariès argues that during the European Middle Ages, children might have been loved and cared for, but their lives were largely undifferentiated from those of adults. His account of the Enlightenment "invention of childhood" as a distinct social category shows how figuring the child as different from the adult sanctions the learned classes now needed to train the young and privatizes the family now needed to protect the innocent. In narrating how the concept of childhood was forged in early modern Europe, Ariès does not present a progress narrative. The alternately "coddled" and "disciplined" childhoods that emerge have in their different ways lost much of the autonomy and latitude that he identifies in the lives of premodern children (1962, 329). Thus the vulnerabilities associated with modern conceptions of childhood prove double edged: they elicit tenderness and care, but they also disallow agency. Such trade-offs characterize the ways that age is valued not only across time but also across place.

Globally, coming-of-age rituals differ in both the age of initiates and the skills required—for example, the scriptural knowledge of the bar mitzvah or of Khatam al-Koran, the pain endurance of Masai circumcision or of Fula tattoos, the survival skills of the Australian walkabout or of Inuit outcamps. Economic dependence is another frequent marker of childhood, although again one with extraordinary class, gender, and national variation. During Europe's Industrial Revolution, small dexterous fingers and the capacity to squeeze down mine shafts turned young children into cheap mill and mine workers during the very period when school expectations increased for children in the middle classes (Tuttle 1999). National and regional disparities over child labor remain among the most contested areas for the enforcement of the UN Convention on the Rights of the Child (Hanson, Volonakis, and Al-Rozzi 2015).

Rendering these rights as a kind of children's literature, UNICEF disseminates the fifty-four articles of this treaty in a "child friendly language" poster decorated with monkeys, lions, and giraffes.

The conflation of ideas about child development with models for the development of human civilization has had enormous implications both for child-rearing practices and for Western colonial rule (Stoler 1995). Douglas Newton's assertion that "the world-wide fraternity of children is the greatest of savage tribes, and the only one which shows no sign of dying out" (quoted in Opie and Opie 1959, 2) undergirds the study of childhood play as a field of folklore. Such equations spawn American "Indian"–themed summer camps and even more dangerously infantilize Indigenous people (Paris 2008). Colonial exploits are a frequent trope of nineteenth-century European juvenile adventure stories (Bristow 1991), but these associations continue to manifest in the contemporary children's literature market through the packaging of stories rooted in the oral traditions or religious practices of disparate cultures. Gerald McDermott's recasting of trickster tales from Africa, Asia, and America into award-winning English-language picture books is just one of the more recent manifestations of this long-standing tendency.

John Locke's ([1690] 1964) influential image of the child's mind as a "white paper void of all characters" (89) conflates child and page—a trope that is particularly illuminating for a discussion of children's literature. The success of John Newbery's line of "toy books" in the 1740s depended on this new conception of childhood (Avery 1995). The very notion that there should be books produced specifically for child readers in itself indicates a great deal about the evolution of the idea of childhood.

Shifting conceptions of childhood also seed quite different assumptions about the most appropriate stories to tell children. As Samuel Osgood advised, "We have ceased to think it the part of wisdom to cross the first instincts of children, and to insist upon making of them little moralists, metaphysicians, and philosophers, when great nature determines that their first education shall be in the senses and muscles, the affections and fancies" (1865, 725). Such changes in the content and purpose of childhood reading prove formative not only for the individual but for the culture. As Gillian Brown (2001) details, Locke's pedagogical models did as much or more than his political theories to inform American Revolutionary conceptions of governmental authority and consent. Striving from his exile in New York to foster Latin American cultural development, José Martí would consider publishing a children's magazine as an important tool of national formation. In *La Edad de Oro* (1889), the gold seems to be childhood itself. With his children's magazine, *The Brownies' Book* (1920–21), W. E. B. Du Bois primed for leadership African American "children of the sun."

The mid-nineteenth-century Euro-American flourishing of children's literature as a golden site for fantasy and play treated childhood less as a period of preparation for adult life than as a time wonderfully separate from it. Childhood from this vantage appears so different from the rest of life that it becomes another place entirely. Virginia Woolf's lovely phrase for it—"that great Cathedral space which was childhood" ([1939] 1985, 81)—is loaded not only with awe and beauty but also (this is Woolf, after all) with ironic iconoclasm. All the magical places of children's literature (Wonderland, Neverland, Narnia, Oz, where the wild things are) understand childhood in these topical terms as a distant someplace else. There is obvious class bias in the luxurious abundance of these fantasies that can sentimentalize and absolve inequalities.

The sense of childhood as a time and space of enchantment intriguingly mirrors the development of psychoanalysis (Blum 1995). Psychoanalytic theory gave new primacy to childhood as the origin of the adult self and its inchoate desires. Freud's account of infantile sexuality and the processes of its repression served to correlate the unconscious with childhood. Carolyn Steedman (1995) goes so far as to credit the figure of the child with grounding the modern concept of the self with its personal history and individual interiority. Thus by the late nineteenth century, childhood had become a locus of memory and imagination, a "secret garden" whose characteristics are in many ways shared with those of fiction itself (Burnett [1911] 1951).

By the end of the twentieth century, such an idealized romance of childhood appeared to many cultural critics as something lost or on the verge of loss. The hectic pace of modern life, the stress of high-stakes testing, the juvenilization of poverty, and the commercialization of desire seem to threaten the sacred pastoral of childhood. Television and video games besiege the golden citadel of children's literature (Postman 1994), and the ravaged figure of the child soldier explodes the myths both of childhood adventure and of childhood security (Jimmie Briggs 2005). Resisting childhood's essentialism, recognizing the constructed nature of this idyll, puts the language of crises in historical perspective. Pub signs and other commercial interests infiltrated alphabet primers from as early as the seventeenth century (Crain 2000), and as William Blake's *Songs of Innocence and Experience* insist, romantic celebrations of childhood were always shadowed by grim alternatives. Anne Higonnet (1998) urges that we replace the investment in childhood innocence with the recognition of the "knowing child," a figure aware of the world's threats and desires but still deserving of adult protection. We would do better at tending to the real needs and situations of children if we forgo our miraculous faith in any essential and singular idea of childhood. The historical record reveals the broad array both of ideas of childhood and of children's ways of living it. Contemporary "American society is unique in its assumption that all young people should follow a single, unitary path to adulthood," Steven Mintz observes with disapproval (2004, 383). The plural *childhoods* could prove a more honest and productive keyword, and children's literature may help inscribe this change by telling an ever-wider array of new and different stories.

13

Children's Literature
Peter Hunt

Children's literature can describe both a corpus of texts and an academic discipline—often confidently and apparently unproblematically, as in the title of this volume—but the term is what Raymond Williams (1976) would have called "difficult." Its elements cover a huge range of cultural meanings synchronically, diachronically, and internationally. It is still widely regarded as an oxymoron: if *children* commonly connotes immaturity, and *literature* commonly connotes sophistication in texts and reading, then the two terms may seem to be incompatible. Equally, its meaning varies considerably across the world—for example, *kinderliteratur*, *børnelitteratur*, *letteratura per l'infanzia* (or *letteratura giovanile*), *dječje književnosti*, and *literatura infantil* are not exactly equivalent. How can they be, when the concept of child varies culturally in terms of cognitive and physical development, responsibility, relationship to the adult world, and along many other axes? Across the years, the child has been seen as inherently evil, or as a tabula rasa, or as an innocent, "trailing clouds of glory." Today, children leave school (childhood's end?) at the age of ten in Bangladesh and eighteen in Argentina; children go to school (perhaps another childhood's end) at the age of seven in Finland and five in Australia. In Western countries, the concept of childhood as a protected space occupied by a protected, distinctive creature—the child—may be a predominantly twentieth-century phenomenon whose time is past. Similarly, *literature* (or its "equivalent") does not always have the primary connotation of cultural value that it carries in British and American English; it is widely used to mean any written text or specialist material, and there are also considerable differences in attitudes to, and the status of, the concept (Williams 1976).

Children's literature is, as keywords go, highly unstable.

It first appeared in English in an anonymous article in the *Quarterly Review* in January 1860, and by then, texts produced specifically for the entertainment of children were well established in Britain. However, elsewhere the idea of such noneducational texts, and therefore the need for a term to describe them, has emerged at widely different periods—perhaps as early as the Sumerian period (fourth century BCE; see Adams 1986). Such texts appeared more widely in the late eighteenth century in the Netherlands and in the early nineteenth century in Russia; in China, a "new awareness of a literature for children came about after the establishment of the Commercial Press in Shanghai in 1902" (Ho 2004, 1031), and in Iran, this developed not before the Constitutional Revolution of 1906. Children's literature in any form was not common in most of South America until the twentieth century and until the second half of the twentieth century in much of Africa. The totalitarian regimes that controlled many countries, notably in eastern and southeastern Europe until comparatively recently, regarded (often accurately) children's literature as subversive and a matter for rigorous state control. Although such control has been eroded by the internet, the idea that children's literature (often based on or consisting of national and nationalistic folk tales) must carry a strong ideological agenda persists in countries such as Iraq and Vietnam.

Children's literature, then, has become a blanket term, covering both educational and purely entertaining material and texts designed for children and "young adults." This latter categorization goes back at least as far as Sarah Trimmer's *The Guardian of Education*, in which she distinguishes between "'Books *for Children*' and 'Books *for Young Persons*.' . . . We shall take the liberty of . . . supposing all young gentlemen and ladies to be *children*, till they are *fourteen*, and *young persons* till they are at least *twenty-one*" (1802a, 22). Similar age-range prescriptions linger today, if only for administrative and publishing purposes. John Rowe Townsend's observation in 1971 remains true: "the only practical definition of a children's book today—absurd as it sounds—is 'a book which appears on the children's list of a publisher'" (1971, 10).

The broadest definition of *children's literature*, "any text read by any child," is of little practical value. Similarly, definitions that rely on the characteristics of texts, however subtle (see Nodelman 2008) founder either on exceptions—texts for children cover virtually all forms and genres—or on the problem of what "child readers" can perceive. More fruitful are definitions based on identifying the "implied reader" (Wall [1991] 1994; Weinreich 2000), which lead on to definitions centering on *intent*. Clémentine Beauvais considers "children's literature to be all texts for which the associated writing, publishing, mediatory, critical, and readerly practices display an awareness of the audience as primarily located within the symbolic childhood of their time" (2014, 8). Peter Hollindale, coining the term *childness* in 1997, felt that "children's literature" partakes of a certain jouissance and can be seen as an "event" involving author, text, and child: "This definition recognises a doubleness that we have to live with, namely that children's literature is characterized both by textual status and by readership, and its uniqueness is evident at the point where they meet" (1997, 50).

But what of the elements of the term?

The *Shorter Oxford English Dictionary* unhelpfully defines *children* as "boys or girls," and Matthew O. Grenby asks, "Is there such a thing as children's literature?

Might it be more accurate to talk of a boys' literature and a girls' literature?" (2008, 8). The term *children* is being interpreted in this context as "comparatively inexperienced/unskilled readers"; paradoxically, children, and their potential reactions to texts, are increasingly seen as individual at the same time that the increasing commodification of childhood suggests a deindividualization. Because the cultural concept of children (and childhood) changes radically with time, place, gender, and perceiver, a distinction might be made between books that *were* for children and books that *are* for children (see Hunt 1996; Flynn 1997).

Much depends, in the English version of the term, on the possessive *s*: does *children's* mean texts that are *for* children, *by* children, *belonging to* children, or *of* childhood?

Books *by* children and *for* children and therefore genuinely *of* childhood (their characteristics are unlikely to appeal to adults) can be seen as the "purest" form of children's literature. In 2001, Jack Zipes observed that "there has never been a literature conceived *by* children *for* children, a literature that belongs to children, and there never will be" (2001, 40). Time and electronic publishing have shown him to be wrong: the world is being flooded by texts *by* children and *for* children—the extent to which these are *of* either childhood or literature is an issue for children's literature as a discipline to grapple with.

If we take *children's* to mean *for* children but *by* adults, then the term is seen to focus on a complex power relationship. Jacqueline Rose's seminal *The Case of Peter Pan* challenged the traditional idea that "children's literature" *belongs* to children—and argued (a sign of her times, perhaps) that it was *necessarily* and negatively manipulative: "Children's fiction sets up a world in which the adult comes first (author, maker, giver) and the child comes after (reader, product, receiver), but where neither of them enter the space in between" (1984, 1–2). Later critics have found the relationship to be far more subtle and positive (Beauvais 2014; Rudd 2013).

Literature is also a problematic element, especially for children's literature academics trying to establish their credibility in universities. The texts of children's literature are often taken to fall into Raymond Williams's popular literature category in *Keywords*: "they are not 'substantial' or 'important' enough to be called 'works of literature'" (1983b, 186). However, such an argument (which still persists widely) has been undermined by the obvious cultural and commercial importance of texts for children (around 33 percent of all publications in several countries), crossover texts, and the fundamental idea that children's literature as both corpus and discipline is unique—neither comparable to nor in competition with adult literature. It is, as Zohar Shavit puts it, a different literary "system." This is a comparatively recent idea, and much confusion is still caused by the assumption that adult literature (and especially poetry) is the norm to which children's literature should aspire. The nineteenth-century German educationalist Heinrich Wolgast, who believed that children should be given only "real works of literature," observed that "anyone who wishes to swim must enter the water, and young people cannot extract any enjoyment from works of literary art if none are presented to them" (Ewers 2009, 117).

There are many—perhaps a majority—of countries, such as Taiwan, where despite the strength of children's literature texts as an important cultural and commercial fact, children's literature as a study is still marginalized. Elsewhere, as in France and Italy, it is treated with caution, whereas in countries such as Japan, Germany, Sweden, and Australia, it has been wholeheartedly accepted. There are many thousands of undergraduate and graduate degrees awarded in children's literature across the world, although in practice, many have little in common. They range from primary education to abstract theory and from aspects of child psychology to the most arcane bibliography—it is difficult to identify a coherent, or even mutually comprehensible core. The basic division is sometimes seen as one between "child people" and "book people" (a distinction first coined by John Rowe Townsend in 1971); the one sees children as central to the enterprise; the other does not. At the literary end of the spectrum, as Beverly Lyon Clark (2003) points out, the distortion of the term *children's literature* to *kiddie lit* indicates the condescension of some in the academic establishment. Children's literature is marginalized by being excluded from critical and theoretical discourses to which it could contribute vitally (Thacker 2000); this is the more surprising in that it is widely established as an exemplar of interdisciplinary studies.

The reaction of those working within the academic literary field called children's literature has variously been to adopt the critical and theoretical strategies of their peers in adult literature, or to position children's literature as a valuable partner in the cross-disciplinary childhood studies or an essential concomitant to established academic areas such as Victorian studies.

Children's literature, then, as a descriptor of a corpus and an academic discipline, attempts to enfold a system, an event, an intent, and an almost worldwide cultural phenomenon. This is, as David Rudd puts it, "hybrid, or border country" (2004, 39), and it is no wonder that the term continues to provoke confusion and controversy—and, in an international context, a good deal of misunderstanding.

14

Classic
Kenneth Kidd

Classic refers not only to texts but to ideals and aspirations. As Deborah Stevenson says of Lewis Carroll's *Alice*: "Eventually, a children's literature classic masters being beloved without actually being read . . . you do not have to read *Alice*, but you will be deemed culturally illiterate should you not acknowledge it as a children's literature classic" (1997, 126). The classic is imagined variously as a gift, a bribe, a promise, a legacy, and a contract. *Classic* stands for the past but claims relevance for and demands accommodation to the present. It claims continuity across translation in language or form. The classic represents selectivity but circulates widely. The classic binds together time and timelessness, the exceptional and the typical, the historical and the contemporary, the organic and the manufactured, the universal and the personal.

Classic is also a Western construction with particular Anglo-European inflection. It shores up more than disputes the borders of nation and language, rooted in a particular time and place even when it travels and accrues new meanings. Raymond Williams notes that *classic* shares derivation with *class* from the Latin *classicus*, which "had social implications before it took on its general meaning of a standard authority and then its particular meaning of belonging to Greek and Roman antiquity" (1983b, 60). The first definition in the *OED* links *classic* to *class*: "Of the first class, of the highest rank or importance; approved as a model; standard, leading." Both adjective and noun, *classic* came to designate the works of antiquity not only as literary but also as standard and standardizing. A related term is *canon*, derived from biblical discourse. According to the *OED*, *canon* refers not only to sacred books but also to "those writings of a secular author accepted as authentic"; a 2002 draft addition equates *canon* with "the classics." Both *classic* and *canon* suggest a selective heritage, with *classic* linked to classical culture and *canon* to religious tradition.

The meaning of *classic* has been expanded as well as preserved across the centuries. For Sainte-Beuve in the 1850s and then T. S. Eliot in 1944, *classic* means the Roman literary classic and in particular Virgil's *The Aeneid*. Eliot favors "maturity" as the major criterion of excellence but makes the counterintuitive argument that classics tend toward "a common style" ([1944] 1975, 118) and a "community of taste" (119). He also suggests classics are culminating moments not only of mature civilizations but also of dead or dying ones. Though Frank Kermode concurs with Eliot's sense of *classic* as bearing (in Kermode's words) "the assumption that the ancient can be more or less immediately relevant and available, in a sense contemporaneous with the modern" (1975, 15), he also points out that *empire* "is the paradigm of the classic: a perpetuity, a transcendent entity, however remote its provinces, however extraordinary its temporal vicissitudes" (28). Kermode resists Eliot's imperialist conception and allows for the "modern classic," open to accommodation (114). More critical still of Eliot's faith in the perpetuity of *classic*/*empire*, South African novelist J. M. Coetzee calls Eliot's lecture "an attempt to claim a cultural-historical unity for Western European Christendom including its provinces, within which the cultures of its constituent nations would belong only as parts of a greater whole" ([1993] 2001, 5). Coetzee and other postcolonial writers (Walcott, Rushdie, Naipaul) use the question of the classic to interrogate the politics of literary value in a global society that is still marked by

nationalism (Mukherjee 2014). Nations, Benedict Anderson reminds us, are "imagined communities," and both *classic* and *canon* are part of the nation-building enterprise in and around children's literature (Kelen and Sundmark 2013; Kümmerling-Meibauer and Müller 2017). In the first part of the twentieth century, for instance, labor-oriented Zionism required and helped manifest new "classics" for Israeli children (Darr 2017).

Emer O'Sullivan notes that children's classics come from three sources: (1) appropriations of adult works, (2) adaptations from traditional (usually oral) narratives, and (3) works written specifically for children (2005, 133). National traditions feature varying combinations of these categories, depending on the state of children's publishing and the broader situation of print culture. Classic status is bound up with the politics of publishing and translation as well as national identity. Penguin Books Australia, for instance, runs an Australian Children's Classics series of "keepsake editions" of settler-colonial texts with no mention of Indigenous literature. In China, debates about the children's classic are linked to traditions of educational writing and oral literature before and after the Cultural Revolution. Tracing discussion of the children's classic to the 1960s, O'Sullivan points out that most so-called children's classics come from Europe, "primarily north-west Europe, and America. Of all originating languages, English is by far the most prevalent" (133). Through a case study of *Pinocchio*'s translations, she concludes that it is impossible to settle on a world canon of children's classics largely because no text migrates to another culture without modifications in content and meaning. In place of the "world republic of childhood" imagined by Paul Hazard, we have "the worldwide children's market" (151), in which classics "are a market rather than a literary phenomenon" (147), one favoring English-language and especially American titles. Even so, many European classics have found international distribution, albeit in translation, such as the work of Astrid Lindgren, Tove Jansson, Michel Tournier, Michael Ende, and Jostein Gaarder, among others (Beckett and Nikolajeva 2006). Gaarder's philosophical YA novel *Sofies verden* (*Sophie's World*; [1991] 1994) has sold over forty million copies in fifty-nine languages.

Though tethered to empire and nation in unfortunate ways, *classic* is also linked to more progressive efforts. In the US especially, the idea of the children's classic has been useful to librarians, publishers, scholars, and other advocates trying to fashion a public sphere of children's literature. *Classic* in fact entered middlebrow American culture in part through the children's classic in the early twentieth century. As Radway (1997) notes, the first Book-of-the-Month Club selection was Sylvia Townsend Warner's *Lolly Willowes* (1926), often considered a children's book; conversely, the first winner of the John Newbery Medal was Hendrik Willem van Loon's *The Story of Mankind* (1921), one among many popular outlines for the reading public.

Established in 1922, the Newbery was one of the great mechanisms of middlebrow culture and classic making, the brainchild of publishers and booksellers as well as librarians (see Kidd 2007). Other book awards followed, some national and others ostensibly international in scope. Some were established to help bolster the language and literature of smaller nations, as with the Norwegian Ministry of Culture's prizes for children's and young adult literature. Coterminous with those awards were rhetorics of gold, as in "golden treasuries" of children's literature and the influential 1929 book list *Realms of Gold*. This language of gold is at once naturalizing, suggesting that classics are found or mined, and associated with commerce—with coining, minting, and even alchemy—suggesting that classics are not born but rather made (even forged). New

or fast classics were manufactured according to modern demands and tempos. Librarians, booksellers, and publishers all got into the business of making as well as listing classics. Louise Seaman Bechtel, the first woman head of a children's book division within a major publishing house (Macmillan), was particularly adept at the business, leveraging the status of established titles into classic status for new ones (Kidd 2006). In her unpublished memoir, she remarks, "I just needed to put [children's titles] in similar bindings, devise new jackets, and call them classics" (Bechtel, n.d., 6:4). Granted, this culture of children's book promotion took place alongside a general devaluation of children's literature by "serious" literary types (Clark 2003; see also Eddy 2006; Marcus 2008; and especially Lundin 2004).

Given this complicated history, it is no surprise that children's literature critics both champion and oppose the classic(s). Jon C. Stott's 1978 presidential address to the recently formed Children's Literature Association called for the establishment of a canon (Lundin 2004). The *Touchstones* project emerged, a three-volume collection of essays (1985–89) edited by Perry Nodelman. Volume 1 focused on fiction; volume 2 on folk literature, legend, and myth; and volume 3 on picture books. The project was undertaken, as John Cech explains, "not to dictate or mandate certain books while ignoring or rejecting others, but rather, to serve as a starting point" (1986, 177).

The last few decades have brought sharper criticism of the children's classic. Jacqueline Rose's *The Case of Peter Pan, or The Impossibility of Children's Fiction* (1984) is arguably a dismantling of such. Echoing Roderick McGillis (1998–99) and applying Pierre Bourdieu's critique of distinction to the field of children's literature studies, Jack Zipes (2001) holds that the idea of the children's classic distracts us from a more expansive understanding of what children read and write. Not only must we struggle with the classic's debts to empire and nation; there is also the problem of fallen classics—classics that have lost value ideologically, aesthetically, or both. Not a few children's classics are racist, for instance. Others are now less relevant and seem to be fading away. Not all fallen classics are bad, of course. Some might be good books with bad histories or afterlives, as Jonathan Arac (1997) asserts of *Huck Finn*. Problematic children's classics might include Lindgren's *Pippi in the South Seas* (1959) and Jean de Brunhoff's *The Story of Babar* (1931). Confronting structural racism in children's literature, Philip Nel (2017b) recommends we learn to read such texts "uncomfortably."

A possible conclusion here, one reached by Coetzee, is that *classic* productively encompasses the debate it engenders. "The classic defines itself by surviving," proposes Coetzee, and therefore "the interrogation of the classic, no matter how hostile, is part of the history of the classic, inevitable and even to be welcomed. For as long as the classic needs to be protected from attack, it can never prove itself classic" ([1993] 2001, 16). Bechtel understood that point early on: "The more argument as to what *is* a children's classic *for* children, the better" (n.d., 6:19).

15

Crossover Literature
Sandra L. Beckett

Crossover is a somewhat slippery term, as it is used with a different meaning in a variety of fields. None of the main entries in the *OED*, where the word is spelled with a hyphen, refer to literature or to any other art form; rather, they refer to textiles, women's clothing, railway lines, river currents, and biology. While the final definition of *cross-over*, "that crosses over; characterized by crossing over," allows for applications to literature and other arts, the exemplary quotations are limited to fashion and politics. It is not until a draft addition of December 2006 that the arts are mentioned in a meaning originating in the US, where, since the 1970s, *crossover* has been used to refer to music that finds appeal beyond its niche market with a "different (esp. a wider) audience." In the field of children's literature, the term refers specifically to texts that cross age boundaries. As in music, the word is used both as an adjective and a noun that can refer to either "the process or phenomenon" or "a piece . . . which undergoes this process" (*OED*). The etymology of the word from the verbal phrase *to cross over* explains the lexical tensions of a word that can be applied, with a multiplicity of meanings, to a wide range of subjects. Despite some reservation with regard to a term that is used with different meanings in postcolonial studies, gender studies, comics, and music (Falconer 2004, 557), *crossover* has now been widely adopted, even beyond English-speaking borders, to refer to literature that transcends age boundaries.

Although the term *crossover* is relatively new, the literary phenomenon that it designates has existed for centuries. The term was coined when crossover literature gained a high profile and began to attract widespread public, media, and critical attention after the unprecedented success of J. K. Rowling's first Harry Potter books in the late 1990s. One of the earliest articles to refer to the "crossover phenomenon" in those terms was a 1997 piece titled "Breaking the Age Barrier" (Rosen 1997). Although critics, the media, and the publishing industry began to use the term in the late 1990s, it did not emerge as a common expression until the 2000s. The first monographs to adopt the term in their title were Sandra L. Beckett's *Crossover Fiction* (2009) and Rachel Falconer's *Crossover Novel* (2009).

Further tensions are created by the fact that *crossover* is not the only term that has been coined to refer to literature read by both children and adults. The expression *crosswriting* (or *cross-writing*) was broadly used by critics, even beyond the anglophone world, before the widespread adoption of the term *crossover* (Beckett 1995, 1996–97; Knoepflmacher and Myers 1997; Kümmerling-Meibauer 1999). Although the two terms were initially used synonymously, the majority of critics now reserve *cross-writing* for authors who write for both child and adult audiences but in separate works, as in the case of Margaret Atwood, Colette, Umberto Eco, Selma Lagerlöf, and Virginia Woolf, to name only a few. In 2000, the crossover writer was broadly defined as "the writer who writes for both children and adults" (Cadden 2000b, 132). Such a writer would be a crosswriter unless he or she appeals to both audiences with the same work. The inconsistent usage of *crossover* illustrates the ambiguity or "fuzziness" that Falconer (2009) attributes to the term. Since the 1990s, scholars, critics, reviewers, and publishers have used a variety of other

terms to designate literature read by both children and adults, including *dual address, dual readership, dual audience*, and *cross-audience* (Beckett 1999). The adjectives *intergenerational* or *cross-generational* have also been employed to refer to this literature. The assortment of expressions reflects the general dissatisfaction with any one term and the search for an appropriate descriptor for this literature that had suddenly achieved an exciting, new status. *Crossover* rapidly gained popularity and largely replaced other expressions. The catchy term became a handy label for publishers and a favorite buzzword with the media.

English-language terms were not, however, the first to refer to literature addressed to a diverse, mixed-age audience that can include children, adolescents, and adults. The term *allalderlitteratur* (all-ages literature) was coined in Norway as early as 1986 to describe the works of authors such as Tormod Haugen, who had been appealing to young and old alike since the 1970s. In Spanish, such books are referred to as *libros para todas las edades* (books for all ages). In 1990, the publisher Siruela created a groundbreaking series, whose name, Las Tres Edades (The Three Ages), clearly indicates the perceived inadequacy of terms implying a "dual" audience. One of their first books for all ages was Carmen Martín Gaite's *Caperucita en Manhattan* (Little Red Riding Hood in Manhattan; 1990). A number of countries have adopted terms, sometimes anglicisms, that incorporate the idea of all-age books. In Germany, the expressions *All-Age-Buch, All-Age-Literatur*, and *All-Age-Titel* have been in use since about 2002, although the term *Brückenliteratur* (bridge literature) was coined much earlier, probably following the publication of Michael Ende's *Die unendliche Geschichte* (The neverending story; 1979). In the Netherlands, the term *literatuur zonder leeftijd* (literature without age) gained wide usage after 1993, when it became the title of a journal acknowledging the growing importance of Dutch-language fiction for all ages, notably by authors like Bart Moeyaert and Anne Provoost. The sometimes cumbersome terms coined in other languages serve to illustrate the difficulty of finding a suitable descriptor as well as to explain the adoption of the catchy English term *crossover* in other language areas. In 2008, Matteo Nucci devoted an article to *la letteratura crossover* in *La Repubblica* in Italy, and in 2013, Andrés Lomeña Cantos published an interview about *la literatura crossover* in Spain. "The rise of crossover fiction in Swedish" is the subject of a 2014 article by Agnes Broomé and Nichola Smalley, while the Norwegian scholar Åse Marie Ommundsen discusses "la *crossover* littérature scandinave" in a 2011 issue of a French journal. In French, critics have resorted to expressions such as *la littérature destinée à un double lectorat* (literature aimed at a dual readership), *la littérature pour tous les âges* (literature for all ages), and the anglicism *la cross-fiction* (Beckett 1997, 2009b; Moissard 2005). The expressions forged in other languages are a reminder that crossover fiction is not a phenomenon limited to English-language literature but rather a widespread, international trend. The scope and social importance of crossover literature can only be fully appreciated when it is considered from a global and cross-cultural perspective.

Crossover has often been used in a rather narrow sense to refer only to contemporary children's and young adult fiction read by adults. For many, crossover literature is genre specific, limited to the novel. It is certainly true that attention has been largely focused on the novel (Falconer 2009). Others further restrict crossover to the subgenre of the fantasy novel—that is, to titles such as the Harry Potter series, Philip Pullman's epic trilogy His Dark Materials, and Cornelia Funke's Tintenwelt (Inkworld or Inkheart) trilogy. While the runaway best sellers that played a key role in drawing public and critical attention to crossover literature are fantasy novels, virtually every genre can cross age boundaries, including short fiction, fairy tales, poetry, graphic novels, picture books, and comics. The term *crossover* is now being widely applied to picture books, which have a long history of addressing a mixed-age audience (Beckett 2012). Works by Maurice Sendak, Anthony Browne, Tomi Ungerer, Bruno Munari, Jörg Müller, Stian Hole, Katsumi Komagata, and countless other picture-book artists challenge the misconception that picture books are only for children.

The crossover does not occur in one direction only. Crossover literature is also adult fiction read by young readers. In fact, adult-to-child crossover has a much longer historical precedent. From John Bunyan's *The Pilgrim's Progress* (1678) to Daniel Defoe's *Robinson Crusoe* (1719) to Alexandre Dumas's *Les trois mousquetaires* (1844), adult literature has been appropriated by children for centuries. In the nineteenth century, a significant number of works were marketed to (and even adapted for) young readers, including Herman Melville's *Moby Dick* (1851) and Harriet Beecher Stowe's *Uncle Tom's Cabin* (1852), as well as novels by James Fenimore Cooper and Charles Dickens. This trend continued into the twentieth century, with titles such as Jack London's *The Call of the Wild* (1903) and L. M. Montgomery's *Anne of Green Gables* (1908). Today the rebranding of adult fiction for young readers has made this type of crossover a much more conscious process.

Most often, crossover books are initially published for one audience and subsequently appropriated by another in a process that has been called "cross-reading" (Falconer 2004, 559). The majority cross from child to adult or adult to child audiences. Some books find a new audience when they cross cultural or language borders, as in the case of Jostein Gaarder's *Sophie's World* (1991). However, some books are explicitly written and marketed intentionally for both audiences, as in the case of Mark Haddon's *The Curious Incident of the Dog in the Night-Time* (2003).

Crossover is a conception of literature that blurs distinctions between adults and children. It therefore needs to be seen in a broader cultural context. The crossover phenomenon exists in many spheres of contemporary culture. Well before Harry Potter launched the vogue in the literary domain, visual media were attracting huge audiences of children, teenagers, and adults with television shows such as the original *Star Trek* (1966–69) and *The Simpsons* (1989–); video games like *Super Mario Bros.* (released in 1985); and films such as *Star Wars* (1977), *E.T. the Extra-Terrestrial* (1982), and *Toy Story* (1995). Interestingly, the term *crossover* is rarely used in these fields except by children's literature theorists and critics. A children's literature encyclopedia entry devoted to *crossover literature* defines it as "books and films that cross from child to adult audiences and vice versa" (Falconer 2004). Crossover novels have generated highly successful cross-medial franchises, such as Harry Potter, *The Lord of the Rings*, *The Twilight Saga*, and *The Hunger Games*, which have mass appeal with broad, mixed-age audiences. The website crossoverguide.com is nonetheless one of the few sources to offer a broad definition that embraces several media: "Any book, film or TV programme that appeals to both adults and children is a crossover title." Even in the literary field, where the crossover phenomenon has had a much higher profile, theoretical discussions continue to be almost exclusively within the field of children's literature, as theorists of adult fiction tend

not to "cross over" to children's books (Beckett 2018). Crossover literature is part of a broad cultural trend in which a wide range of cultural forms are increasingly reaching across age groups. The term *crossover* has great potential for cross-disciplinary, cross-medial, and cross-cultural discussion of a phenomenon that has enormous social implications. As critic Andreia Brites suggests in titling an interview "O Crossover como ponte universal" (published in Brazil in 2015), we might see "the crossover as a universal bridge."

16

Culture

Richard Flynn

"Culture," writes Raymond Williams, "is one of the two or three most complicated words in the English language" (1983b, 87). When applied to the study of children and their literatures, it is also one of the most contested, as it sprawls across distinctions between artistic practices and prestige, media, conventions of societal groups, regions, and nations. The Latin *cultura* is derived from the past participial stem of the root word *colere*: "to cultivate," "to worship." The 1805 *OED* definition is the one most relevant to the tensions central to children's literature and culture: "The training and refinement of mind, tastes and manners; the condition of being thus trained and refined; the intellectual side of civilization." Lingering in the definition are the oppositional senses that children can be cultivated like the land or worshipped, as in idealizing the "cult of childhood." The 1805 definition locates this culture at the beginning of the Romantic era, foregrounding the tension between worshipping children for being natural and cultivating them into civilized adults.

Notions of children's acculturation are perceived as being either in concert with or opposed to nature—or frequently both. Largely as a result of the Wordsworthian brand of Romanticism, childhood is equated with innocence and the primitive, while the socializing and "culturing" aspects of child rearing and education are downgraded as artificial. The educating or cultivating of children is analogous to the culturing done under artificial or controlled conditions, as in culturing pearls or microorganisms such as viruses.

Even in such a radically Romantic text as *Émile ou de l'éducation* ([1762] 1911), Rousseau argues that the aim of education is to cultivate the (male) child's natural tendencies in order to avoid the negative effects of "all the social conditions into which we are plunged" because "they would stifle nature in him and put nothing in her place" (5). Although Rousseau's valorization of the innocent child of nature has long dominated the definition of childhood, groundbreaking scholarly work, particularly by Mitzi Myers and Julia Briggs in the 1980s, on late-Enlightenment maternal teacher-writers such as Maria Edgeworth (1768–1849) in England and Mme de Genlis (1746–1830) in France slowly began to erode the image of the Romantic innocent (and ignorant) child. A more nuanced relationship between nature and culture, one emphasizing the development of child agency, is emerging (notably in the essays in *Culturing the Child, 1690–1914: Essays in Memory of Mitzi Myers* [2005], edited by Donelle Ruwe) in constructions of a twenty-first century version of childhood.

Because our tendency is to define culture by its presumed opposite, typical notions of culture have tended to exclude children or relegate them to subcultural status, as Neil Postman argues in *The Disappearance of Childhood* (1982). His default position was premised on the assumption that the child—either originally sinful or innocent—existed in a state of nature upon which adults and adult institutions imposed culture. However, the once distinct borders between nature and culture are becoming more porous, with meanings shifting according to historical and, well, cultural contexts. As Kenneth Kidd (2002) notes, when in the 1990s childhood itself became understood as a cultural invention, distinctions developed between children's literature, children's culture, and childhood studies. As children's literature is typically assumed to disseminate cultural norms, even classic books such as the *Pippi Longstocking* stories or the *Struwwelpeter* verses can cause consternation in their troubling ambivalence toward normative socialization.

The perceived conservatism of the children's canon has spurred scholars to explore what might be termed countercultures, as in Julia Mickenberg and Philip Nel's anthology *Tales for Little Rebels* (2008), Kimberley Reynolds's *Left Out* (2016), Julia Benner's *Federkrieg* (War of words; 2015), and Helle Strandgaard Jensen's *From Superman to Social Realism* (2017). Such works remind us that children's culture is historically a contested site.

While *literature* stands as much of an evaluative term as a descriptive one, children's literature has often been relegated to what Williams calls the "category of popular literature or the sub-literary" (1983b, 186). *Culture* too traditionally carried both elitist connotations of high culture and populist notions of mass culture. In his fascinating but cantankerous manifesto, *The Idea of Culture* (2000), Terry Eagleton complains that while "traditionally, culture was a way in which we could sink our petty particularisms in some more capacious, all-inclusive medium," it now means "exactly the opposite. . . . the affirmation of a specific identity—national, sexual, ethnic, regional—rather than the transcendence of it" (38). *Literature* and *culture* are now frequently yoked, as in Routledge's *Children's Literature and Culture* series.

High/low, literature/culture distinctions began to break down as transnational, migration, and childhood studies emerged as disciplines of their own. Even in its early days, the humanities-based study of children's literature internationally was already engaged in translation, transnational, and cultural studies. Thanks to the efforts of Jella Lepman, the Internationale Jugendbibliothek (International Youth Library) was founded in Munich in 1949, and the International Board on Books for Young People (IBBY) was founded in Zurich in 1953. The International Research Society for Children's Literature (IRSCL), founded in 1970, was conceived at a colloquium in 1969 organized by members of the Institut für Jugendbuchforschung (Department for Children's and Young Adult Literature Research) of Goethe University in Frankfurt (also the home of Walter Benjamin's own collection of children's books). Anne Devereaux Jordan's account of the very first American Children's Literature Association conference (March 1974) notes that the theme was "Cultural and Critical Values in Children's Literature," and the participants included actual cultural workers: writers, publishers, reviewers, and even a member of the Newbery-Caldecott committee. Rare for an American journal at the time, *Children's Literature* 3 (1974) included a survey of Chinese, Austrian, Greek, and Norwegian children's literatures. In 1976, the third IRSCL symposium held in Södertälje, Sweden, set as its theme the "Problems of Translation in the Field of Literature for Children and Young People."

Questioning any "universal" idea of childhood finds affirmation in issues related to translating language and culture, which figures increasingly in the international scholarly work in the field. In her comprehensive essay "Comparative Children's Literature," Emer O'Sullivan charts the distance from Paul Hazard's universalizing "republic" of childhood in *Les livres, les enfants et les hommes* (1932) to cultural and comparative studies "examining texts in their historical and cultural contexts and probing the modes of (non)transfer" (O'Sullivan 2011, 195). She cites Martina Seifert's explanation of why L. M. Montgomery's 1908 Canadian classic, *Anne of Green Gables*, was not published in German until the 1980s: the world of the imaginative small-town literary girl was at odds with the German view of Canada as a rugged wilderness to be conquered by boys and men.

If there is a single most important factor in changing the default image of the child from being an innocent creature of nature to a cultured person able to exercise individual agency, it is probably the open borders created by increased global internet connectivity and access, dating from around the turn to the twenty-first century. One way to mark the shift is through the work of Henry Jenkins. His *The Children's Culture Reader* (1998) excerpted a number of foundational texts, including Philippe Ariès, Jacqueline Rose, Viviana Zelizer, and James Kincaid. While the introduction paid lip service to children's agency, many of the essays therein—with the notable exception of those by media studies scholars Lynn Spigel and Ellen Seiter—relegated children to victim status. Although Jenkins, Ito, and boyd in *Participatory Culture in a Networked Era* (2015) attend to the fact that the rise of internet connectivity has largely overturned the Romantic version of the innocent child insulated from the outside world, it still does not engage sufficiently in the rise in child agency, a feature that has radically changed the critical context for discussions about children's literature and culture. Children born in the internet age have been quick to harness its power to advocate for social change, as demonstrated in the political demands for gun control in the aftermath of the Parkland school shooting of 2018 or Greta Thunberg's ability to galvanize international youth in a call for political action to address the climate emergency.

As Kenneth Kidd (2002) argues, "children's culture and children's studies" rather than "venturing into uncharted territory" are more of a "shift in focus from literature to culture [that] attests to the staying power and adaptability of analysis as a vocation, and of 'culture' as an organizing field" (146). The acknowledgment that childhood is not a universal, transhistorical, and sacrosanct culture of its own necessitated a turn away from belletristic literary appreciation to a more rigorous consideration of history, ideology, and culture. The nature/culture divide has resolved into an acceptance of the notion that a stable or fixed idea of childhood no longer exists—if it ever did.

17

Diaspora

Michelle Martin and B. J. McDaniel

Diaspora, which means "to scatter" or "disperse" in Greek (IdEA, n.d.), combines "the prefix *dia-* (meaning 'through') and the verb *sperein* (meaning 'to sow' or 'to scatter')" (Edwards 2014, 76). While Münz and Ohlinger write that the term "was first used in ancient Greece to characterize the exile of the Aegean population after the Peloponnesian War" (2003a, 3), Edwards says that it originally appeared in the Septuagint, which is "the translation of the Hebrew Torah prepared for the ruler of Alexandria in Egypt around 250 BCE by a specially appointed group of Jewish scholars" (2014, 76). Although the word has historically been used as a self-designation by populations of Mediterranean Jews during the Hellenic period, today we use it to describe those living outside their shared country of ancestry or origin. Both emigrants and their descendants belong to the diaspora of the emigrant, who might or might not maintain strong ties to an ancestral homeland. Those with mixed heritage can belong to multiple diasporic communities (IdEA, n.d.).

Jewish traditions make a sharp distinction between voluntary migration (*diaspora*) and exile (*galut*). According to Haim Hillel Ben-Sasson, "Only the loss of a political-ethnic center and the feeling of uprootedness turns Diaspora (Dispersion) into *galut* (Exile)" (1971, 275). While Münz and Ohlinger note that the evolution of the Jewish diaspora plays an important role in how the term is understood and used today, rarely is a distinction made between voluntary migration (as in emigration from a country of origin to another) and forced migration (as in chattel slavery or exile) in determining whether someone belongs to a diaspora. Hence how people enter the diaspora may not impact whether they belong to a particular diaspora, but their means of entry might influence how connected they remain to their homeland.

As we raise definitional questions about what constitutes a diasporic text, we will argue that the idea of *sankofa* plays a significant role; this Ghanaian word from the Akan tribe means to "go back to the past and bring forward that which is useful" (SIU Department of Africana Studies 2018). In children's literature, these texts typically recall the homeland and/or home culture as characters seek to integrate their experiences into a new culture—a process that Guyanese British poet Grace Nichols articulates aptly in *The Fat Black Woman's Poems* (1984): "I have crossed the ocean / I have lost my tongue / From the root of the old one / A new one has sprung" (64). Conversely, African American poet Countee Cullen writes about resistance to *sankofa* in his 1925 poem "Heritage": "One three centuries removed / from the scenes his fathers loved / Spicy grove, cinnamon tree / What is Africa to me?" ([1925] 2013). As someone with enslaved ancestors who knew Africa intimately, this speaker asks why he should concern himself with Africa. Cullen's poem highlights the tensions between those who seek to honor the vital connections with their respective homelands, those who acknowledge but resist these connections, and even those who still live in the homeland but perhaps long to become a part of the diaspora.

If we define diasporic youth literature by audience rather than by authorship, its definition should be based on the age and background of readers. However, if this generic categorization builds on authorship (as do adult texts), then its diasporic qualities may reside in the content of the text or the author's experience or background. Sharon Draper is African American. Is her novel *Out of My Mind* (2010)—which never mentions the race of the characters—as much a diasporic text as *Copper Sun* (2006), her work of historical fiction about the Middle Passage and southern US slavery? Is Jane Yolen's *The Devil's Arithmetic* (1990) diasporic because it tells a Holocaust story, or because Yolen is Jewish, or both? Is *The Arrival* (2006) by Australian writer-artist Shaun Tan diasporic because it imagines a fantasy world that intentionally alienates readers to help them understand the difficulties of emigration even though Tan still lives in Australia? These questions underscore the complexities of defining diasporic texts and their potential role in helping readers negotiate the intersections of identity that occur when texts explore race, nationality, sex, gender, religion, age, and other vectors of identity.

While we acknowledge that authors who write outside of their own cultural experiences can write world literature, we believe that only authors who originate from the countries they write about or who are descendants of those who do can write diasporic literature. In recalling a culture and a set of experiences and values that are ultimately tied to the author's life and ancestry, diasporic texts perform *sankofa* regardless of readership. Hence although *children's literature* points to audience, we posit that *diasporic children's literature* points more to authorship. Therefore, although these are eye-opening and informative, we do not consider them diasporic texts: Patricia McCormick's YA novel *Sold* (2006), about sex trafficking in Nepal and India; Tara Sullivan's *The Bitter Side of Sweet* (2016), about child laborers on a cocoa plantation in Ivory Coast; or Sullivan's *Golden Boy* (2013), about albinism in Tanzania. These authors do not come from the countries or belong to the diasporas about which they write in these texts. Depending on how closely the story ties back to the culture of origin, diasporic texts seem to fall into three primary categories

that can provide a useful lens for examining this genre, though these categories are by no means exhaustive. Diasporic stories focus on (1) transition/displacement when characters move from the homeland to the new country, (2) integration/cultural collage within the new culture, and/or (3) hybridity/intersectionality. Representing a progression of experiences, these stories explore aspects of the characters' home culture as they emphasize tensions, challenges, and triumphs.

The International Diaspora Engagement Alliance (IdEA) confirms that over 3 percent of the world's inhabitants live outside their homelands, and "if migrants made up a single country, they would be the 5th largest in the world" (IdEA, n.d.). In the winter 2018 issue of the *Children's Literature Association Quarterly*, Philip Nel adds, "Today, 244 million people live outside the country of their birth. . . . Nearly 22.5 million are refugees. Over half of all refugees are under the age of eighteen. Of the world's 10 million stateless people, one third are children" (357). Exposing young people to diasporic texts—an increasingly significant genre, given the international statistics on migration—helps broaden their worldview and expose them to diverse cultures and to the stories of children who have been displaced. Furthermore, as Nel notes, "Such literature can affirm the experiences of children in those communities, letting them know that they are not alone" (2018, 358). A few examples follow that illustrate the important role these texts play in enabling young people to explore diaspora vicariously.

Highly impactful for its child's-eye view of war, Bana Alabed's middle-grade autobiography, *Dear World: A Syrian Girl's Story of War and Plea for Peace* (2017), gives readers one perspective on how displacement looks, feels, and sounds. She writes of her beautiful childhood surrounded by family and how, when she was just three, that life was shattered as bombs began to fall in Aleppo. Bana's story is punctuated by the narratives of her mother, Fatemah, offering a parent's perspective on family life in war-torn Syria. Bana became well known for her pleas for peace on Twitter, which also made her family a target of the Syrian Army. Bana's moving story ends with her displacement: a relief agency evacuated her family to Turkey just before Bana's eighth birthday.

Jewish American Pamela Ehrenberg's *Queen of the Hanukkah Dosas* (2017), illustrated by Indian British Anjan Sarkar, presents a fine example of a cultural collage, layering culturally Jewish and Indian language and references into both text and illustrations. The main character's father, mother, and Amma-Amma (grandmother) all help shape a Hanukkah that does not look like other traditional celebrations but emphasizes the broad reach and impact of the Jewish Diaspora. Intergenerational interactions emphasize the representation of a family that has successfully integrated myriad cultural experiences into their unique lifestyle. Traditions (lighting the menorah), recipes (*dosas* and mango *lassi*), and landmarks (Little India Market and Hebrew school) that are implicitly and explicitly cited in the book—though their geographical location remains unspecified—may be traced to separate origin spaces, but their integration is intentional and self-defined by the story's multiracial, multinational family. Resisting stereotypes and embracing many different kinds of diversity, this picture book affirms the characters' position within at least two diasporas.

Tracing five generations of one African / African American family from the US to Liberia and back, Shannon Gibney's YA novel *Dream Country* (2018) embodies a sankofic consideration of an often-unexplored history of subjugation and intradiaspora conflict among Black Americans, Liberians, and citizens from other countries within Africa. Perspectives from characters escaping the effects of slavery in 1827 Virginia, only to replicate the cruelty of that system in Liberia, are juxtaposed against Liberian refugees adjusting to life as "too Black" for White people and "not Black enough" for African Americans in early 2000s Minnesota. Gibney's positionality as an African American transracial adoptee raised by white parents, who now mothers Liberian American children, emphasizes an understanding of diaspora as a spectrum of experiences with emotional as well as literal movement. Gibney shows that the literary threading of hybrid intersections within diasporic experiences need not include resolution or assimilation to acknowledge and respond to cycles of trauma.

Writers of diasporic texts tap into their knowledge and experience of the history, culture, language, stories, and sensibilities of the culture about which they are writing and to which they belong. As diasporic writers perform *sankofa*, they connect with the past to influence the present and future. In so doing, these authors widen the world for young readers.

18

Didactic

Clémentine Beauvais

All that *didactic* means, etymologically, is "instructive" or "skilled at teaching" (*OED*: διδακτικός). That meaning has persisted, neutrally, in some languages, where a *departamento de didáctica* or *département de didactique* simply refers to an education faculty, or *Didaktik* labels the theory of teaching. But the term, today, in English, is generally used polemically. To call a children's book didactic is to accuse it of trying to impart a "message"—generally of a moral nature. *Didactic*, in children's literature criticism and reviewing, is often synonymous with *moralizing, authoritarian, totalitarian, propagandist*. The term is also its own superlative: rarely is a book deemed "too didactic"; *didactic* generally suffices to condemn it.

Yet "the didactic" (or didacticism) remains seldom defined in children's literature criticism: it is an I-know-it-when-I-see-it sort of vice. The only solid definitional anchor for didacticism is historical. Didactic literature for children—namely, for religious and moral instruction—was the origin of children's literature itself: didacticism is in the DNA of children's literature (Grenby 2009). François Fénelon's *Télémaque* (*Telemachus*; 1699), traditionally acknowledged to be the earliest example of children's literature in the West, was written to entertain but also educate intellectually and morally the young Duke of Burgundy. In the seventeenth and eighteenth centuries, one would not bat an eyelid at the remark that a children's book was didactic. It better be; if not, what would be the point? Certainly, entertainment

was also important—for instance, in John Newbery's conception—but the educational responsibility of a children's text was strong. Samuel Johnson argued that literature, especially when conceived for young people, must select its representations carefully so as to be an embellishing mirror, telling of aspirations rather than reality: "The purpose of these writings is surely not only to shew mankind, but to provide that they may be seen hereafter with less hazard" (Johnson 1750).

In the course of the nineteenth century, and then more so in the twentieth, didacticism in literature became increasingly perceived as a defect rather than an expectation or quality. With the advent of a Kantian perception of art as what has been dubbed "for art's sake," texts that openly sought to educate were gradually considered coercive and of inferior aesthetic merit (Higonnet 2000). Wolfgang Iser (1974) argues that the advent of literary fiction as a replacement for didactic texts occurred with the emergence in novels of gaps, or blanks, for the reader to fill. The presence of these gaps, and the readerly freedom they imply, separates Samuel Richardson's didactic *Pamela* (1740) from Henry Fielding's freer *Tom Jones* (1749)—a view critiqued by Cerny (1992). Authors began to shirk from using fiction as an open means to instruct, and *didactic* became an insult, as in this observation by Edgar Allan Poe, who talked of a phenomenon that "may be said to have accomplished more in the corruption of our Poetical Literature than all its other enemies combined. I allude to the heresy of *The Didactic*" (1850). On the children's literature side, F. J. Harvey Darton's 1932 survey of children's books in England mapped the evolution from "The Moral Tale: Didactic" to what he perceived as a liberation of the genre post-1880. "To-day: Freedom," he claimed—freedom, that is, for the child to enjoy the reading experience rather than be edified by it ([1932, 1958] 1970). Lucy Pearson (2013) has shown, and aptly critiqued, these pervasive scholarly narratives that contend children's literature has progressed from *didactic* to *enjoyable*.

Three parameters seem to frame "the didactic" as used informally by theorists and reviewers. First is the presence, on the speaker's part, of an explicit intention to communicate a specific moral or ideological message in the hope that it will convince the addressee to adhere to it. This is what Peter Hollindale calls "active ideology" (1988, 10) and Sutherland "the politics of advocacy" (1985, 145) in their essays on ideology in children's books. Second, there is the implication that this message aspires to exclude parallel viewpoints—that it "serves the aims of indoctrination, *urging* a particular value system or course of action" (Sutherland 1985, 146). Third, *didacticism* implies that the mode and content of the communicative event make it impossible for the addressee to engage critically with it; they are "leaving little to the imagination" (Latimer 2009).

A tentative definition of the term could be as follows: *didactic* tends to be attributed to texts that are seen as striving to carry a single message in a way that makes the addressee unable to respond with critical distance. The distinction between didactic and non-didactic texts tends to be formulated as a distinction between texts that give space to many voices and those whose closedness constrains the recipient. In contemporary criticism as in everyday discourse, *didacticism* can now be viewed as an umbrella term under which to cluster forms of literature that are monological, excluding, intentionally instructional, or threatening to reduce plural viewpoints to a single perspective.

But such definitions are necessarily frail because the term is very undertheorized and generally mentioned flippantly rather than profoundly: it more often serves rhetorical than analytical purposes. In literary criticism, definitions of *didacticism* as a property of text are rare. In 1987, William Casement argued that the growing condemnation of didacticism in literary circles was due to "three main themes that are integral parts of the mindset from which we operate today: contemporaneity, subjectivism, and relativism" (110), theorizing the distaste for didacticism as a distinctly modern concern. Charles Repp, analyzing didacticism as a polemical term, distinguishes several meanings encapsulated by the accusation—namely, dogmatism, intellectual arrogance, and prejudice. What we imply when we talk of a didactic text, he says, is that we are in "bad company" with the author, that the writing is "bad taste," and that our readerly pleasure is spoiled (2012). The history of that last accusation is at least as old as the Romantics; in Keats's famous words, "We hate poetry that has a palpable design upon us" (1818).

Do we really hate it always? Scholars in children's literature have pointed to the possibility that young readers might read against, around, or even alongside the didactic elements and still gain pleasure from the text (Nodelman 2000a, 41–42). Even when we identify some features of text that might signify a didactic impulse, it is far from established that they preclude enjoyment. One of the hallmarks of didacticism, for instance, is the presence of an adult and child characters engaged in pedagogical exchange, as in Norwegian author Hanna Winsnes's *Aftenerne paa Egelund* (The evenings at Egelund; 1852) or Jostein Gaarder's well-loved mise en abyme novel *Sophie's World* (1991), in which a young girl, in an epistolary relationship with an older man, is playfully but firmly taught about canonical philosophy. The didacticism of the novel, however, was evidently no obstacle to its enduring international success and critical praise. And many contemporary best sellers for children make use of Socratic dialogue–like devices, which leave just enough space for the child narratee or character to respond yet not quite enough for the response to be outlandishly outside the adult character's plan for the direction of the conversation. Every single Harry Potter novel (Rowling 1997–2007), for instance, ends with such a dialogue, yet it is rumored that at least some children have enjoyed that series.

Even if we tolerate that didactic texts might sometimes seduce children, are they good art? The accusation of "bad taste" or that didacticism nullifies aesthetic power remain very strong in children's literature criticism and leads to conceptual difficulties. Maria Nikolajeva's (2010) use of the term *literary-didactic split* to characterize children's literature hints at a field of study and a corpus of texts that are intrinsically uneasy about their own identity and unsure about which side to value more. Artistic merit and instructiveness do not cohabit peacefully in children's literature. Preoccupation with some kind of balance between the artistic and the didactic, conceptualized as separate, is not new: *Télémaque*, while widely appreciated, elicited the following critique by Boileau: "I should wish [the author] had made [*Telemachus's Mentor*] a little less of a predicator, and that the moral be spread across his work a little more imperceptibly and with more art" ([1699] 1893). Today, similar thoughts are routinely uttered by children's literature scholars; some genres appear to be particular magnets for that type of criticism, such as biographies for children (e.g., Nel 2010) or literature striving to impart an environmental message (e.g., Echterling 2016).

There are correlations between the modern vision that a didactic text cannot be art and the slow emergence of children's literature criticism. As Margaret Higonnet (2000) argues, the assumed lack of literary merit in any text with an educational purpose has long sidelined children's literature as a worthy object of literary study. Indeed, because didacticism is a theoretical blind spot in literary theory, corpuses of novels chosen for study by literary scholars have historically excluded didactic texts. Wayne Booth, in the very first sentence of the *Rhetoric of Fiction* (1991), states that he is not concerned with "didactic fiction, fiction used for propaganda or instruction" (xiii). That kind of premise, generalized to the discipline, leaves untouched vast quantities of fictional works, including children's literature.

The theoretical orientations of children's literature scholarship today bear the marks of critical disdain and distrust for didacticism. There is strong critical emphasis on features of texts that preclude closure: "gaps," for instance, are at the core of picture-book aesthetics. While there is a plethora of work on postmodern books for children, the aesthetics of openly didactic texts are little developed. Nonfiction for children, evidently instructive in purpose, has only recently started to elicit serious interest (e.g., Sanders 2015). The same could be said of politically committed children's fiction. Gradually, however, we are seeing children's books with a clear political or social message gaining critical praise for *both* their aesthetic and ideological features. The peaceful cohabitation of the didactic, the beautiful, and the enjoyable is fairly uncontroversial—for instance, in Antonio Skarmeta and Alfonso Ruano's story of resistance to totalitarianism in *The Composition* (2000), Gro Dahle and Svein Nyhus's haunting picture book on domestic violence *Sinna Mann* (Angry man; 2003), Shaun Tan's tale of immigration in *The Arrival* (2007), or Armin Greder's less optimistic variation on the same theme in *The Island* (2007).

Recently, children's literature scholars, creators, and activists have directly and indirectly given more critical space to new forms of the didactic in children's literature. The #WeNeedDiverseBooks campaign, the rise of awards for books celebrating social change (Kidd and Sanders 2017), and the emergence of independent publishers with committed editorial lines can be read as a revalorization of the didactic drive in the production, distribution, and reviewing of children's texts. In academia, too, there has been in the past fifteen years a rise in studies on politically "radical" or "committed" texts with clear didactic dimensions (Mickenberg 2006; Mickenberg and Nel 2008; Abate 2010; Hubler 2010; Curry 2013; Beauvais 2015; Reynolds 2016). An important recent development is Louise Joy's (2019) theorization of the aesthetics of didactic children's literature. The potentially transformative nature of children's literature is being reconsidered, and we are increasingly able to think of messages without necessarily concluding to a lack of aesthetic merit or readerly pleasure. If this ethics and aesthetics of commitment, both in criticism and in creation, continue to develop, then the term *didactic* might gradually become descriptive again rather than polemical.

19

Disability
Nicole Markotić

Etymologically, the prefix *dis-* suggests lack and reversal: a *dis*ingenuous person lacks sincerity. Where the noun *ability* indicates the state of "being capable of doing," *disability* implies "inability, incapacity," or "weakness" (*OED*). The prefix *dis-* indicates a kind of *undoing*. For many people, being disabled means an undoing of the body's whole, originary state, making any illness, age, or injury that moves the body away from its supposed normality undesirable. Conflating disability with illness, the "medical model" assumes individual or pathologized responsibility for corporeal difference and seeks to "cure" any such differences. In contrast, the "social model" looks to environmental barriers that exclude physically, cognitively, and developmentally disabled people. Historically, *disability* has indicated "a physical or mental condition that *limits* a person's movements, senses, or activities" (*OED*; my emphasis)—a *disadvantage* whether because of birth or accident or imposed by social law.

Theorizing the body as a mutable, unstable form, disability studies challenges the assumption that bodily variations are defects to be cured. Emerging as a discipline first in the social sciences via Erving Goffman's *Stigma: Notes on the Management of Spoiled Identity* (1963), the field soon began to examine the historical parameters upholding an able-bodied norm. Disability studies interrogate categories of oppression based on corporeal difference, whether that difference be social, cultural, gendered, racialized, class-based, ageist, homophobic, or ableist.

The disabled body presents an ambiguous site where outward appearances have denoted inward pathos or even vice. As Susan Wendell (1996) explains, disabled bodies historically have been "feared, ignored, despised, and/or rejected in society and its culture" (85). In canonical English and European children's literature, disability plays a fixed and primarily metaphorical role—one that has not celebrated what Rosemarie Garland-Thomson calls "extraordinary rather than abnormal" (1997, 137). Often, representations of disabled characters in children's stories presume a social and cultural standard of normalcy that renders images of ageing, illness, or disability abnormal within an ableist paradigm and that differentiates bodies via categories of "able" and "less able," "handicapped" and "normal."

Addressing a prevalent contradiction between the ubiquitous appearances of disability in literature and the relative critical and audience silence on the topic, James Porter claims that "a disabled body seems somehow too much a body, too real, too corporeal" yet at the same time "seems too little a body, a body that is deficiency itself" (1997, xiii). From Raff Brinker in Dodge's *Hans Brinker* (1865), to Long John Silver in Stevenson's *Treasure Island* (1881), to Eeyore in Milne's *Winnie-the-Pooh* (1926), to the Oompa Loompas in Dahl's *Charlie and the Chocolate Factory* (1964), to Toothless (and ultimately Hiccup, too) in *How to Train Your Dragon* (2010), disability is everywhere and yet nowhere. Disabled characters proliferate in literary narratives that simultaneously diminish their importance; these works compartmentalize disability by reinscribing difference as absolute and making the disabled character an icon of individual tragedy or a pathologized problem. So readers may "read past" disabled characters by understanding them as metaphor only, lacking a lived reality. In children's literature, the category of the normal body creates (and is often posed as re-creating) an able-bodied norm that assumes disability as a lesser state of being, invariably tied to illness or corruption.

In folk and fairy tales, disability allegorizes difference: stepmothers become evil witches, ogres eat people and livestock, trolls steadfastly guard bridges and threaten travelers, one-eyed and three-eyed sisters torment and oppress their two-eyed stepsister. Many children's tales center on disabled characters who come across as especially malevolent. Almost as frequently, texts depict "ordinary characters" whose disabilities—in and of themselves—transform them into noble or "special" people (supercrips) with exceptional powers. These extremes frequently convey certain disability types: evil antagonists (the blind witch in "Hansel and Gretel"), sympathetic or wretched victims (Andersen's "The Little Mermaid"; Disney's version of Hugo's *The Hunchback of Notre Dame*), courageous heroes (Andersen's "The Steadfast Tin Soldier"), or avenging villains (Captain Hook in Barrie's *Peter Pan*). Character extremes built on disability portrayal also convey metaphorical glosses for the more prominent "normal" character's narrative. For example, in *Finding Nemo* (2003), though Nemo has a foreshortened fin, it is his father, Marlin, who must overcome his pusillanimity.

As frequent moral metaphors in fairy tales, disability characters must be contained or destroyed: in "Snow White," the accommodating dwarfs remain isolated in the Enchanted Forest. Main characters who become disabled are magically restored by the tale's end: in "The Maiden without Hands," the title character's hands grow back; in "Rapunzel," the blinded prince regains his eyesight. Of *Grimms' Fairy Tales*, Beth Franks notes that—often against their own best interests—disabled characters aid and assist human protagonists. Rumpelstiltskin is so enraged when the miller's daughter speaks his name that he stamps through the floor, tearing himself in half. Ultimately, he completes the heroine's task of spinning straw into gold as well as defeating *himself*. "As soon as disability presumes to normalcy," remarks Franks, "it must be ripped in two" (2001, 249).

As a physically "flawed" protagonist, the one-legged title character of "The Steadfast Tin Soldier" (1838) must "heal" or perish. The story concludes with the soldier thrown into the fire and a draft pulling his beloved paper ballerina in after him. David Mitchell and Sharon Snyder argue that the soldier dies in part as punishment for desiring "someone physically perfect and therefore unlike himself" (2000, 56) and, in part, for being disabled in the first place. As Lois Keith writes about nineteenth-century "girls' books," "There were only two possible ways for writers to resolve the problem of their characters' inability to walk: cure or death" (2001, 5). When children suffer a disabling injury or illness, their plight invokes the sublime, and historically, most narratives conclude with absolute healing or ultimate demise. In Burnett's *The Secret Garden* ([1911] 1951), Colin throws off the rug covering his legs and stands "upright—upright—as straight as an arrow" (268). At the end of Spyri's *Heidi* (1880–81), Clara walks after Peter spitefully pushes her wheelchair over a precipice. And at the end of Turner's *Seven Little Australians* (1894), a falling tree branch kills Judy.

Conventionally, child characters who fall ill or become "permanently" injured must learn a moral lesson, and that lesson is tied to their miraculous healing: Katy in Coolidge's *What Katy Did* (1872) wholly recovers from paralysis brought on by a spinal injury after learning to become the cultivated matriarch of the household. She is the "blessed invalid" (Foster and Simons 1995, 76) who must learn the lesson of patience and the value of suffering, as do the seriously injured title characters of Alcott's *Jack and Jill: A Village Story* (1880), Colin in *The Secret Garden*, and the protagonist of Porter's *Pollyanna* (1913). In the process, these characters (and their readers) learn

to be proper young ladies or gentlemen. Frequently, the story presents a dying character as the "sacrifice" that makes others whole. Judy's death in *Seven Little Australians* allows her father to be more tolerant, and Beth's in Alcott's *Little Women* (1868) facilitates Jo's maturity.

A Janus trap often rests on a dying character who either is called "home" by God (other characters in *Little Women* regard Beth as too good for this world) or undergoes an astonishing recovery through a bettered spirit and resolve (Katy, Clara, Colin, Pollyanna). Writing of a literature that emerges from a US history entrenched in the exceptionalist tenet that industrious individuals magically defeat social disadvantage, Beauchamp and colleagues note, "A common idea is that those [disabled characters] who are unable to cure themselves either didn't try hard enough or that the disability is really a blessing in disguise" (2015, 62). In most novels from the mid-nineteenth century through the first half of the twentieth, protagonists rarely remain disabled *and* live: Beth dies, Katy fully recovers, the hunchback dies, Pollyanna recovers. A notable exception is Craik's *The Little Lame Prince and His Travelling Cloak* (1874); although Prince Dolor's disability seems to cause the death of both his parents, he not only survives but regains his lost throne.

Second only to the death of a parent or guardian, disability or illness often serves as the impetus for fictional worlds. The story of *Mulan* (1998) and Ellis's *The Breadwinner* (2000) offer narratives of girls who must masquerade as boys to thrive as a hero, but both narratives *also* rely on the frailty of the girls' fathers as narrative instigation. Zevin's *All These Things I've Done* (2012)—a story that imagines a prohibition era against chocolate—hinges on the sixteen-year-old protagonist embracing the family business because of her older brother's brain injury and her grandmother's budding dementia. Richardson's *After Hamelin* (2000) relies on its protagonist's deafness to help defeat the evil Pied Piper. The 2016 Governor General Award winner for young people's literature, Leavitt's *Calvin* (2015), has the teen protagonist walking across a frozen Lake Erie in search of a magical cure for his schizophrenia.

In children's literature, as Lennard Davis argues in a different context, the disabled subject is not so much a character using a wheelchair but a "set of social, historical, economic, and cultural processes that regulate and control the way we think about and think through the body" (1995, 3). The category of disability is not simply an "add-on" to a representational taxonomy of identity (race, gender, class, sexuality, etc.); rather, the analysis of disability in children's books reveals historical, political, and social agendas that fuel other modes of marginalization. Historically, homosexuality has been labeled a disease, women "lack" prerequisite body parts, and racialized characters often appear as mentally (or morally) degenerate. While literary theorists investigate and celebrate the unstable or unruly body, most neglect the disabled body (and mind), seemingly unaware that representations of disability intertwine, influence, and often establish characters introduced as "Other."

Disability theory, then, troubles the opposition between disabled and able-bodied. Throughout the latter twentieth and early twenty-first centuries, an abundance of picture books designed to teach supposedly able-bodied children tolerance for disabled children underlines Garland-Thomson's insistence that the representation of disability resides "not in inherent physical flaws, but in social relationships" (1997, 7). Levi's *A Very Special Friend* (1989), Carlson's *Arnie and the New Kid* (1992), Shriver's *What's Wrong with Timmy?* (2001), Moore-Mallinos's *My Friend Has Down Syndrome* (2008)—to name only a very few—endeavor to teach children acceptance and tolerance for this "new Other." Happily, an increasing number of children's picture books embrace the possibilities of protagonists who happen to have disabilities: Stuve-Bodeen *We'll Paint the Octopus Red* (1998) and Wills's *Susan Laughs* (2000) show disability more as an aside to the narrative than as pivotal to the characters' identities, and Small's *Imogene's Antlers* (1988) and Tan's *The Lost Thing* (2010) entice with intriguing tales of unusual bodies. Texts for middle readers, such as Philbrick's novel *Freak the Mighty* (2001), Bell's graphic novel *El Deafo* (2014), and the animated films *Princess Mononoke* (1997) and *Inside Out* (2015), invite children into engaging situations—only some of which have to do with disability or illness. Contemporary young adult novels especially present complicated and well-rounded protagonists, such as the anorexic Lia in Anderson's *Wintergirls* (2010), the autistic-spectrum narrators in Haddon's *The Curious Incident of the Dog in the Night-Time* (2003) and Stork's *Marcelo in the Real World* (2011), Ben who has cerebral palsy in Koertge's *Stoner & Spaz* (2011), or both protagonists, Amy and Matthew—who have cerebral palsy and OCD, respectively—in McGovern's *Say What You Will* (2014).

Michael Davidson recounts an anecdote wherein performance poet Aaron Williamson, upon being asked about his hearing loss, replied, "I choose not to say when I lost my hearing but rather when I gained my deafness" (2008, 33). More contemporary stories reach beyond unsophisticated body-positive representations, allowing disability to become one of many narrative elements. In such texts, disability emerges as yet another everyday issue—oftentimes the least of the characters' "problems." As children's and YA writers acknowledge and celebrate diversity, let us look to a future wherein such narratives also include stories that do not focus on a loss of ability but rather encourage readers to imagine a disability gain.

20

Diversity

Ebony Elizabeth Thomas

While the word *diversity* is old, the way that we are using it today in children's literature is quite new. *Diversity* came into contemporary English usage from the medieval French word *diversité*, which at the time meant "difference" (*OED*). However, the ultimate origin of the word comes from the Latin *diversitatem*, which means "contrariety, contradiction, disagreement." The very etymology of the term captures its inherent polarities. Conversations about diversity unwittingly appropriate a very old word for new purposes during our age of discursive volatility.

When it comes to considerations of diversity in children's literature, location and identity matter. Former settler-colonial nations, such as the US, Canada, and Australia, conceive of diversity as existing within the nation's borders. Though these countries have long histories of legal discrimination, their concept of nation is more heterogeneous: diversity refers to differences (ethnic, racial, religious, etc.) *within* national borders. In contrast, European nations tend to discuss diversity in terms of "integration" or "assimilation" within an individual nation, and in their senses of national identity, the populations of European countries seem comparatively more homogenous. Our different discourses illuminate these differences. European *imagology* explicitly opposes national stereotypes. American, Canadian, and Australian *multiculturalism* opposes a wider variety of stereotypes. Beyond the West, diversity refers to ethnic, religious, and/or linguistic minorities, with their own traditions of stories for children and conversations about the need to represent every child (Edward 2018; Menon 2006). And all over the world, Indigenous peoples provide even more nuances of what it means to be diverse. All these complexities matter for considering diversity in children's literature.

Diversity in US children's literature begins with centuries-old movements to shift the depictions of Black children away from caricature and toward positive representation (Brooks and McNair 2009; Harris 2003). Although Nancy Larrick's landmark article "The All-White World of Children's Books" (1965) is often cited as the first major examination of the depiction of race in children's literature (Forest, Garrison, and Kimmel 2015; Pescosolido, Grauerholz, and Milkie 1997), this vital work of humanizing children omitted from or distorted in literature goes back much further (Bishop 2007; Sims 1982). The antislavery movement, both international and interracial in scope, featured moments of protest against negative caricatures of people of African descent, from the eighteenth-century Danish newspaper for children *Avis for Børn*, to the troubling "Story of the Inky Boys" by German writer Heinrich Hoffman, to Helen Bannerman's infamous *The Story of Little Black Sambo* (Christensen 2017; Martin 2004). African American parents, educators, and clergy were noting and writing about racist representations of Black people in children's books as early as the late eighteenth century (Capshaw and Duane 2017; Bishop 2007; Connolly 2013; Martin 2004). To address the pervasive erasure and caricaturization of Black children, church publications such as the African Methodist Episcopal Church's *Christian Recorder* and the *Repository* contained material for children and youth, offering counternarratives based on community strength. These early publications were often didactic and evangelical in tone, intended to convey Victorian-era morals to their young audience.

With the first breath of the Harlem Renaissance came the NAACP's *Brownies Book* (1920–21), where luminaries such as Langston Hughes first were published. Hughes, along with contemporaries Arna Bontemps and Countee Cullen, were among the first to produce children's literature and poetry eschewing racist caricatures to address real-life Black children's wants, needs, hopes, and dreams.

Meanwhile, Charlamae Hill Rollins at the Chicago Public Library (starting in 1927) and Augusta Braxton Baker at the New York Public Library (starting in 1937) did much to influence the development of the field (Yokota 1993), as did the rise of Dr. Carter G. Woodson's Negro History Week, which later evolved into Black History Month. During and after the Harlem Renaissance, writers began to position African Americans as active agents fighting for their own physical, social, and economic liberation from stifling oppression. As Katharine Capshaw observes, "The major writers of the time were deeply invested in the enterprise of building a Black national identity through literary constructions of childhood" (Smith 2004, xiii). Thus much of the impetus of midcentury African American children's literature during the civil rights era and Black Arts Movement was reparative, telling celebratory tales about the victories and the achievements of African Americans in spite of collective trauma and monumental odds, promoting a bourgeois ideology of racial uplift and encouraging young people to lead the race politically and socially toward American ideals of progress and individual achievement.

At the same time, there were notable parallel movements in other communities to represent the experiences and lives of children who were neither White nor Black. To provide two examples, Debbie Reese notes that Pequot author and activist William Apess wrote about problematic representations of Native Americans in the early 1800s. The work of Marilisa Jiménez García and others highlights the efforts of the first New York Public Library librarian of Puerto Rican descent, Pura Belpré, whose career began in the 1920s and spanned storytelling and authorship (Jiménez García 2014). The multicultural education and ethnic studies movements of the 1960s and 1970s also led to a push toward greater inclusion of greater racial diversity in children's books (Banks and Banks 2009; Enciso 1997; Nieto 2002). More recently, the need for children's literature that is both critical and multicultural has been articulated by educators seeking what Chinua Achebe once called a "balance of stories" in classrooms, schools, and communities (Botelho and Rudman 2009; Cai 2008; DeNicolo and Franquiz 2006). Within the past decade, websites like *Latinxs in Kidlit* (edited by Cindy L. Rodriguez et al.), the *Brown Bookshelf* (by Paula Chase-Hyman et al.), and *American Indians in Children's Literature* (by Debbie Reese) have become treasure troves for those seeking historic and contemporary perspectives on multicultural children's books.

The shift in terminology from *multicultural* and *multiethnic* to *diverse* children's literature mirrors similar shifts in the larger educational world as well as in the North American academy (Europeans still favor the term *multicultural*). *Multicultural* was initially intended as a term inclusive of cultures beyond race and ethnicity, but it did not sufficiently address recent attention to growing awareness of differences in gender, sexual orientation, religion, and immigration status; cultural and linguistic differences; disabilities; and Native peoples as sovereign nations. As these other intersectional factors became more essential, the term *diverse* emerged as a way to include a broader range of identity in literature. This shift in terminology is notable, but it also fails in our purportedly postracial era to challenge White privilege and structures of race and power. Since it often functions as a synonym for *nonwhite*, the term *diversity* can occlude the difference it strives to make visible by not naming the many varieties of human experience that its users want literature to include.

Although the use of *diversity* as a term to describe children's literature is relatively recent, conversations *about* diversity in children's literature are not new. *New York Times* op-eds written by the late pioneering Black children's author Walter Dean Myers and his son Christopher Myers in the spring of 2014 were among the latest signature developments in decades-long struggles over disparities in children's publishing and media (C. Myers 2014; W. D. Myers 2014). Their powerful essays, "Where Are the People of Color in Children's Books?" and "The Apartheid of Children's Literature," both cited statistics collected by the University of Wisconsin's Cooperative Children's Book Center (CCBC), which has analyzed trends in children's publishing on an annual basis for more than two decades. The CCBC has found that every year, over 85 percent of all children's and young adult books published feature White characters—a statistic that has barely moved since the 1960s.

Historically, diverse books only emerge when activists confront the silence that sustains the status quo. After the Myers' editorials appeared, a number of the largest publishers remained silent until authors Ellen Oh, Malinda Lo, and Aisha Saeed launched a bold new campaign on social media, #WeNeedDiverseBooks, in response to BookCon's choice to feature white male authors on their children's literature panel. Other prominent voices within the children's publishing industry, including Jason Low (founder and CEO of the multicultural publisher Lee and Low Books) and Stacy Whitman (publisher and editorial director of the diverse science-fiction and fantasy imprint Tu Books), helped move social media conversations on diversifying children's

literature into the public discourse. These recent efforts revive a protest tradition launched decades ago by children's literature diversity pioneers such as Augusta Baker, Pura Belpré, Nancy Larrick, Jella Lepman, Rudine Sims Bishop, and many other authors, librarians, educators, and community activists.

Advocates for diversity understand that representations are always about power. When characters of color appear in children's publishing and media, many are often demeaning, as recent controversies about picture books featuring smiling slaves demonstrate (Schoenberg 2016). The stereotyping and marginalization of people of color, poor and working-class children and families, gender and sexual minorities, immigrants, and other minoritized groups have persisted throughout children's literature's long history (Bradford 2001; Forest, Garrison, and Kimmel 2015; MacCann [1998] 2001; McGillis 1999). Additionally, the CCBC's annual reports show a troubling trend in books that feature diverse characters not being written by authors from that background, leading to questions about who has the right to tell diverse stories. So as author, creative writing professor, and activist Daniel José Older points out, publishers should use their power to promote diverse stories:

> The question industry professionals need to ask themselves is: "How can I use my position to help create a literary world that is diverse, equitable, and doesn't just represent the same segment of society it always has since its inception? What concrete actions can I take to make actual change and move beyond the tired conversation we've been having for decades?" (Older 2014).

When diversity decolonizes children's literature, it can liberate stories and their readers. In her powerful case for decolonizing children's literature, Canadian literary critic Shaobo Xie argues that the rise of children's literature during the Victorian era served to make young people into proper subjects who knew their place, much like Said's (1993) argument that the rise of the novel was tied to imperialism. Keeping in mind that "decolonization is not a metaphor" (Tuck and Yang 2014), Xie's words are nonetheless quite persuasive for those who strive for educational and societal equality, and they have served as my personal mission statement since I first read them as a fifth-grade teacher seventeen years ago:

> To most Westerners, "the source of the world's significant action and life is in the West," and "the outlying regions of the world have no life, history, or culture to speak of, no independence or integrity worth representing without the West" (Said, *Culture* xix). . . . If children's literature and the criticism of children's literature take upon themselves to decolonize the world, they will prove the most effective postcolonial project in the long run, for the world always ultimately belongs to children. If today's children grow up with postcolonial education, and if they are encouraged to understand and appreciate racial/ethnic difference, that would tremendously expedite the progress towards a globalized postcoloniality. (Xie 2000, 13)

Since childhood stories transmit troubling discourses of colonialism and supremacy, it is absolutely critical that these functions of children's literature are revealed, historicized, and interrogated. After all, in her influential TED Talk "The Danger of a Single Story" (2009), Chimamanda Ngozi Adichie reminds us "how impressionable and vulnerable we are in the face of a story, particularly as children." In light of responses to recent human rights conflicts in the US and around the world, from Black Lives Matter to the Syrian refugee crisis, it is clear that, as Xie notes, children are "most violently subjected to colonialist ideas of racial-ethnic Otherness at the most formative years of their life" (2000, 13). In contrast, if today's children grow up with literature that is multicultural, diverse, *and* decolonized, we can begin the work of healing our world through humanizing stories.

21

Domestic

Claudia Nelson

Domestic derives from the Latin *domus* (house) through the Middle French *domestique*. The *OED*'s earliest usages are in sixteenth century, by which time the word already had multiple meanings: quasi-familial intimacy, as in the 1521 supplication "make hym domestique / Within the heuyns," but also homegrown rather than foreign. While *domestic* always implied closeness, the extent of the sphere of proximity varied. That sphere might be the individual (Norris's 1707 *Treatise on Humility* defines *domestic ignorance* as "the ignorance of . . . what passes within our own breast" [*OED*]); the household, as in *domestics* meaning "servants"; the nation, as in *domestic policy*; or humankind generally, since *domestic animal* includes livestock in other countries and eras. What the domestic excludes—wild animals, strangers, foreigners—partakes of the alien, a binary enabling hierarchy, conflict, and exploitation.

In children's literature, *domestic fiction* denotes a genre emerging in the eighteenth century—namely, realistic stories of family life. It may be blended with other genres, including the historical novel and the animal story, but classically it examines a contemporary household, perhaps with neighbors who, in the sixteenth-century sense of the term, become "domestic" within the principal family. Etymologically, the domestic tale is the opposite of the adventure, a category derived from the Latin *advenire*, "to come to," with all this word's implications regarding the external world; adventure heroes travel, while the protagonists

of domestic fiction often stay put. While domestic tales remain popular, the term is now commonly applied to the fiction of earlier days, particularly the nineteenth century, when much girls' fiction urged acceptance of home duties and proper deportment even by naughty girls, as in Catherine Sinclair's *Holiday House* (1838) and the Comtesse de Ségur's *Les malheurs de Sophie* (1858).

Yet even nineteenth-century domestic novels often chronicle domestic problems. Hector Malot's *En famille* (1893) tells of a girl who is hardly "among family," since she must cross the country alone, establishing home in an abandoned hut, before reconciling with the grandfather who has repudiated her because she is biracial; his physical blindness is a metaphor for his obtuseness about others. Johanna Spyri's *Heidi* (1880–81), Switzerland's best-known literary production, similarly contains a grandfather who has rejected his son and must be reconciled to and reformed by his little granddaughter. Like Malot's, Spyri's novel lovingly describes domestic arrangements: beds made from hay, meal preparation, the contrast between Alpine hut and urban mansion. Both novels, while interrogating what constitutes home and how it is to be achieved, employ the term *domestic* differently from some English-language fiction. Malot uses *domestique* exclusively for servants or domesticated animals; Spyri uses the German words *häusliche* once (of "domestic affairs") and *heimlich* only for a secret blow with which Aunt Dete reprimands Heidi.

Associating the term *domestic fiction* with middle-class Victorian girls occludes not only non-Anglophone examples and discussions of nontraditional family life—such as Francesca Lia Block's magic-realist Dangerous Angels series (1989–2012) and Paula Fox's *The Eagle Kite* (1995), about a boy's response to his father's AIDS—but also the multicultural domestic novels that began proliferating in the twentieth century. Some of the latter examine the tension between *domestic* and *foreign*. They include Rosa Guy's *The Friends* (1973), whose protagonist deals with being a West Indian in Harlem, with her mother's terminal illness and her father's difficult nature, and with guilt at failing a friend; Geraldine Kaye's *Comfort Herself* (1984), in which, after her English mother dies, Comfort joins her father in Ghana and must decide which country is home; and even Dori Sanders's *Clover* (1990), which describes how, when Clover's father is killed hours after remarrying, ten-year-old Clover bonds with her white stepmother despite community disapproval. Whatever the culture, domestic fiction often raises serious issues. The light tone of Jeanne Birdsall's *The Penderwicks* (2005) belies its focus on a mother's attempts to dominate her fatherless son, while Kyoko Mori's *Shizuko's Daughter* (1994) describes the difficult adolescence of a girl whose mother has committed suicide, leaving her upbringing to her distant father and hostile stepmother.

Because *domestic fiction* is generally associated with girls, however, many readers have scorned it as sentimental. Elizabeth Vincent commented in 1924 that Louisa May Alcott pleases girls with "a natural depraved taste for moralizing" (Keyser 1999, 20); Humphrey Carpenter suggests that one might misread the Marches as "a rather saccharinely portrayed but otherwise unremarkable family" (1985, 93). Providing a useful sample of Victorian male litterateurs' attitudes, Wilkie Collins satirically describes the effect of "this fatal domestic novel," Charlotte Yonge's *The Heir of Redclyffe*, on a girl fan: "She reads for five minutes, and goes up-stairs to fetch a dry pocket handkerchief; comes down again, and reads for another five minutes; goes up-stairs again, and fetches another dry pocket handkerchief . . . the case baffles the doctors. The heart is all right, the stomach is all right, the lungs are all right, the extremities are moderately warm. The skull alone is abnormal" (1858, 50).

Since the rise of feminist criticism in the 1970s, Victorian juvenile domestic fiction has received more respect. Elizabeth Thiel's argument is characteristic: "The ambiguities that clearly exist within nineteenth-century texts for children—sometimes overt, sometimes implicit, but invariably present—may have been attempts to tell the truth about domestic life in a world that celebrated idealism" (2008, 155). Thiel is not the first to see nineteenth-century domestic fiction as a covert dialogue among sisters who dared not speak plainly about women's pain.

This emphasis on femininity makes sense, since most writers and readers of domestic fiction have been female, yet it also obscures the form's connections with masculinity. Many classic domestic sagas divide their attention between the genders, as in Eleanor Estes's Moffat series (1941–83), Elizabeth Enright's Melendy quartet (1941–51), Ethel Turner's *Seven Little Australians* and its sequels (1894–1928), and Mary Grant Bruce's Billabong books (1910–42), and some have male protagonists. A classic example of the male domestic novel protagonist is Frances Hodgson Burnett's *Fauntleroy* (1886). Other instances include displaced East German teenager Christoph in Margot Benary-Isbert's *The Long Way Home* (1959), who unites the family that takes him in by reforming his malcontent adoptive mother; Manny in Victor Martinez's *Parrot in the Oven: Mi Vida* (1996), who contemplates a home that "my mother spent so much energy cleaning and keeping together, and . . . my father spent so much energy tearing apart" (215); the title character of Yang Hongying's Ma Xiaotiao books (2003–), whose unruliness does not threaten family harmony; and Kip in Sarah Ellis's *Odd Man Out* (2006), who, given permission to trash his grandmother's home before its demolition, finds a notebook from his dead father's teenage years and gains new perspective thereby.

Ellis's image of the destroyed house acknowledges that *domestic* may not imply "bliss." Kimberley Reynolds dates to the mid-twentieth century the readiness to perceive "threats to child characters' wellbeing . . . as coming from within the family" (2008, 201), just as *a domestic*, per the *OED*, is twentieth-century slang for a violent altercation between family members. But earlier domestic novels also frequently acknowledge that intimacy need not promote peace. The "domestic drama" of *Little Women* involves bitter quarrels between Jo and Amy, and Marmee reveals that she is "angry almost every day of [her] life" (Alcott [1868–69] 1998).

Tracing the concept of "home" in children's literature from the eighteenth century forward, Reynolds (2008) argues that children's fiction has always identified domesticity as something to be contested or redefined at need. Freud, too, acknowledges this contest in his discussion of the overlap between *heimlich* and *unheimlich*, the domestic and the uncanny: "*heimlich* is a word the meaning of which develops in the direction of ambivalence, until it finally coincides with its opposite, *unheimlich*" (Freud [1919] 1955, 111), so that "what is ultimately most frightening and *unheimlich* is what is most intimate and personal" (Nelson 2003, 111). This paradoxical instability is apparent in the shifting emotional connotations of *domestic*. Some girls' writers celebrate the word: Alcott's *An Old-Fashioned Girl* ([1870] 2008) calls Mr. Sydney's "domestic traits and virtues . . . more engaging to womanly women than any amount of cool intellect or worldly wisdom." Others acknowledge that many women despise it. In L. M. Montgomery's *Jane of Lantern Hill* (1937), Jane's grandmother sneers that Jane "fancies herself as domestic," inasmuch as "she likes to hang about kitchens and places like that." The narrator adds, "Grandmother's voice implied that [Jane] had low tastes and that kitchens were barely respectable."

The source of the *barely respectable* here is not purely a matter of class but an outgrowth of the tension between tradition and progress. In *Marm Lisa* (1896), Kate Douglas Wiggin satirizes activist women's assumption "that no woman could develop or soar properly, and cook, scrub, sweep, dust, wash dishes, mend, or take care of babies at the same time. . . . They were willing to concede all these sordid tasks as an honourable department of woman's work, but each wanted them to be done by some other woman." This comment points to the source of much of the juvenile domestic novel's energy: the awareness that achieving and maintaining the domestic, whether defined as intimacy, familiarity, or housewifery, is often neither easy nor pleasant.

22

Fairy Tale / Märchen

Vanessa Joosen

Taken literally, the term *fairy tale* and its French counterpart *conte de fées* refer to "a tale about fairies" (*OED*). While that definition may still have applied when the genre was established in the French salon culture of the late eighteenth century, many of the most popular fairy tales today—think of "Snow White," "Little Red Riding Hood," or "The Ugly Duckling"—do not contain any fairies. In German and Dutch, the diminutives *Märchen* and *sprookje* refer to oral, spoken tales. The origin of fairy tales in oral narratives is disputed, however, and so is the criterion of length (Haase 2008, 323; Zipes 2002, 27–29). Perhaps the diminutive should rather be taken as an indication of the belittlement of fairy tales by the literary establishment. Fairy tales have been considered to be trivial narratives that may entertain simple people like children or commoners but do not count as proper literature. Yet propagators as varied as Romantic philologists, psychoanalysts, and esoteric philosophers have lauded fairy tales for capturing the essence of humanity in writing. By all means, fairy tales have proven to be particularly resilient narratives and currently count as some of the oldest stories that many children still read and enjoy today.

The term *fairy tale* produces considerable semantic confusion. *Fairy tale* and *folktale* are often used as synonyms but are not necessarily the same. Folktales are oral narratives told by "the folk" that usually have a long tradition and hence exist in different variants: tellers may forget or invent new passages and adapt the stories to their own context and needs. While some fairy tales have their roots in folklore, others are the product of a single author's imagination. Scholars distinguish between *Volksmärchen* (folktales), which are usually short and simple in form, and the more elaborate and sophisticated *Kunstmärchen* (literary fairy tales). There is, however, considerable overlap between the two types. Hans Christian Andersen wrote literary fairy tales that were often inspired by folk motifs—for example, "The Princess and the Pea" and "The Emperor's New Clothes." Folklorists also differentiate between fairy tales (secular) and myths (spiritual), although there is considerable overlap in motifs and characters between these types of folktales (Valk 2008, 653).

Folktales and fairy tales occur in various parts of the world, and some tale types are popular in different continents. Aantti Aarne provided groundbreaking work with his fairy tale index from 1910, which was later expanded and revised by Stith Thompson (1961) and Hans-Jörg Uther (2004). Specific regional trends can be distinguished in fairy tales as world literature both in the concrete shape that certain tale types take and in the genre as a whole. The Chinese Cinderella, "Yè Xiàn," for example, gets help not from a fairy godmother but from a fish that is her reincarnated mother. The beast from "Beauty and the Beast" can take various animal shapes in the "animal groom" tale type. In South African variants, the heroine falls in love with a crocodile and a five-headed snake; in a Russian variant, she loses her heart to a snotty goat (Silver 2008, 41). Whereas the most popular Western fairy tales have young protagonists, in Japan, the main characters are often older people (Murai 2018).

As the Aarne-Thompson-Uther index also makes clear, fairy tales are a very heterogeneous group that includes various subgenres, such as the religious fairy tale, the erotic tale, and the jest. Most of the classic fairy tales of the West belong to the so-called wonder tale. Typical of these stories is that magic occurs without raising surprise—this is what Tzvetan Todorov calls "the marvelous" (1975, 41). Carlo Collodi's *Pinocchio* (1883) and Lewis Carroll's *Alice's Adventures in Wonderland* (1865) are sometimes called fairy tales, but strictly speaking, they are not. Because of their length, "looser and more wandering" (Tiffin 2008, 161) structure, and the inclusion of dreams and secondary worlds, they rather belong to fantasy. The confusion between the genres results from overlapping features of fairy tales and fantasy (in particular, the occurrence of magic) and from the fact that *Pinocchio* and *Alice's Adventures in Wonderland*, like many fairy tales, have been adapted by Disney into popular animated films.

In addition to the question of what defines a fairy tale, the origin of fairy tales has raised considerable debate. The discussion pivots around the question of whether fairy tales featuring bourgeois and noble characters and themes (many of which are part of the fairy tale canon) originated in oral folk culture and served as the bases for written tales or whether it was the other way around (Bottigheimer 2009; Zipes 2012). What came first, the oral tales or the written texts? This is ultimately also an issue of ownership and appropriation. Fairy tale authors and collectors cannot always be trusted when they address the genesis of their work. Charles Perrault first published his fairy tale collection *Histoires et contes du temps passé* (*Stories or Tales of Times Past*; 1697) under the name of his son. It came to be known under the nickname of Mother Goose, who featured on the frontispiece and was presented as a female storyteller of the folk. One can question, however, the extent to which Perrault acted as an intermediate for folktales (Shavit 1999, 323). Marina Warner (1994a, 182) suggests that Mother Goose may have merely served as a cover to dissociate the courtier Perrault from the vulgar tales whose content and style were associated with everything that he was not: the common, the childlike, the female.

The history of the genre is fraught with corruptions and appropriations that are questionable by contemporary standards. As the stories have been perceived as a common good, many authors have taken the liberty to adapt them as they saw fit and claimed authorship (Haase 1999). Those adaptations often catered to young audiences, or rather to what parents and educators considered suitable for children. As a genre that already thrived in the Middle Ages (Zipes 2006, 45), the fairy tale predates the period in which children's literature became an established literary field. Early collections such as Straparola's *Le piacevoli notti* (*Delectable Nights*; 1550–53), Giambattista Basile's *Pentamerone* (1634–36), and the fairy tales by seventeenth-century French *conteuses* were primarily shared among adults. The audience of Charles Perrault's collection is ambiguous. Children feature on the frontispiece of the book, as they are listening to Mother Goose. Yet Zohar Shavit argues that Perrault was simply "availing himself of the common conception of the child as a source of amusement" for adults rather than writing for children (1999, 324).

Whether intended for children or not, with the publication of Perrault's collection, fairy tales did enter children's literature, as various references and chapbook versions from the eighteenth century make clear. While popular with children, Perrault's magical and sexually suggestive stories bothered many educators and parents. The Brothers Grimm adapted the tales in *Die Kinder- und Hausmärchen* (1812–57), which was originally conceived as a way of preserving German folktales, to accommodate children—or rather, bourgeois adults who were concerned about children's reading. They had criticized some stories in the Grimms' first edition, such as the tale in which children play at butchering and one child's throat gets sliced. While the Grimms were often considered as exemplary folklorists and inspired many abroad to tread in their footsteps (Joosen and Lathey 2014), their methods of collecting, rendering, and adapting the tales are problematically liberal according to later standards and have been revealed to be highly ideological (see Bottigheimer 1978, 2009; Tatar 2003; Schmiesing 2014).

As the reception of their tales makes clear, however, the Grimms' adaptations were not considered radical enough to make the tales suited for children, and various passages were further altered or deleted when the tales entered the children's canon. Few fairy tale collections on twentieth-century children's shelves contained the passage in which Cinderella's stepsisters cut off their toes and heels to fit the glass slipper, for example, or the gruesome punishment of Snow White's stepmother, who is forced to dance herself to death in iron shoes that have been heated with fire. While fairy tales are among the most popular stories for children in the world, translators often adapt the narratives freely. The same is true for adaptations in other media, with Disney as the prime example. According to Jack Zipes, Disney's approach to the fairy tale is marked by "sexism, sentimentality, and sterility" and reduces the fairy tale's subversive power (2002, 129). While one might deplore the perceived necessity of changes and deletions to the fairy tale's course of events and criticize the way they have been appropriated, their adaptability can be argued to be inherent to the fairy tale's history and a vital element in their success (Joosen 2014). If we conceive of the literary field in Darwinist terms, as a system that operates according to the law of the "survival of the fittest," then the fairy tale's flexibility can be considered a vital factor in its survival.

The development of the fairy tale in recent decades illustrates this process once more. In the 1970s, the dated ideology of tales like "Snow White" and "Cinderella" was subject to feminist and Marxist criticism, with some scholars questioning their inclusion in the children's canon (Haase 2004). Postcolonial scholars criticized the Western representation of and domination over fairy tales from the rest of the world (Bacchilega 2004, 179–82). The same period also witnessed the surge of postmodern fairy tale rewritings, for both adults and children, that tackled the fairy tale's ideology and made it the subject of revision and intertextual play. Angela Carter's *The Bloody Chamber* (1979) and Roald Dahl's *Revolting Rhymes* (1982) are famous examples. Over the past decades, fairy tale rewriting has established itself as a vibrant and flexible genre in its own right, which manifests in various media (including internet memes, manga, and telenovelas) and does not remain limited to the West. In the late 1990s, Japan witnessed a "Grimm Boom," which led to an interest in the suppressed content of earlier Grimm tales and to "a rediscovery of Japanese and other cultures' folktales as sensational literature for adults" (Murai 2014, 167). Although the dominance of Western fairy tales continues to be subject to criticism, Sung-Ae Lee and Anna Katrina Gutierrez point out that they are subject to processes of "glocalisation" (Gutierrez 2017) and "intercultural conceptual blending" (Lee 2014) when they travel: Western elements are mixed with local forms and motifs into cultural hybrids that are rich in meaning. This process illustrates once more that ideals of purity do not apply to the fairy tale as a genre and that these narratives' popularity and openness allow for their continued proliferation, which is not expected to cease any time soon.

23

Family
Elisabeth (Lies) Wesseling

Family figures prominently in literature and science as the primary shaping influence on the next generation. In modern western Europe, the term generally refers to the nuclear family, consisting of a father, mother, and one or more children. While most cultures acknowledge the family as the core unit of society, deep-rooted notions of family vary across the globe. In the global South, Afrocentric and Indigenous communities usually invoke a wider concept of family, one that includes grandparents, uncles, aunts, and their progeny, with extensive practices of fostering and adoption taking care of orphaned children within extended families (Mazzucato and Schans 2011).

Family, however, remains a contested concept: the winnowing of *extended family* to *nuclear family* is a relatively recent semantic development. As its origins indicate, the word included a much larger group, including "household, household servants, troop (of gladiators) . . . group of persons connected by blood or affinity" (from the Latin *familia*) and "group of people living under the same roof" (from Middle French *famile* in the fourteenth century). By the fifteenth century, *family* could refer to what we today consider the nuclear unit but retained its more expansive senses of "group of people living as a household," "any group of people connected by blood, marriage, adoption, etc.," and "lineage" (*OED*). The shift in meaning from a household to a closely knit unit of parents and children only became established usage in the early nineteenth century. Given

this etymology, it comes as no surprise that vestiges of older meanings linger on in late-modern discourses on family, including children's literature.

The tensions between nuclear and extended definitions of *family* also emerge in another fault line in cultural understandings of the term—namely, the tensions between genetic and elective belonging. On the one hand, family seems to be an obvious fact, defined by a genetically circumscribed group into which one is born (filiation). On the other hand, if a family is chosen through marriage, adoption, fostering, or comparable cultural practices of affiliation, the genetic determinism of the word seems much less certain (Scheffler 1985). The question of which ties are most deserving of the honorific title *family*—those determined by genes or those created by daily love, care, and togetherness—remain unresolved, as demonstrated by the ongoing debates about international adoption (Homans 2013; Perreau 2014; McLeod 2015) and about the harm caused, especially in the 1960s and 1970s, of the adoption of Indigenous children by non-Indigenous families. These tensions fold into each other without fully coinciding, the one (genetic/elective) defining the foundation and the other (nuclear/extended) the scope of *family*. Those who favor elective belonging tend to advocate for extended concepts of family, while those who put a premium on "blood ties" tend to associate these with the nuclear family, but not necessarily so. Western adoptive parents usually aspire toward the norm of the nuclear family while extolling elective over genetic belonging.

As children are considered to be dependent on family, narrative fiction about the adventures of child characters is a crucial cultural site at which the tensions between genetic versus elective belonging and nuclear versus extended versions of family are negotiated. Ann Alston claims that "over nearly two centuries . . . the ideology of the nuclear family still remains central to children's literature but it is a largely unexamined ideological presentation of a normative family life" (2008, 8). Others argue that Victorian authors of children's books were already preoccupied with representations of the "transnormative family," defined by "the temporary or permanent absence of a natural parent or parents, often by the presence of a surrogate mother or father, who may or may not be related to the child, and, frequently, by the relocation of the child to an environment outside the 'natural' family home" (Thiel 2008, 8). According to Elizabeth Thiel, literary representations of transnormative families enabled Victorian authors to expose the tenuous nature of middle-class ideals of domesticity. These contradictory claims illustrate that children's literature is a frequently visited arena for pitting conflicting views on family against each other so as to assess their relative merits.

Some nineteenth-century genres of children's literature are fully devoted to propagating the heteronormative ideal of the nuclear family, especially genres that address girls. Sentimental domestic novels, or *Backfischromane* (Wilkending and Kirch 2003), feature tomboys who gradually learn to reconcile themselves to the role society holds out for them—that is, marriage and procreation. Louisa May Alcott's *Little Women* (1868) provides a world-famous example, with Jo learning to let go of her boyish ways through numerous punishments and mishaps before she is ready for wedlock and motherhood. *Little Women* was a major source of inspiration for the Joop ter Heul novels (1918–25) by Dutch author Cissy van Marxveldt (Setske de Haan), who lives on in cultural memory because Anne Frank styled her diary *Het achterhuis* (The secret annex; 1947) after this model. The picture becomes more complex when the heroine is an orphan, as in Johanna Spyri's *Heidi* (1880–81), L. M. Montgomery's *Anne of Green Gables* (1908), or Frances Hodgson Burnett's *The Secret Garden* (1911). These plucky heroines may count at best on cold and distant relatives—or on no

relatives at all—but they manage nevertheless. Marriage does not necessarily figure as a reward for good behavior here, while friendship proves to be a greater support than family, in combination with the sustenance of nonhuman benefactors (comfort delivered through the natural beauty of plants, animals, or the outdoors at large).

The nuclear/extended tensions visible in stories about female orphans also appear in stories about male orphans. Even when boys are finally reunited with their relatives, orphan stories do not necessarily sing the praises of the nuclear family and genetic belonging, as in Frances Hodgson Burnett's *Little Lord Fauntleroy* (1886) or Hector Malot's naturalistic novel *Sans famille* (1878). Although the hero in the latter, Rémy, eventually turns out to be the son and heir of an aristocratic British family, he remains fully devoted to his elective family members from the lower walks of life. Indeed, this novel drives the message home that affiliation creates equally vital—perhaps even stronger—ties as filiation, since only it crosses the divides of class and ethnicity.

As the twentieth century progressed, a new type of character became popular: the autonomous child, living quite happily without relatives. *Eloise* (1955) by Kay Thompson and Hilary Knight is a famous American example of a child who lives more or less on her own, though in Eloise's case, in the Plaza Hotel in New York. Astrid Lindgren's Pippi Longstocking, who shares her home with only a monkey and a horse, epitomizes this type, as does the young hero of *Pluk van de Petteflet* (*Tow-Truck Pluck*; 1971) by Lindgren's soulmate, Annie M. G. Schmidt. Pluk lives all by himself in a tower that crowns a high-rise apartment building, the Petteflet. There is no tragic story about the loss of his parents to explain his self-reliance, which is presented as perfectly normal and fully satisfactory. All sorts of people are living in the Petteflet, and Pluk befriends quite of few of them, most notably the children of two single-parent families, but the nuclear family is categorically absent in this cheerful antiestablishment novel, without anyone coming to harm.

In the late twentieth century and into the twenty-first, the relative merits of filiation and affiliation become increasingly topical, with contemporary authors facing relatively new forms of family such as transnational families emerging from global migration, interracial families forged through intercountry adoption, single-parent families, "patchwork families" developing in the wake of divorce, and same-sex families that accompanied the legalization of gay marriage and the emancipation of gay couples in some, but by no means all, parts of the world (Daubert 2007).

Transnational migrant families loom large in Kirsty Murray's tetralogy *Children of the Wind* (2003–6), a series of four historical novels about the role of Irish child migrants in the settlement history of Australia. The series begins in mid-nineteenth-century Ireland, whose inhabitants were set adrift by the infamous potato blight, and it ends in twenty-first-century Australia, featuring a Chinese Irish heroine. Strikingly, the displaced child characters in this series never find fulfillment through reunion with their blood relatives or through marriage and procreation. They seek to belong not in one particular place, the family home, but rather in a "chronotope" (Bakhtin 1981), weaving a web of familial relationships that stretches back in time and across a wide array of different places, generating a genealogy as an ongoing work in progress.

A niche market that started to emerge in the 1990s is one catering to adoptive parents looking for books about adoption to share with their adopted children. These books are designed to provide adoptees with origin stories in answer to the inevitable questions about where they came from. Adoption narratives often pivot around notions of destiny. Ed Young's *The Red Thread* (1993), Liao Yanping's *El hilo rojo: Cuento popular chino* (The red string: A popular Chinese folktale; 2006), Grace Lin's *The Red Thread: An Adoption Fairytale* (2007), and Ana Folguiera's *En algún lugar de China* (Somewhere in China; 2009) suggest that adopters and adoptees were meant to be with each other. The "red thread" of fate—a barely disguised substitute for the umbilical cord—supposedly ties them together from the moment the adoptee was born (Gonzalez and Wesseling 2013).

In the late twentieth and twenty-first centuries, children's books that expressly cater to LGBTQ families, moving beyond nuclear families and genetic belonging altogether, have found a place on library and bookstore shelves. When published, Susanne Bösche's *Mette bor hos Morten og Erik* (*Jenny Lives with Eric and Martin*; 1981) and Lesléa Newman's *Heather Has Two Mommies* (1989) received censure from self-appointed guardians of the family merely because the books sympathetically depict the daily lives of children with gay parents. Today, there are many more books that celebrate queer families. It is too early to identify classics in this sphere, but the author who probably sums up the current state of the art is the Berlin-based "media acrobat" WoMANtís RANDom, creator of the German-English picture book *Gummiband-Familien / Rubberband Families* (2016). It visualizes different family constellations that have literally been crafted out of rubber bands in all colors, shapes, and sizes, playing with neologisms such as *mapa* (single parent) and *spuncle* (sperm donor). The image of the rubber band—so very different from the naturalizing image of the blood-colored "red thread" in adoption narratives—underscores the variability of family concepts and practices. As the author puts it, "Rubber bands exist individually or together, in different sizes. They accompany our everyday life. Sometimes they move to the foreground, they endure a lot and sometimes they break. Rubber bands are dynamic, flexible, reusable as well as binding. Just the right material to create a family book!"

24

Fantasy
Deirdre Baker

The story of fantasy in relation to children's literature is one of forceful contradictions: it is criticized for being fraudulent, irrational, frightening, and overly imaginative; for being formulaic, escapist, and not imaginative enough; for being suitable only for children and for being suitable only for adults. The seeds of this energetic debate take us into the very source of story making: imagination and reason.

The origin of the word *fantasy* lies in the Greek φαντασια (*phantasia*), "a making visible" or "to show." It begins its career in written English as both *fantasy* and *fancy* (derived from spellings *fantsy, fansy, fancie*). Its early primary meanings refer to a faculty of mind: "mental apprehension of an object of perception; the faculty by which this is performed" or "the image impressed on the mind by an object of sense." A primary sense of fantasy in the early modern period is "imagination; the process or the faculty of forming mental representations of things not actually present" (*OED*).

Imagination is the Latin translation of the Greek *phantasia*: in the seventeenth and eighteenth centuries, *fantasy, fancy,* and *imagination* are virtually interchangeable. In meaning, they relate to the faculty of forming mental representations and to the way the mind examines and orders those images, turning them into story or sense (Svendsen 1956; Stevens 1984). Fantasy is not at odds with reason; rather, it is "subject to and governed by reason, or at least should be" (Burton [1621] 1886). When fantasy is distinguished from imagination, it is understood to be the creative faculty that combines and arranges images gleaned through sensory experience. Thus fantasy, fancy, or imagination—as involuntary as the senses of taste or touch—is necessary to reason and to our apprehension of reality.

But in sleep, fantasy can "misjoin shapes" and produce the "wild work" of dreams, as Milton's (1667) Adam tells Eve, and therein lies its danger. Its dream work is "sudden," La Primaudaye writes, "for it . . . taketh what pleaseth it, and addeth thereunto to diminisheth . . . mingleth and unmingleth so that it cutteth asunder and seweth up againe as it listeth. . . . Fancie breeds the fact which it imagineth" (quoted in Svendsen 1956). Fantasy is thus volatile and influenced by desire, drawing one into to its own artful constructions and confusing reason. Hence it is associated with an inability to distinguish the imagined from the "real": note *fantasy/fancy* as an "illusory appearance; delusive imagination; a whimsical or visionary notion or speculation, caprice" (*OED*) or the Japanese term for fantasy literature, *gensou bungahu*, "illusion literature." *Fantasy/fancy* is also associated with "inclination, liking, desire" (*OED*), for it takes what pleases it, as La Primaudaye notes—an impulse that resonates with its usage in psychology and psychoanalysis (Bettelheim 1976).

The *OED*'s first citation for *fantasy* as "a genre of literary composition" dates to 1949 in the *Magazine of Fantasy and Science Fiction*. Only around then is *fantasy* replacing the umbrella term *fairy stories*, which until that time encompassed traditional fairy tales, myths, legends, and what current usage deems literary fantasies, such as *Alice's Adventures in Wonderland*. In discussing *The Lion, the Witch and the Wardrobe*, C. S. Lewis (1952) remarks that "within the species 'children's story' the sub-species which happened to suit me is the fantasy or (in a loose sense of that word) the fairy tale"; he goes on to use *fairy tale* and *fantasy* as synonyms.

Shifting assessments of fantasy's value for or potential harm to children arise out of new Enlightenment theories concerning childhood and education and continue into our present day. To some, the "fancies" (visual imagery of magic—ogres, giants, etc.) in fairy tales threaten to undermine rational behavior and proper understanding. "Why should the mind be filled with fantastic visions instead of useful knowledge?" Maria Edgeworth (1796) wonders, criticizing fairy tales for their improbability. Sarah Trimmer declares fairy tales likely to confuse "little children whose minds are susceptible of every impression; and who from the liveliness of their imaginations are apt to convert into realities whatever forcibly strikes their fancies" (1803). Edgeworth's and Trimmer's vehemence against fancy and the fantastic can be attributed in part to efforts to tout their own more realistic writings (Grenby 2006) and to very real concern for children's terrors (Tucker 1997). But it is fantasy's potential—the child's "fancy"—to wildly, freely "mingle and unmingle" images, to arouse desire and fear and to confuse understanding, that consistently underlies educators' uneasiness over fantasy for children up until our present day. The young child "cannot distinguish between the real and the imaginary, between things that are possible and things that are merely 'made-up,'" claims Maria Montessori (1919; quoted in Goodfellow 2014); in the so-called Fairy Tale Wars (Marcus 2008), Lucy Sprague Mitchell (1921) argues that the young are apt to find fairy tales confusing in subject matter and symbolism. As for claims that fairy tales are necessary for children's imaginations, Mitchell, Montessori, and Montessori's followers insist that children's imaginations thrive without them.

But many defenders claim fancy and fantasy to be a vital domain for children: Samuel Johnson, Thomas Carlyle, James Boswell, and Samuel Coleridge all praise fancy's pleasures and benefits for the young. William Godwin, writing under the pseudonym William Scolfield, complains that rationalist children's writers "have left out of their system that most essential branch of human nature the IMAGINATION . . . everything is studied and attended to, except those things which *open the heart*" (1802). Fancy/fantasy is declared essential to sympathy and understanding, to the development of the child's mind, and even to national interests. Publishing his Home Treasury editions of fairy tales and nursery rhymes, Henry Cole (1843), using the pseudonym Felix Summerly, claims that "the many tales sung or said from time immemorial" appeal to vital aspects of a child's mind: "its fancy, imagination, sympathies, [and] affections." Charles Dickens defends "the fairy literature of our childhood" because "a nation without fancy, without some romance, never did, never can, never will, hold a great place under the sun" (quoted in Cruikshank 1854). In part, these claims for romance and fancy/fantasy undergird a view tailored toward Romantic masculinity, a pejorative attempt to deride arguments for imaginative realism made by female educators (Myers 1999), but a century later, writers still argue for fantasy's practical benefits. "Fantasy is the most valuable attribute of the human mind," argues Soviet children's poet Kornei Chukovskii. "Without imaginative fantasy there would be complete stagnation in both physics and chemistry . . . the value of such tales [is] in developing, strengthening, enriching, and directing children's thinking and emotional responses" (quoted in Lynn 2005).

The question of whether fantasy by its very nature belongs to children or adults generates a complex tangle of debate about the role of fantasizing in human cultural evolution. For Victorians, "fairy literature" encompasses not only folk and traditional fairy tales but also adventure stories, nursery rhymes, Arthurian romances, Gulliver's visit to Lilliput, and literary fairy tales. In his preface to *The Heroes; or Greek Fairy Tales for My Children*, Charles Kingsley (1856) considers "the *Eddas*, and the *Voluspa*, and *Beowulf*, and the noble old Romances" equally to be fairy tales (quoted in Kamenetsky 1992). This "fairy literature" is understood to pertain to children and the "childhood of man." "All nations [love fairy tales] when they are young: our old forefathers did, and called their stories 'sagas,'" Kingsley (1856) writes, reflecting prevailing attitudes toward civilization and cultural maturity. Anthropologists and folklorists (Jacob and Wilhelm Grimm, Andrew Lang, Joseph Jacobs, Peter Asbjørnsen, and Jørgen Moe) brought fantastic tales forward in abundance, suggesting a rich relationship between fantasy, imagination, childhood, and culture. But while anthropology considers stories' fantastical elements to be evidence of an immature intellect or culture, one that should eventually mature into superior adult rationality, for George Macdonald ([1893] 1973), true maturity is the retention of a youthful openness to fantasy. "For my part, I do not write for children, but for the child-like, whether five, or fifty, or seventy-five," he writes in "The Fantastic Imagination." "He who will be a man, and will not be a child, must . . . become a little man, that is a dwarf." Thus he begins to wrest fantasy from nursery and schoolroom, claiming it not for the underdeveloped, but for the spiritually mature. He opens the way for J. R. R. Tolkien (1938/1947), who reclaims the fairy tale for adults, and for Lewis (1952), who echoes Tolkien in stating that "the whole association of fairy tale and fantasy with childhood is local and accidental." Montessori and Mitchell agree, but for their own reasons: fairy tales "are adult fancies," writes Mitchell (1921). In fairy tales, "it is we (the adult) who do the imagining," says Montessori (1919); "the child only listens." Current children's writers claim fantasy for both children and adults. "Fantasy writers who are published for children hardly ever write *for* children;

they write for themselves," says Susan Cooper (2017), noting that her own fantasies, although published on children's lists, have always been read by adults as well as children. That critical discourse on fantasy often considers children's and adult literature together (perhaps the only literary field to do so as a matter of course) is evidence of the rich, unresolved questions fantasy continues to provoke—about realism, reason, maturity, and modes of imagination (Attebery 2014; Mendlesohn 2008).

Of all contested meanings in the realm of fantasy literature—whether for children or adults—perhaps the most enduring is that of definition. For Brian Attebery (1992), following Tolkien's template means that "nonformulaic" fantasies involve some violation of what the author believes to be natural law, they are comic in structure, and they provoke a response of wonder or estrangement in the reader. Farah Mendlesohn, quoting Tzvetan Todorov, points to a "moment of hesitation" between the *marvelous* and the *uncanny* in the context of fantasies by Diana Wynne Jones, while Gary K. Wolfe conceptualizes fantasy's "collective world view" as "the geography of desire." Natalie Babbitt (1987) claims that fantasy "aims to define the universe," and in her guide to fantasy literature for children, Ruth Nadelman Lynn (2005) cites many fantasists' attempts to define it—from Jane Langton's assertion that "fantasy novels are 'waking dreams'" to Susan Cooper's statement that fantasy is a "most magnificent bubble." Ursula Le Guin (1973/1979) writes that fantasy is "a different approach to reality, an alternative technique for apprehending and coping with existence. Fantasy is nearer to poetry, to mysticism and to insanity than naturalistic fiction." She claims the role of the child to be central to the creation of fantasy worlds. "The fundamental premise of fantasy," writes Attebery (2014), "is that the things it tells not only did not happen, but *could* not have happened. In that literal untruth is freedom to tell many symbolic truths." This diverse sampling of definitions of *fantasy* points to the playful, complex, and poetic capacities of this faculty of mind, making little or no distinction between children's and adult literature.

The ground prepared by nineteenth-century fantasists (E. T. A. Hoffmann, Lewis Carroll, Hans Christian Andersen, George Macdonald, Carlo Collodi, Juliana Ewing, Mary Louisa Molesworth) and further tilled in the first half of the 1900s (E. Nesbit, L. Frank Baum, J. M. Barrie, Penelope Delta, Antoine de Saint-Exupéry) produces with new abundance in the burgeoning children's publishing industry from the 1950s to the present. Tove Jansson, Astrid Lindgren, C. S. Lewis, William Mayne, Philippa Pearce, L. M. Boston, Susan Cooper, Alan Garner, Tomiko Inui, Joan Aiken, Diana Wynne Jones, Tonke Dragt, Edward Eager, Michael Ende, Norton Juster, Lloyd Alexander, Virginia Hamilton, Ursula K. Le Guin, Cornelia Funke, Otfried Preußler, Margaret Mahy, and many others publish children's and young adult fantasies in the decades after World War II. In the wake of the popularity of *The Lord of the Rings*, Tolkien-derivative "epic," "heroic," or "sword and sorcery" fantasies proliferate, and fantasy is given another boost with the sensational "crossover" popularity of J. K. Rowling's Harry Potter series. Female heroes, once excluded from the very romances whence contemporary fantasy arose, are now free to take the lead in works by, among others, Robin McKinley and Lene Kaaberbøl, and at long last, racially and culturally diverse heroes and literary models are finding a valued place in fantasy literature in works by Nnedi Okorafor, Gene Luen Yang, Cherie Dimaline, Nalo Hopkinson, Octavia E. Butler, and others.

In the face of the thousands, even millions, of children's fantasies that have been written, translated, sold, and read in the past fifty years, parents and educators still debate whether fantasy draws young readers into unhealthy escapism and fosters an inability to manage in the "real world." Some protest "occult" or heterodox content in series such as Philip Pullman's His Dark Materials and Harry Potter. In critical discussion, Ebony Elizabeth Thomas explores the role racial difference plays in fantasy, suggesting that the "Dark Other" is "the engine that drives the fantastic" (2019, 25) and proposing ways to liberate the fantastic from "its fear and loathing of darkness and Dark Others" (29). The vigor and plenty of youthful enthusiasm for fantasy has turned critical debate toward a rich array of perspectives and issues, including fantasy's complex aptness for adolescent readers (MacRae 1998; Coats 2010); its function as poetic language, whether metaphor or metonymy (Stephens 1992; Attebery 2014); its modes (Mendlesohn 2008); and most enduringly, the peculiar, ineffable mysteriousness of the way that it works.

25

Gender

Elizabeth Marshall

Gender within children's literature studies is an analytic concept that names and sorts a constellation of bodies. According to the *OED*, the term *gender* historically classifies words and bodies into a particular "sort or kind." Indo-European languages include pronouns and nouns classified as feminine, masculine, or neuter and bodies categorized into male or female, as in "the collective attributes or traits associated with a particular sex, or determined as a result of one's sex. Also: a (male or female) group characterized in this way" (*OED*). Since the twentieth century, *gender* operates as a verb "to assign or attribute a gender to; to divide, classify, or differentiate on the basis of gender" (*OED*). These definitions define social classifications within and beyond literature for the child.

From its inception in the eighteenth century, children's literature enforced ideas about biological sex as synonymous with a gender that required specific behaviors. In 1744, John Newbery published *A Little Pretty Pocket-Book* in two editions, one for little Master Tommy and the other for pretty Miss Polly; it included a pincushion for Miss Polly and a ball for Master Tommy. By the mid-1800s, British magazines like the *Girl's Own Paper* and the *Boy's Own Paper*, and school stories like Sarah Fielding's *The Governess, or The Little Female Academy* (1749), and Thomas Hughes's *Tom Brown's Schooldays* (1857) solidified a gendered literary market with two separate readerships that linked femininity to stories of romance and domesticity and masculinity to stories of adventure and empire. While school stories originated in Britain, the genre circulated globally. Girls' school stories, for instance, "engaged in an extended and transnational dialogue about idealized femininity for girls and young women" (Moruzi and Smith 2013, xv). Recent international best sellers *The Dangerous Book for Boys* (Iggulden and Iggulden 2006) and *The Daring Book for Girls* (Buchanan and Peskowitz 2007) suggest that the gendering of childhood into two separate readerships continues to drive the marketing of children's texts.

Representations of gender in children's literature reflect and produce a politics about bodies, power, and socialization that extends beyond its pages. Theorizing bodies as sites of cultural inscription challenges the claim that gender denotes an objective difference between male and female. Therefore, gender engages multiple meanings, encompassing a range of masculinities and femininities and elaborating a fluidity that exceeds biological binaries. Attention to the production of gender in literature for children suggests that the fictional child is a complex site for examining which bodies have power and which do not and who gets to decide.

To this end, adults often lift children's literature out of the nursery and use it as a tool in a fight for (or against) the empowerment or visibility of certain bodies. During the women's movement in the 1970s in the US, feminist critics like Judith Fetterley (1978) became "resisting readers" of the literary canon, including children's literature. Marcia R. Lieberman (1972) argued that "a close examination of the treatment of girls and women in fairy tales reveals certain patterns which are keenly interesting not only in themselves, but also as material which has undoubtedly played a major contribution in forming the sexual role concept of children, and in suggesting to them the limitations that are imposed by sex upon a person's chances of success in various endeavors" (384). As a critical term, *gender* works in two ways in this example. First, Lieberman's critique assumes a link between biological sex and one's gender and extends it to include the social and political implications of that lived distinction. The *OED* notes that modern "(esp. feminist) use" of *gender* has been "a euphemism for the sex of a human being, often intended to emphasize the social and cultural, as opposed to the biological, distinction between the sexes." Second, Lieberman's work and much of the early criticism on gender in children's literature assumes girls and women as the subject of analysis, focusing on their misrepresentation and absence (Dixon 1977; Liljeström 1972; Nilsen 1971; Weitzman et al. 1972). The critique of stereotypes and the different treatment of male and female subjects endures into the present (McCabe et al. 2011). Feminist analyses of gender, especially of girls and women in children's texts, map onto other examinations that consider the gendering of boys (Stephens 2002; Kidd 2004), the ways in which visual and verbal discourses construct gender (Paul 1998; Marshall 2004, 2018; Sunderland 2004), or how acts of parody, cross-dressing, and other performances challenge or reaffirm gender binaries (Flanagan 2008; Mallan 2009).

In tandem with feminist scholarship and movements for equity throughout the 1970s and beyond, writers and illustrators of children's texts revised and fractured familiar narratives built around independent, predominately white, cisgender girls who save the prince and/or refuse the heterosexual plot. Robert Munsch and Michael Martchenko's *The Paper Bag Princess* (1980) or Babette Cole's *Princess Smartypants* (1987) remain popular examples of this strategy. In *The Paper Bag Princess*, Elizabeth fights a dragon and saves the prince but in the end dances alone into the sunset. Princess Smartypants "enjoyed being a Ms." and outwits several suitors so that she might lounge in a red bikini under an umbrella sipping a cool drink while surrounded by her pets. The overturning of familiar fairy tale tropes—like beauty or heterosexual marriage as reward—continues to resonate with contemporary audiences. Extending the essential work of interrupting an industry of stories in which "girls win the prize if they are the fairest of them all; boys win if they are bold, active, and lucky" (Lieberman 1972, 385), Louise O'Neill's *The Surface Breaks* (2018) offers a feminist retelling of Andersen's "The Little Mermaid," and Bethan Woollvin's *Rapunzel* (2017) deletes the prince character.

The critique of gender stereotypes as a means to a more equitable future assumes a relationship between reading and socialization. However, as Sherrie Inness (1997) demonstrates in her reading of the Nancy Drew series and Beverly Lyon Clark (1996) argues in her reading of the "crossgendering" of the school story, openings for subversive readings of gender exist within texts. Moreover, readers may also contest progressive messages about gender equity, as Bronwyn Davies (1989) found in her study of Australian preschoolers' responses to *The Paper Bag Princess*. Although studies continue to assume that literature informs the production of gendered identity, it remains difficult to tease out how this happens, especially given that children's texts do their work amid a larger cultural pedagogy.

The idea that gender is a political category, open to interpretation in ways that reinforce or challenge dominant discourses of hegemonic gender relations, builds from philosopher Judith Butler's (1988) highly influential concept of "performativity"—the idea that gender is "real only to the extent that it is performed" (527). Performativity is less about an individual's choice to pick whether to be a girl or a boy in a particular moment; rather, gender lies in the repetition or imitation of dominant norms that make it seem real. The "I" emerges "only within and as the matrix of gender relations themselves" (Butler 1993, 7). This definition differs from those studies that pursue the differences between male and female characters, attending instead to disruptions to "heterosexuality's claim on naturalness and originality" (125). Children's books like *10,000 Dresses* (Ewert 2008) or *Morris Micklewhite and the Tangerine Dress* (Baldacchino 2014) that feature boys who wear dresses unsettle "masculine" behaviors, representing acts that may or may not be linked with a male body. These texts interrogate gender rather than sex and/or sexuality but do not always disrupt familiar binaries. As Victoria Flanagan (2008) points out, cross-dressing moments in children's texts are not necessarily subversive, as they can both challenge and reify normative understandings of masculinity and femininity. That is, seemingly stable gender categories are a fiction. Lisa Chu Shen analyzes a contemporary Chinese school story, Yang Hongying's *Jia Xiaozi Dai An* (Tomboy Dai An; 2010), a text "meant to construct girlhood and boyhood in accordance with socially and culturally accepted norms, purporting to serve as manuals for heteronormative gender roles" and finds that "despite its conservative constructions of femininity and gender, *Tomboy Dai An* inadvertently brings the reader's attention to the artifice and artificiality of such constructions, thereby simultaneously subverting what it sets out to endorse" (2019, 280). Similarly, queer theorists propose additional strategies for interpreting the inherent instability of gender in mainstream children's texts, such as the practice of "reading perversely" (Hurley 2011, 119) in order to examine "nonnormativities more broadly" (Forrester 2016, 120). Some authors writing for a young audience make the fluidity of gender visible, as in the middle-grade novel *George* (2015), written by genderqueer author Alex Gino. The book centers on a transgender girl named Melissa. The narrator calls Melissa by her birth name, George, but uses female pronouns to speak about Melissa, who wants to play Charlotte in the school play of E. B. White's *Charlotte's Web*

(1952). Her teacher tells her that she cannot try out because she is a boy. Other characters around Melissa use male pronouns, and through this tactic, Gino captures the violence of language as it seeks to define Melissa's subjectivity in normative and biologically bound terms.

Studies of gender in children's literature generally obfuscate other intersectional identities, and the majority of books that feature empowered heroines or gender-fluid characters also persistently reproduce whiteness as the norm. In her intersectional analysis of sixty-eight picture books from four Western countries, Jasmine Z. Lester (2014) finds that the majority "tell the stories of upper middle class White queers with binary gender identities" (259). Similarly, Vivian Yenika-Agbaw (2013, 238) argues that scholarship in children's literature often prioritizes gender, failing to consider messages that "white cultural products" are sending to children of color. Postcolonial and Indigenous scholars (Simpson 2014b) draw our attention to the ties between colonialism and the gendering of bodies and in turn call into question the idea that gender equity narratives are liberating for all readers. *My Princess Boy* (Kilodavis 2009), in which a brown child "is neither defined nor restricted by his gender nonconformity" (Lester 2014, 260), and Canadian artist Vivek Shraya's *The Boy & the Bindi* (2016), a picture book that features a gender-creative South Asian child, provide intersectional narratives that capture the complexity of lived experiences.

These exemplary texts suggest that the term *gender* is on the move. Lois Gould's *X: A Fabulous Child's Story* (published in *Ms. Magazine*'s "Stories for Free Children" in 1972 and as a picture book in 1978) uses *it* as a gender-neutral pronoun to name protagonist X, a child deliberately raised without reference to its gender. In 2012, the Swedish publishing house Olika released a children's book that uses the gender-neutral pronoun *hen* (a substitute for *hon*, "she," and *han*, "he") in Jesper Lundqvist and Bettina Johansson's *Kivi & Monsterhund* (2012). This controversial book reignited a larger cultural debate about gender (Rothschild 2012), returning us to the entwining of words and bodies inherent in the origins of the term. Books such as *Kivi & Monsterhund* and Maya Christina Gonzalez's *Call Me Tree / Llámame árbol*, a bilingual middle-grade novel about a Chicana child that uses the gender-neutral pronoun *tree*, move beyond binaries to envision youth on a gender spectrum. These projects are a reminder that the term *gender* is also a verb meaning "to form, come into existence" (*OED*), an act of becoming that captures the complexity of embodied experience and resists a history of linguistic violence that seeks to discipline the body through words, including those written for children.

26

Genre
Karin E. Westman

The January/February 2012 issue of *Poets and Writers* magazine recounts the "Cinderella" publishing tale of novelist Adam Mansbach, independent publisher Johnny Temple of Akashic Books, and the unexpected success of their *Go the Fuck to Sleep* (2011). Mansbach's book is alternately described by its author, publisher, and readers as "an illustrated children's book" (85), a *New York Times* best seller (85), "the go-to gag gift for your cool best friend's baby shower" (85), "a popular gift book" (86), and "a novelty book" (89). Having gone through "seven printings and earned revenues of more than two million dollars in its first three months" (88), *Go the Fuck to Sleep* occupies one of several cultural spaces, including one titled "profane children's bedtime books."

Even as individual titles may elude a single genre's grasp, genre is both ubiquitous and inimical to the history of children's literature, dominating and vexing systems of classification in terms of form, theme, audience, and material production. If, as Peter Hunt (2001) remarks, "one of the delights of children's literature is that it does not fit easily into any cultural or academic category" (1), children's literature is consequently everywhere and nowhere on the generic landscape. It lacks "generic purity," happily "subsuming and assuming other forms" (3), and is either lauded or disparaged for such flexibility, such generosity, such omnipotence. The cultural history of children's literature circulates around this intergeneric potential, as considerations of genre organize responses to individual texts and determine questions for the field: When did children's literature begin? What text is worthy of an award? For whom is children's literature written? Is children's literature its own genre or only the intersection of others?

As a keyword for the field of children's literature, *genre* plays a constitutive if contested role. As a literary term, *genre* is an amorphous category whose definition shifts over time and context.

Derived from the French word *genre*, meaning "kind" or "type" (Murfin [1831] 2000), the term also has origins in ancient Greek classifications (Abrams 1993). However, *genre* no longer denotes an objective, stable set of categories to which one can assign a text according to its formal characteristics. In the twentieth century, critical interest turned to the one who applies the taxonomy. For contemporary theorists like Jonathan Frow (2005), genre is "a set of conventional and highly organized constraints on the production and interpretation of meaning" (10). Those constraints might be formal, thematic, or material—or, most likely, a combination of those three in relative proportions, according to the expectations of an audience within a particular historical moment. This more recent view, developing from the work of Tzvetan Todorov, considers genre as discourse or speech act. For Todorov, "the literary genres . . . are nothing but such choices among discursive possibilities, choices that a given society has made conventional" (1990, 10). Identifying genre as social convention, Heather Dubrow observes that "Generic prescriptions also resemble social codes in that they differ from culture to culture," noting how genre functions like "a social institution, such as an established church or legislative body": "It is often possible to challenge such institutions, sometimes overthrow them, but it is virtually impossible simply to exclude them from our lives" (1982, 3).

This view of genre as a culturally constructed social institution coincides with Raymond Williams's goals in *Keywords* (1976). Though Williams does not select *genre* for discussion, his genealogies for the words *formalist, structural,* and *conventional* pose questions similar to the ones asked by contemporary theorists of genre: how a text's formal characteristics and content serve as the starting point for discussions of ideology, how form and content reflect perception and belief. Genre thus becomes a "set of expectations" that readers bring to the text based on past experiences and current conditions (Cobley 2001). As Amy Devitt explains, "Defining genre as a kind of text becomes circular, since what we call a kind of text depends on what we think a genre is" (2004, 7). Instead, Devitt suggests, genres are better viewed as "shorthand terms for situations" (7). Echoing Devitt's approach, Michael Goldman theorizes genre as drama, focusing on in the drama of generic recognition: "In the heat of the moment, we respond to genre as if it were taxonomical," but we really "experience it as something looming or fading, definite or disrupted, something more like an expectation or occasion," and "we become aware of it as a phenomenon of performance" (2000, 5). Like a performance, a text's generic classification is site-specific, contingent on an audience's expectations and response as much as the text's form and content. Past, present, and future audiences establish, maintain, or change generic expectations, which emerge from a negotiation between convention and innovation.

Children's literature's complex relationship to audience augments the field's reliance on genre as an organizing principle. Even if younger readers are the intended addressee, adult writers, readers, publishers, scholars, teachers, and librarians influence production and reception of these texts through their performance of generic expectations. In turn, genre becomes a way to map the history of children's literature and the relative aesthetic value of children's and adult literary texts. As the editors of the *Norton Anthology of Children's Literature* note in their preface, "Typically, the term *literature* has excluded children's literature—that is, children's literature has generally been marked as separate from 'real literature'" (Zipes et al., 2005, xxxii). Perry Nodelman pursues a related, if less pejorative, taxonomy when he names children's literature as a "distinct and definable genre of literature, with characteristics that emerge from enduring adult ideas about childhood" (2008, 242). Children's literature can thus bear the label of a "genre," much like romance or science fiction or the western, even if such use of the term *genre* requires many other designated genres—poetry, drama, dystopian novels, nonsense, and so on—to squeeze uncomfortably under that same label.

Much scholarship on children's literature revolves around categories of genre rather than chronology. This organization may be a consequence of the earlier days of children's literature scholarship—shaped by librarians, teachers, and publishers who sorted books according to the child reader's age and reading ability. The resulting categories divided picture books from middle-grade readers and middle-grade readers from chapter books (Lundin 2004). Such distinctions continued in the teaching and scholarship of children's literature, as the *Norton Anthology* demonstrates: it is organized first by genre and then by chronology. Unlike Norton's anthologies for English or American literature (now in their tenth and ninth editions, respectively), this first anthology for children's literature maps its subject not by centuries but by genres such as "Alphabets," "Primers and Readers," "Fairy Tales," "Animal Fables," "Fantasy," "Verse," "Plays," "Books of Instruction," "Adventure Stories," "School Stories," and "Domestic Fiction." The editorial apparatus does not forget history, but the organizing principle is genre—that is, considerations of

form, content, and audience—rather than the passage of time.

Given this intellectual framework, genre can confound the origins of children's literature. For many years, as Gillian Adams (1998) and others have noted, Philippe Ariès's *Centuries of Childhood* (1962) has held sway, corroborated by others who also located the start of children's literature in the seventeenth or even eighteenth century. Within this historiography, genre serves as the organizing principle, with Johann Amos Comenius's *Orbis Sensualium Pictus* (Latin and German, 1658; English translation, 1659) finding its place as the first picture book for children. For Adams, Ariès's and others' historiographic error resides in a false horizon of generic expectations: if didactic texts fail to qualify as "literature," then children's literature scholarship has inappropriately foreshortened the narrative timeline of its history and must instead look back to earlier centuries (1998, 4–5). Yet the dominance of genre as an organizing principle persists. Daniel T. Kline's edited collection on *Medieval Literature for Children* (2003) uses genre to structure its insights: "Didactic and Moral Literature," "Courtesy and Conduct Literature," "Educational and Instructional Literature," "Religious Literature," and "Entertainment and Popular Literature" (6–9). Even while acknowledging that the collection is "divided somewhat artificially into five parts, based on similarities of form and purpose" (6), Kline uses generic parameters to tell this newer history.

Of course, a genre's relative value and definition can shift over time. The perceived need in 1980 for the Children's Literature Association to appoint nine colleagues to a "ChLA Canon Committee," charged with identifying "touchstones" of children's literature, speaks to the Association's need to set boundaries of "excellence" (Nodelman 1985, 7). The resulting list of sixty-five titles—some a single picture book, others a series or collection of stories—officially presents itself, by way of genre, as inclusive of the variety within the field of children's literature. Committee member Perry Nodelman notes how aesthetic preferences created hierarchies of generic value: the selected titles favor "complexity," "American and British," "linguistic distinction," and "realistic styles of art" (1985, 8–9). The list's "main usefulness," Nodelman concludes, may well be the opportunity to reveal "the limitations of [their] consensus" (9): it is a temporary marker of generic expectations, already open to renegotiation.

That perpetual renegotiation of generic expectations is therefore bounded by cultural privileges of race, ethnicity, nation, gender, class, and sexual orientation. As Philip Nel (2017b) notes, "Genre functions as a form of segregation, restricting non-White children to only certain types of stories" (27) when, for instance, "history, realism, and nonfiction dominate lists of African American and Native American literature" (174). If "genre helps us see structural racism" (181) within a particular national literature, it also reveals a nation's cultural differences. In an editorial for the *New York Times* (2018) about "What Dutch Children's Books Can Teach Adults," Michael Erard identifies generic similarities between the Dutch *zoekboek*, the German *Wimmelbuch*, and the seek-and-find books popularized in the US by *Where's Waldo*, but the cultural specificity of each text dominates his reading, maintaining national boundaries more than crossing them.

Awards, too, highlight genre as the means of negotiating aesthetic and cultural value. In the US, the Caldecott Medal goes predominately to picture books of fiction rather than nonfiction or poetry; the Newbery Medal goes predominately to books of historical fiction, realist fiction, and fantasy rather than nonfiction, folklore, or poetry. Yet as a genre's relative value and definition shift over time, awards become a location

where generic value gets contested and redefined. Brian Selznick's *The Invention of Hugo Cabret* (2007) stretched the conventional bounds—literally—of the Caldecott Award's expectations, presenting itself to readers as a "550-page picture book" (Selznick 2008). Its intergeneric and intermedial qualities—Selznick's desire to "create a novel that read like a movie," his turn toward the picture book to accomplish this artistic goal, and the result volume of pages he required—demonstrate how, in Selznick's words, "we are still passionately debating what exactly a picture book is" (2008). What readers expect a picture book to be—in terms of size, shape, content, and audience—has a new generic horizon following Selznick's Caldecott win. The definition of *children's literature* is thus continually under negotiation, often through the parameters of genre.

Like Selznick's *Hugo Cabret*, Rowling's Harry Potter series defied late 1990s conventions for readers, authors, and publishers of children's literature in terms of its physical size and its intergeneric narrative. Its success with child, young adult, and adult readers also prompted a redefinition of the audience for children's literature. Imagining her series as "one big book" (Anelli and Spartz 2005), Rowling offers a seven-volume study of one character's development—a bildungsroman of Harry's life from age eleven to seventeen. The series's generic hybridity illustrates its significance in terms of literary form as well as critical response. Drawing on traditions of psychological realism, mystery, the gothic, the school story, the family story, satire, and fantasy, Rowling's compelling narrative prompts both sympathetic engagement and critical reflection. Individual genres are invoked, stretched, and transformed, creating new iterations and relations of literary forms that defy easy classification. Rowling's generic blending also bends the expected narrative conclusions for literature and literary history, testing our established categories for these individual genres and for children's literature. Rowling is hardly the first author to craft a hybrid text: Astrid Lindgren's *Pippi Långstrump* (1945) includes elements of nonsense, fantasy, realism, and the adventure story; Morten Dürr and Lars Hornemann's graphic novel *Zenobia* (2016) mixes realism, myth, and travel narrative; and Tove Jansson's Moomin novels (1945–71) blend fable, fairy tale, and the family story. However, the overwhelming popularity of Rowling's series with readers of all ages has challenged generic conventions about child readers, adult readers, children's literacy, children's book publishing, the publishing industry, the role of marketing, and the role of the fan. Eroding any clear distinction between *popular* and *canonical*, between one genre and another, Rowling's Harry Potter series prompts debate about boundaries—their efficacy and their necessity—for our experience, enjoyment, and critical history of children's literature.

Rowling's success and the subsequent shift in expectations demonstrate how children's literature and adult literature continue to occupy negotiated generic territories, each with their particular ideological weights. Such reinscription of generic lines—literature for adult readers on one side, literature for child readers on the other—reminds us that the boundaries are never fixed and that genre will continue to be at center stage in the performance of children's literature.

27

Girlhood
Jacqueline Reid-Walsh

"Well! WHAT are you?" said the Pigeon. "I can see you're trying to invent something!"

"I—I'm a little girl," said Alice, rather doubtfully, as she remembered the number of changes she had gone through that day.

"A likely story indeed!" said the Pigeon in a tone of the deepest contempt. "I've seen a good many little girls in my time, but never ONE with such a neck as that! No, no! You're a serpent; and there's no use denying it."

—Lewis Carroll, *Alice's Adventures in Wonderland*

There is no all-encompassing definition of *girlhood*. Nor is it a static or universal state. In *Alice's Adventures in Wonderland* (1865), by asserting she is a little girl, Alice demonstrates the mutability of girlhood. The exchange—concluding with the conflation of Alice with the seductive serpent in Genesis—highlights problematic interrelations between *girl* and *girlhood* in Anglo-American culture.

According to the *OED*, *girlhood* has been used from the mid-eighteenth century with overlapping meanings: "the state of being a girl; the time of life during which one is a girl. Also: girls collectively." The first citation in British literature occurs in Samuel Richardson's novel *Clarissa* (1748), where the virtuous heroine, barely past childhood, is placed as a commodity on the "marriage market" and chooses death after being raped. The linking of girlhood and virginity continues.

Girlhood is based on *girl*, with contradictory definitions extending back to the Middle Ages (*OED*). The variability undermines one age, sex, or gender being associated with the term. In the 1300s, *girls* (usually plural) referred to a child or young person of either sex. In the late 1300s, *girl* began to be associated with the female sex: some matter-of-fact and some derogatory terms refer to a young or relatively young woman, a woman of any age, a female child, a sweetheart, a prostitute, a female servant, a female slave, and an effeminate man. Different theories have been proposed: *girl* either is a diminutive of the Middle Low German word for small child, *Gör*, *Göre*, or derives from the Old English term for dress or apparel, *gyrela* (*OED*). The link between girls, clothing, and dolls has been entrenched in European culture since *Émile, ou De l'éducation* (1762), where Jean-Jacques Rousseau stated, "The doll is the special plaything of the sex. Here the girl's liking is plainly directed towards her lifework . . . the art of pleasing finds its physical expression in dress. . . . But the time will come when she will be her own doll" (quoted in Mitchell and Reid-Walsh 2002). The same connections continue today, though definitions of *girl* and *girlhood* remain conflicted.

Is a singular term, *girl*, even valid? Perhaps pluralizing is better, as Karen Sánchez-Eppler (2011a) does in defining *childhood*. Catherine Driscoll (2002), in *girls*, proposes a "genealogy of girlhood" where, following Michel Foucault, researchers do not trace sequential development, turning girls into passive objects (4). Driscoll investigates "how knowledge about girlhood has shaped what it means to be a girl and how girls experience their own positions in the world" (4). The focus in that construction is on the ability of girls to seize (limited) agency, to define themselves (Walshaw 2007, 71). But the question of how girls are defined by others—including language—remains. Some Western countries possess no terms for girlhood or boyhood but one for both, as in *barndom* (in Swedish, Danish, and Norwegian) and *Kindheit* (in German). In Spanish, *niñez* or *infancia* refers to the childhoods of both genders.

Given the amorphous nature of girlhood, it is unsurprising that scholars approach the subject from a wide range of positions. Some emphasize chronology or psychological development so that age is offered as a "universal" criteria despite cultural and economic realities. Others emphasize cultural constructions. Does it matter if a girl is of preschool age, between the ages of ten and fourteen (a "young adolescent" as defined by the Population Council [McCarthy, Brady, and Hallman 2016]), or eighteen, the age of consent in many countries? If the UN's definition of *youth* is applied to a girl, the age limit rises to twenty-nine—so then women's experiences are valid to an understanding of girlhood (Gonick and Gannon 2014). If participating in girls' cultures qualifies, then the age rises further (Fuchs 1999). The question of who is included and is excluded from girlhood intersects with geography, culture, race, and ability. A female in sub-Saharan Africa may spend her childhood looking after her siblings because their parents have died of AIDS. Girls of First Nations communities in Canada and Australia may live circumscribed by poverty, substance abuse, and remoteness (Lea and Driscoll 2012). The unearned privileges of birth determine whether girlhood includes forestalling adult responsibilities or protecting virginity.

Historically, Anglo-American girls' fiction has promoted a normalized girlhood validating social conventions or showing acceptable ways of subverting expectations. In late nineteenth- and early twentieth-century North America, "girls' books" flourished: among the most famous are Alcott's *Little Women* (1868–69), Coolidge's *What Katy Did* (1872), Wiggin's *Rebecca of Sunnybrook Farm* (1903), Burnett's *A Little Princess* (1905), Montgomery's *Anne of Green Gables* (1908), and Porter's *Pollyanna* (1913). These explore the vitality, playfulness, and unconventional childhood of the heroines (Reynolds 1990). Initially tomboys, they grow up to accept conventional female norms, serving as fictive conduct manuals (Vallone 1995).

Heroines embraced as feminist reveal fissures in that term. Astrid Lindgren's Swedish tomboy Pippi Långstrump (Pippi Longstocking) subtly challenges conventions of girlhood, even if the third novel in that series, *Pippi Långstrump i Söderhavet* (*Pippi in the South Seas*; 1948), affirms colonialist stereotypes. Laura Ingalls Wilder's Little House books (1932–71) confirm the resourcefulness of White girls and women on the American frontier but also dehumanize Native Americans, refiguring the theft of their land as benign industriousness. In contrast, David Robertson and Julie Flet's *When We Were Alone* (2016), a powerful Canadian picture book based on a Cree girl learning about her grandmother's residential school experiences, shows how Indigenous Canadians resisted cultural genocide (Reid-Walsh 2018b).

Challenging heteronormative femininity directly or subtly, queer girlhoods chart topographies of longing and belonging. Often embraced as a protoqueer character, the title character of Louise Fitzhugh's *Harriet the Spy* (1964) manifests a queerness, Robin Bernstein suggests, more from her youth than from her tomboyishness, the sexuality of her creator, or her status as a childhood role model for lesbians. As Bernstein argues, heterosexuality constructs womanhood "in binary opposition to" both manhood and girlhood: lesbians are both genderqueer and "agequeer," and Harriet is more the latter than the former (2011a, 115). Genderqueerness more typically emerges in YA fiction like Nancy Garden's *Annie on My Mind* (1982), in which a same-sex relationship precipitates the protagonist's discovery of a her homosexuality. A recursively structured work that parallels the queer histories of the author and her (closeted) father, Alison Bechdel's graphic memoir *Fun Home* (2006) reflects on the family secrets that ripple through her girlhood and young womanhood.

In its intersections with many matrices of identity, the lived experiences of girls map gender's entanglement in competing hierarchies of power. Cassie, the title character of Faith Ringgold's semiautobiographical *Tar Beach* (1991), imagines herself flying above the barriers of American racism (such as a Union that rejects her father as a "half-breed Indian"). In Cece Bell's graphic memoir *El Deafo* (2014), the author's anthropomorphic rabbit avatar makes visible the social and environmental barriers faced by a deaf girl navigating a world designed for hearing persons. The violence—both psychological and physical—of patriarchal fundamentalism shapes the girlhoods depicted in Marjane Satrapi's *Persepolis* (2000–2003) and Malala Yousafzai and Patricia McCormick's *I Am Malala: How One Girl Stood Up for Education and Changed the World* (2014; the "young adult" version of her *I Am Malala: The Girl Who Stood Up for Education and Was Shot by the Taliban*).

A rich source is reading texts *by* girls—past and present, material and virtual, manuscript and published—that respect the agency of the creators (Mitchell and Reid-Walsh 2008). Juvenilia is identified with famous writers and artists, but scholarship needs to fill this gap in representation, lest its neglect contribute the further marginalization of children. Some work seeks to fill this gap by focusing on writing by ordinary and marginalized girls. Manuscript materials are found only in archives (Reid-Walsh 2016; Weikle-Mills 2011), but published examples of little-known girls' poetry include those by teenage Northern black girl Ann Plato published in 1841 (Sorby 2017) and poems by Kali Grosvenor in her sixth and seventh years about growing up black in New York (1970). Reading widely, deeply, and thoughtfully will educate us about girls and their multiple girlhoods.

28

Graphic Novel
Charles Hatfield

Comics have traditionally marked the gap between adult-sanctioned children's literature and self-selected children's reading. Though internationally popular and crucial to the literacy narratives of many, they have been doubly stigmatized, viewed as both a danger to children and yet the quintessence of childishness. However, in anglophone cultures, comics have at last rebounded as a children's genre, spurred by enthusiasm for the graphic novel: the bulwark of comics' recent claims to literariness, or at least legitimacy. The graphic novel ideal has recuperated comics in anglophone children's literature circles (Abate and Tarbox 2017) even as it threatens to eclipse a good part of comics' history. In short, the graphic novel has proven a great legitimizing force for comics—though at the same time a mystifying circumlocution for what is, after all, an old form.

The history of comics is contentious and unsettled, shaped by conflicting formal, definitional, and nationalist agendas. How far back to go, where to look for points of origin and aesthetic breakthroughs, and even the very question of what makes comics distinct—these basic questions remain up in the air. The most convincing scholarly histories of comics in the West (Kunzle 1973, 1990; Smolderen 2014; Gordon 1998; Gardner 2012) have argued for the modernity of the form: comics' essential links to the spread of print, new modes of political and social satire, and an accelerating, industrialized mass culture rooted in consumerism. Comics historiography has tended to waver between local narratives of origin, such as the now discredited claim that comics are an "American" invention, and exogamous narratives that acknowledge the form's transnational lineage. Histories of manga often enact a tug-of-war between the long history of Japanese visual culture and an acknowledgment of crucial American influences in the Meiji and later periods (Schodt 1986; Ito 2005). Exogamous narratives more persuasively frame comics, by whatever name the form is known, as a global phenomenon.

Among the key figures in histories of early comics, two satirists illuminate the roots of the debate over the age of comics' readers: William Hogarth, the English painter and printmaker whose moralizing "novels in prints" (1732–50) established a popular and collectible mode of sequential visual narrative, and the more whimsical Rodolphe Töpffer, a Swiss schoolmaster influenced by Hogarth whose seven *histoires en estampes*, or comic albums (1833–45), are often credited as the prototypes of the modern comic book and graphic novel. Neither Hogarth nor Töpffer published works "for" children, though Töpffer's comics were initially seen and encouraged by his young students. The claim that the nineteenth-century comics medium was emphatically "for adults" and only later banished to the children's press (Groensteen [2000] 2009) is debatable. The newspaper strip genre launched on the cusp of the twentieth century trafficked in images—both satirical and sentimental—of children, from R. F. Outcault's Yellow Kid and Buster Brown, to Rudolph Dirks's Katzenjammer Kids, to Winsor McCay's Little Nemo (Hatfield 2011; Saguisag 2018). As Santiago García ([2010] 2015) notes, early comic strips were populated by socially "marginal characters," particularly vagrants and kids, and the kids persisted; newspaper strips' continuing emphasis on child protagonists "decisively reinforce[d] the relationship between the medium and the childhood audience" (44–45). The world's most popular and influential comics have always been rooted in ideas about childhood and have had millions of child readers. For comics to be recognized *now* as an important children's genre requires an act of historical amnesia.

Linguistic differences in terminology map competing histories and uses of the medium. *Comics* abbreviates *comic papers* or *comic weeklies*—that is, journals that published humorous cartoons—and thus highlights the medium's links to jokes (see Harvey 2009). *Manga*, the Japanese term, is composed of two kanji (logographic characters) that mean, respectively, "whimsical" or "impromptu" and "pictures." The French term for sequential art, *bande dessinée*, means "drawn strips." The term for comics in Danish and Swedish are, respectively, *tegneserie* and *tecknade serier*, which literally mean "drawn serial," emphasizing the seriality of the medium.

The histories of American, European, Japanese, and other comics cannot easily fold into one, but a transnational perspective on comics does circle around the question of the child. To what extent have comics influenced and been influenced by childhood, both the lives of actual children and the ideological constructions of childhood within a given culture? Consider: popular serials are often targeted at children, and the omnipresence of transmedial characters, often drawn from comics, is a defining feature of current children's culture. Moreover, the delegitimization of comics often parallels the critical marginalization of children's texts and pastimes, and censorship regimes seldom fail to promise protection "for the children." Deemed trivial on the one hand, dangerous on the other, comics have had to run a tight gauntlet culturally, and this has everything to do with values and concerns vested in an idealized childhood.

In the US, the newly legitimized "graphic novel for young readers" is terribly ironic, because the *graphic novel* label first gained traction as a strategy for conferring adulthood on the allegedly childish comic book. The label's etymology and use reflects its fuzzy borders and origins. *Graphic* means "of or pertaining to drawing or painting" and *novel* a "long fictional prose narrative" (*OED*), but the phrase's popular usage merely reflects a desire to ditch the troublesome word *comics*. Of *graphic novel*'s three main origin stories, the best-known centers on Will Eisner's *A Contract with God and Other Tenement Stories* (1978): though among the first books to bill itself as a graphic novel, and indeed the most widely celebrated candidate for "first," it is not a novel but a short-story cycle based in a common locale. A second, lesser-known origin story centers on fan historian Richard Kyle, who around 1964–65 began using the phrases *graphic story* and *graphic novel*. Other origin stories revolve around George Metzger's *Beyond Time and Again*, Richard Corben's *Bloodstar* (both 1976), and other pre-Eisner underground-derived comics that billed themselves as graphic novels (see Harvey 2001). In the years after Eisner, myriad other publications not originally billed as graphic novels came to be remembered, and sometimes republished, under that tag. None of this publishing activity had children or children's books in mind.

The term *graphic novel* describes neither a discrete literary genre nor a specific publishing format. Rather, it denotes a sensibility: an attitude taken toward comics. As cartoonist-historian Eddie Campbell (2001) has said, the acceptance of the term "embod[ied] the arrival of an idea." This idea aligns comics with a literary aesthetic of seriousness but may be invoked by readers coming from multiple perspectives: those who see comics as deserving literary recognition; aesthetes interested in comics as a type of visual art; publishers and booksellers, for whom the graphic novel is new turf for commercial exploitation; and proponents of children's reading, who see comics as the linchpin of a new visual literacy (though they are in fact the resurgence an old genre). The *graphic novel* label, then, is not so much a single mind-set as a coalition of interests that happen to agree on one thing—that comics deserve more respect.

Some advocates of the graphic novel are paradoxically driven by both a Romantic assertion of the individual artist, aloof from any commercial considerations, and the notion that marketplace popularity confers respect upon artistic creations. These competing interests have found common cause only because comics, as they have morphed into graphic novels, have become recognized as a "serious" form (see Beaty and Woo 2016). This consensus has come just in time to align with other trends in our culture, including abiding concerns about children's putative illiteracy, the hyping of "new" visual literacies, and growing anxiety among publishers about the decline in traditional book reading. Together these factors have legitimized comics as a new focus of publishing in general and children's publishing in particular—with a decided push toward children's graphic novels over the past roughly fifteen years.

Graphic novels are the offspring of comic books—which, from the mid-1930s, were both a staple of US youth culture and objects of scorn. The moral panic came to a head in the early 1950s even as sales remained sky high (Gabilliet 2010 estimates that in 1952 roughly a billion comic books were sold). The industry reacted by collapsing into severe self-censorship. The Comics Code, adopted by a majority of comic book publishers from late 1954, was a desperate rearguard move by the publishers to shield themselves from the consequences of their indifference to making honest distinctions between children's and adult comics. In the early 1950s, *Walt Disney's Comics and Stories* had sat on newsstands alongside Grand Guignol horror and titillating romance comics, all of them accessible ten-centers tossed together higgledy-piggledy in a generative, arguably subversive, stew. A massive and censorious moral campaign—in which children's publishing professionals, teachers, and librarians played major roles—damped down the comic book medium's troublesome vitality, confining it to the margins of the culture, where it languished (Beaty 2005; Hajdu 2008; Nyberg 1998). This postwar furor was not confined to the US but mirrored by moral panics elsewhere—for example, in Canada, Britain, and western Europe (Lent 1999). In America, recovery from this tempestuous period would be long, strained, and never quite complete.

Recovery came via areas from which young children were pointedly excluded: the radical politics, hippyesque hedonism, and sheer fury of underground comix; the growth of a connoisseur culture via a network of comic book shops for older hobbyists, which depended on a specialized distribution system known as the direct market; and the resultant rise of alternative comics for adults. Together these factors nurtured an ethos of individualistic, even radically Romantic, self-assertion among comics artists as well as an intense sense of belonging to a subculture—that is, fandom (Hatfield 2005; Gearino 2017). With its roots in these decidedly adult venues, the graphic novel's recent emergence as a work for children is paradoxical—embodied by Jeff Smith's *Bone*. As its inaugural offering, Scholastic's Graphix published *Bone* in nine volumes (2005–9). Yet Cartoon Books, Smith's own small outfit, first published *Bone* as a series of traditional comic books (fifty-five issues, 1991–2004), then as a series of trade-paperback compilations (nine volumes, 1993–2004), and finally as a single 1,300-page volume (2004). *Bone* was thus a "children's" comic birthed in an "underground" self-publishing tradition. The series has since sold millions worldwide in a reported thirty languages.

Novel-length comics' long history may explain why so many comics devotees and stakeholders dislike the *graphic novel* label. Outside of anglophone markets, witness the European *bande dessinée* album format, born out of a now obsolete tradition of magazine serialization (see Miller 2007), or collected Japanese manga (in *tankobon* form), similarly born out of a now diminished though still fairly prolific (and increasingly digital) magazine industry (Kinsella 2000; Gravett 2004). Those cultures, despite supporting long-form comics, have not privileged the idea of the graphic novel as the guarantor of comics' legitimacy. Francophone criticism has not widely adopted the *roman graphique* as a legitimizing label (French discussions of the *roman graphique* tend to be about the term's currency in anglophone contexts). Similarly, Scandinavians generally prefer *comics* (*tegneserie* [Danish], *tecknade serier* [Swedish]) to *grafisk roman*, which they consider purely a marketing term. Nor has a literal Japanese equivalent of *graphic novel* become a keyword for manga criticism: the *gekiga* movement toward adult manga (which arose from the rental manga industry of the late 1950s) encouraged long narratives but did not invoke literary precedents particularly.

If in America and its sibling markets the graphic novel ideal somewhat effaces the history of comics, it also potentially opens new possibilities for appreciating comics and comics history from around the world. Graphic novel culture in fact represents a dovetailing of traditions drawn from myriad centers of comics worldwide. The US graphic novel market is part of a global circulation of comics that has served to educate readers in many countries. Readers of English-language comics are increasingly aware of European comics, even those produced by small presses and avant-gardists—an awareness fostered by North American publishers of graphic novels such as Drawn and Quarterly, Fantagraphics, NBM, and First Second. Even more obviously, consider the assertive exportation of Japanese manga into many markets, including East Asia, Latin America, and western Europe, where manga is said to have as much influence as it has had in the US—which is considerable.

If, as Jorge Luis Borges observes, artists create their own precursors, then it is safe to say that the past of the graphic novel is continually being re-created and extended, not in a way that obeys a strict historiography, but in an unpredictable accumulation: a continual layering of precursors and inspirations that takes in a huge range of cartooning and comics originally far distant from today's graphic novel ideal. The graphic novel has been independently invented or anticipated in multiple nations and cultures, and work conceived without graphic novels in mind has since been claimed as part of the genre's inheritance. The eclecticism of the graphic novel, then, not only extends to what is being made available (often across national boundaries) today; it also extends to the very history of the genre. Positing something as a forerunner or early example of graphic novels is a radical act of reframing that has become common—a move that historically decontextualizes and makes possible the discovery of new lineages, new lines of influence, and ultimately, new histories. The graphic novel's currency and clout may yet open up new ways of taking varied historical traces and international influences seriously—of reviving interest in old comics, awakening awareness of comics across cultural borders, and discovering the rudiments of an international visual language.

29

Home

Mavis Reimer

The word *home* comes into English through the Teutonic languages of northern Europe, carrying with it the multiple meanings of "world," "village," "homestead," "dwelling," and "safe dwelling," as well as indicating a direction, as it continues to do in a phrase such as *go home*. The primary meaning in contemporary usages of the word is "the seat of domestic life and interests" (*OED*). In this sense, the word is close to the Latin *domus*, from which the adjective *domestic* is derived. As well as referring to a building or place, however, *home* simultaneously refers to the quality of feelings associated with that place so that home is, as the *OED* notes, "the place of one's dwelling or nurturing," which can include members of a family or household, "with the conditions, circumstances, and feelings which naturally and properly attach to it." But *home* can also designate the local (home team), an institution (children's home), a nation (homeland), or the origin and destination of play in games (home base). Not surprisingly, then, it is identified as one of the one thousand most commonly used words in the online version of *Collins Dictionary*.

A nurturing and safe family home is a primary setting of many texts of children's literature, with kitchens and bedrooms within that dwelling often used metonymically to convey the core emotional qualities ideally associated with home. Maurice Sendak's picture book *Where the Wild Things Are* (1963) neatly compresses the qualities of nurturance and safety into the space of the bedroom to which Max returns from his imaginary voyage to find his hot supper waiting for him. The implication that it is his mother who has prepared his supper points to the connection common in children's texts between mother and home. In L. M. Montgomery's *Anne of Green Gables* (1908), Anne can claim the house of Green Gables as home only after she has roused the latent maternal instincts of the spinster Marilla Cuthbert. In the more displaced version of this story in Frances Hodgson Burnett's *The Secret Garden* (1911), Misselthwaite Manor becomes a place to which Mary Lennox belongs after she has learned to coax her dead aunt's enclosed garden into bloom.

As Burnett's narrative demonstrates, houses are often used as both literal and figurative sites for young people to nurture themselves in children's books, as they do in two quite different ways in Astrid Lindgren's *Pippi Långstrump* (1945) and Philippa Pearce's *Tom's Midnight Garden* (1958). Motherless Pippi takes confident possession of Villa Villekulla as a base for her adventures while she awaits the return of her sea captain father, while Tom, exiled from home because of his brother's illness, grows in his understanding of the mysteries of human life through his nightly explorations of the old house in which he must spend the summer with a prosaic aunt and uncle. The metaphorical equivalence between the house and the mother can also be exploited for more unsettling effects in children's texts. In Neil Gaiman's *Coraline* (2002; Selick 2009), Coraline's passage through the brick wall behind the locked door in the front parlor—which her mother has shown her as the absolute limit to her desire for exploration—takes her into the world of her other mother, which is horrifying in its resemblances to and differences from her originary home. Such a text instantiates Freud's observation that the experience of the uncanny, or *Unheimlich*, resides precisely in that which is most familiar, or *heimisch*—the primal example of which he assumes to be the body of the mother (1919).

The linkage of the house to the psychology of self has a long history in Western cultures, according to Witold Rybczynski, who observes the coincidence in the seventeenth century of the evolution of domestic comfort with "the appearance of the internal world of the individual, of the self, and of the family" (1986, 35). The use of the family home as a primary setting in children's literature, then, is one indication that the project of this body of texts is to facilitate the development of the sense of self of young readers. In this reading, the feelings of being "at home" that typically attend the resolution of narratives for young people are privileged over the ultimate arrival at a dwelling place.

Whether as place or feeling, *home* continues to mark the narrative destination of many texts for children. As a place of departure, it also marks the beginning of many of these texts. Indeed, the circular "home-away-home" story has been posited as the central organizing principle of the genre of children's literature (Nodelman and Reimer 2003, 186–91). This use of *home* as holding a structure in place is consonant with its use in the language of games and computers.

Psychological interpretations of children's literature typically privilege the emotional over the material and, in doing so, screen the socioeconomic implications of linking house and home. That a house is, or should be, the center of family life is an idea at the foundation of the contemporary systems of consumer capitalism that are taken to be normative in the societies of the developed world. Seen in this light, the intense interest in home in children's literature situates this literature within the dominant ideologies of its societies. Rosemary Marangoly George, for example, has argued that imagining home in fiction within the English tradition should be understood as "a display of hegemonic power" and that characters who can claim or return home should be analyzed in terms of "the power wielded by [their] class, community and race" (1996, 6). Such interpretations of the homes represented in children's literature often require critical readers to read against the grain of the texts, looking for the unspoken premises subtending the narrative. A few children's narratives themselves perform such readings. Jan Needle's *Wild Wood* (1981) rewrites Kenneth Grahame's *The Wind in the Willows* (1908) to reveal the arrogant assumptions about his entitlements that underwrite Mr. Toad's claim to his eponymous home, Toad Hall. In *M.C. Higgins, the Great* (1974), Virginia Hamilton builds a picture of a home that is not safe but nevertheless nurturing by focalizing the narrative through the young mountain boy. While readers become aware of some of the judgments of the "normal" world of town and city through M. C.'s conversations with the strangers he meets, the cabin on Sarah's Mountain clearly occupies the place of home both at the beginning and at the end of the narrative. A novel such as David Almond's *Skellig* (1998), however, is more typical. Much of Almond's story focuses on Michael's complicated relationship with the indeterminate being—part human, part animal, part angel—whom he finds in the garage behind his house, but the story ends with the reconstitution of his family and his silence as the adults around him conclude that a vagrant has been squatting in the dilapidated outbuilding and that this is reason to demolish it.

Almond's novel is one of a large number of late twentieth-century and early twenty-first-century narratives that demonstrate the structural linkage between ideas of home and homelessness. The first use of *homelessness* recorded in the *OED* is by Charles Dickens in *Dombey and Son* (1848); now as then, homelessness designates the lack of the condition of being at home and, in this opposition, secures the idea of home as one of plenitude. Contemporary texts for young readers internationally are exploring the borderlines between the inclusions and exclusions used to build the idea of home: examples include *Wild Child* by Taiwanese writer Chang Ta-Chun (1996), *Breaking the Wishbone* (1999) by Irish writer Siobhán Parkinson, *Tom Finder* (2003) by Canadian writer Martine Leavitt, *Sleep Rough Tonight* (2004) by Australian writer Ian Bone, *Paranoid Park* (2006; Van Sant 2007) by American writer Blake Nelson, and *No and Me* (2007) by French writer Delphine de Vigan. The interest of these novels in "street kids" and in the institutional homes that claim to serve them suggests that one of the boundaries being tested for its permeability is that between staying and going, dwelling and journey. Itinerants and vagrants are only two of many categories of subjects on the move in the globalizing world: others include migrants, immigrants, refugees, travelers, and tourists. In the context of these times, David Morley suggests, home is being retheorized as "a mobile, symbolic habitat, a performative way of life and of doing things in which one makes one's home while in movement" (2000, 47). But the controversy generated by the publication of Sendak's *We Are All in the Dumps with Jack and Guy* (1993), a picture book about homeless men and children, suggests that confounding the borders between home and homelessness in books for children is widely understood as a challenge to fundamental cultural values.

The refugee crisis that faces the world at the beginning of the twenty-first century has exacerbated this challenge. As Philip Nel notes, more than half of the world's stateless people at present are young people under the age of eighteen, some of them traveling alone or in the company of predatory adults, and the "visual metaphors" of children's picture books seem to be an ideal vehicle for "voicing that unsettling feeling when something unbelievable suddenly becomes true" (2017a). Such books are appearing in many countries, among them *Akim Court* (Little Akim; 2012) by Belgian writer Claude K. Dubois, *Flickan från långt borta* (The girl from far away; 2014) by Swedish writer Annika Thor, *Two White Rabbits* (2015) by Colombian writer Jairo Buitrago, and *The Journey* (2016) by Italian Swiss writer Francesca Sanna.

The current interest in mobile subjects and in the relation of mobility to home is not unprecedented. Postcolonial theorists have demonstrated how European explorers, adventurers, and travelers prepared the ground for colonization, settlement, and other imperial practices. In fact, the sense in which *home* is used to designate "one's own country, one's native land" or "the mother-country" is identified in the *OED* as formulated by British subjects abroad and residents of former British colonies, with instances of such usage clustered in the nineteenth century, the time when the generic patterns of children's literature in English were set. Both the boys' adventure stories and the girls' domestic stories that proliferated during this period participate in linking the political project of home to the psychology of home. That the British Empire might be understood as a homemaking project on a large scale is an argument that has been made in relation to Daniel Defoe's *Robinson Crusoe* (1719), notoriously the only novel Jean-Jacques Rousseau judged to be suitable for children (O'Malley 2008). For the Indigenous inhabitants of the places being claimed by the colonizers, the consequence of such imperial homemaking was displacement, a loss of home to which children's literature by contemporary Aboriginal writers for young people in Australia and Canada, for example, testifies. But home can also function as a site of resistance to imperial culture: in colonial India, its status as a private sphere permitted the home to nurture the birth of Indian nationalism, according to Tony Bennett (2005, 164).

As the context of European colonization reminds us, home is an idea that can be thought in many languages, although not all concatenate the various possible senses of home in the same ways. *Home* has been available as a French word since the middle of the nineteenth century, for example, but French speakers typically separate the concepts of house (*maison*), family home (*foyer*), the place of belonging (*chez moi*), country (*pays*), and homeland (*patrie*). Whatever the language of home, it is clear that children's literature of many cultures is deeply invested in the overlapping symbolic, structural, historical, material, psychological, gendered, and political meanings that circulate around the idea of home.

30

Identity
Karen Coats

The term *identity* has undergone many changes since 1690, when John Locke introduced the idea that a sense of personal identity is composed of a relatively stable and enduring consciousness. The word *identity* derives from the Latin *idem*, meaning "same," thus creating a theoretical conundrum for contemporary theorists who have adopted the more current usage from twentieth-century ideas of identity as a personal possession, open to change and negotiation in dialectic interaction between self and society, between biological and cultural determinism and choice. The representation of identity in children's literature reflects this historical shift in its gradual evolution from perceiving its readers' identities (1) as faithful or aspiring adherents to the dominant religious ideology of their society, (2) as members of a family who support and abide by specific cultural and national traditions, (3) as persons with some degree of psychological depth and conflict, and (4) as self-reliant individuals responsible for constructing their own identities sometimes within, and sometimes over and against, the dominant ideologies of their cultures.

In 2015, cultural critic Wesley Morris observed that *we* (a contentious pronoun but in this case largely referring to North Americans) are "in the midst of a great cultural identity migration. Gender roles are merging. Races are being shed. In the last six years or so, but especially in 2015, we've been made to see how trans and bi and poly-ambi-omni we are." Comparably, the once default identity of much Western children's literature (white, male, Christian, heterosexual) has yielded to a more complex and inclusive range of possibilities.

Morris canvasses a range of adult media in support of his claim, but the obsession with the representation of cultural identities in children's literature and media made headlines over the same period and continues into the present. Morris's article is accompanied by a slide show of international images that includes the fictional version of twelve-year-old Taiwanese American Eddie Huang, who challenges model minority stereotypes in the TV series *Fresh Off the Boat*, as well as a character from Pixar's *Inside Out* with the caption, "Pixar teaches kids that our selves are fluid, determined by power struggles among the emotions that live in our heads" (2015). Scholars and activists, primarily based in the US but expanding to Europe as well, called for the publishing industry to once and for all face up to the persistence of the "all-white [and cisgendered, heteronormative, able-bodied] world of children's books" (Larrick 1965, 63) and actually *do something* about it by publishing more books by and about people of color, Indigenous people, people who are neurodiverse, people with disabilities, people whose embodiments fall outside normative parameters, people whose genders range across a spectrum, and people who embrace various religious or areligious traditions. To ensure that these representations avoid inaccuracies and stereotyping, a new industry has arisen for similarly diverse "sensitivity readers" to do prechecks for the books that publishers bring to market in an effort to respond to social media activists whose critique has resulted in books being withdrawn both pre- and postpublication. Indeed, much contemporary academic criticism of youth literature is devoted to the assessment of not just if and how particular identities are portrayed but how well.

Underlying these claims is the firm belief that identity is molded and shaped, for better and worse, by the kinds of representations children find or do not find in the cultural narratives made available to them. Building on John Locke's notion of the child's mind as a tabula rasa, social constructivists and cultural determinists have viewed personal identity not as something inherent or bequeathed but as something we achieve over time and through experience and experiment. However, the new understanding of transgender identity and sexual orientation as inborn identities marks a return to a discourse of authenticity based on embodiment rather than cultural interventions or scripting. As Andrew Solomon (2012) notes in discussing his own experience growing up gay, "Many conditions I had thought of as illnesses emerged as identities in the course of my research. When one can experience a condition as an identity, one can find pride and satisfaction in it. People who don't share such a condition with their parents must build horizontal identity among others who do share it."

In fact, this generative function of representations—with which children can identify or use to fashion their own multiple identities—creates both optimism and anxiety for people seeking something that can be experienced and/or theorized as a stable, authentic identity. As Solomon argues, today we experience ourselves in the contexts of both vertical and horizontal identities—vertical ones that we share with our parents and ancestors through genetic inheritance and horizontal ones that we form through self-chosen communities of affiliation. These identities may conflict with one another and yet still coexist, as we find them metaphorically represented in Jessica Sima's *Not Quite Narwhal* (2017). Kelp is a unicorn born into a family of narwhals. He is loved despite his physical and temperamental differences, but it isn't until he encounters real unicorns that he understands that there are others like him, that his narwhal family knew he was a unicorn all along, and that he doesn't have to choose between either identity. Both vertical and horizontal identities are supported by our participation in multiple "figured worlds" that function as dynamic social contexts wherein identities and social roles emerge, fluctuate, and evolve (Holland et al. 2001, 40–41). Social scientists from multiple disciplines agree that identities everywhere are formed "dialectically and dialogically" across these "landscapes of action" (Schwimmer, Clammer, and Poirier 2004, 109) as people create and interact with cultural artifacts that become vehicles for building and expressing dynamic identities.

This belief that identities are formed in transactional relationships with cultural scripts and images manifests itself in two critical perspectives that are perhaps paradoxical. On the one hand, we regularly find representations in children's literature of "how trans and bi and poly-ambi-omni we are" (Morris 2015). Chih-Yuan Chen's *Guji Guji* (2004) tells the story of a crocodile, reared in a family of ducks, who eventually embraces his identity as a "crocoduck"; one can't help but be reminded of Dr. Seuss's Horton, whose patient care of a bird's egg results in the emergence of a creature who is both bird and elephant. *Ein schräger Vogel* (*Odd Bird Out*; 2008) by Helga Bansch features a raven who rejects the characteristics and modes of behavior that he shares with his raven family. Dick King-Smith's *The Sheep-Pig* (1983), about a pig who handily takes on the role of sheepdog, seems to view identities that are self-chosen rather than tied to biological inheritances as necessary for literal survival. Other examples of species-transgressing animals abound, such as Rachel Vail's *Piggy Bunny* (2012), which features a pig who insists that he will become the Easter Bunny, and Jessie

Sima's previously mentioned *Not Quite Narwhal*. Such texts seem to privilege the creation of horizontal, intersectional identities free from genetic inheritance or cultural scripting. Instead, like children's dæmons in Philip Pullman's His Dark Materials (1995–2000), young people's identities are unstable, migratory, experimental, and ultimately, self-chosen on the way to adulthood.

On the other hand, sociologists, anthropologists, social psychologists, and literary critics often refer to cultural identities as if they were distinct, monolithic, and determinative, especially in comparative work. Such generalizations build on children's tendencies to adopt widely shared understandings of their cultures as cognitive schemas against which they judge their own and others' behaviors and self-presentations as either normative or deviant. For instance, the general consensus among many social scientists and humanities scholars is that East Asian identities are communitarian, enculturated in and through a society that values obligation and modesty even in the face of personal success and deflecting attention away from the individual self onto a relational identity within culture at large (see, for instance, Heine et al. 1999). We might locate this tendency in Chinese author Cao Wenxuan's various responses to winning the 2016 Hans Christian Andersen Award. In several on-camera interviews, he immediately deflects attention away from his own achievement with some variation of this sentiment expressed on CCTV News: "Of course I'm proud, but I think I'm also proud of all of the Chinese literature for the children" (Poland 2016). And indeed, Wenxuan's *Feather* (2017) focuses on finding a community of belonging based on vertical identity. However, works from Western cultures, which anthropologists view as valuing individualism, emphasize similarly vertical themes, such as P. D. Eastman's *Are You My Mother?* (1960), Marc Pfister's *The Rainbow Fish* (1992), and Piret Raud's *Härra Linnu lugu* (Mister Bird's story; 2009), where solitary creatures' experiments with identity lead them back home to find happiness in species solidarity.

These two critical perspectives—the celebration of horizontal, self-chosen, hybrid identities versus the affirmation of vertical, culturally determined, largely monolithic identities—reflect some of the pluralism that informs our contemporary understanding of identity. Contemporary critics, for instance, take *intersectionality* to be a belated acknowledgment of an already existing truth about identity, but even that term is understood in different ways. One is a benign or even celebratory acknowledgment that everyone fits in different vertical and horizontal communities; another usage highlights the ways in which possessing more than one culturally devalued identity has a multiplying effect on oppression. To study identity as it is represented in youth literature, then, critics must look beyond the characters themselves to the historical and sociocultural beliefs about children that inform their portrayals. Alternative ontologies create alternative possibilities and schemas through which identities are constructed. A fluid, unstable, transient identity may be embraced and celebrated by some cultures and in some time periods as a necessary and even salutary stage of child development, whereas for others it is seen as a cause for anxiety and even threat, as it may represent a loss of cultural distinctiveness. Books and other youth-directed media featuring makeovers; various kinds of ethnic, gender, and posthuman hybridity; and the questioning of cultural ideologies and norms have proliferated in and across cultures. On the one hand, we may revel in the ways contemporary children's books encourage the development of horizontal identities based on communities of affiliation. On the other, we must acknowledge that understanding identity as "plural, open-ended, creative and transgressive" (Elliott 2015, 3) results in mandates for continual self-fashioning and reinvention that can lead to feelings of inauthenticity and insecurity. Throughout the world, the question "Who am I?" has never been met with more radical uncertainty and hopeful possibility, but today's children's books tend to favor the latter.

31

Indigenous

Niigaanwewidam James Sinclair

In the breaking day of Friday, October 12, 1492, Cristóbal Colón (Christopher Columbus) encountered the Taíno people. On first meeting them, Colón remarked that they

> appeared to me to be a race of people very poor in everything. They go as naked as when their mothers bore them, and so do the women, although I did not see more than one young girl. All I saw were youths, none more than thirty years of age. They are very well made, with very handsome bodies, and very good countenances. Their hair is short and coarse, almost like the hairs of a horse's tail. They wear the hairs brought down to the eyebrows, except a few locks behind, which they wear long and never cut. They paint themselves black, and they are the colour of the Canarians, neither black nor white. Some paint themselves white, others red, and others of what colour they find. Some paint their faces, others the whole body, some only round the eyes, others only on the nose. (1893, 37–38)

Commenting on their lack of clothing, weapons, and religion, Colón concludes, "They should be good servants," promising to bring "six natives" back to Europe so "that they may learn to speak." As Stephen Greenblatt remarks, "The idiom has a life of its own; it implies that the Indians had no language at all" (1976, 563).

The Taíno, no matter what Colón described, had language—and a rich and vibrant culture. They had complex politics, philosophies, and senses of history. They had clothing and tools to farm, fish, and fight. They also had aesthetics, senses of beauty and expression (manifested in gesture and spaces like hair), stories, and a dynamic spirituality. The Taíno had—and indeed still have—these things (Poole 2011). Taíno beliefs, for example, centered on the worship of *zemís* (spirits or ancestors) in the lands and waters around them. One of the most important embodiments of *zemís* was by painting one's skin or getting piercings and tattoos. In front of Colón's eyes were writing systems and literatures with bodies as texts. The problem was that Colón was illiterate, unable to read Indigeneity. The colonial subaltern—the subordinated and nonconsenting subject—had reached America.

This is precisely the challenge with defining the term *Indigenous*: the use of preexisting, constraining, and limiting ideas, languages, and conclusions outside of Indigenous perspectives, politics, and space. This is very tempting—and in some ways human and inevitable—but displaces Indigenous peoples, threatening to displace, remove, and erase Indigenous voices. The *OED*, for example, defines *Indigenous* as "native," "belonging naturally," or "people regarded as the original inhabitants of an area." None of these adequately define what *Indigenous* means, for all are determined by what they are not—dependent on premises like "settler," "unnatural belonging" (a.k.a. "colonizing"), or "unoriginal." *Indigenous*, simply, is not definable by these terms.

The fact is that Colón did not invent Indigenous peoples; we define ourselves. This is a familiar tale told in stories of "first contact" such as Thomas King and William Kent Monkman's *A Coyote Columbus Story* (1992). In playful narrative and vibrant colors, King and Monkman frame Colón's arrival as a mistake instigated by Coyote, a creator figure who lives in contradiction and wordplay. Depicting the invading Europeans not as heroes but as grotesque clowns, Colón's ideas here are laid bare for the constraining, restrictive, and nonsensical notions they are. Indigenous peoples are more complex than that.

Indigenous is a term that collapses complexity—when complexity is the hallmark of Indigeneity. There are 370 million Indigenous people belonging to over five thousand different groups and nations worldwide, each with distinct cultures, languages, and histories (Cultural Survival, n.d.). It might be best said that Indigenous communities are defined by their self-definitions, the criteria they use to name, identify, and situate themselves. This relies on the specific spatial and temporal relationships Indigenous carry, found best in their ancestral languages and endonymic ethnonyms—names a people use to refer to themselves. Much of the history of human contact has resulted in the renaming of peoples by other peoples; Colón named the Taíno "Indians," for example, and European settlers in North America called the Anishinaabeg "Chippewa" or "Ojibway." In all cases, the endonymic ethnonym of a people should be sought and used. This makes defining the term *Indigenous* more an exercise in identifying the ways a people define themselves than creating definitions for them.

Still, *Indigenous* is a term that carries much weight and has become the acceptable word communities use when working cross-culturally or internationally. The United Nations Permanent Forum on Indigenous Peoples (2007) uses the following criteria to define an individual or group calling itself "Indigenous":

- Self-identification as indigenous peoples at the individual level and accepted by the community as their member.
- Historical continuity with pre-colonial and/or pre-settler societies.
- Strong link to territories and surrounding natural resources.
- Distinct social, economic or political systems.
- Distinct language, culture and beliefs.
- Form non-dominant groups of society.
- Resolve to maintain and reproduce their ancestral environments and systems as distinctive peoples and communities.

This definition is inherently inclusive and forms a language for Indigenous communities to work together in pursuing shared interests and goals. It also allows for a fluid understanding of the multiple ways Indigenous nations self-identify. One of the most important criteria is more about what you *do* than what you *are*. Despite historical attempts to make it so, blood quantum is not a primary determinant of membership in an Indigenous society. Rather, membership is determined by how one interacts with citizens, carries responsibilities, and performs work for the community. This is a perfect example for why having an Indigenous grandparent does not make one Indigenous; it is determined by how one acts in relationship with community.

The issue of identity and/or what makes something Indigenous is arguably the most central theme in Indigenous writing. This is why most Indigenous writers use ancestral languages, politics, and themes in their work. Choctaw writer LeAnne Howe writes that "Native stories are power. They create people. They author tribes. America is a tribal creation story . . . a tribalography" (1999, 118). Through Indigenous stories, Indigenous peoples learn who we are, why we are here, who can help us, and where are we going. Indigenous writing by Indigenous creators demonstrate essential lessons on how Indigenous lives has been lived, are living, and can live in the future.

Still, while the UN definition centralizes how a people self-identify as Indigenous in specific ways and means, two issues arise. First, how do we critically analyze Indigenous identity if self-declaration is the pre-eminent criteria? Second, how are Indigenous rights, territorial claims, and laws discerned (which inevitably involve non-Indigenous peoples and nonhumans) when only Indigenous-derived criteria are used? These are crucial questions that illustrate the centrality of relationships to Indigenous nationhood and how Indigeneity is an ongoing process of self-determination. An Indigenous nation is constantly moving; its people are influenced by geography, time, and politics but not determined solely by the tangible. *Indigeneity* is best defined as creativity in action. Indigenous leaders can articulate laws online and in lodges, for example, or elders can deliver traditional teachings by a fire or through email. This illustrates the innate strength of Indigenous nations and peoples to adopt, adapt, and continue over time, growing and changing while remaining Indigenous.

A definition of *Indigenous* is perhaps best found through the interactions we have with Indigenous stories—the offerings and gifts Indigenous peoples offer themselves and the world. As the structural motif of the "coming-to" story in Cherie Dimaline's dystopian YA novel *The Marrow Thieves* (2017) makes clear, stories enact expressions of Indigenous becoming and embody the processes Indigenous peoples use to engage and understand the world. By interacting with these responsibly, ethically, and consistently, one gains insight into what is Indigenous via the processes of Indigeneity and Indigenous nationhood.

The most intellectual vessels that articulate Indigenous tenets are creation stories, the narratives used to explain origins, relationships, and purposes. Often embodied in songs, traditional texts, and the (inadequately named) "oral tradition," these stories are the articulations of the most seminal Indigenous knowledges, experiences, and histories. They are vessels that must be told and shared, for they are inevitably about creation, action, and life. While appearing as having "fictional" elements, these stories are anything but; they are laws, institutions of governance, and scientific principles all at once. Interaction with these stories—whether through "orality" or text—comes with great responsibility for the reader/listener, for he or she is being given a window into the ongoing creation of a people. This is why Indigenous creation stories continue to be told, retold, and sometimes resist capture in orthography and books, for they are movement itself. Examples of these reside in Simon Ortiz's *The People Shall Continue* (1977), Edward Benton-Benai's *The Mishomis Book: The Voice of the Ojibway* (1988), and Maria Campbell's *Stories of the Road Allowance People* (1995). An unfortunate result of misunderstanding these intellectual gifts is that they are seen as fiction, legends, or myths or located in lesser-respected areas of bookstores and libraries.

More recently, Indigenous creators have turned to poetry, novels, and other narrative forms like graphic novels to tell stories. Via a narrative peppered with song lyrics, Facebook posts, and text messages, Niviaq Korneliussen's *Homo Sapienne* (2014)—told in a Greenlandic prose punctuated with both English and Danish slang—juxtaposes the stories of five young queer protagonists discovering and developing their identities. Her novel and other novels by Indigenous writers are a continuation of Indigenous literary traditions—particularly when text and image are juxtaposed, multiple aesthetics are combined (like sound and performance), and an expansive notion of Indigeneity is expressed (incorporating other worlds and universes, for example). Today, Indigenous writers like Lee Maracle, Richard Van Camp, Duncan Mercredi, Jeanette Armstrong, Kateri Akiwenzie-Damm, and Jennifer Storm perform the same critical task that writers who wrote on skin, rock, and birch bark did in the past.

Their expressions articulate how rich and dynamic cultures and nations continue in authentic, adaptive, and innovative ways—regardless of invasion, colonization, and genocide. Criticism and theories that contribute to this movement by articulating the complexity that resides in Indigenous stories—even in reactions and resistances—participate in the ongoing growth of Indigenous communities. One of the best comprehensive forums in North America where this is found in Indigenous children's literature is on Nambé Pueblo scholar Debbie Reese's website American Indians in Children's Literature.

Indigenous is best thought of as a verb, not a noun. It is something Indigenous peoples live every day in vibrant, legally definable, and self-determining nations in relationship with humans, nonhumans, and the universe. Indigenous is not reducible but exists rather in specific spaces and times by peoples struggling to continue while facing political, social, economic, and geographical forces. It is in this often contentious but always complex space where Indigenous is found, for it is here that names are found, conflict is overcome, and lives are made, whether it be in making love, scaling a mountain, or overcoming colonial invasion. To be Indigenous is to live as Indigenous nations always have—as rich, complex, and beautiful people regardless of the languages, ideas, and conclusions we face. It has been this way for millennia and will continue to be.

Indigenous may not be an Indigenous word, but it is the language we now use to articulate ourselves; so thus it has become one. *Miigwech.*

32

Innocence
Marah Gubar

A little girl stares at us from an advertisement in a 1970s American magazine. Her spotless white dress and cuddly teddy bear mark her as an appropriately childlike spokesperson for a line of perfume products scented with baby powder. But her artfully styled hair, heavy makeup, and come-hither gaze carry an erotic charge, as indicated by the ad's tagline: "Love's Baby Soft. Because innocence is sexier than you think" (Caputi 2004; Collins 2013). While yoking purity with eroticism might seem bizarre, this tendency stretches back to a transatlantic, nineteenth-century "cult of the child" (Kincaid 1992; Gubar 2016a) and forward to our present moment (Mohr [1996] 2004; Walkerdine 1997; Giroux 2000). From television programs that capitalize on our desire to see tarted-up tiny girls perform in beauty contests to fashion models whose waif-like slightness exalts early youth as the epitome of attractiveness, contemporary Western society furnishes disturbing proof for cultural historian James R. Kincaid's contention that "our culture has enthusiastically sexualized the child while denying just as enthusiastically that it was doing any such thing" (1998, 13).

Defining *innocence* solely in terms of its antonyms contributes to this problem. The *OED* describes it as "freedom from sin, guilt, or moral wrong . . . freedom from cunning or artifice." On this account, innocence is all about what you lack, a negative vision that evolved from a similarly negative etymology: *in-nocens* means "not harming" (being unable to injure anyone). No wonder, then, that childhood innocence sometimes gets equated with emptiness, a "hollowing out of children by way of purifying them of any stains (or any substance) [that] also makes them radically different, other. In this empty state, they present themselves as candidates for being filled with . . . desire. The asexual child is not . . . any the less erotic but rather more" (Kincaid 1992, 175).

Intent on countering the common assumption that the asexual, asocial child is a wholly natural and admirable phenomenon, Kincaid and other childhood studies scholars excoriate childhood innocence as an adult fantasy that does more harm than good. Yet we can absorb the most compelling aspects of their critique without flipping from one extreme (unwary celebration of innocence) to the other (dogmatic denunciation). To map out a more moderate position, it helps to distinguish between better and worse ways of thinking about innocence, moving away from conceptions that stress the deficiency or alterity of children and toward one that emphasizes their kinship with adults as vulnerable human beings who depend on other people to exist and thrive.

Those who regard children as originally innocent are often surprised to learn how deeply many people in the past believed in the doctrine of original sin, which held that human beings are born already tainted by depravity inherited from Adam and Eve (Bunge 2001; Clark 1994; Jacobs 2008). Anxious for children to attain the ability to seek salvation, adults who believed in original sin did not celebrate the child's difference from adults but instead strove to speed young people's passage into maturity and enlightened piety. For example, seventeenth-century parents who regarded crawling as indicative of the primitive "inadequacies of infancy" tried to prevent it by placing infants in leading strings and standing stools, which forced them to adopt an upright position (Calvert 1992, 31). Early intellectual development was also encouraged, sometimes by means of corporal punishment (Greven [1990] 1992). The child speaker in Isaac Watts's children's poem "Praise to God for learning to read" (1715) calls himself "a wretched Slave to Sin" but finds comfort in the fact "that I was taught, and learnt so young / To read [God's] holy Word" ([1715] 1769, 159–60). Other early children's writers, influenced by the philosopher John Locke, moved away from the notion of the child's innate depravity and instead imagined the child's mind as an "empty Cabinet" (Locke 1690, 55) or "white Paper, void of all Characters" (104).

Many historians of childhood point to the eighteenth century as the time when Western culture shifted away from conceiving of children as deficient adults-in-the-making and toward the notion that they were exemplary beings to be cherished for their primal otherness and authenticity (Cunningham 1995). Romantic writers such as Jean-Jacques Rousseau, Friedrich von Schiller, and William Wordsworth enjoined adults to stop rushing children into adulthood and instead to cherish and try to preserve the child's alluring alterity. In his "Ode: Intimations of Immortality from Recollections of Early Childhood" (1807), Wordsworth rejects the infancy-as-deficiency model in favor of portraying babyhood as the time when we are closest to God, nature, and our "Star"-like "Soul," an inner essence of selfhood that "hath had elsewhere in its setting, / And cometh from afar" ([1807] 1983, 273).

Idealizing children as otherworldly beings untouched by the culture they inhabit tempts us to regard them as an unrealistically homogenous and autonomous group. Profound socioeconomic inequalities prevented all children from experiencing early youth as the carefree period of "delight and liberty" described by Wordsworth ([1807] 1983, 275). Yet when the Romantic

"Child of Nature" got transplanted to popular novels (Wordsworth [1802] 1983, 231), poor as well as rich children began embodying this vision of innocent otherness. Sensitive souls such as Charles Dickens's Oliver Twist and Little Nell tenaciously hang on to their angelic purity despite being parentless, homeless, and subjected to endless abuse by callous, corrupt adults. Similarly, being born into a slaveholding family in no way inhibits Harriet Beecher Stowe's delicate Little Eva from spending her short life as a beacon of enlightened egalitarianism.

The weird imperviousness of these internationally famous child exemplars paves the way for a full-blown cult of the child in which innocence gets increasingly commercialized, disassociated from vulnerability, and aligned with a dopey obliviousness drained of ethical or religious content. Whereas Dickens, Victor Hugo, Clara Zetkin, and Alexandra Kollontai used the figure of the pitiable child to protest the toll that industrialized capitalism was taking on the bodies and minds of the poor and disenfranchised, many fin de siècle artists, advertisers, and cultural commentators represented children as adorable autocrats who wrap everyone they meet around their little fingers. Far from being harmed by systemic social problems, the child heroes of Johanna Spyri's *Heidi* (1880–81), Frances Hodgson Burnett's *Little Lord Fauntleroy* (1886), and Annie Fellows Johnston's *The Little Colonel* (1895) solve them by melting hearts and bringing together members of previously opposed groups.

Ironically, the monotone racial identity of such celebrated child characters—and film star Shirley Temple, who embodied many of them on-screen—itself attests to a deeply entrenched structural problem: racism. As cultural historian Robin Bernstein's *Racial Innocence* (2011b) documents, the late nineteenth and early twentieth century witnessed an increasing tendency to portray innocence as the exclusive province of white children and to depict black children as unfeeling "pickaninnies"—grotesque imps incapable of being harmed by even the roughest mistreatment. The viciously dehumanizing depictions of nonwhite children analyzed by Bernstein (2011b) and Donnarae MacCann ([1998] 2001) are especially libelous. But as well as being racist, they are also part of a more general phenomenon. From "The Little Boy Who Can't Be Damaged" (child vaudevillian Buster Keaton) to indomitable orphans such as Annie and Harry Potter, representations of disadvantaged white kids whose bodies and minds remain oddly unscathed by serious abuse or neglect imply that they too are magically indestructible.

Perhaps the ubiquity of such "Teflon kids" makes it easier for apathy about structural inequalities to coexist with the rhetorical exaltation of childhood innocence (Gubar 2020). Over the course of the twentieth century, for example, American claims to care about children's well-being were belied by the adoption of economic policies that caused the child poverty rate to soar (Jenkins 1998; Sealander 2003). Recent studies have found that approximately 41 percent of US children are living in low-income families (Koball and Jiang 2018). Contrary to cultural myths that emphasize the poor child's imperviousness, social science research suggests that growing up in poverty raises children's risk of being harmed by a wide range of health problems that can permanently impair their physical, intellectual, and emotional development (Hair et al. 2015). Worldwide in 2018, approximately 5.3 million children under the age of five died from largely preventable causes (UNICEF 2019).

Because the gap between rhetoric and reality is so wide, the concept of innocence is "regularly reviled" by childhood studies scholars, who view it as a "pernicious abstraction" that does more harm than good (Davis 2011, 379, 380). Yet the moral calculus on innocence is complicated, as shown by what happened when a photograph of Alan Kurdi—a dead three-year-old Syrian refugee washed up a beach—went viral on social media in 2015. Convinced that the deployment of such images is deplorable (Edelman 2004), cultural critics objected that using the figure of the innocent child victim metonymically—as a stand-in for a more diverse group of victims—obscures crucial aspects of the big picture, including the broader geopolitical conditions that created the current refugee crisis and our own potential complicity in them (Snell 2016). Such critiques are useful, but to characterize the photograph's primary effect as mystifying is to ignore that it "brought much-needed attention to the Syrian war and the plight of its refugees, which resulted in short-term but important increases in individual aid and refugee policy changes in many countries" (Slovic et al. 2017, 640).

Demonizing the concept of innocence obscures its history as a driver of incremental progress toward more humane treatment of vulnerable groups. In the 1980s, American politicians allocated zero federal dollars to helping communities devastated by HIV/AIDS, in part because this epidemic was associated with gay people and drug users. Desperate to secure passage of the Ryan White Comprehensive AIDS Resources Emergency Act in 1990, its proponents highlighted in congressional hearings how the disease was affecting heterosexual women and children such as White, a hemophiliac who had contracted it via a blood transfusion (Poindexter 1999). The villain in this story is not the concept of innocence but the homophobia and callousness to human suffering that made this shift in focus integral to the bill's success. Recognizing this, the AIDS activist group Gran Fury began posting signs that declared, "All people with AIDS are innocent." Rather than objecting to the fact that people whom we deem vulnerable often engender our compassion, they called

on the public to extend such mercy outward to cover more people.

In so doing, they followed in the footsteps of the Romantics, whose adherence to the idea of the child's alterity was intermixed with another way of thinking that emphasized childhood's continuity and kinship with adulthood. Even Wordsworth sometimes wrote about children who, like adults, are prone to "doing wrong and suffering, and full oft / Bending beneath our life's mysterious weight / Of pain, and doubt, and fear" ([1850] 1979, 175; Robson 2001; McGavran and Daniel 2012). Meanwhile, William Blake endorsed the radical idea that the joy, delight, and liberty often associated with early youth ought to be shared by people of all ages, classes, races, and religions. In his *Songs of Innocence and of Experience* (1789/1794), fully human child characters such as "The Little Black Boy" and "The Chimney Sweeper" are prevented from partaking in such pleasures and freedoms by unjust social circumstances. Like the adult characters around them, their sense of self is formed not in a vacuum but in conversation with various cultural and familial influences that enable as well as oppress (Richardson 1990).

Far from being empty, then, Blake's conception of innocence aligns with a vulnerability at once shared by all human beings and distributed unequally among different social groups. His moral indignation at the exploitation of enslaved and poor people led him to fault both capitalist nation-states and organized religion for failing to live up to the radically egalitarian example set by Jesus in the New Testament (Makdisi 2003). As religious studies scholars point out, Jesus does not welcome children into his company because he regards them as intrinsically different from and superior to adults. Rather, this move is part of a larger "countercultural disruption" whereby he rejects traditional status hierarchies that devalue the most vulnerable members of the human community: not just children but also sex workers, the ill, the poor, and strangers (Carroll 2008, 186). Rather than conceiving of caregiving as something done only by individual families, Jesus "extends kinship relations to the whole community" (Horsley 2001, 197).

When Blake insists that "every thing that lives is holy" ([1793] 1982, 51), he is at once emulating Jesus and anticipating the efforts of AIDS activists. Eschewing the binary thinking that exalts some social groups over others, he recognizes likeness across difference, celebrating the heterogeneity of a human community in which "heathen, turk, [and] jew" share with followers of Christ the same "divine" form and ability to access the simultaneously human and godlike qualities of "Mercy Pity Peace and Love" ([1789] 1982, 13, 12). Children are not superior, inferior, or utterly alien to adults but rather akin to them: Blake acknowledges that early youth is a time of heightened vulnerability but also suggests that depending on the support of others does not end as we age, nor do we lose the capacity to embody harmlessness and guiltless pleasure. This inclusive vision of innocence is enabled by Blake's rejection of the repressive sexual mores of his day, including rising homophobia and the habit of equating chastity with godliness and sex with defilement (Hobson 2000; Bruder and Connolly 2010).

The history of sexuality suggests that shifting away from a deficit-based conception of innocence and toward a kinship-based one benefits young people. Regarding children as devoid of sexuality has fueled violently intrusive efforts to punish them for masturbating and engaging in consensual sex play with peers, activities that social science research indicates is routine even for children under the age of six (Egan and Hawkes 2010; Levine 2002; Okami, Olmstead, and Abramson 1997). Adopting a kinship-based view of innocence would allow us to view human sexuality as a continuum, an integral part of our lives from birth to death that manifests itself in varying ways over time. That approach has already been recommended by sex education experts such as Deborah M. Roffman. In *Sex and Sensibility* (2001), Roffman advises caregivers to regard children not as "empty vessel[s]" whose cluelessness must be protected but as active learners who seek to know more about their bodies and the sex-filled world they inhabit (27). Listening and responding honestly to children's own questions helps caregivers know when and how to share what information. Many studies show that children who grow up in families in which sexuality is openly discussed make healthier choices (Roffman 2001, 4–5).

This kinship-based vision of innocence is in tune with the tradition of secular liberalism that affirms the value of all people regardless of their ethnicity, class, gender, or sexual orientation. It also aligns well with some religious worldviews, including Martin Luther King Jr.'s call for the creation of a "beloved community" in which poverty and prejudice are not tolerated ([1956] 1991, 140). No wonder, then, that many creative writers around the globe—including Annie M. G. Schmidt, Maurice Sendak, Hayao Miyazaki, and Anna Maria Machado—repurpose rather than reject innocence.

In *The Hate U Give* (2017), for instance, Angie Thomas associates African American characters of all ages—not just infants but also adolescents and adults—with light-giving stars (256), gardens (37), and even the scent of baby powder (12). Her portrayal of how systemic racism and economic inequality blight new life and those who nurture it in Garden Heights proves that representations of innocence under siege do not inevitably mystify the cultural complexities of children's lives. Often, they alert us to undeserved harm being done to vulnerable people, serving as a vital component of activism aimed at eradicating the social injustices that poison our communal life.

33

Intermedial

Ute Dettmar and Anna Stemmann

The adjective *intermedial* derives from the term *intermediate*. The latter has been used since the late sixteenth century (*OED*) to describe something as being in the middle or in between. By contrast, *intermedial/intermediality* is a more recent term that has spread internationally in research since the 1980s and that generally (as the prefix *inter-* implies) describes interactions that—implicitly or explicitly—occur between different media. In this sense, the term *intermediality* transfers Julia Kristeva's (1986) term *intertextuality* into a media-related context. Jürgen E. Müller speaks in this respect of "crossing borders between media and media disorder" (1996, 16). However, one problem in defining *intermediality* is that the media can be defined narrowly or broadly (Wolf 2005, 252). And this is coupled with the question of what constitutes a distinct medium in the first place. Werner Wolf's answer relies on the underlying semiotic system: "Intermediality deals with media as conventionally distinct means of communicating cultural contents. Media in this sense are specified principally by the nature of their underlying semiotic systems . . . and only in the second place by technical or institutional channels" (2005, 252). Following this semiotic definition, intermedial phenomena in the broadest sense denote processes, couplings, interferences, and overlaps between at least two different media that traverse the boundaries between them (see Wolf 2005, 252; Rajewsky 2010, 51). Reflecting the fluid nature of intermedial exchange, related research takes place not just in the context of literary studies but also in film, media, music, theater, and art studies (see Kaye 2000; H. Jenkins 2006; Grishakova and Ryan 2010; Rippl 2015; Bruhn 2016). A literary perspective, however, foregrounds various processes of intermedial exchange in the field of children's and youth literature.

There are three basic levels under consideration: materiality, the relationship between mode of presentation and narrative method, and the thematic, content-related dimension. In line with this approach, Irina Rajewsky delineates among three phenomena of the intermedial as follows: (1) medial transposition, (2) media combination, and (3) intermedial references (see Rajewsky 2010, 55; 2002, 15–18).

1. One very widespread example of the first phenomenon—medial transposition—is the transformation of narrative content into another medium, something that is also referred to as adaptation (Hutcheon 2006). Although these processes of transfer and transformation may in principle emerge in very different media and in different directions, the adaptation of literary works into plays and films is especially common. In particular, children's literary classics (such as *Alice in Wonderland, Peter Pan, Pinocchio, Pippi Longstocking, Krabat, Heidi, Le petit Nicolas*) have been transformed over the decades into many and varied cinematic iterations.

Note that media changes and adaptions differ from "transmedia storytelling"—another currently much debated term. *Transmedia* refers to a narrative transcending media boundaries. In this process (and the narrative universe surrounding J. K. Rowling's Harry Potter series is a prime example), dynamically growing, open narrations emerge that are not separate and should be regarded as a total narrative—unlike the literary adaptation, which is intermedially related to the initial text but an independent artistic form. Henry Jenkins, who significantly influenced the term and the concept of transmedia storytelling, defines it as "unfold[ing] across multiple media platforms, with each text making a distinctive and valuable contribution to the whole" (2006, 97–98).

However, in the intermedial, media changes may be closely or only loosely related to the original. They offer interpretive scope and differ in the range of their references to the original text. For example, the entire plot or just individual strands may be transferred. By no means a new phenomenon, changing the medium of individual stories, material, and figures goes back a long way in the world of children's and youth literature. L. Frank Baum's *The Wonderful Wizard of Oz* (1900) appeared shortly after publication in musical, theater, and film versions (see Kelleter 2012). In Germany, the best-known example is Erich Kästner's novel *Emil und die Detektive* (*Emil and the Detectives*; 1929), which as early as 1930 was adapted for the stage by Kästner himself. In 1931, the first film version (with a screenplay by Billy Wilder) was released, with many more films to follow. And in 2013, German illustrator Isabel Kreitz published a comics version. In addition to theater, comics, and film, the radio play is another popular form of adaptation of children's literature, which in recent decades has been joined by computer games as well as apps for smartphones and tablets. The shifts associated with medial transposition mainly concern the plot level, with specific content being adapted and retold in different media. Those media changes can be found in different times and national contexts. In the 1940s and 1950s, Norwegian author Thorbjørn Egner first presented his stories on radio, then on stage, as illustrated books, and as records. Today's children can meet the scenery on stage, in books, and at the amusement park Cardamom Town while they are on vacation.

2. Media combinations conjoin the structures or sign systems of at least two media while preserving their original material form. Media combination is not a new phenomenon either; it has a long history in a variety of combinations of texts and images, ranging from emblematics, to visual poetry, to (musical) theater, and to cinema. As far as children's literature is concerned, combinations play the most prominent role in picture books and comics.

The most conspicuous combination of two different media is that of texts and images. These days, elements are frequently integrated into the narration. Susan Schades and Jon Buller's Fog Mound (2006–9) children's trilogy intersperses small illustrations within the narrative text and uses comic sequences to interrupt prose passages. This hybrid form opens up the boundaries of the literary text. An exciting story arc unfolds, mixing the visual elements of two media yet still preserving the materiality of both. In Jeff Kinney's Diary of a Wimpy Kid (2007–) series, the external form is based on a diary: the pages are lined, and the typography is reminiscent of handwriting, dissolving the form of the "traditional" novel. However, it augments its simple chronological plot via image sequences, speech bubbles, and sound words borrowed from comics. Image and text merge here to create an entertaining hybrid narrative evoking (including in its subject matter) the comedic genre of funnies in comics. Meanwhile, Frank Cottrel Boyce's *The Unforgotten Coat* (2011) supplements the narrative text with printed Polaroids, adding an additional layer to the narrative space. These graphical elements tell an alternative version of the (apparent) biography of the two main characters.

Not confined to children's books, media combinations also emerge in young adult literature. In *The Selected Works of T.S. Spivet* (2009), Reif Larsen uses a diary form expanded by Ben Gibson's sketches, drawings, and charts. Gibson's art is more than mere illustrative subtext: the content of the pictorial elements responds to and supplements the narrative text. Narrative and theme neatly correspond to each other, since the processes of drawing and the drawings themselves act as media of reflection and expression for the main character.

3. Intermedial references, on the other hand, preserve the materiality of the main medium yet clearly refer to another medium and imitate its specific way of narration. A typical example is the "cinematic narrative" in a literary text, in which cinematic methods are simulated by focalizing ("camera eye"), varying the speed of the narrative, and changing scenes. Anthony McCarten's novel *Death of a Superhero* (2005) generates meaning via its numerous intermedial references and its formal imitation of influences from films, video games, and especially comics. Beyond thematic references within the plot, the intermedially formed narration contains action sequences borrowed from the superhero genre and sound words, typographical variations, and imitated speech bubbles imported from the medium of the comic. The novel has now also experienced a media change to film, which in turn uses intermedial references. For example, live-action movie sequences frequently give way to animated sequences with comic figures being embedded in the realistic setting.

Tamara Bach employs a cinematic approach in the road novel *Busfahrt mit Kuhn* (Bus journey with Kuhn; 2007). Based on the film genre of the road movie, the book's plot and narrative mimic a film script. Tracking shots, dialogues, scene changes, director's commentary, and a narrated audio track intermedially shape the text of the novel. In this condensed form and explicitly referring to the screenplay as a cinematic pretext, Bach's novel occupies a prominent position. Approaches that subtly simulate the narrative mechanisms of the film medium are not a genuinely new phenomenon, for they have occurred in children's and youth literature since the late 1920s, including the Berlin novels by Wolf Durian and Erich Kästner.

Mapping distinctions among intermedial transposition, combination, and reference helps create a new scholarly language for discussing children's literature. Texts can be interpreted within processes of media transfer; texts and media can intertwine using different senses and in complex aesthetic configurations. When playing with intermedial references, surprising turns, parodistic ruptures, and multiple encodings are possible—and can address different groups of users. Attending to distinct audiences, to intermedial allusions, and to the shifting meanings created by variant media requires a multilayered approach that crosses material and formal boundaries. Arthur Conan Doyle's figure Sherlock Holmes (1887) has been adapted in, for instance, the Japanese manga series *Detective Conan* (1994–) and hence shifted to a different cultural context. Benjamin Lacombe populates many of his picture books with imagery from popular culture. He includes various pictorial quotations in his adaptation of *Snow White* (2011), presenting the text of the Grimms' fairy tale against a backdrop of popular icons, such as Hitchcock's *Psycho* (1960) and the Disney film *Snow White and the Seven Dwarfs* (1937). Finally, other aesthetic forms of intermediality are being created in the "new media," such as enhanced e-books containing links to videos and websites. The ways in which the digital age is changing and being changed by literature are still unfolding.

34

Irony

Bettina Kümmerling-Meibauer

In Lemony Snicket's *The Bad Beginning* (1999), the custodian of the three Baudelaire orphans, Count Olaf, after hearing that the children had been asked to contact a family friend about him, deplores their difficulties in adjusting to the life he had graciously conceded to them. His words seem to express concern for the children's welfare. However, up to this point of the novel, he has mostly scolded and yelled at the children, even threatening their lives. His confession does not match his previous actions and demeanor. The very next sentence emphasizes his vile character: "His face was very serious, as if he *were* very sorry to hear that, but his eyes were shiny and bright, the way they are when someone is telling a joke" (73). This ambiguous facial expression and the italicized word are additional cues for the reader that Count Olaf's allegation is purely ironic. He has asserted something that is the opposite of what he actually means.

Irony is a rhetorical device used in everyday discourse as well as literature. The word derives from the ancient Greek εἰρωνεία (*eirōneía*), whose literal meaning is "dissimulation." The most common and frequent definition—saying something that is contrary to what is meant—is attributed to the first-century Roman orator Quintilian, who introduced irony as a trope typically used for a "humorous or emphatic effect" (*OED*). The word came into English as a figure of speech in the sixteenth century (*Encyclopedia Britannica*) and broadens its coverage over the course of time, leading to the distinction between verbal irony, situational irony, and dramatic irony (Colebrook 2004). While verbal irony is saying the contrary to what is meant, situational irony refers to a situation in which the outcome is incongruous with what is expected. Finally, dramatic irony is understood as the "incongruity created when the significance of a character's speech or actions is revealed to the reader but unknown to the character concerned" (*OED*).

Over the centuries, the category of irony merges with several different figures of speech, such as sarcasm, understatement, rhetorical question, and hyperbole, which make the recognition of irony even more challenging (Booth 1974). Irony thus has become a keystone of literary poetics, considered optionally as a mode of consciousness or a philosophical stance. In terms of this change in meaning, irony serves multiple functions, such as mockery, detachment, and even involvement. Whether intended to criticize or perhaps insult someone (equated with ironic criticism) or to compliment someone in a humorous manner (regarded as ironic praise), irony reveals an emotional dimension, since it simultaneously indicates something about the unbalanced relationship between the speaker and the addressee. It is not without reason that Linda Hutcheon (1994) classifies irony as edgy: it particularly discloses the speaker or narrator's judgmental attitude.

However, as Hutcheon (1994) points out, perceiving irony depends on many factors—including a reader's ability to detect tone, use context, and participate in the same interpretive community as the ironist. How do we know when a speaker or narrator is not sincere? Why should a speaker decide to express a blatant falsehood in order to convey a truth? How do we acquire the sort of knowledge that allows us to interpret an utterance or a text as ironic? And on top of all this, are children generally able to understand irony?

For more than forty years, psychologists and linguists have been trying to determine when children begin to understand irony. From a linguistic perspective, irony is a metalinguistic device, since it requires the listener to reflect on what is said and what is actually meant (Gombert 1992). From a cognitive perspective, modeling irony in this way demands the attribution of second-order mental states—that is, to infer a speaker's belief and intention. This capability goes hand in hand with the acquisition of theory of mind, another hallmark in the child's cognitive development. Theory of mind is the ability to attribute mental states, such as feelings, desires, knowledge, and thoughts, to others and to understand that other people may have beliefs, intentions, and feelings that are different to one's own (Marraffa 2011). A crucial watershed is the age of four, when children usually acquire a basic understanding of theory of mind; however, this ability continuously develops over childhood up to adolescence and beyond. Since irony relies on second-order beliefs, children's difficulties with irony are related to their struggles to infer a speaker's intention. Any failure to recognize it leads to an interpretation of irony as a literally true statement, an error, or a lie (Dews et al. 1996, 3083).

There are conflicting beliefs regarding the age at which children master a full understanding of irony. Some argue that irony comprehension emerges in early adolescence; others find evidence of understanding in middle childhood or even earlier (Winner 1988; Nakassis and Snedeker 2002; Creusere 2007). Experimental studies show that children usually do not reliably understand irony until at least five to six years of age, when they are able to understand simple forms of verbal irony. Only at the age of six to eight or perhaps even later are children capable of recognizing a speaker's intention to criticize or tease. Since irony is a gradual phenomenon, ranging from rude to subtle and depending on

contextual clues to infer the speaker's intention, there are many parameters involved, such as an awareness of the communicative functions of irony and the distinction between ironic criticism and ironic praise (Pexman and Glenwright 2007). This is all the more true when it comes to situational irony, which is usually not grasped before the age of ten to twelve, since it requires the capability to understand other people's life conditions and to infer the situational context (Glenwright and Pexman 2003).

These observations may suggest that irony lacks a significant role in children's books that are targeted at children younger than ten years of age. Yet the opposite is the case: irony already appears in picture books for preschool children and constantly emerges in children's books addressed to children from the age of four onward. Typical examples are Pat Hutchins's *Rosie's Walk* (1968) and Ellen Raskin's *Nothing Ever Happens on My Block* (1966). Both picture books are based on a tension between the superficially dull narrative and the pictures that convey a different, even contradictive story (Kümmerling-Meibauer 1999).

A study by Jennifer Dyer and colleagues (2000) on the representation of mental states in children's literature finds that a third of ninety storybooks surveyed display ironic remarks, with a preference for the depiction of situational irony. However, we know next to nothing about whether children really understand the meaning of the ironic statements in children's books. Since in written texts, there is no prosody, no "ironic tone of voice" that may give readers a clue about the actual intention of the ironic expressions, they might run the risk of not being understood by the child audience. To go a step further, one may even suspect that ironic statements are merely addressed to the adult mediator—behind the backs of children. Will preschool children really get the meaning of the narrator's ironic comments in A. A. Milne's *Winnie-the-Pooh* (1929), as, for instance, when the narrator points to the discrepancy between Owl's alleged astuteness and his inability to spell words correctly?

Moreover, it is not at all common practice that children's books directly refer to the ironic meaning, as a rare example in Edith Nesbit's *The Story of the Amulet* (1906) demonstrates: "The children took this to be bitter irony, which means saying the exact opposite of what you mean in order to make yourself disagreeable; as when you happen to have a dirty face and someone says: 'How nice and clean you look!'" (1975, 87). However, even this passage, which follows a dispute between Old Nurse and the children, reveals a double twist, as the children get the ironic statement totally wrong due to their incomplete world knowledge (Walsh 2016).

Children's books focusing on the pranks of little rascals are quite popular and can be found in almost all national literatures. In German, there is even a specific term for this genre: *Lausbubengeschichte*. Most often told from the rascals' point of view, the humorous effects of the stories emerge from the contradiction between the naive perspective of the first-person narrator and the reactions of other characters. Very often, the first-person narrators understand ironic comments as literally true statements, thus causing misunderstandings and sometimes even a total mess. Prominent examples are *Just William* (1922) by Richmal Crompton, the popular French series on *Le petit Nicolas* (1960) by René Goscinny and Jean-Jacques Sempé, and the Chilean diary-novel *Papelucho* (1947) by Marcela Paz.

The understanding of verbal and situational irony is highly context bound and demands the reader to reflect on the implicatures of the ironic statements, since they usually violate communicative rules (Colston and Gibbs 2007). The child reader's ability to grasp meaning depends on the subtlety of irony and its degree of indirection, even though there are always some textual markers that serve as clues, such as repetition, echoic mention, quotation marks, typographic changes, and litotes and hyperbole as modes of under- or overstatement. However, even this markedness raises the question of literary interpretation, which implies that the reader knows what an expression means according to its context.

A case in point is the last chapter in Erich Kästner's detective novel *Emil und die Detektive* (1929; trans. *Emil and the Detectives*, 1931), in which Emil's family discusses whether there is a moral to the story. Emil's grandmother has the final say by declaring, "Money should always be sent by money order" (256). The ironic undertone can only be grasped if the reader considers the possible consequences of this assertion: Emil would never have experienced his thrilling adventures in Berlin and caught the bank robber with the help of the children's gang if his mother had followed the grandmother's advice. Kästner's novel is infused with ironic dialogues and comments from the very beginning, which mostly rely on verbal irony, while the final twist is a prime example of situational irony, since it demands a consideration of the story's context.

The matter of irony becomes even more complicated in young adult novels. The first-person narrator in Justine Larbalestier's *Liar* (2009) proves to be a notorious liar who makes extensive use of ironic statements. For instance, when reprimanded for having told lies to the school's principal, the main protagonist comments on the essay she has to write: "My second essay for the principal was on the virtues of honesty. I ran out of things to say on the first page" (33). Later on, she states, "Now I must confess to a lie. Everything I've told you so far has been completely true except for the tiny matter of Great-Uncle Hilliard. Hilliard's alive" (109–10). By using the narrative strategy of unreliable narration, the reader is never quite sure whether the narrator has told another lie or merely made an ironic comment, thus contributing to the reader's increasing puzzlement. The connection of irony and lying is also at the fore of Rosie Rushton's *Love, Lies and Lizzie* (2009); however, this young adult novel makes this issue even more difficult. As a modernized adaptation of Jane Austen's *Pride and Prejudice* (1813), Rushton's novel plays with irony on two levels. It transfers the original book's ironic statements into contemporary times and ironically comments on the now obsolete ideas hidden in these ironic statements at the same time.

When discussing children's books, literary critics usually mention irony only in passing, noting its presence in L. Frank Baum's *The Wonderful Wizard of Oz* (1900), Astrid Lindgren's *Pippi Långstrump* (1945), and Roald Dahl's *Matilda* (1988). That said, researchers have addressed the didactic aspects of teaching irony to children (Stott 1982), the depiction of irony in picture books (Rasmussen 1987; Kümmerling-Meibauer 1999), the complicated connection of irony and social power relations (Cadden 2000a; Walsh 2011, 2016), and irony as a category of humor (Cross 2011). The question remains: Can children's books teach irony to children by familiarizing them with specific story conventions and scripts, which in turn may help them recognize ironic statements' deviations in meaning?

The more they read children's books that rely on verbal irony or situational irony, the better children may ascertain that irony disrupts common expectations, foregrounds out-of-place or unconventional ideas, and encourages reflection on other people's beliefs and intentions.

35

Liminality
Michael Joseph

The phenomenon of liminality appears in the earliest children's texts, but the term itself is a coinage from Scottish anthropologist Victor Turner (1969), who drew on *liminaire*, a term used by Arnold Van Gennep in his ethnographical writings on preindustrial societies to designate the middle, transitional stage of a three-stage paradigmatic rite of passage: "rites which accompany every change of place, state, social position and age" (quoted in Turner 1969, 94). Joseph Campbell adapted this construct as a basis for *The Hero with a Thousand Faces* (1949), an example of Turner's long shadow on literary studies.

Liminality describes the quality of being socially segregated, set apart, and divested of status and relates to characteristics and qualities associated with this condition: indeterminacy, ambiguity, selflessness, and becomingness among them. Though Turner gives the Latin *limen* as its root, *liminality*'s origins precede the early Bronze Age in the Egyptian word for "port," "harbor," "haven," and "port city"—*mni*—which appears during the second millennium BC in the Middle Kingdom and later becomes transposed into the Greek *limen*, also meaning "harbor."

As Campbell adapted the rite of passage to a Jungian interpretation of myth and fantasy, Turner adapted liminality to the study of religious patterns in contemporary culture, elaborating on Émile Durkheim's theory of religious functionalism. Like Campbell's, Turner's work was stimulated by literary interests, which included children's literature. Edith Turner notes that her husband saw liminality in works by C. S. Lewis, Mark Twain, and Robert Louis Stevenson as well as in the innumerable children's stories with passage to adulthood as their theme (Turner 1990).

During the 1990s, *liminal* appeared frequently in research touching on adolescence, generally qualifying an adolescent subject with regard to the ambiguousness of their social position and/or sexual identity. In 1997, Reuven Kahane used the phrase *postmodern liminality* in arguing that postmodernity had institutionalized liminality, providing adolescents with a buffer zone in which to move playfully and spontaneously between normative and antinormative behaviors, thereby offsetting the tensions (and judgments) of a complex society. In his work, postmodern liminality becomes a metonym of adolescent agency, which persists in the criticism of young adult literature.

What may be the earliest link between liminality and preadolescent children appears in Dennis Todd's 1995 discussion of objects acquired by gentleman collectors—specifically "monstrous children, in their deceased form." Todd calls these exceptional collectibles "liminal creatures" (156) because they straddle boundaries between categories and thus neutralize conventional definition. The overlapping of identities of children and monsters is an ironic commonplace in contemporary culture and indeed in children's literature. Like monsters, literary children dismayingly breach boundaries in their passage into adulthood, as Lynne Vallone's *Big and Small: A Cultural History of Extraordinary Bodies* (2017) insightfully demonstrates. They symbolize both chaos and order, antistructure and structure. One glimpses the face of invisible affiliation in the historical shifting of the similarly transitional gothic romance (such as Mary Shelley's *Frankenstein*) into children's literature and the congeries of monsters in fairy tales: Madame Leprince

de Beaumont's "Beauty and the Beast" (1756) perhaps the earliest fairy tale composed for children, asks, What is a monster? This is a question containing the question, What is a child?

After 2000, scholars began to discuss liminality more widely in representations of childhood, children, and child culture. The adjective *liminal* appeared with greater improvisation and richness of use, generally indicating states of being "in between," "bounded," or "hybrid." Liminal space emerged as a flexible concept in which space can refer (extensively) to literary time-space or to something more abstract: for example, Hogwarts and Crusoe's island are both liminal spaces because they are projected outside of society and symbolize a borderland through which the protagonist or the community of liminal beings—"the *communitas*" (Turner 1969)—passes to reenter structure. On the other hand, liminal space can also be used (intensively) to signify an interior state—a projection of creative power, yet another metaphor of the imagination. The broadly pervasive importance of liminal space to children's literature becomes immediately evident when noting its iteration in the titles of canonical texts: *Alice's Adventures in Wonderland* (1865), *The Wonderful Wizard of Oz* (1900), *The Chronicles of Narnia* (1950–56), and *Moominland Midwinter* (1958, translation of *Trollvinter* [1957]).

Scholarly discussions of liminality in children's literature expanded exponentially in the opening years of the twenty-first century. *Liminal consciousness* appears partly to describe Randall Jarrell, who, "obsessively revisiting his grim recollections of a childhood trauma," envisions an escapist fantasy scene of a boy lying abed, between sleeping and waking, in whose "liminal consciousness" the terrifying details of a Grimms' fairy tale his mother is telling him become woven into a dream (Knoepflmacher 2005, 173–74). Liminal consciousness, like liminal space, represents a condition of interiority. This usage evokes the late nineteenth-century psychological notion of the *limen* as a "threshold of consciousness," although challenging the customary dyadic psychological structure that recognizes only "subliminal" and "supraliminal" states. In so doing, a compound or fused liminality forms, one that modifies the self with a condition of contingency that is both private, or phenomenological, and public—relating to socially constructed selves.

Liminal carries two common meanings when coupled with *being*. The primary one, implying a person or character experiencing liminality, has a robust and growing presence in discussions of multicultural children's literature, often pendant to the phrase *liminal existence*. Raphpee Thongthiraj (2006) uses the term to describe Jinda's dilemma of being torn between the rural world and westernized Bangkok in Minfong Ho's YA novel *Rice without Rain* (1990). The second usage, a variant of *liminal character*, appears in the domains of folklore and speculative fiction and defines a fantasy character who combines antithetical states. These doubled beings are granted an elevated status by force of their unique perspective and knowledge, but they are also viewed as unpredictable and dangerous. Gandalf, the wizard who leads Bilbo and then Frodo away from the Shire, is a liminal being because he is both dead and alive (Clute and Grant 1997). Cyborgs, like Ted Hughes's Iron Giant (Iron Man in the UK), are also liminal beings. Posthumanist theorists map this derivative meaning of *liminal being* onto the original so that cyborgs symbolize women and, potentially, other social categories that are disempowered or liminalized by normative humanistic values. Children's literary critics Roni Natov (2001), Christopher Parkes (2006), and Anna Panszczyk (2016) have described Harry Potter, Robinson Crusoe, Alice, and Pinocchio as liminal characters (symbols of liminality), echoing Turner, who identified Tom Sawyer and Huck Finn as liminal characters. E. Turner also considered

Lewis Carroll, "with his dream world," a "liminal person" (1990, 167), a description that reflects Victor Turner's seminal insight into the presence of ritual and representation in everyday life.

Someone whose personhood is liminal lives beyond the pale of society or structure. For such persons, liminality is neither conventionally ritualized nor transitional but an open-ended way of life qualified by sets of cultural demands, ethical systems, and clashing processes that are irreconcilable.

Liminal persons fall into two of three categories, both of which nourish children's literature. Ritual liminality anticipates the reincorporation of the liminal being into social structure. (Alice wakes up; Pinocchio becomes flesh; Katniss becomes a mother.) Outsiderhood and marginality, two types of liminality explored in recent narratives for adolescents, define stuckness: lives that are permanently or semipermanently destructured. This quarantined condition is the virtual opposite of Kahane's (1997) notion of liminal adolescence as a "safe space." The "outsider" (a term readers will identify with S. E. Hinton's *The Outsiders* [1967], said to be the first work of young adult fiction) retains an element of choice. While the temporary marginality of childhood finds expression in many children's texts as a defining characteristic of childhood, as something positive if occasionally tedious or frustrating for all concerned, the prolonged marginality of childhood into adolescence depicted in adolescent literature is an unnatural condition that threatens structure and reads as cultural critique. Lewis Carroll typifies outsider liminality because, according to Turner (1990), he set himself apart—he governs his dreamworld. Holden Caulfield, in J. D. Salinger's *Catcher in the Rye* (1951), is more problematic: Is he an individual who cannot resolve social ambiguities and assimilate into structure, liminalized by psychological quirkiness, or is he a category? Does he represent a coherent critique of society as someone who would be termed a "marginal"?

"Marginals" comprise a liminality category popular in multicultural children's narratives of the adolescent children of immigrants or Indigenous people, often paired with the phrase *liminal existence*. In their analyses of socially constructed identities, recent children's literature and criticism seem to be increasingly interested in the bases for asserting status as a marginal. Existence connotes continuity rather than social affiliation and reinforces the idea that a marginal's daily life is determined by a crucial disjunction, even opposition, between the values and expectations of the notional homeland and the oppressive new world. For marginals, liminality is all consuming and a priori: liminality precedes existence. The term also catches at the ontological contractedness of such a state. In marked contrast to the landscaped liminal spaces designed for native-born adolescents to experience ecstasy (as in the context of the Twilight series [2005–8] by Stephenie Meyer and other vampire-erotic fantasies), the circumscribed spaces of first- and second-generation adolescent immigrants or Indigenous peoples epitomize stasis—brutally imposed by a social order whose absorptive rites of passage for the privileged allow, possibly even demand, a hostage population of permanent exiles.

Such a troubled status animates many texts published for children in postcolonial Africa, often within stories based on folktales. In Chinua Achebe's *The Drum* (1977), based on a traditional Igbo and West African tale, the miserable state of the populace at the story's conclusion—"they scattered in every direction of the world and have not yet stopped running" ([1977] 1998, 33)—rhetorically suggests the disintegrative, neither/nor status of a people, like postcolonial Nigerians. In *The Diamond Ring* (1989) by Kenyan author Asenath Bole Odaga, the journey of young Rapemo to visit his "grandfather, the great chief, who live[s] many miles away across a wide stretch of thick forest" (7) similarly codifies in a traditionally coded text the liminality of a people divided from both traditional and modern identity.

The Absolutely True Diary of a Part-Time Indian (2007), winner of the National Book Award, portrays the youth of the Spokane Tribe, whose definitively marginal lives are afflicted by poverty and hopelessness. Arnold Spirit, the book's protagonist (whose nickname, Junior, suggests the reduced and subordinate stature of the reservation), daringly enrolls in a high school removed from the reservation, choosing a harder, less restrictive outsider status to the "stuckness" of marginality. Arnold's eventual passage into the social structure is symbolically predicted by his acceptance into the *communitas* of the high school basketball team. His choice to assimilate into the dominant culture by asserting his individual abilities—to reject the soft identity as "junior" and to embrace a differently liminalized status as a "part-time Indian"—suggests a Romantic conceit of the individual, or the "spirit," triumphing over social constraints. Undoubtedly, it represents the philosophy of the author, Sherman Alexie, whose own choices have earned him a wide reputation as a uniquely gifted poet, author, and filmmaker while also garnering disturbing accusations of insensitive and abusive behavior.

Whether as a context to explore monstrosity, state change, social disintegration, individual growth, personal and cultural identity, or other questions concerning existence and meaning, the literature for children and young adults continues to yield itself productively to liminal studies. In fact, one would almost be tempted to assert—were one unaware of the dynamics of confirmation bias and idioplasty—that children's literature primarily exists as an ideal space in which to critically represent the multifarious meanings of *liminality*.

36

Media

Naomi Hamer

Because *media* is in a moment of cultural transition, it is a quintessential keyword, its meaning "contested or conflicted" (Nel, Paul, and Christensen 2021). Traditionally, in children's literature studies, *media* designates texts produced in forms other than print codices, thus subtly creating a hierarchical distinction between the nonliterary (media) and the literary. Yet since the early twentieth century, the term *media* has also been strongly associated with its definition as "the main channel for mass communication, as newspapers, radio, television, etc.; the reporters, journalists, etc., working for organizations engaged in such communication" (*OED*). This definition highlights the development of new technologies for mass communication, beginning with newspapers and other print media in the seventeenth century, radio and television in the twentieth century, and digital modes of communication into the twenty-first century. In response to those scholars who use this definition to elevate the literary above such allegedly nonliterary media, the fields of cultural studies, media studies, and digital media studies have reclaimed the term *media* to challenge the literary as a dominant cultural value, draw attention to the book as print media, and examine the audience cultures of engagement across channels of communication (Williams 1983b; Hall and du Gay 1996).

Children's literature scholarship, framed by fandom and digital media studies, particularly challenges the separation of children's literature from digital and popular media cultures. Analyses of Harry Potter slash fanfiction (Tosenberger 2008) and the transmedia cultures of Lewis Carroll's *Alice* (Kérchy 2016) conceptualize the print media source as only one point of multiple entries within a transmedia narrative world. Scholars of picture books and other visual/verbal works also challenge dichotomies of the literary and mass media to reveal strong connections between older and newer media (Mackey 2007; Høyrup 2017). More current and expansive characterizations define *media* as any means of communication, as an "intermediate agency, instrument, or channel; a means; *esp.* a means or channel of communication or expression" (*OED*). This definition of *media* places the book in codex format alongside newer and older channels for communication.

Although challenges to the primacy of print media and the conceptualization of the book have a long history in literature for the young, the emergence of digital and mobile media technologies in the 1990s has resulted in the flourishing of cross-media hybrids: a combination of new versions of childhood, "new 'texts,' new views of literacies, and new ecologies of reading" (Høyrup 2017, 101). As Robin Bernstein points out, rather than defining these hybrids as distinct species of children's literature, a reconceptualization of the field should acknowledge that the "history of children's literature exists not in opposition to, but in integration with, the histories of children's material culture and children's play" (2013, 459). Such an integrated history of children's literature, material culture, and play illustrates the ways that children's literature has long been imbricated in material culture and other media beyond print codices.

Beginning with the origin of the hornbook in the fifteenth century, media have played central roles in the production and consumption of children's literature.

Even prior to John Locke, there are multiple examples of mobiles, cards, paint-by-number educational books, dissected maps, and other media that blur definitions of books, games, and interactive toys used within the domestic sphere (Julia Briggs 2005; Paul 2011). John Newbery's marketing of children's books alongside toys in the eighteenth century and small-sized books such as Anna Barbauld's *Lessons for Children* (1778–79) predated Beatrix Potter in the design of books as interactive print media for young readers with small hands (Paul 2009, 133). The movable book constituted a popular format for texts geared at young people during the eighteenth and nineteenth centuries, indicating a close connection historically among books, toys, and games. As Jacqueline Reid-Walsh observes in her analysis of eighteenth- and nineteenth-century flap books and paper-doll books, "Movable books came to be associated with children in the period of burgeoning commercial publishing for children during the Enlightenment, partly through the popularity of John Locke's ideas concerning the importance of visual images and playthings in the promotion of literacy" (2016, 213).

Over time, children's picture books have incorporated new technological developments from the introduction of chromolithography for multicolor illustrations in the nineteenth century to the recent remediation of picture books for electronic readers, producing hybrid communicative media. Indeed, the blurred lines among toys, games, and children's books have consistently defined the interactive, multimedia character of children's literature. In the nineteenth century, stage versions of *Alice in Wonderland* (Brooker 2004), children's dishware depicting characters from *Robinson Crusoe* (O'Malley 2012), and Peter Pan postcards and greeting cards by Mabel Lucie Attwell all exemplify transmedia storytelling (H. Jenkins 2006) before the advent of early twentieth century advertising

or branding and licensing in children's cultures (Tilley 2015). By the mid-twentieth century, a youth niche market was the target for a range of products, including children's and infant clothing (Cook 2008), the Golden Books series's retelling and promoting of Disney films (Marcus 2007), media tie-ins (from children's literature adaptations on radio, television, and in film) such as Shirley Temple paper dolls dressed in costumes from the films of *Heidi* (1937) and *The Little Princess* (1939), and phonograph records that played children's stories and music (J. Smith 2010).

Embodied and material play with dolls and toys has often characterized engagement with children's literature and folkloric narratives. Meredith A. Bak, like Bernstein, argues for a theoretical frame that looks at the significance of how "fairy tales are kept aloft not only through reading, hearing and seeing but also through doing, through acts of embodiment and performance that material objects can facilitate" (2018, 329). Many children's book exhibits and children's story museums provide a range of media for material and virtual play with children's literature. Miyazawa Kenji Dowa Mura (Village of Fairy Tales) in Iwate, Tohoku, Japan, offers video and soundscapes alongside a fairies' trail in a wild plant garden to engage with the work of Japanese poet and children's author Kenji Miyazawa (Hamer 2018). This embodied play expands further in the transnational *Anne of Green Gables* fandom of Japanese tourists in Prince Edward Island and Canadian theme parks in Japan (Bergstrom 2014). Often transmedia adaptation, consumption, collection, and other forms of material play take place over multiple decades across a range of media. Since the publication of Tove Jansson's illustrated Moomin books (1945–77), they have been adapted into an animated series, dishware, linens, toys, and a Finnish theme park. These material and physical media have been extended into the online Moomin shop, blog, and social media accounts, including a Twitter account with more than fifty thousand followers in January 2019.

Young people are often perceived as victims of commercialized children's publishing and the children's culture industry more generally (Kline [1993] 1995; Quart 2003). Since 2009, the majority of the news articles on apps for young people reflect anxiety about the effects of screen usage on the development of cognitive and motor skills (Quenchua 2014). The term *media* carries with it competing perspectives of children as both passive consumers and active participants empowered through media (Gee 2003; Tapscott 1997). In contrast, new media literacies scholars Colin Lankshear and Michele Knobel argue that "new literacies" include practices that draw on new technical affordances and cultivate a "new ethos" that is often defined as "participatory," "collaborative," and "distributed" (2007, 9). Henry Jenkins's (2006) conceptualization of "convergence cultures" has been central to addressing the merging of old and new media and the blurring roles of consumer and producer in digital cultures. However, the "new ethos" and "convergence cultures" are not unique to media such as picture books apps: convergence, participation, collaboration, and mass distribution have long been characteristics of print picture books too.

The picture book app refashions the multiple modes of the picture book by remediating design elements and associated discourses from other influential forms such as film, comics, video games, and theatrical performance (Hamer 2017; Bolter and Grusin 1999). While mobile platforms to some extent exemplify a return to both the design and function of earlier forms such as the hornbook, media discourse on picture book apps often sentimentalizes the loss of the material qualities of the print codex. Following Alan Liu's argument that digital media brings with it a need for a "genealogy of mediated

experience—bookish, online, or otherwise—that shuttles uncannily between old and new" (2007, 16), some picture book app features engage with the affective attachment to the physical wear and markings of print media in conjunction with new media affordances such as the mobile camera. For example, the *Goodnight Moon* app (Loud Crow Interactive 2012) offers an option for readers to sign their names and photograph a photo of their own on the picture book title page image as one of the app features. The *My Very Hungry Caterpillar* AR app (Storytoy 2017) extends the material experience of reading a print picture book with augmented reality (AR). The AR focuses on the user's experience of feeding and nurturing a caterpillar in the physical environment. Drawing on new technological innovations, the app imitates the practices and discourses of tie-in toys and educational games associated with Eric Carle picture books from predigital media eras. The My Moonlite story projector (https://mymoonlite.com) uses the affordances of the flashlight and audio features of a mobile phone to expand the reading experience through the projection of picture-book images. While employing the technological advantages of the mobile app and smartphone, the projector and cardboard reels offer a remediation in form and function of a View-Master stereoscope (the 1930s version designed to feature Kodachrome color film for children).

Other new apps draw on the affordances of digital media and echo play and pedagogies from the history of children's literature and culture. While remediating an illustrated print text, the adaptation of the Indigenous print picture book *Pîsim Finds Her Miskanaw* (Dumas 2013) also aims to remediate elements of Indigenous oral storytelling, Cree language, song, and land-based practices and pedagogies. To address the limitations and advantages of the app, the project drew on an advisory board of researchers, community partners, and Rocky Cree knowledge keepers in the design of audiovisual elements—particularly the voicing of Cree language, map-oriented activities, and simulated game activities related to land-based practices. Through these connections to audio, visual, and other performative components of storytelling, the Pīsim story app (more than the print picture book) reflects a return to protocontact ancestral experience, exemplifying the potential for digital media to address recent Indigenous movements of radical resistance that champion a return to land-based pedagogy and education (Simpson 2014a).

Digital media in the form of apps provide potential for the subversion of dominant narratives without sentimentalizing or discounting older forms of media. Various tie-in texts and fan cultures offer interruptions of the dominant discourses of identity—often of gender and sexuality—rooted in the earlier texts. Such intersectional, transgressive fandom emerges in Catherine Tosenberger's (2008) work on Harry Potter slash fan fictions and Thomas Xavier Sarmiento's (2014) exploration of *Glee* and queer Filipina/o American identity. Digital fan communities and practices, such as "manga scanlation," where producers scan, translate, and edit comics from one language to another (Lee 2009), have challenged understandings of copyright and authorship historically linked to the print codex. However, the most potential for digital media cultures continues to be harnessed by adolescent and adult participants with access to and capacity for user-generated material that can disrupt networks of surveillance. The potential for transmedia practices and cultures to support activism, critical reflection, and subversion of children's literature has not been fully explored. However, the transmedia histories of children's literature, play, and material culture at least offer a framework to address these gaps in examinations of both historical and contemporary media.

37

Modernism
Kimberley Reynolds

Arguably, no word maps the kind of cultural shifts in language that Raymond Williams (1976, 1983b) was documenting better than *modernism*. At its simplest, this is because of its roots in the word *modern*. Inevitably, what is modern at one time eventually becomes dated and of its time. So from the first recorded use of that root word in 1500, to the appearance of the word *modernism* itself in 1737, to the fin de siècle, it was a shifting signifier, referring to the current present of any given period rather than a specific historical moment or movement (*Shorter Oxford English Dictionary*). There have been, then, many modernisms, at some level all suggesting "a sense of forward-looking contemporaneity" (Wilk 2006). Toward the end of the nineteenth century, however, a new set of understandings started to come into play, and eventually the meaning of *modernism* became more fixed. It is now widely used to refer to a movement that was particularly active across Europe (including pre- and postrevolutionary Russia) and North America from the late nineteenth century to the middle of the twentieth century. This movement embraced all the arts and resulted in practitioners, critics, and philosophers turning away from classical and traditional forms, styles, and modes of expression and creativity. Their aims were far from cohesive, and the word embraces both those groups who were pessimistic about a technologized future and those who saw science and technology as capable of realizing utopia for all. Nevertheless, together they comprise a "movement towards sophistication and mannerism, towards introversion, technical display, internal self-skepticism, [which] has often been taken as a common base for a definition of Modernism" (Bradbury and MacFarlane 1976, 26). Most avant-garde artistic movements from this period display many features of modernism and so are included in this discussion.

If modernism itself pulls in several directions, the relationship between children's literature and modernism is convoluted and contradictory. This condition came to the attention of those who teach and research in the area of children's literature studies when Jacqueline Rose (1984) argued that writers for children have consciously rejected literary modernism as part of a strategy to resist cultural change. The result, she suggests, is that by the middle of the twentieth century, children's literature provided a refuge for writers in retreat from modernism. As evidence, Rose cites Isaac Bashevis Singer's declaration, "I came to the child because I see in him the last refuge from a literature gone berserk and ready for suicide" (Rose 1984, 10). Since Singer makes clear through references to Kafka and *Finnegans Wake* that it is specifically the impact of modernism from which he is retreating, his views support her case. She might also have pointed to the fact that some modernist writers deliberately excluded children from their audience. Henry James ([1889] 1990), for instance, dismissed both juvenile and female readers as "irreflective and uncritical" and so incapable of appreciating the intellectually driven, self-conscious work of modernist writers like himself.

Perhaps because she only deals with works written in English and mostly published in Britain, Rose fails to recognize many examples of modernism in publishing for children throughout the last century. Britain was generally more ambivalent about modernism than the US or most European countries, and especially in relation to children (A. Harris 2010; Reynolds 2016), despite the fact that modernism itself is highly indebted to the idea of the child as transcendent and inspirational. Charles Baudelaire was one of those who pointed to the way: "Children see everything afresh. . . . There is nothing that more closely resembles what is called inspiration than the joy with which children absorb shape and color. Genius is merely childhood rediscovered at will" (quoted in Lloyd 1998).

Like Baudelaire, modernists in all media were interested in ideas of play, the untrained eye, and the intuitive, intense perceptions of childhood. Modernist artists and practitioners around the globe drew on ideas, activities, and attributes associated with children and childhood in an effort to break away from traditional ways of seeing, thinking about, and representing the world (Kinchin, O'Connor, and Harrod 2012). Foremost among the characteristics of childhood that spoke to modernist sensibilities and aspirations is play, which came to be seen as the basis for imagination, fantasy, and creativity—all vital for the modernist project of revisioning the world (Warner 2005)—as typified in work by Giacomo Balla, Joseph Cornell, Marc Chagall, Wassily Kandinsky, Ernö Goldfinger, Vladimir Lebedev, Henri Matisse, Pablo Picasso, and Kurt Schwitters.

As contributors to *Children's Literature and the Avant-Garde* (Druker and Kümmerling-Meibauer 2015) show, the early years of the twentieth century saw the publication of numerous modernist children's books in many countries that make use of objects and experiences that are familiar to children—such as toys, shapes, drawing materials, and dreams—to create stories that do not flinch from either the ideological or the aesthetic extremes of modernism. A good example is Russian-born artist El Lissitzky's *About Two Squares: A Suprematist Tale* about *Two Squares in Six Constructions* ([1922] 2000). Lissitzky's short tale, dedicated "To children, to all CHILDREN" (the capitalized, repeated use of *children* elevating the term and including all who retain the capacity to be childlike), uses geometric shapes and flat planes to celebrate revolution and reforms associated with it as symbolized by the appealing red squares, which triumph over the grayness of disorder. Leo Lionni's *Little Blue and Little Yellow* (1959) uses irregular circles of primary colors to create a parable about friendship and tolerance. Both stories have underlying utopian themes, a powerful strand in modernist thought equally evident in Lewis W. Hine's *Men at Work* (1936). This collection of photographs showing muscular men working with machines to create the architectural future also speaks to modernist preoccupations with the healthy body and the heroic nature of workers.

Modernist writing's concern with the nature of language, the problem of rendering subjective experience on the page, and its engagement with science and technology as forces that reshape and destabilize the world are evident in writing for children from the 1920s onward. Richard Hughes's *The Spider's Palace and Other Stories* (1931), Gertrude Stein's *The World Is Round* (1939), Norton Juster's *The Phantom Tollbooth* (1961), Russell Hoban's *The Mouse and His Child* (1967), and the picture books created from stories extracted from Eugène Ionesco's memoirs ([1968] 1978, 1970, 1971, and 1973, the first two illustrated by Étienne Delessert, the third by Philippe Corentin, and the fourth by Jean-Michel Nicollet) are all predicated on wordplay that calls into question the tenets of realism, particularly its dependence on chronological linearity.

Visual aspects of children's literature have been an important area of modernist experimentation, as they allow the kind of fusion and cross-fertilization of the arts that so interested the early modernists. Colors, graphics, cutouts, and images work with text to produce seemingly simple works that convey complex ideas. Tove Jansson's *Hur gick det sen? Boken om Mymlan, Mumintrollet och Lilla My* (1952; trans. *The Book about Moomin, Mymble and Little My*, 2004) uses cutouts to bring past, present, and future times (pages) together on a double-page spread, while its antinaturalistic palette conveys atmosphere and emotions without recourse to language. Especially in combination with elements such as flaps and overlays that break up images, illustrations can disrupt linearity, juxtapose incongruous elements to inhibit straightforward readings, and offer multiple viewpoints. These devices often function in ways similar to dreams, internal monologues, framing narratives, focalization, and other techniques used to render interiority and the fragmented nature of experience in modernist fiction for adults. The combination of words, images, textures, and even scents (scratch-and-sniff books) and sounds (audio accompaniment) mean picture books in particular can be highly innovative and synesthetic, qualities central to modernism.

There is, then, a well-developed tradition of modernist children's literature; indeed, arguably, modernism is a product of children's literature (Dusinberre 1987). As Dusinberre explains, those at the forefront of literary modernism were also the generation that grew up reading *Alice's Adventures in Wonderland* and its successors; modernists' concerns with "mastery over language, structure, vision, morals, characters and readers" (1987, xvii) have their basis in their childhood reading. The influence of modernism, often crossing over into postmodernism, is now unmistakable. Writing that employs devices such as mise en abyme, chronological fluidity, sophisticated wordplay, metafictive self-consciousness, unreliable or limited focalizers, and stream of consciousness can be found across the range covered by children's literature. Meanwhile, critical work on the relationship between children's literature and modernism has largely followed Dusinberre's (1987) lead, demonstrating that far from turning its back on modernism, children's literature has always been a fertile area for modernist thinking and avant-garde experimentation (Boethius 1998; Natov 2003; Reynolds 2007, 2016; Westman 2007 Druker and Kümmerling-Meibauer 2015).

38

Multicultural
Debra Dudek

The first usage of the word *multicultural* in 1935 articulated tensions about belonging and alienation, which still resonate today. In "The Problem of the Marginal Man" (1935), Everett V. Stonequist engages with Robert E. Park's notion of the "marginal man," a figure Park defined in "Human Migration and the Marginal Man" (1928). Park describes this figure as one who is "living and sharing intimately in the cultural traditions of two distinct peoples, never quite willing to break, even if he were permitted to do so, with his past and his traditions, and not quite accepted, because of racial prejudice, in the new society in which he now seeks to find a place" (892). Stonequist expands Park's definition to claim, "The marginal man arises in a bicultural or multi-cultural situation" (1935, 1). Park and Stonequist identify key issues that continue to inform debates about multiculturalism, in particular the marginalization and prejudice that can occur when different cultural groups live in proximity to one another.

After World War II, multiculturalism flags a connection between language and culture. In 1949, German journalist and activist Jella Lepman founded the International Youth Library in Munich and then the International Board on Books for Young People (IBBY) in 1953 as a means of promoting international understanding and peace. In 1957, fourteen educators and thirteen business representatives met in New York City at a conference organized by the Foreign Language Program and

Modern Language Association to discuss the role of foreign languages in international business and industry. In his contribution to the report on the conference, Edward A. Medina—director of elementary education and supervisor of Spanish in New Mexico's Department of Education—first used the word *multiculturalism*. Speaking about how Indigenous peoples, Americans of Spanish descent, and "Anglos" have daily contact in New Mexico, Medina argues, "The key to successful living here, as it is in Switzerland, is multilingualism, which can carry with it a rich multiculturalism" (*OED*). This connection between multilingualism and multiculturalism is also highlighted in the influential 1965 *Preliminary Report* of the Royal Commission on Bilingualism and Biculturalism, in which the authors equate multiculturalism with the "Canadian Mosaic."

In the 1960s, the words *multicultural* and *multiculturalism* point more directly to a connection between nationalism and multiculturalism, indicated when several Western democracies took a so-called multicultural turn in their approach to managing diversity. As the Multiculturalism Policy (MCP) Index at Queen's University (Canada) demonstrates, this turn can be measured by evaluating multicultural policies designed to assist immigrant-origin ethnic groups, historic national minorities, and Indigenous peoples. In their study of multicultural policies in place from 1980 to 2010 across twenty-one Western countries, researchers found there was little repeal of multicultural policies, contrary to popular belief. Despite the continued presence of multicultural policies, however, German chancellor Angela Merkel famously declared in 2010 that attempts to create a multicultural society had "utterly failed" (Weaver 2010).

Nationalist anxieties about integrating foreign populations shape and continue to inform debates about how best to embrace difference and to oppose prejudice.

In *The Crisis of Multiculturalism in Europe* (2017), Rita Chin argues that anxious responses to foreign populations occurred inside nation states as early as the late nineteenth and early twentieth centuries. She draws on Stuart Hall's distinction between multicultural and multiculturalism to inform her analysis. According to Hall, multicultural describes "the social characteristics and problems of governance posed by any society in which different cultural communities live together and attempt to build a common life while retaining something of their 'original' identity" while multiculturalism denotes "the strategies and policies adopted to manage and govern the problems of diversity and multiplicity which multi-cultural societies throw up" (quoted in Chin 2017, 18–19).

In North America and Australia, national identity was discussed via this conceptual lens of multiculturalism, and in Europe, the concept of imagology was more influential in these discussions. A multicultural lens focuses on differences *within* a nation, and imagology looks at differences *between* nations. Furthermore, imagology works "primarily on literary representations, [and] furnishes continuous proof that it is in the field of imaginary and poetical literature that national stereotypes are first and most effectively formulated, perpetuated and disseminated" (Leerssen 2007, 26).

This process of looking at how national, racial, and cultural identities are represented in texts for children informs discussions about multicultural children's literature. Multicultural children's literature developed in tandem with multicultural education, which grew out of ethnic studies in the late 1960s and early 1970s in America (Schwartz 1995). However, as early as 1938, African American librarian Augusta Baker began listing books that were appropriate for African American children. Following Baker's lead, in 1953, the Jane Addams Children's Book Award recognized books that "most effectively promote peace, social justice, world community, and the equality of the sexes and all races" (Rudman 2006, 112). This effort to call attention to the dearth of children's books that represented racially diverse characters in positions of power came to the foreground with the publication of Nancy Larrick's oft-quoted and reprinted article, "The All-White World of Children's Books" (1965). Similar to Larrick's criticism of books published in America, Karen Sands-O'Connor (2003) finds a tendency to represent racialized characters as originating from outside England in books published in Britain in the 1950s, '60s, and '70s. She argues that "fiction for older children and young adults remained steadfastly uniform in their depiction of white characters only" and that in Susan Cooper's *Silver on the Tree* (1977) and John Christopher's Tripods trilogy (1967–68), "nonwhite people all originate *outside* the borders of England. Citizens of England—and saviours of the planet—are white" (Sands-O'Connor 2003, 45). Sands-O'Connor posits that since only the mid-1990s has literature for children addressed the idea of Britain as an inclusive multicultural society. Ingrid Johnson, Joyce Bainbridge, and Farha Shariff (2007) see a similar yet earlier trend in Canada, with the 1970s privileging a Eurocentric perspective and children's books in the late 1980s and early 1990s beginning to represent cultural diversity beyond a White mainstream with the publication of Freda Ahenakew's *How the Mouse Got Brown Teeth: A Cree Story for Children* (1988), Paul Yee's *Tales from Gold Mountain* (1989), and Michael Kusugak's *Baseball Bats for Christmas* (1990).

Multicultural children's literature succeeds in varying degrees to represent cultural differences to young readers. In the best cases, such as Shaun Tan's wordless picture book / graphic novel *The Arrival* (2006), readers negotiate a complex, culturally diverse community and may emerge with a stronger understanding of and respect for cultural differences and for the effect those differences have on individual and group identities. At the other end of the spectrum are texts that gesture toward an acceptance of cultural difference but reinscribe an ideological position in which sameness—or assimilation—seems the desired outcome of multiculturalism. Mem Fox's *I'm Australian Too* (2017), for instance, celebrates an optimistic, ideal view of Australia: it is a peaceful country that welcomes people from across the world, including from Ireland, Italy, Greece, England, Lebanon, Vietnam, China, Somalia, Afghanistan, and Syria. Covertly, however, the book advocates for assimilation: the person from Vietnam speaks "just like an Aussie," and the Chinese family in Canberra "call out, 'G'day mate!'" *I'm Australian Too* struggles to represent a diverse nation populated by Indigenous peoples, Australian-born non-Indigenous people, immigrants, refugees, and asylum seekers.

Words that constellate around *multicultural*, then, include *difference, assimilation, integration, tolerance, acceptance*, and *nationalism*, with *diversity* and *diverse* now often standing in place for and expanding *multiculturalism* and *multicultural*. At a grassroots level, the nonprofit We Need Diverse Books (2006) responds to a continued lack of diversity in children's books by creating an invaluable resource that "advocates essential changes in the publishing industry to produce and promote literature that reflects and honors the lives of all young people." In the mainstream, Yohana Desta's (2016) *Vanity Fair* essay announces 2016 as "The Year Disney Started to Take Diversity Seriously," citing *Moana, Queen of Katwe*, and *Zootopia* as examples. Debates about cultural authenticity and cultural stereotyping seem the most heated in relation to Disney's animated films, perhaps because they have such wide impact globally. For *Moana*, the Disney studio created an Oceanic Story Trust to try to ensure cultural authenticity, while *Zootopia* attempts to avoid these issues by portraying a mammal world divided into predators and preys with nary a human in sight. As we move further into a twenty-first century that sees political leaders becoming more concerned about protecting national borders while the number of people who have been forcibly displaced worldwide reaches an all-time high, the representation of diverse cultures in texts for young people becomes even more important. The study of multicultural children's literature intersects with human rights and social justice discourses as more readers, authors, teachers, and critics advocate for the critical analysis of texts for young people as a way to understand and to shape the diverse world in which we live.

39

Nature

Peter Hollindale

The word *nature* derives from Latin *natura*, which in turn is rooted in the verb *nasci*, "to be born." It denotes the primal and original condition of all things, including human beings. In essence, nature can be seen as the default condition of planet earth if freed of human impact and of humans (essentially children) before socializing and "civilizing" influences are brought to bear on them.

Nature is a complex word with many meanings; the *OED* sets out three intertwined, indispensable definitions. First, *nature* is defined as "the creative and regulative physical power which is conceived of as operating in the material world and as the immediate cause of all its phenomena." This is nature as perceived by the Romantics in the eighteenth and nineteenth centuries and in modern times may be variously titled God, Mother Nature, Gaia, or evolution. Second, *nature* is "the material world, or its collective objects and phenomena, especially those with which man is most directly in contact; frequently the features and products of the earth itself, as contrasted with those of human civilization." This definition separates humanity and its artifacts from "wild" nature. Third, *nature* is "the inherent and innate disposition or character of a person (or animal)."

The contrast between *human nature* (which appears in the third definition) and *good-natured* highlights the word's ability to oscillate between the general (all humans) and the particular (smaller group of humans). When we talk of human nature, we commonly take it to cover all people and qualities such as instinctive desires that are innate and universal features of our species. However, when we say somebody is good natured, we are picking out an individual characteristic, not a universal one.

Each of us, we now know, has a unique as well as a common genetic inheritance. The good-natured characters of children's literature are often depicted as spirited, individualistic, even antiauthoritarian, as is Anne in L. M. Montgomery's *Anne of Green Gables* (1908). Such free-spirited behavior by good-natured children may be shown approvingly in the text but deemed subversive by the parent culture. Thus the antiauthoritarian behavior of Pippi Longstocking (Lindgren 1950), though well regarded in her native Scandinavia, was censored in postwar France, and the private policing exploits of Emil and his friends in Kästner's *Emil und die Detektive* (*Emil and the Detectives*; 1929) were banned in Nazi Germany. Good nature in action runs the gauntlet of prevailing cultural and social norms.

For centuries, the condition of the child at birth has been debated. Are children born in innocence or sin? Whatever the answer, this primary state of nature is then modified by nurture, or physical, intellectual, and moral upbringing. In Shakespeare's *The Tempest*, Prospero describes Caliban "as a born devil, on whose nature / Nurture can never stick." We are not far here from original sin, the idea that untutored humanity is innately savage, even evil. The critic Frank Kermode observes, "Caliban represents . . . nature without benefit of nurture" (1954, xxiv). The contrast between nature (as generic, inborn, animal being) and nurture (as education, moral guidance, civilizing influence) underpins children's literature in succeeding centuries. A hundred years after *The Tempest*, Isaac Watts wrote *Divine Songs Attempted in Easie Language for the Use of Children*. Watts was a comparatively humane inheritor of the Puritan

tradition but sturdily believed that wickedness was the primal condition of all untutored children, as in "Satan finds some mischief still / For idle hands to do" ([1715] 1789, 51).

The eighteenth century, which saw the birth of children's literature as we know it, also saw the flourishing of natural sciences and such revolutions in thinking, as in Rousseau's *Emile* (1762). Rousseau rejected the doctrine of original sin, believed in childhood innocence, and held that the first impulses of nature are always right. He disapproved of much reading prescribed for children's improvement but enthusiastically embraced Defoe's *Robinson Crusoe* (1719) as "the best treatise on an education according to nature" (Rousseau [1762] 1911, 147). Under Rousseau's influence, *Robinson Crusoe* was adopted into children's literature, and to it we owe the "Robinsonade," now a classic narrative tradition of children in wild places. An early example is Joachim Heinrich Campe's *Robinson der Jüngere* (1779). Hugh Cunningham notes that "the child-nature link was being formed, with enormous implications" (1995, 67) for the future of childhood. Meanwhile, around 1780, the boy William Wordsworth was at large in the English Lake District, experiencing adventures that became the locus classicus of Romantic childhood in *The Prelude* ([1805] 1997, [1850] 1979). Wordsworth came to perceive nature as a quasi-parental force of benign severity, educating mind and conscience, and praised "the means which Nature deigned to employ/Whether her fearless visitings, or those/That came with soft alarm . . . or she may use/Severer interventions."

By 1800, the world "could no longer be regarded as having been made for man alone, and the rigid barriers between humanity and other forms of life had been much weakened" (Thomas 1983, 301). The understanding of nonhuman nature was radically changed by the work of naturalist and explorer Alexander von Humboldt, who "gave us our concept of nature itself" (Wulf 2015, 8) by effectively founding the science of ecology and the concept of a world ecosystem. Von Humboldt, in his South American exploration (1799–1804), also first drew attention to the perils of deforestation and manmade climate change. It was against this background of new scientific understanding that a children's literature of children in the wild first grew.

In the twentieth century, these several concerns—original sin (the darkness of man's heart), the child as species and as individual, and the natural environment—came together in Golding's *Lord of the Flies* (1954), which, like *Robinson Crusoe*, is a children's book only by adoption and is itself a kind of catastrophic Robinsonade. It has been hugely influential on children's literature and the culture of childhood. Most of the marooned boys on their island revert to a primitive state of tribal savagery, but three retain various features of civilization (moral, rational, social or spiritual). Though individuals, the three characters taken together form what Maria Nikolajeva (2002) terms the "collective protagonist." Dependent as the boys are on wild nature for their survival, in a microcosm of human behavior, they end up by destroying it. Geneticist Steve Jones (2007) observes, "For Golding, man's basest instincts triumph in the end and life on an island colonised by children is destroyed by an inevitable struggle for existence. His view of human nature descends directly from *The Origin of Species* and the notion of universal strife."

A more positive echo of Darwinian thought is the story of successful adaptation and survival in the wild. At its extreme, this is the test undergone by the feral child, famously represented by Mowgli in Kipling's *The Jungle Book* (1894, 1895). There are also children who fall accidentally into solitary or group self-reliance in wild places, as in Scott O'Dell's *Island of the Blue Dolphins* (1960). Meg Rosoff's *How I Live Now* (2004) memorably

places two children dependent on foraging in her futuristic vision of political catastrophe. But there are also children who deliberately choose nature, the children of the classic Robinsonade, as in Jean Craighead George's *My Side of the Mountain* (1959). This attractive Robinsonade is distinguished for its demonstration that lone survival depends on the union of qualities conventionally separated by gender: the boy hero must be androgynous in his repertoire of skills.

Unlike Robinsonades, literatures rooted in extreme environments are characterized by their often conflicted relationships with the modern world. Markoosie's *Harpoon of the Hunter* (1970) is a case in point. Written in Inuktitut and self-translated into English, it evokes a former self-contained Inuit world where nature means weather as much as nonhuman fauna. Like the father in Jean George's story of an Inuit girl, *Julie of the Wolves* (1972), Markoosie himself lived a modern, compromised Inuit life as a pilot. A similar phenomenon in the Native American world is the work of Zitkala-Sa, who depicts a childhood culture rooted in nature but adulterated by colonial "improvements" (Suhr-Sytsma 2014). The story of Australian Aboriginals under colonial invasive pressures is now widely told by both Aboriginal and insightful non-Aboriginal writers, notably Anthony Hill in *The Burnt Stick* (1994). Inuit, Native American, and Australian Aboriginal writers all depict a history of children in cultures steeped in nature, both practically and spiritually, many of whom are transplanted or abducted to colonial institutions to be "civilized" in acts of cultural deracination and what Morgenstern (2015) has termed "demonization of the Native Other."

Children in nature now face two new risks, one present and domestic, one future and apocalyptic, both of which are reflected in the literature offered them. A prizewinning Arabic picture book, Walid Taher's *Al-Nuqtah al-Sawda* (The black dot; 2009), has been praised for viewing the natural environment as empowering for children: there are no adults, and "children act freely and independently of adult supervision and control. . . . Landscape provides a chance for fun, freedom and development—a depiction that also evokes the Western concept of 'the child in nature'" (Aisawi 2013, 34–35). Ironically, this happy development coincides with a major contraction of such freedoms in most Western societies. A range of environmental prohibitions, fear of litigation, and risk-averse adult concerns about harm and injury to unsupervised children are leading to "de-natured childhood" (Louv 2005, 26), our period's special version of the long-term "de-naturing of man" (Coveney 1967, 239). Children deprived of free play in nature are suffering what is termed "nature-deficit disorder" (Louv 2005, 99). Likewise in fiction, the novel of playful and safe apprenticeship to a life in nature, such as Arthur Ransome's *Swallows and Amazons* (1930), is giving way to fictions in which nature is hostile and dangers and risks are all too real, as in Ransome's *We Didn't Mean to Go to Sea* (1937).

We now have, and need, a flourishing dystopian literature that explores a second, vaster risk—that of damage to the human species and all others on our planetary spaceship as a consequence of human actions. As environmentalist Bill McKibben (1990) is one of many to point out, nature in the traditional sense (a biodiverse world independent of human beings) no longer exists because no life-forms or natural phenomena are now untouched by people. Of all the dystopian stories, Peter Dickinson's *Eva* (1988) is still one of the most powerful, with its vision of human overpopulation and the minimal survival of other life-forms. This and many other texts could equally stand with Kimberley Reynolds's comment on Rosoff's *How I Live Now*: "It remains to be seen whether Rosoff's readers will take up the challenge and avoid the frightening future she sees in prospect. . . . If they are to do so, however, they need more texts that warn them of the risks, problems and assorted environmental and political time bombs that have been set by previous generations" (2007, 154). Perhaps the youth-led global climate strikes of 2019 augur an activist awakening that will meet that challenge. As then fifteen-year-old Greta Thunberg said at the October 2018 Extinction Rebellion protest in London, "There are no gray areas when it comes to survival. Either we go on as a civilization or we don't. We have to change."

40

Nonsense
Michael Heyman and Kevin Shortsleeve

What is Nonsense? I know when you do not ask me.
—Edward Strachey

In his introduction to *The Chatto Book of Nonsense*, Hugh Haughton comments, "Nonsense is a bit of a problem" (1988, 2). Haughton is alluding to a set of semantic and literary "difficulties" that have surrounded *nonsense* since the term came into common usage in the seventeenth century, when the word was used mostly in its literal sense, meaning "that which makes no sense" or that which is "worthless" (*OED*). Over the next two hundred years, a new meaning emerged, referring to a particular literary mode or genre. The discussion of nonsense as a genre was pioneered by Elizabeth Sewell in her seminal *The Field of Nonsense* (1952), in which she works exclusively with the poems of Edward Lear and Lewis Carroll and posits that nonsense can be identified by a playful tension between sense and non-sense. Wim Tigges worked to further refine this definition in his *An Anatomy of Literary Nonsense* (1988). Critical discussions that broach the topic suggest subcategories such as "literary" nonsense and "folk" nonsense (Heyman 2007). Some attempt to describe a canon ostensibly composed of a sort of "pure" literary nonsense; in Tigges's (1988) forty-eight-page chapter "What Nonsense Is Not," nursery rhymes find themselves excluded from the canon, while Sewell (1952) drops certain poems by Lear

and Carroll that she finds too emotional. Meanwhile, Susan Stewart (1979), Tigges (1988), and Malgorzata Bien-Lietz (1998) have broken the discussion down to to formalistic devices such as topsy-turvyness, non sequiturs, neologisms, portmanteau words, puns, and impossibilia.

What today we classify as the genre of literary nonsense has an ancestral connection to medieval carnivalesque traditions examined in Mikhail Bakhtin's *Rabelais and His World*. Bakhtin describes a "grotesque" genre of "absurd compositions" (1984, 471) that revel in "linguistic freedom," illogical sequences, and the "inside out" (424). Over several hundred years, variant meanings of *grotesque* include "rugged," "unpolished," "distorted," "irregular," "fantastically extravagant," and "bizarre" (*OED*). In this same period, *grotesque* begins describing literary works considered quaint or immaterial, ludicrous or fantastically absurd, and by 1822, "very amusing." Reflecting these varied meanings, *grotesque* became the favored term for literary nonsense when it grew popular in Victorian England. In 1868, when Carroll was casting about for illustrators for *Through the Looking Glass*, W. S. Gilbert came to mind because, as Carroll wrote, "his power in grotesque is extraordinary" (quoted in Stedman 1996, 28). Emile Cammaerts's *The Poetry of Nonsense* (1925) uses the term *grotesque* almost interchangeably with the word *nonsense* to describe that which is rough, childlike, sketchy, or exaggerated.

Bakhtin's study suggests that in the eighteenth and nineteenth centuries, there was a splintering in the meaning of the term *grotesque*, one as an ascendant gothic vision that is horrifying or disgusting and the other as merely joyful and gay. Understandings of what we now label *nonsense* can be split along similar lines. Like *grotesque*, the term *nonsense* is associated with that which is unnatural, distorted, bizarre, ludicrous, or fantastically absurd, while simultaneously, *nonsense* is also understood as that which is amusing, quaint, and immaterial—a place for simple, joyful fun (Shortsleeve 2007, 20–21).

In the seventeenth century, as Noel Malcolm (1998) notes, there was a fashion for poems we retrospectively identify as "literary nonsense," such as John Taylor's "Sir Gregory Nonsense His Newes from No Place" (1622) or "Mercurius Nonsensicus" (1648). Yet the poets of the time were just as likely to use other terms to classify their works, such as John Hoskyns's "Cabalistical Verses" (1611) or Taylor's "Poem in the Utopian Tongue" (1630). Seventeenth-century anthologies of light verse would include some nonsense, yet the volumes were often labeled "drolleries" and made no distinction between nonsense and other humorous poems.

While nursery rhyme publishers of the eighteenth century such as John Newbery used *nonsense* to advertise their publications, the first *OED* quotation entry for the phrase *nonsense verses* occurs in 1799, from Richard Phillips's annual, *Public Characters*: "Although few *men* in England could equal him in writing *sense* prose, yet many *boys* might surpass him in writing *nonsense* verses." While *nonsense* here has made the leap to being attached to *verse*, it still denotes an inconsequential art form. The 1799 example also shifts the word from representing the sophisticated, adult parodic nonsense of the seventeenth century to a child's creation, a move that parallels the development of emerging conceptions of childhood. In this association with children, *nonsense* aligns itself with another troubled term, *innocence*.

John Morgenstern (2001) throws doubt on the popular notion that the emerging vision of the "innocent" child gave birth to the children's book industry in the eighteenth century. Instead, Morgenstern argues that the children's book industry gave rise to the idea of the innocent child. Newbery's success, then, as one who advertised books with "nonsense" in them,

recommended a semantic connection between *nonsense* (the content of the books) and *innocence* (the ideal state of the child reader; Shortsleeve 2007, 17). This connection has led to trouble in how nonsense literature is perceived and discussed. Just as we routinely underestimate the resilience, independence, rebelliousness, and sexuality of a supposedly innocent child, critics correspondingly underestimate the complex nature of nonsense literature (Shortsleeve 2007, 20). Lear biographer Vivian Noakes denies any provocative qualities to Edward Lear's nonsense and describes his works instead as a haven of "safety and imagination" (2001, xxvi). *Nonsense*, *imagination*, and *innocence* thus come tumbling together in a semantic muddle.

The history of this muddle now includes a number of distracting descriptors, such as *senseless*, *worthless*, *grotesque*, and *innocent*, all of which undermine a clear understanding of the genre. These unfortunate semantic connotations suggest that as a genre, *literary nonsense* is poorly named. (Nonsense literature, then, might better be described with an original portmanteau phrase, a phrase freed from the semantic shackles of its overly negative cousin-meanings. We would suggest *literwordsy absurdifusion*. Really.)

The most influential step in the word's evolution came when Lear featured *nonsense* prominently in his book titles: *A Book of Nonsense* (1846); *Nonsense Songs, Stories, Botany and Alphabets* (1871), *More Nonsense, Pictures, Rhymes, Botany, Etc.* (1872), and *Laughable Lyrics: A Fourth Book of Nonsense Poems, Songs, Botany, Music, Etc.* (1877). In the years between his first and his final volume, the descriptor shifted from *nonsense* to *nonsense rhymes* to *nonsense poems*, indicating its elevation from the lowest level of literary output, nonsense in its literal meaning, to the highest, poetry. Strachey noted this trend, proclaiming Lear "the creator of a new and important kind of that Nonsense for the honors of which the pen and the pencil contend" (1888, 357–58). Like his contemporary, Lewis Carroll, Lear *was* doing something new: reclaiming a sophisticated adult parodic literary nonsense in the style of John Taylor and combining it with folk nonsense from the now established children's tradition. The resulting hybrid produced what are routinely classified as classics of the genre, such as Carroll's "Jabberwocky" (1871) or Lear's "The Owl and the Pussycat" (1871).

The nineteenth-century public, hungry for nonsense but unable to articulate what exactly it was, became susceptible to misunderstandings. Starting in the 1860s, Lear's books sparked limerick contests (Baring-Gould and Hart-Davis 1969, 39), but the texts submitted were not the kind made famous by Lear; rather, they were modern limericks—stylized jokes complete with a witty punch line. However, it has since been established that the defining features of nonsense limericks are an absurd circularity and linguistic, graphic, and logical tension rather than wit and ingenuity of rhyme (Cammaerts 1925, 5–8; Tigges 1987, 124–26). To the uninitiated, or those who might take the *OED* to heart, there is a tendency to assume that fantasy, riddles, and light verse are nonsense. Yet by the widest definition of the genre, they are not. Editors, authors, and critics routinely misrepresent nonsense in so-called nonsense anthologies. Collections such as William Jay Smith's *Laughing Time: Collected Nonsense*, which includes the poem "Round or Square / Or tall or flat / People love / To wear a hat" (1990, 10), or Carolyn Wells's *A Nonsense Anthology* (1902), which includes Tennyson's "Minnie and Winnie," offer examples of nonsense being confused with other styles of poetry.

If we cast our net beyond England and America, nonsense emerges worldwide along two lines. One is colonial—that is, derivative of English Victorian nonsense, as evidenced by the English word *nonsense* used in foreign languages: in the Dutch, *nonsens*; French, *le nonsense*; German, *nonsensverse*; Polish, *nonsensu*; and Japanese, *nansensu*. The other is the homegrown, as evidenced by a myriad of native varieties. The collision between colonial and native nonsense is well represented in twentieth-century Indian authors, who assimilated aspects of Lear's and Carroll's works to create hybrid nonsense as a site of resistance to English colonialism. Sukumar Ray, perhaps the best-known Indian nonsense writer, gives us "Article Twenty-One" (Ray and Ray, 2007), a poem that is indebted to Carroll's style but aims its critique at an oppressive, absurd system where sneezing "before six is a crime," and the punishment is twenty-one snuff-induced sneezes. Importantly, native Indian nonsense predates the colonial period, as implied by Ray's suggestion that nonsense represents a heretofore unrecognized category within India's ancient aesthetic codification system (Heyman 2007). The spiritual significance of unreason in ancient Indian holy texts can be seen in Kabir, a fifteenth-century poet saint, whose "twilight verse" rejected linear discourse in the path to enlightenment. An explicit link between nonsense and spirituality—in addition to what Satyajit Ray sees as a more intense connection to the domestic and everyday, with its "drought, clay pots, rice, buffalo, rupees . . . and Indian village life" (quoted in Heyman 2007, xxxvii)—seems a particular trait of native Indian nonsense.

The Luo people of western Kenya express nonsense via intentionally humorous and lyrical personal introductions like *pakruok*: a concatenated name, such as "The-flour-is-the-beauty-of-the-house" (Odira 2010), that can include pieces of disconnected narrative or a loose portmanteau that pushes many words into one. The *pakruok* often contain other nonsense elements that utilize the performative nature of the "text," including exaggerated gestures, motions unclearly connected to or at odds with the words, and humorous, grotesque facial expressions. While the *pakruok* would never be called *nonsense* in the native language, the Kenyan and English traditions share certain nonsensical manipulations of language and logic.

Perhaps because *nonsense* resists translation, these international varieties are not well known in the English-speaking world, where there is a tradition that assumes nonsense is peculiar to English culture. As Cammaerts notes, "There is ample evidence to show that . . . nonsense is practically neglected in other countries" (1925, 79). If Cammaerts had looked more diligently, he would indeed have found ample evidence of nonsense literature in many other languages, such as French (Alfred Jarry) or German (Christian Morgenstern). What was once understood as a uniquely English tradition is, it turns out, a universal urge and pops up like varieties of wheat: a worldwide staple known locally under a thousand different names.

41

Nostalgia
Boel Westin

Nostalgia is related to feelings of loss and longing, memory and remembrance, pain and sadness. The desire to look back or return to something experienced or imagined is essential. Nostalgia is an amalgamation of two words from Greek, *nostos*, which means "returning home," and *algos*, "pain." Etymologically, it derives from postclassical Latin (*OED*). The word-concept *nostalgia* was first used by medical student Johannes Hofer in his *Dissertatio medica de Nostalgia, oder Heimwehe* (1688). This dissertation considered painful homesickness (*Heimwehe*) among Swiss soldiers (displaced by war) as a medical condition of such severity as to put sufferers at risk of serious illness. Hofer thus establishes nostalgia as a pathological discourse. Jean Starobinski, interpreting Hofer in the essay "The Idea of Nostalgia" (1966), states that nostalgia is linked by its roots to the trauma of deprivation and loss. Starobinski points to Kant and his observation in *Anthropologie in pragmatischer Hinsicht* (1798). In Starobinski's words, "what a person wishes to recover is not so much the actual *place* where he passed his childhood but his youth itself" (Hodgkin 2016, 115; Starobinski 1966, 94). Time, unlike space, cannot be returned to. Nostalgia becomes the reaction to that sad fact.

As such, nostalgia is part of medical history but even more the history of emotion. The changing view of nostalgia goes from an "occasional disease" to a "cultural aesthetic": it works as "a way of producing and consuming the past" (Austin 2007, 2). The meaning of *nostalgia* refers to both spatially and temporally based emotional activities: an acute "longing for familiar surroundings" or "homesickness," a sentimental "longing *for* or regretful memory of a period of the past, esp. one in an individual's own lifetime," or simply "something, which causes nostalgia for the past" (*OED*). In Susan Stewart's view, the nostalgic longs for longing: "This point of desire which the nostalgic seeks is in fact the absence that is the very generating mechanism of desire . . . the realization of re-union imagined by the nostalgic is a narrative utopia that works only by virtue of its partiality, its lack of fixity and closure: nostalgia is the desire for desire" ([1984] 1993, 23). This often-cited definition has been criticized by later scholars who argue that "the specific objects of nostalgia—lost or imagined homelands—represent efforts to articulate alternatives" (John Su, cited in Johanson 2016, 14). Childhood could be considered metaphorically as a lost homeland.

Nostalgia is a "sentiment of loss and displacement, but it is also a romance with one's own fantasy," Svetlana Boym declares in *The Future of Nostalgia* (2001, xiii). She distinguishes between a restorative kind of nostalgia and a reflective kind: the first "puts emphasis on *nostos* and proposes to rebuild the lost home and patch up the memory gaps," while the latter "dwells in *algia*, in longing and loss, the imperfect process of remembrance" (41). This is also a split between the individual and the collective, where restorative nostalgia evokes "national past and future," while reflective nostalgia is about "individual and cultural memory" (49). They may use the same triggers of memory and symbols, but the stories told are different.

Children's literature as a concept might itself be considered a subject of nostalgia, a place of fiction (imagination) where ideas or pictures of a past childhood are preserved and relived. The desire to return to a familiar place and the longing for home recurs in folktales, fairy tales, and Fénelon's classic, *Les Aventures de Télémaque* (*The Adventures of Telemachus*; 1699), in which Telemachus searches for his father, Ulysses. As Katherine Hodgkin says, childhood "is often seen as the natural object of nostalgic emotion" (2016, 116). In her critique of children's literature criticism, *The Case of Peter Pan, or The Impossibility of Children's Fiction* (1984), Jacqueline Rose claims that the story of Peter Pan always has been "assigned with the status of a truth (lost childhood, nostalgia or innocence)" (137). The child in in children's literature is, according to Rose, an adult fantasy.

The "golden age" of English children's literature—defined by classics like Carroll's *Alice's Adventures in Wonderland* (1865), Milne's *Winnie-the-Pooh* (1926), and Grahame's *The Wind in the Willows* (1908)—has been characterized as a "nostalgically configured period" coinciding with the rise of psychoanalysis. According to this view, nostalgia is "a function of the imagination, steeped in temporal and spatial longing, and the illusive object of that longing is childhood" (Hemmings 2007, 55). The memory of childhood might be seen as an expression of nostalgia, as in the epilogue of *Alice's Adventures in Wonderland*, where Alice's sister pictures Alice as a grown woman, keeping "the simple and loving heart of her childhood," passing on the story of Wonderland to her children (Carroll 1990, 127). The initial poem of the "golden afternoon" in the book also evokes the story of Alice as "childish," describing it in terms of a lost dreamland: "And with a gentle hand / Lay it where Childhood's dreams are twined / In Memory's mystic band" (8). As for *The Wind in the Willows*, the nostalgic power exists in "a combination of familiarity and permanence" (Hemmings 2007, 70). A. A. Milne's second book about Winnie-the-Pooh, *The House at Pooh Corner* (1928), ends the story about the boy and the bear with a picture of a place of fictional eternity, forever possible to relive or reread: "But wherever they go, and whatever happens to them on the way, that enchanted place on top if the Forest, a little boy and his Bear will always be playing" (1957, 314). This can be interpreted as an example of reflective nostalgia, a creation of a both individual and cultural memory in Boym's (2001) conceptual view. But it might at the same time reflect an idealized idea of childhood. Or as Robert Hemmings puts it, "The interiorized village to which the adult writer, and also the reader, regresses is not only the imaginative space but also the time of childhood" (2007, 55).

Modern nostalgia is more about loss than return. It has been explained as a "mourning for the impossibility of mythical return, for the loss of an enchanted world with clear borders and values" (Boym 2001, 8). The final novel about the Moomins by Finnish Swedish author Tove Jansson, *Sent i november* (*Moominvalley in November*; [1970] 2011), develops this sense of loss. Driven by memories and longings, a number of characters return to an empty valley, normally inhabited by the Moomin family and their friends. Their desire is to somehow evoke the past in the present, but the place they once knew or thought they knew turns out to be, if not different, then quite another thing than they experienced in their individual memories, dreams, or ideas. The process of facing the present and the future pervades feelings of nostalgia. A later example might be the young adult novel *How I Live Now* (2004) by Meg Rosoff, in which war shatters the young protagonists' ideas about home, nature, friendship, and love. The imperative to return is generally viewed as a nostalgic impulse, connected with home as a place where you get food and are nourished, mostly by a mother or a motherly figure. In Rosoff's novel, the young people are forced to nourish themselves. Another example is the characterization of Singaporean children's literature from the 1980s and onward as "a nostalgic recollection of past times and places" (Kong and Tay 1998, 141).

A new kind of critical reevaluation aims to question the reading of nostalgia as a "stable, backward-facing realm of irrecoverable fantasy" (Johanson 2016, 15; Schwyzer 2016; Hodgkin 2016). One question is whether people might have been nostalgic before the word was invented. In her essay "Childhood and Loss in Early Modern Life Writing" (2016), Katherine Hodgkin discusses childhood autobiographies from the seventeenth century, accounts of departures from home as the place of nourishment. The point is to understand nostalgia in a "broader sense to evoke a structure of emotional and memorial patterns; a desire to dwell on the past that is both painful and pleasurable" and "a sense of unfinished emotion" (117). One of her examples is the journal of Edward Barlow (1659–1703), a young man leaving home. When he looks back at his mother, who is asking him to stay with her hand reaching out for him, the decision is made: "Yet with all her persuasions she could not entreat me to stay" (quoted in Hodgkin 2016, 125). The picture of this scene (the journal is in both words and pictures) shows the son in one corner and the mother in front of their house with a clear gap between them. Barlow departs not just from home but from the mother and the "maternal sphere." Barlow's "connection," Hodgkin argues, "between food, home and maturity provides an oblique link to the Swiss soldiers diagnosed by Hofer, who suffered from the loss of maternal nourishment and familiar flavours" (126). But the young Barlow rejects the food of the motherland.

Nostalgia in relation to children's literature is mainly linked to stories of home and what Svetlana Boym calls "imagined homelands" in her distinction between restorative and reflective nostalgia (2001, 258). The imperative to return and the longing for home are fundamental, clearly linked to emotional history and change. Summarizing nostalgia's impact on children's literature, Robert Hemmings concludes with the desire for home:

"From Swiss soldiers to Victorian, Edwardian, and post–Great War adult writers, to postmodern adult readers who still attend to fetishized objects—'classics'—from a past itself constructed retrospectively and nostalgically as a 'golden age,' nostalgia embodies a yearning for home" (2007, 76). Yet as Kristine Johanson suggests, nostalgics' yearning directs affect both backward and forward: "Ultimately, nostalgia is Janus-faced: standing in the present, looking at the past and the future, the nostalgic can either flee from the future to shelter in the past, or see the idealised past as a starting point, a source of invigoration of that future" (2016, 14). Here, she picks up an argument of Susan Stewart's. Nostalgia is always like a future-past.

42

Performance
Robin Bernstein

The word *performance* is often traced to the twelfth-century Anglo-Norman and Middle French word *parfournir*, which means "to carry out," "to fulfill," "to accomplish," or "to execute" (*OED*; Turner [1982] 1992, 13). Later, in the sixteenth century, the word became associated with mimesis, or bodily imitation, mimicry, or repetition. Today, the word *performance* carries the legacy of these apparently contradictory meanings. Performance can refer, in the older sense, to performing an action, to completing an operation—that is, to making something, to causing something to exist. We invoke this meaning when we speak of "performing one's duties" or of a worker's "high performance." In the newer sense, however, performance can refer to theater, to acting. Performance scholar Richard Schechner (2013) has pithily described these distinct meanings as "making" and "faking" (Turner [1982] 1992, 93). Both these meanings—separately and together—have profound implications for the study of childhood.

To think about childhood through performance in the newer, theatrical sense is to find a rich array of potential sites of analysis—many of which are understudied. Most obviously, of course, are children on the professional stage. Individual child stars, or prodigies, have been popular for hundreds of years: stars such as Shirley Temple or Michael Jackson had precedents in Cordelia Howard, who originated the role of Little Eva in *Uncle Tom's Cabin* (1852); Kate and Ellen Bateman, who performed Shakespearian roles throughout the mid-nineteenth century; and "Blind Tom" Wiggins, an enslaved musical prodigy who played piano in the antebellum and postbellum US. Child choruses are also an enduring and widespread form of entertainment: to name but two examples, the Children of the Chapel (later Children of Blackfriars) was a chorus and later an acting troupe of boys who performed in the English royal court in the sixteenth and seventeenth centuries, and in the early twentieth century, a troupe of African American children, led by Belle Davis, toured the Austro-Hungarian Empire, Germany, Russia, and the Netherlands before settling in Paris (Brown 2008, 19–20). Child acting troupes are also common, as in the case of the US-based Marsh Troupe, which staged plays in venues across the American continent and as far away as Australia (Vey 2015). Some well-known plays such as *Really Rosie* and *Runaways* usually feature mostly or all-youth casts.

Amateur theater is a second realm in which children routinely perform. Schools, religious communities, and summer camps commonly stage plays. As Angela Sorby (2005) has demonstrated, students widely recited poetry in nineteenth-century American schools, and these recitations became a key site for the articulation of American identity; similarly, Anna Mae Duane (2010) has documented the importance of children's recitations of poetry and prose in the African Free School in New York City in the early nineteenth century. Educational drama has been a crucial site for many communities. French educator Mme de Genlis published the first of her influential four-volume *Théâtre à l'usage des jeunes personne* (Theater for young people; 1779–80) with the explicit purpose of allowing children to play out the possibilities of acting in an ethically responsible way. Popular in England, Genlis's drama directly influenced Maria Edgeworth's *Little Plays for Children* (1827). In the second half of the eighteenth century, German author Christian Felix Weiße published educational comedies for children, intended for performance and entertainment in family circles (Dettmar 2002). These plays were published in his widely read magazine *Der Kinderfreund* (*The Children's Friend*; 1775–82), which—thanks to its translations into French, English, Danish, Russian, and other languages—influenced the development of children's drama internationally. Katharine Capshaw Smith has shown how, during the New Negro movement, African Americans created pageants and history plays that "combated biased schoolbooks and prejudiced assumptions about black cultural achievement" and "helped shape the identity of local and national communities" (2004, xxiv). Children also regularly engage in home-based entertainments: they may perform scripted or self-authored puppet shows, skits, parlor dramas, magic shows, and more (Dawson 2005).

Theater for young audiences (commonly called TYA), which may or may not include child actors, is a vast and important aspect of world theater. The Association Internationale du Théâtre pour l'Enfance et la Jeunesse (ASSITEJ; International Association of Theatre for Children and Young People) networks youth-oriented theaters and practitioners in approximately one hundred nations, hosts a world conference and festival, publishes a magazine, and advocates internationally for children and the arts. In the US, the association Theatre for Young Audiences (www.tyausa.org) organizes individual and institutional practitioners, publishes a journal, and hosts a biennial festival and conference, among other activities. The robust global phenomenon of theater for young audiences receives less scholarly attention than it deserves. Books have been published on children's theater in countries ranging from Austria to Yemen and across regions from North and South America to Europe, to Africa, to Asia, and to the Middle East; however, many of these books are decades old, out of print, and inaccessible. As Marah Gubar argues in the April 2012 special issue of *Lion and the Unicorn*, the field of children's literature is ripe for greater engagement with children's theater.

The older set of meanings of *performance*—"to make," "to execute," "to bring forward"—also opens a vast field for analyzing childhood. Judith Butler (1988) famously argues that gender is made real through repetitions of stylized acts that shape the body over time. We sit, walk, or talk in ways that are marked as masculine or feminine, and as we repeat these actions over time, they come to feel natural and even physically affect our musculature; thus our repeated acts—our performances—make gender on our bodies. Age, too, can be understood to be made real through performance. This view foregrounds the fact that human bodies have objectively observable or measurable qualities that include genitals and number of years lived, but the *meanings* attached to these features are culturally produced—and much of this cultural production occurs through bodily performance.

Among the many meanings that have historically attached to chronological age, innocence is one of the most tenacious. In *Racial Innocence: Performing American Childhood from Slavery to Civil Rights*, I argue that for the past two centuries, Western cultures have heavily associated childhood with innocence. As a result, displays of innocence can become necessary if a juvenile human is to be recognized—and protected by the state—as a child. This "childhood innocence," however, has been persistently raced white, which has caused children of color often to be excluded from innocence and even from the category of childhood (Bernstein 2011b). A recent psychological study shows that adults tend to perceive black boys to be 4.53 years older and Latino boys to be 2.19 years older, on average, than they are and that black children are perceived as "significantly less innocent than other children at every age group, beginning at the age of 10" (Goff et al. 2014, 531, 532, 529). Another study finds that adults are likely to view black girls as "less innocent and more adult-like than their white peers" and "suggest[s] that the perception of Black girls as less innocent may contribute to harsher punishment by educators and school resource officers" (Epstein, Blake, and González 2017, 1). In other words, if a culture associates innocence and childhood with whiteness, it becomes difficult for the everyday performances of children of color to be read as innocent. When children of color engage in normal childhood behaviors, such as throwing tantrums or talking back, adults may interpret those actions as evidence not of childishness but instead of adultlike, and even criminal, threats.

One area of future research—play—has special potential to integrate the fields of childhood studies and performance studies. Play is a major subject of interest in performance studies: the topic occupies a full chapter in Richard Schechner's *Performance Studies: An Introduction* (2013) and a five-essay section in Henry Bial's *The Performance Studies Reader* (2007). Some scholars even consider play to be "the heart of performance" because "performance may be defined as ritualized behavior conditioned/permeated by play" (Schechner 2013, 89). Performance scholars have investigated play in games with rules (such as sports or board games), in acts of pretending on stage and in everyday life ("playing a role"), and as a mode of social communication ("playing the dozens"). These scholars of course acknowledge the importance of children to the subject of play, but most focus their research on adult players. Only a few scholars have delved deeply into the relationship among play, childhood, and performance. Kyra Gaunt (2006) has written a superb study of performance-based games, such as double Dutch and hand-clapping games, that black girls have played over the past two hundred years; Gaunt's work provided the foundation for Irene

Chagall's equally excellent film, *Let's Get the Rhythm: The Life and Times of Miss Mary Mack* (2014), which traces the global history of girls' hand-clapping games. In *Racial Innocence*, I argue that children's representational play with racialized dolls constitutes an important factor in US racial formation since the nineteenth century (Bernstein 2011b). Much work remains to be done, however. The deliberate union of performance studies and childhood studies provides a powerful new basis for the analysis of play, from playing house or playing doctor, to the material culture of toys, to the built environments in which children and youth play. Even more significantly, however, play, as a topic, has the potential to draw childhood studies and performance studies ever closer together, demonstrating the necessity of each to the other and harnessing the strengths of both.

43

Picture Book

William Moebius

No keyword in children's literature could be quite as fluid in its application as the one-word *picturebook* or the two-word *picture book*. The cultural medium to which this locution refers is itself quite malleable and can be stretched to include nonprint pictorial media for children or adults on the internet, picture-book "format" or "a type of visual encyclopedia," and humorous simulacra for adults such as Adam Mansbach's *Go the Fuck to Sleep* (2011). Or it can simply be a book with pictures in it, as Henry James in 1900 called his illustrated travel book *A Little Tour in France* (1883–84) a "picture-book," a hyphenated form recognized by the *OED* and defined as "a book consisting wholly or partly of pictures, esp. for children." Barbara Bader's definition of the picture book in 1976 still stands as comprehensive, making room for the child reader's experience while acknowledging the book's physicality ("an item of manufacture") and exchange ("a commercial product") and historic value ("a social, cultural, historical document" [1976, 1]).

Bunching together the words *picture* and *book*, after *Bilderbuch*, some academic specialists (e.g., Bader 1976; Nikolajeva and Scott 2000; Moebius 1986) have attempted to zero in on a particular configuration or historical modality of books for children in which pictures and words together are treated as semiautonomous and mutually attractive chains of meaning rather than as fixed images serving as a supplement to meanings fixed in words. This particular configuration emerges with the advent of cinema and the comic book, and may also have ties with theater, opera, vaudeville, and dance. While this working hypothesis has gained adherents, those who retain the separation of *picture* and *book* in a collocation (hyphenated or not)—still recognized by the *OED* and print media such as the *New York Times* and the *New Yorker* as well as critics like David Lewis (2001) and a host of librarians—may well have the history of the book itself in mind. One reason to keep the two words separate is to retain traces of that history of the "book" (at least in Europe) as one that, while favoring the written word, seems to foster images in the margins, at the incipits of verses, and intermingled with text. This practice diversifies the reader's experience as a stimulus and call to reading and enhances the reader's memory, as has been noted by philosopher Paul Ricoeur (2004) and by medievalists such as Carruthers and Ziolkowski (2002).

What, as part of print media, is to be called a *picture book* or *picturebook* depends very much on a particular reader's memories, expectations, and affinities; an artist/writer's intentions and historical moment; the marketing strategies of book editors and publishers; or the trade or academic connections of book critics, librarians, or children's literature specialists. As a keyword, *picture book* is a contested term and has gone from being an artifact of childhood (evoked by the French locution *album de jeunesse*, as something of a memory book long out of print) to become a staple of print culture, mass marketing, and official scrutiny—a sustainable commodity ratified by national media and local teachers and librarians as well as parents. In this respect, the picture book becomes malleable in a different way. If it is Helen Bannerman's *The Story of Little Black Sambo* (1899), Jean de Brunhoff's *The Story of Babar* (1931), H. A. and Margret Rey's *Curious George* (1941), or Lesléa Newman's *Heather Has Two Mommies* (1989), if its stereotypes

and caricatures are perceived to cast a shadow on a particular population or demographic, it may cease to own its place in the world of the picture book and become an instant cultural artifact available only to historians and specialists in children's culture. Though comics have influenced picture books (notably Maurice Sendak's *In the Night Kitchen* [1970], Raymond Briggs's *The Snowman* [1978], and Régis Faller's Polo books [2002–]), the comic book until the early 2000s was deemed to be in a register unworthy of the American Library Association or the professional organizations of educators and critics. It was, as McCloud (1993) once pictured it, confined to the lower regions, while the picture book hovered on the wings of cherubs.

Such medieval theodicy aside, the picture book may be seen as a descendant of the European propaganda wars that paradoxically attached the Counter-Reformation spirit of the Baroque, as French critic Jean Perrot (1991) has documented so well, and its pictorial turn to the ardent advocacies of literacy that followed the spirit of the Reformation, notably in the compendious proto children's picture book of Johann Amos Comenius, *Orbis Sensualium Pictus* (1657). The hieroglyphic turn of the pre-seventeenth-century alchemy book, or grimoire (cognate with *grammar*), may also anticipate the rebus and alphabet books for children of later centuries. From the middle of the nineteenth century in Europe, visual artists made drawings or paintings that were used as illustrations in picture books—for instance, painter Lorenz Frölich's illustrations to *La journée de Mll Lili* (Miss Lili's day; 1862). No matter where it has emerged and whether in the service of nation, culture, or religion, the picture book as a medium for children has tended also to be identified with public decency and right thinking, even if the message, as in a Maurice Sendak book, seemed to be subversive. But in France and Belgium, what in the US would be called a kind of comics has enjoyed no such stigma; whether as *Bécassine*, *Astérix*, *Suske en Wuske*, *Tintin*, or *Lucky Luc*, the *bande dessinée* has shared respectability in the public sphere since the 1900s with what in anglophone countries is called the picture book.

There are two prevailing views in the critical literature of what this experience means. On the one hand, it is seen as one of "the drama of the turning of the page," as Barbara Bader (1976) says, and thus conducive to notions of theatricality, dynamism, performance, presentational process, staging, miniaturism, ritual, choreography, carnival, and the allure of advertising, in which the play of the body in motion is key. Such a view may also be found in Moebius (2020), Reinbert Tabbert (1999), Nikolajeva and Scott (2000), Renaud (2007), and Van der Linden (2000). On the other hand, some readers and producers—led by Jane Doonan (1993), Molly Bang (1991), and paradoxically, Quentin Blake (1995)— see the picture book as a site for "absorption." For this school of thought, the turning of the page is not as urgent as the lingering on the single image on each page, plumbing its depths, understanding its multiple dimensions and messages, and interrogating the feelings of its characters. While one school seems to favor the exciting possibilities of montage, the jump cut, the close-up, and the panorama, the other favors a respect for color, shape, texture, and artistic medium as sufficient rewards for the picture *beholder*, a word Doonan (1993) chooses over *reader*. Certain picture books—those of Allen Say, Mitsumasa Ano, Jane Birkert, and Molly Bang herself—would appear to meet the absorption/ contemplation test. Recent picture books by Quentin Blake highlight the significance of the traditional tableau or easel art as something worth pondering. Other picture books such as those of Dr. Seuss, William Steig, Posey Simmonds, and Tomie dePaola lend themselves to a comedic response for which turning the page is an indispensable part of the picture book's success. It is not necessary to choose sides in this case (the paradigm for which may be found in art historian Michael Fried's *Absorption and Theatricality: Painting and Beholder in the Age of Diderot* [1980]), but one should take the picture book's aesthetic as a guide to its own best reading and acknowledge the tension described by Lawrence R. Sipe (1998): "There is thus a tension between our impulse to gaze at the pictures—to forget about time in creating an 'atemporal structure'—and to not interrupt the temporal narrative flow. The verbal text drives us to read on in a linear way, where the illustrations seduce us into stopping to look" (101). As a subtext in this contest, the rivalry of the museum school and the commercial art academy plays itself out.

Picture books do not arise ex nihilo out of a picture-book generator; they draw on thousands of years of human visual representation, filtered through the creative facilities of the adult imagination of a picture-book maker—or makers. In picture-book discourse, authorship is often a collaboration between word maker and image maker. In such a collaboration, how does one assign credit? In questions of authorship of Broadway show tunes, it is usually the composer (George, not Ira, Gershwin; Hoagy Carmichael, not Sydney Arodin) who earns the credit. Until recently, the author of the verbal text was deemed to hold chief responsibility for the picture book, while the image maker would be viewed as secondary.

Another complex issue related to picture-book discourse derives from the presumption of adult authorship and the recognition that the picture-book experience is "constructed," the result of multiple acts of representation that cannot be credited to the mind of a child. The suggestion of cross-writing is an inevitable consequence, especially since adults usually judge which books get published, reviewed, or bought. However "constructed," a picture book in circulation for more than one generation may also come to be revered as a site of memory despite invidious stereotypes, power relations, or questionable representations of violence (e.g., Wilhelm Busch's *Max und Moritz* [1865]).

An abiding faith in linearity in the guise of sequential narrative may lead some critics of the picture book to assume that a picture book, in order to mobilize the reader, must adhere to a narrative logic and that therefore the picture book is subject to linear models of narrativity. However, a given picture book may be beholden not to any narrative logic but rather to processes associated with poetry, rhetoric, and choreography—processes such repetition, alternation, augmentation, and diminution. As Nathalie op de Beeck (2010) suggests, the picture book is a hybrid, borrowing from many media and forms: "It has the relative shape and feel of a book, the images and oversize words of an advertisement, editorial cartoon, or store catalog, and the iconography of nursery songs and stories" (10–11). Perhaps for this reason, it is not uncommon in the picture book world to bump up against the non sequitur, the "good night nothing" of Clement Hurd and Margaret Wise Brown's *Goodnight Moon* (1947), or the provocative juxtapositions of Chris Van Allsburg's *The Mysteries of Harris Burdick* (1984). The critical question here is whether such representational gambits mimic child behavior and child thought for adult amusement (the child as ignorant savage) or engage in and address the cognitive uncertainties of the child as a thoughtful future survivor of childhood.

Critical vocabularies for the picture-book experience are now fairly well established, but some debate remains in respect to the application of critical analogies to other practices, whether hermeneutics, music, or translation. While some critics (Nikolajeva and Scott 2000; Moebius 2020) find these critical analogies useful and edifying, some, like Lewis (2001), find them anathema. Is a picture in a picture book an "interpretation," or an illustration, or a silencing of a few words? Is the interplay of pictures and words a kind of "counterpoint" (Nikolajeva and Scott 2000) or is it best described as a kind of "ecology" (Lewis 2001)? What are the roles of culturally specific images and verbal formulations in the translation of the picture book? The epistemology of the picture book is still being written, but it is clear that the verbal text alone will not suffice, and the term *iconotext* (Hallberg 1982; Nikolajeva and Scott 2000) may eventually take its place in common parlance.

The picture book may be best viewed as an experiment for the child and even for an adult student of literature. Picture books such as those of Arnold Lobel or Peter Catalanotto may serve as testing grounds for thought about the world. The uses of the picture book—be they psychotherapeutic, sedative, role modeling (gender), mathematical skill building, or memory building for geography, cultural heritage, or history—are, to echo Barbara Bader (1976), limitless.

44

Play

Stine Liv Johansen

The purpose of play is play. Play might have positive side effects, such as physical activity, general well-being, creativity, or even some sort of formal or informal learning. But while you play, you do so with the purpose of playing. Play is related to aspects of our being, which adults may often prefer to understate or perhaps even hide. In a time when our efforts are measured by utility, tensions arise around children's play, since play has no measurable outcome. Still, play continuously pops up in the lives of children and adults, crosscutting domains like media, literature, and education regardless of political and pedagogical paradigms.

The term *play* describes activities that are free of external purpose (*OED*). *Play* is autotelic, carrying its purpose in itself. Definitions of *play* emphasize its relation to bodily movements: play has to do with operations, with doings, and with practice, such as jumps and dance. The term also refers to stage play—and as such, to performance—and is in several ways related to the term *game* (in Danish: *leg* [play] and *spil* [game]). Attempts to make precise distinctions between the two have puzzled scholars for centuries, pointing to one of play's many ambiguities (Sutton-Smith 1997).

Play balances tensions between purpose and purposelessness, meaning and meaninglessness, rules and transgression, winning and playing for the sake of the play, and rationality and absurdity. We are only to our fullest extent human when we are playing, as Friedrich Schiller ([1793] 2016) wrote, presenting one of the most famous statements on play ever made. Johan Huizinga considered play as the origin and foundation of human cultural history in his classic book *Homo Ludens* ([1938] 1971). When play and its forms and rules are no longer considered important, culture deteriorates, Huizinga writes, continuing Schiller's line of thought and locating play at the center of our humanity. Huizinga also encapsulates the understanding of play as taking place besides, or even outside, daily life—in a "magic circle" or as an intermezzo between other activities. Recent studies of play in relation to digital culture (Frissen et al. 2012) question this, pointing to the ways in which digital technologies blur the separation of play from other parts of life, being always accessible and offering opportunities for play. Similar points can be made regarding the relation between literature and play, whereas literature may function as a way for the player to become playful and to immerse him- or herself in playful moods (Karoff 2013). Then and now, definitions of play always seem difficult to make, or as Sutton-Smith (1997) puts it, play is ambiguous.

Play is related to the carnivalesque and is associated with the silly, the frivolous, and the transgression of what is normally considered well behaved and acceptable. When playing, people have the opportunity to imagine a world that is different from the everyday. It is suddenly possible to turn things on their heads, to sneer at good taste and proper behavior, and to flirt with violence, death, and sexuality (Sicart 2014). What might to an outsider seem out of order may seem perfectly meaningful for those who are in play. When I was a child in the 1970s, the prime minister of Denmark exposed a rather unusual haircut—he was bald on the top and the back of his head but had small tufts of hair above both ears. When I was dressing or undressing, I sometimes put my panties on my head so that my hair would stick out of the two holes for each leg and imagined that I was the prime minister (whom I, by the way, considered a fine and kind man, looking a little like my grandfather).

A proper analysis of this behavior, which must have had a certain significance, since I still remember it almost forty years later, might focus on the satirical aspects—making fun of a politician and doing so using an artifact that normally has absolutely no business on top of a little girl's head. In the specific situation, however, it made perfect sense. As such, this incident points to some very important aspects of what play is and why it is so important for us. When you play, you take what is at hand, and you turn it into a situated meaningful expression, regardless of the original purpose of the things, tools, texts, and materialities you use. You can "play anything," as Bogost (2016) explains in his book of this title. Being good at play is about being able to immerse yourself in your surroundings and the possibilities they provide.

Mouritsen (2003) puts significant emphasis on these aspects of children's lives as well as on their use and production of texts. His focus on the nuances, rhythm, and structures of children's play specifically emphasizes how these are influenced and inspired by the texts that they use. Through empirically based analysis, he points to the connections between literary traditions and children's own verbal and bodily performances. Mouritsen specifically underlines the significance of frivolous play—the ways in which play and playfulness can transgress everyday mundanity and as such function as a "free" space where different rules apply. Similar connections between the aesthetic dimensions of children's play and poetry is made by Thomas (2007) in his studies of "playground poetry," focusing on the significance of nonsense in written and verbal texts in literature as well as in children's play.

Play is a matter of mastering play practices but not (necessarily) about winning. When you practice play,

you do so with the purpose of becoming good at it so that you can play more and in more advanced ways. You don't have to wait for mastering to occur before you can act and perform in play, though—mastery is achieved through practice. Whether or not you step on the lines between the tiles, you still play "don't step on the lines between the tiles." Actually, play is particularly fun when you don't succeed and when things turn out to be different than expected. Mastering play can be exactly about overruling the intentions of a computer game or reading a literary text in a silly, maybe even frivolous, way. Such play requires literacies beyond what is needed to read and understand the text. Texts may provide an inspiration for play, which readers, viewers, and listeners can perform through practices of interpretive reproduction (Corsaro 2017).

Understanding playfulness requires an in-depth understanding of play as a practice. The medium—a book, a movie, or a YouTube channel—does not disclose whether its content will be subject to playful practices. Whether the tool used to play with is digital or analog (Johansen 2018), shaped as a book or a plush toy (Bernstein 2013), does not in itself determine what kind of play will happen. Play depends on the user (reader, listener, viewer) and the social settings in which he or she acts. And it depends on the affordances of the play tool—whether this is a book, a toy, or a combination of different artifacts—within an overall narrative framework. Through different materialities, which can be configured in different combinations, literature and play can be seen as related and intertwined. Not only has literature always functioned as an inspiration for children's role-play, but children's literature and toy industries (or, more broadly, material culture) have been mutually dependent, as Bernstein (2013) demonstrates. A thorough understanding of children's play in relation to adult-made commodities, whether these are books or toys, should encapsulate what Bernstein points to as main characteristics: "Children's play is simultaneously compliant and unruly. It is not simplistically resistant; rather, it is creative, symptomatic, anarchic, ritualistic, reiterative, and most of all, culturally productive. Children receive mass-produced material culture, but they adapt it: they chop hair off dolls, apply stickers to toy trucks, endow plastic blocks with names and personalities. They play in ways that are socially sanctioned and they play otherwise" (2013, 460)

Why is play important, then? Why should adults take play more seriously and give more room for play—with or without playful texts—in different institutional settings? Playful people are better at adjusting to a society where fundamental norms and traditional regulations have undergone severe changes. First of all, because play engages people in relations with one another, it builds networks and makes people take positive advantages of one another's ideas, skills, and competencies. Second, being playful makes you think about how things might be done differently. It has a close connection to creativity, innovation, and critical mind-sets. But third, and perhaps most importantly, being playful makes you able to laugh at it all—to understand the absurdity as well as the beauty of the mundane and to transform this into a sense of meaningfulness. Play may be ambiguous, but it is nevertheless part of what makes us human.

45

Poetry
JonArno Lawson

In 1984, African American poet Audre Lorde described poetry as "the quality of the light within which we predicate our hopes and dreams toward survival and change . . . the way we help give name to the nameless so it can be thought" ([1984] 2007, 37). Lorde's twentieth-century version of poets giving "name to the nameless" reverberates with exactly what poets from classical times onward have tried to express about their craft. The Ancient Greek word *poesis*, from which our modern word *poetry* is derived, means "the activity in which a person brings something into being that did not exist before" (Polkinghome 2004, 115). Variations on *poesis* survive in modern Spanish as *poesia*, in French as *poesie*, and in Danish, Norwegian, and Swedish as *poesi*. In Old English, however, the words for *poetry—sangcraeft* (art of the song) and *léoðweorc* (work of the lay)—emphasized the musicality of verse. The concepts of both music and naming the nameless are central to the *OED*'s definition of poetry as "the expression or embodiment of beautiful or elevated thought, imagination, or feeling, in language adapted to stir the imagination and emotions . . . such language containing a rhythmical element and having usually a metrical form." The music of verse stands at the beginning of poetry for children.

In most—maybe all—cultures, infants are introduced to less prosaic forms and uses of language through song, particularly lullabies and, in many cases, nursery verse and dandling rhymes. Their exposure to verse quickly grows exponentially into playground rhymes, television theme songs, songs from musicals, sports chants, pop music, and hymns and prayers. What constitutes children's poetry specifically is harder to define, partly because the genre has grown out of changing constructions of childhood and variations in cultural norms. Both a lullaby sung by an adult to an infant and a bawdy playground rhyme addressed by an eleven-year-old to his peers are categorized as children's poetry. Though there is a strong taboo against adults speaking to children using smutty or suggestive language, children, in their playground poetry, speak to one another in this way. It is tempting to finger the breeching of taboos—as in "Miss Susie Had a Steamboat"—as a defining feature of children's poetry because that kind of verse is often categorized as childish. Western cultures, as David Pendlebury points out in his introduction to the works of the twelfth-century Persian poet Sanai, tend to categorize "the fascination of secret codes, rhyming, punning, spoonerisms, etc." (1974, 62) as inherently childish and immature. But that is not the case in Eastern cultures, as he explains in his discussion on Sanai. The sixth-century BCE Hebrew Bible, with its use of wordplay (puns, acrostics, and alliteration) and gematria (alphanumeric codes) provides a parallel example.

Given the impossibility of identifying universally distinctive features of children's verse, a look at the ways in which shared national and linguistic characteristics function provides some defining insights. Though Canadian children know poems (or songs) by Dennis Lee, Pakistani children know those by Allama Iqbal, and children in the Philippines know those by Felipe Padilla de León, but not one of them is likely to be recognized outside his own country. In fact, it is very unusual for a children's poet or for any of his, her, or their books of poetry to be known outside of the country of origin. Dr. Seuss is an exception, being well known in most of the English-speaking world. In contrast, Michael Rosen is virtually unknown outside the UK. Halfdan Rasmussen is a children's poetry hero only in Denmark, as is Inger Hagerup in Norway and Lennart Hellsing in Sweden. On the other hand, there are notable examples of sung poems that have spread to countries sharing a language, but the authors of these sung poems are usually either unknown or known only to scholars: "Twinkle Twinkle Little Star" is known and sung all over the English-speaking world, "Los Pollitos dicen" throughout the Spanish-speaking world, and "Chiku Chiku Chacha / Chichu Chichu Chacha" all over the Hindi- and Urdu-speaking worlds. "Lún chē pǎo dé kuài" is sung by Mandarin speakers regardless of where they live.

In the end, it may be the musicality of the linguistic structures that determines how children's poetry becomes geographically fixed. Vocabulary, accent, and sentence melody are easily lost in translation partly because those features are internalized so early: newborn babies even cry in a way that mirrors the language or "accent" of their mothers, as Charles Fernyhough explains in *The Baby in the Mirror* (2008). The ever-evolving nature of how languages are spoken stands as one reason why there are few long-term survivals, even of lullabies, as time passes (rarely more than a few hundred years). But there are cultural reasons too that are related to changing constructions of children.

In the English tradition, the rationale for shifting fashions in children's poetry is reflected in its history. It does not become a distinct genre until the late seventeenth century, and when it does, it is in the instructive mode primarily geared to religious indoctrination, as in John Bunyan's *Country Rhimes for Children* (1686) or Isaac Watts's *Divine Songs* (1715). The first books of lilting original secular verse begin in the early nineteenth century. Ann and Jane Taylor's *Rhymes for the Nursery* (1806) is an early example, and Christina Rossetti's *Sing-Song* (1872) is a later one. Robert Louis Stevenson, in *A Child's*

Garden of Verses (1885), is credited with introducing the voice of the speaking (singing) child into the genre, a technique later adapted by A. A. Milne in *When We Were Very Young* (1924). And it is only in the late nineteenth century that nonsense verse for children comes into vogue, especially in the works of Edward Lear and Lewis Carroll, who exploit, as Michael Heyman (2007) writes, the "sheer joy in the musicality of language, its sound and rhythm" (xxvii). Discovering and/or capturing compelling sounds and rhythms in linguistic form is no small part of naming otherwise nameless energy and transferring it in ways both physical and cerebral.

The dominant poetry movements of the last hundred years in English have sometimes, perhaps inadvertently, driven a wedge between deadly serious, often obscure cerebral poetry and poetry that is more accessible and humorous. These movements have emphasized divides not only between poetry for children and for adults but within children's poetry itself—between verse that is more literary, such as Robert Graves's *The Penny Fiddle* (1960), and verse that is intended to be more playground oriented, as Shel Silverstein's *Where the Sidewalk Ends* (1974) or Jack Prelutsky's *New Kid on the Block* (1984). Poets writing for children in the twenty-first century have added distinctive features to the genre. The rise of the "verse novel" is an example of a genre that sometimes works (in the tradition of epic poems), as in Jacqueline Woodson's *Brown Girl Dreaming* (2014), but all too often slips into an excuse to leave a lot of white space on a page. There is also a new interest in embracing non-English languages and cultures into children's poetry, with the strongest input coming from African diasporic traditions. Poets such as Benjamin Zephaniah in the UK and Marilyn Nelson in the US have expanded the register beyond the middle-class, white, and predominantly male and conservative face of children's verse.

The renewal of poetry, whether for adults or for children, always takes place through spoken (and sung) language—from the repetitions and imitations that allow us to consolidate what we know to the explorations and innovations (sometimes fully conscious, sometimes resulting from slips of the tongue) that allow us to explore what we don't yet know, what hasn't yet been named. Issues of authorship and authenticity frequently become irrelevant in the fluid world of poetry and songs written for (and sometimes by) children, as the best thoughts most enjoyably said simply enter the oral tradition, existing and transforming there anonymously—a shape-shifting gift from humanity to itself.

46

Postcolonial
Clare Bradford

The word *postcolonial* refers to (1) a period or state following (i.e., "post") colonialism and (2) the effects of colonization on cultures, peoples, places, and textuality. The terms most often associated with *postcolonial* are *imperialism*, denoting the formation of an empire, and *colonialism*, which refers to the establishment and control of colonies by an imperial power. The first usage of *postcolonial* (or *post-colonial*) identified in the *OED* occurs in 1883 in the *Century Illustrated Monthly Magazine*, where it is defined as "occurring or existing after the end of colonial rule." This association of the word with the practice of periodization is sustained well into the twentieth century; for instance, the *OED* cites this quotation from Gavin Black's *The Golden Cockatrice* in 1975: "If there's one thing worse than rampant colonialism . . . it's post-colonial dictatorship." By the late 1970s, literary critics used *postcolonial* to refer to the effects of colonization and to reading strategies capable of interrogating the (often naturalized) manifestations of colonial discourse in texts of all kinds and times. Although Edward Said did not use the term *postcolonial* in *Orientalism* (1978), his characterization of Orientalism as the discourse that constructed the Orient for Europeans afforded a model for the analysis of relations between colonizers and their colonized others (Dirks 2005).

In *The Empire Writes Back* (1989) Ashcroft, Griffiths, and Tiffin use the term *post-colonial* to "cover all the culture affected by the imperial process from the moment of colonization to the present day" (2), and this usage is generally accepted within postcolonial theory and postcolonial literary studies. While all periods of history and all continents have been marked by imperialism, it is also the case that "different empires have historically produced different imperialisms" (Huggan 2013, 28). Postcolonial studies seeks to understand and interpret these past imperialisms and their consequences and ramifications in the present. Emer O'Sullivan notes in *Comparative Children's Literature* (2005) that postcolonialism offers strategies capable of informing comparative studies of literature as well as investigations of national literatures. O'Sullivan uses the examples of African and Irish children's texts to argue that the histories, economies, and cultures of these nations have produced distinctive postcolonial literatures that must be understood in their own terms. Critics are divided on whether the US is a postcolonial society. Elleke Boehmer (1995) argues that the US is not postcolonial because it gained independence long before other former British colonies, and its literature developed along a different national trajectory. However, other scholars maintain that the doctrine of American exceptionalism merely covers the imperial and colonial history that shaped the national identity of the US and (arguably) provided the preconditions for its neocolonial enterprises in modern times (Janiewski 1995; Hulme 1995; Hage 2003).

In contemporary nations where Indigenous peoples experienced the traumatic events of colonization, their descendants commonly experience the lasting consequences of colonization through material effects such as poverty, loss of territory, and injustice (Logan 1999; Lucashenko 2000; MacCann 2001). While it is never safe to generalize across all postcolonial societies, many of these societies manifest a sense of unease about their nations' origins, often visible in children's texts that address histories of colonization and questions of individual and national identities (Bradford 2001, 2007). Thus Svein Slettan's (2013) analysis of Norwegian young adult books of the 1930s points to the ambivalence that marks representations of the Sami people who lived in northern Scandinavia at this time and who were subjected to forced assimilation, deprived of their language and culture.

Publishing for children in Europe and the New World developed rapidly during the nineteenth and early twentieth centuries, just as European imperialism was at its peak. It is thus inevitable that children's texts of this time engaged with some of the key concepts and ideologies that informed colonialism. Chief among these were a belief in the superiority of European culture, a high regard for "progress" (especially in industrial and economic terms), and a conviction that Indigenous peoples did not deserve territory because they failed to use it so as to generate wealth (Seed 2001). Authors such as G. A. Henty, Frederick Marryat, and W. H. G. Kingston produced stories of empire featuring boy heroes; school stories beginning with Thomas Hughes's *Tom Brown's Schooldays* (1857) were directed toward boys who would grow into imperial men; Daniel Defoe's *Robinson Crusoe* (1719) spawned scores of Robinsonades, narratives in which young adventurers both engage in colonial enterprises and domesticate the New World by reproducing British, middle-class homes in the midst of unhomely territories (O'Malley 2008). If *postcolonial* refers to all culture from the moment of first contact between colonizers and Indigenous peoples, these are postcolonial texts, but they are informed by colonial discourse, which advocates the values of imperialism. Nor are contemporary texts necessarily exempt from colonial ideologies, which retain their potency long after nations have achieved political independence.

As Bill Ashcroft says, *postcolonial* refers to "a *form of talk* rather than a *form of experience*" (2001, 13), a form of talk that moves beyond historicist approaches, where texts are analyzed in relation to whether they depict life as it "really" was (Fisher 1986). Postcolonial discourse theory, drawing on the work of Foucault and Said, adopts poststructuralist methodologies by refusing to locate "truth" or "reality" in societies, institutions, or textuality. Rather, postcolonial readings of texts (whether historical or contemporary) seek to dismantle the signifying systems of colonialism by identifying the tropes and rhetorics whereby texts construct "truth"—for instance, the "truth" of colonial hierarchies that rely on binaries such as civilized/savage and modern/premodern. In addition to the historicist approaches commonly used in children's literature criticism, discussions of colonial texts often treat the authors of these texts as merely "men [sic] of their time"; thus, Dennis Butts, discussing Henty's *With Clive in India*, argues that Henty's historical novels "reflected the ideology of a late-Victorian British imperialist" (2003, 82). Rather, postcolonial discourse analysis considers the strategies of concealment and denial that manifest in even the most self-confident colonialist texts. Colonial authors were not necessarily conscious of the fissures and inconsistencies that marked their writing, since colonial discourse permeated language and culture.

Textual production for children by Indigenous authors and illustrators (sometimes originating from Indigenous publishers) now comprises a sizeable body of postcolonial children's literature. Some of these texts, like Louise Erdrich's *The Birchbark House* (1999), Thomas King and William Kent Monkman's *A Coyote Columbus Story* (1992), and Gavin Bishop's *The House That Jack Built* (1999), reclaim Indigenous histories, telling the past from the perspectives of peoples formerly objectified by colonial discourse. In *A Coyote Columbus Story*, King and Monkman engage in what Stephen Slemon refers to as postcolonial counterdiscourse (Slemon 1987) through its mockery of Christopher Columbus and his colonial enterprise, and Bishop's treatment of the wars that raged between Maori and European invaders in *The House That Jack Built* dismantles triumphalistic accounts of settler achievements in New Zealand. Indigenous texts including Sherman Alexie's *The Absolutely True Diary of a Part-Time Indian* (2007), Lee Maracle's *Will's Garden* (2002), and Meme McDonald and Boori Monty Pryor's *Njunjul the Sun* (2002) locate their Aboriginal protagonists in cross-cultural settings. The concept of hybridity is a complex one in postcolonial theory (Bhabha 1994), and these novels refuse to accede to simplistic notions of an untroubled "mixing and matching" of values and practices from European and Indigenous cultures. Rather, their protagonists construct new ways of being Aboriginal as they engage in multiple negotiations, positive and negative, with the dominant culture.

Researchers in children's literature began to draw on postcolonial theory from the 1990s, when essay collections (McGillis 1999; Khorana 1998) and monographs (Bradford 2001, 2007; E. Jenkins 2006) began to appear. These publications focused, in the main, on Australian, Canadian, and African texts for the young. More recently, postcolonial approaches have informed analyses of children's texts from Britain (Grzegorczyk 2014), New Zealand (Feingold 2015), Taiwan (Chen and Duh 2013), and India (Goswami 2012). A lingering area of debate surrounds the idea, proposed by Perry Nodelman in 1992, that relations between Orientalists and Orientals offer a parallel to relations between adults and children. This analogy has been accepted far too uncritically, leading to assertions such as that "children are colonized by the books they read" (Kutzer 2000, xvi). It is, of course, the case that colonial discourse constructs colonized peoples as children, lacking the intelligence or autonomy of their (colonizing) superiors. However, the reverse paradigm—that children are similar to colonized peoples—assumes an homogenized version of childhood and "the child" that denies the possibility of childhood agency (ironically, this effect is similar to Said's account of how Orientalism operates). Moreover, the analogy occludes any reference to race and racism, whereas the concept of "race" as a system of classification based on genetics and physical appearance was a founding principle of imperialism from the early modern period. The worst effect of the analogy is its capacity to trivialize the violence and oppression of colonization and its lasting effects on Indigenous peoples; the white, middle-class child readers who comprise the principal audience of children's literature do not occupy a comparable position either politically or symbolically.

Like other critics, Donnarae MacCann (2001) argues that postcolonial studies is an abstract body of theory far removed from the lived experience of colonized peoples and their descendants and carried out by European scholars who conduct a form of neocolonialism over colonized peoples. In her famous essay "Can the Subaltern Speak? Speculations on Widow Sacrifice" (1985), Gayatri Spivak says that the voices of subaltern people are lost in the noise of Western theorists as they talk *about* the colonized, and Dipesh Chakrabarty (1992) contends that postcolonial theory is inevitably incorporated in a Eurocentric historical master narrative. Nevertheless, postcolonial literary studies constantly reinvents itself, connecting with studies of globalization, transnationalism, and environmentalism. In addition, postcolonialism now aligns itself with critical race theory and whiteness studies, thus enabling comparative and historicized approaches that consider both national literatures and the global conditions in which they are produced.

47

Posthuman

Zoe Jaques

The word *posthuman* can engender anxiety. Like all *posts-*, the prefix suggests transition, rejection and moving beyond what came before. The posthuman, then, implies an existence *after* the human—a prospect evolutionary biology teaches any species to eschew. That the *OED* traces its first use (as the hyphenated *post-human*) to a discussion of eugenics in Maurice Parmalee's *Poverty and Social Progress* (1916) does little to mitigate such disquiet. The dictionary's secondary descriptors are hardly more buoyant: "abstract, impersonal, mechanistic, dispassionate" (*OED*). In the face of such a dismal ontological state that we, as the humans in question, are taught to resist, is it any wonder that we might be skeptical of a term that seems distancing at best and outright apocalyptic at worst?

Yet *posthuman* is tied to an important *ism* that might be said to shift the emphasis away from these detached, futuristic definitions and toward a more provocative, liberating domain that very much relates to our human present and, indeed, to history. Posthumanism is the critical discourse invested in interrogating the posthuman subject or condition; its etymological root, as *after* humanism, provides the key to understanding exactly what is being rejected. First used in the 1970s, the term speaks to what cultural critic Ihab Hassan saw as "five hundred years of humanism . . . coming to an end" (1977, 843). While humanism is no more a homogenous ideology than its disputant posthumanism, its history

(emerging forcefully in the Renaissance) glorifies man as unified, transcendent, rational, enlightened, and most importantly, distinct from the rest of the world. The humanist subject is invested in drawing lines between itself and "others," enforcing binary oppositions not just between humans and other beings but also within humanity itself. It inevitably describes difference hierarchically. The posthumanist subject, conversely, rejects an anthropocentric worldview that essentializes "man" (in both its species-based and gendered terms) and instead sees the human as an "assemblage" (Nayar 2013, 4), entangled with technology, other species, and our environments as part of a shared, coevolving planet. As such, it does not necessarily imagine a literal *post*human future in which technology has supplanted humanity in favor of that "abstract" alternative to which the *OED* refers but rather probes and critiques long-standing and debilitating humanist assumptions.

Nevertheless, the anxiety-ridden definition of *posthuman* tends to garner attention in children's literature scholarship, particularly in terms of how young adult literature has imagined—and opposed—the possibility of human decline. Noga Applebaum perceives an "increasing technophobia in children's fiction" (2010, 15); Clare Bradford and colleagues venture that "in children's literature so far, the prospect of a posthuman future is invariably aligned with notions of dystopia, shaped by a humanistic hesitation about or suspicion of . . . developments within information theory and cybernetics" (2008, 155). Dystopian visions of mechanistic life, such as the "stalkers" of Philip Reeve's Mortal Engines (2001–6) or the "Mutts" from Suzanne Collins's Hunger Games (2008–10), are in keeping with this paradigm; that these hybrids unite dead human bodies with machine or animal parts forcibly images the end of man alongside the evolution of "unnatural" technologies.

Operating in similar terms are Scott Westerfeld's critique of technologically "enhanced" beauty in the Uglies series (2005–7) and M. T. Anderson's satirical vision of the brain "improved" by the internet in *Feed* (2002). These critical takes on bodily augmentation speak to, invert, and reject the cybernetic origins of posthuman philosophy. As first imagined in the 1960s, the cyborg was merely another mode by which man might extend his anthropocentric dominion beyond the limitations of his physical, earthbound body. Posthuman philosophy, however, upends such visions, with thinkers like Donna Haraway seeing in the cyborg the utopian possibilities of a creature without genesis and thus unencumbered by the debilitating binaries whereby humanity constrains itself. Rethought again in texts like *Feed* and the Uglies series, the cyborg loses the liberating potential it finds in posthuman thought, becoming a docile, interpellated shadow of a valorized, whole, human(ist) subject. Thus while both these texts *depict* posthuman futures, neither *reflects* the central tenets of posthumanism. Victoria Flanagan contends that "authors are beginning to produce narratives about technology in much more life-affirming and positive ways" (2014, 2), but she too emphasizes that change is slow, developing only in a small number of texts since the mid-2000s. Such arguments echo the long-standing sense that children's literature is firmly grounded in the humanist tradition (Stephens and McCallum 1998).

What emerges thus far are two important points from scholarship on children's literature and the posthuman. First, texts that embrace the more celebratory possibilities of posthumanism emerge rarely, recently, and against the tide of mainstream children's fiction. Second, both positive and negative responses to the posthuman are primarily focused on technoscience, in keeping with the modern era to which the term seems tied. I venture, however, that neither point is wholly sound. In *Children's Literature and the Posthuman* (2015), I argue that posthuman conceits have circulated in children's fiction from much earlier dates; its very history is founded upon teaching young readers what it means to be human—rather ironically—via a willing attentiveness to a spectrum of imagined and alternative subjectivities that stretch humanistic boundaries. Lewis Carroll's nineteenth-century chess pieces and playing cards, alongside animal characters determined to poke holes in Alice's sense of herself as rational and discreet, are just as provocatively posthuman as Peter Dickinson's *Eva* (1988), wherein readers are asked to reflect critically on the conflicted subjectivity of a human-chimp hybrid made possible by futuristic technology. Narratives of objects-come-to-life more generally have long been popular tales for young audiences: E. T. A. Hoffmann's *Nussknacker und Mausekönig* (*The Nutcracker and the Mouse King*; 1816), Hans Christian Andersen's *Den standhaftige Tinsoldat* (*The Steadfast Tin Soldier*; 1838), and Carlo Collodi's *Le avventure di Pinocchio* (*The Adventures of Pinocchio*; 1883) might be read as providing something of a prehistory to the posthuman. Conceived in this light, the posthuman potential of children's literature might, in fact, emerge wherever hierarchies of being are questioned—from the (partial) queering of gendered normative in *And Tango Makes Three* (2005), to the carnivalesque delights of the liminal boundary figures of Anansi and Br'er Rabbit, to the playful mockery of Cartesian ideas in Salman Rushdie's mechanical Hoopoe bird from *Haroun and the Sea of Stories* (1990).

That all these examples feature animal subjects speaks to the crucial and conflicted place the animal occupies in the human imagination—at once "us" (humans are, of course, animals) and "other" (the human so often defined in distinction to the animal). Posthuman philosophy is committed to recognizing and valuing polymorphous animal subjectivities, in keeping with Derrida's (2002) famous case against the "sin" of thinking about animality in singular terms. The "immense multiplicity" Derrida locates in the animal kingdom emerges in children's literature's wealth of animal characters (2002, 416); sixty-five of the ninety-three titles nominated to the Kate Greenway Medal in 2017 feature animal protagonists ranging from bears, to badgers, to bees. Such volume is significant; as Tess Cosslett (2006) and Amy Ratelle (2014) have explored, our earliest training in the workings of human society is mediated through animal encounters.

Yet surely that abundance does not imply that *all* texts for children featuring nonhumans address posthumanism's concern with boundary dissolution. Texts like David McKee's *Tusk Tusk* (1978) or the similarly conceived *Green Lizards vs. Red Rectangles* (2015) by Steve Antony are meant to be read as commenting on wars between humans rather than on the subjectivities of elephants, lizards, or—indeed—abstract shapes. While these texts do seek to dissolve arbitrary and debilitating boundaries *within* a human social order, reading or rendering animals only as ciphers does little to address humanity's disconnection from the nonhuman world. Steve Baker (1993) argues that the animal is repeatedly and deliberately belittled in contemporary culture—a position with which children's literature scholarship might sympathize—underscored by a sense that "worthwhile" animal narratives have deeper, human-centric meanings.

While such a reading of the animal story is pervasive—responding to a long tradition of fiction deploying animals allegorically or satirically—a posthumanist stance might venture that animals cannot be "used" so straightforwardly. First, they fundamentally resist universalizing symbolism. Erica Fudge points

out that dogs are "the most storied of all pet animals" (2008, 10); while true in the context of Western understandings of canines as human companions, Middle Eastern attitudes differ markedly (Foltz 2006). Second, anthropomorphism cannot avoid challenging (at some level) a case for human distinctiveness. Beatrix Potter's *Tale of Peter Rabbit* (1901)—which positions Peter as sometimes a naturalized bunny, other times a naughty child—provocatively exposes connections between one and the other. Max's desire for, but eventual discomfort with, colonializing dominion in *Where the Wild Things Are* (1963) attends to the implications of viewing humans and animals across ideological fault lines. More overt examples include Katherine Applegate's *The One and Only Ivan* (2012) and Anthony Browne's *Zoo* (1992), which like Dickinson's *Eva* or Swedish author Jakob Wegelius's *Mördarens Ape* (*The Murderer's Ape*; 2014) invite readers to perceive their interconnections with imagined animal subjectivities via the first-person narration of a captive gorilla or through playful and powerfully poignant postmodern imagery. The point here is that children's literature's commitment to thinking with and through the animal—for whatever purpose—inevitably and potently problematizes any sense that there are easy or uncontested boundaries defining the world.

The keyword *posthuman* provides a model for understanding the universe not from the perspective of a human-centered order that sets "us" apart from a great many "thems" but through connecting humanity to a wider ecosystem of bodies, both organic and mechanistic. Children's literature studies has long been attuned to boundaries, particularly a perceived rupture between adult and child. While we are rightly cautioned against seeing children as themselves "others" (Gubar 2013), we might equally attend to John Betjeman's case that "childhood is measured by sounds, smells / And sights before the dark hour of reason grows" ([1960] 1989, 38). Childhood is a potent and distinctive state not yet fully inscribed by humanist agendas and thus more open to taking *"pleasure in the confusion of boundaries"* (Haraway 1985, 66) that posthumanism enjoys. Children's literature's delight in imagining and prioritizing the subjectivity of the nonhuman thus offers a crucial site for posthuman thinking, introducing young readers to ideas that trouble at the edges of dominant humanist ideology, whether that troubling is intentional or not.

48

Postmodernism
Philip Nel

Postmodernism literally means "after modernism." But the dates don't work. While modernism is said to have ended, variously, in 1939, 1945, or 1950, *postmodernism* first emerged in 1870, when English painter John Watkins Chapman applied it to art that (he claimed) was more avant-garde than French impressionism (Storey 2005). Despite its anomalous dating, *postmodernism* by the 1940s defined a new period in literature or architecture. Though the term gained wider currency in the 1960s, its arrival depended on where you lived. Postmodernism in Japan began somewhere between the late 1970s and mid-1980s and in China and Romania in the 1980s (Shaoyang 2013; Dirlik and Xudong 1997; Schneider 2014). It appears at different times because the onset and nature of postmodernity (the historical condition to which it responds) varies by location. Romanian censors delayed postmodernism's arrival and changed its flavor; in its precapitalist economics, China's postmodernism appeared more as "aesthetic expectation" and less as symptom of (or challenge to) late capitalism (Schneider 2014; Dirlik and Xudong 1997, 9). Even more confusingly, *postmodern* (a stylistic designation) is often conflated with *postmodernity* (a historical condition or cultural logic).

Though geography predicts which meanings the term might encompass, two formal postmodernisms became popular in North American and western European children's literature in the 1970s, 1980s, and 1990s: narrative fragmentation and metafiction. Remy

Charlip and Jerry Joyner's *Thirteen* (1975) and David Macaulay's *Black and White* (1990) each launches simultaneous narratives—the latter book refracting one story into four perspectives, unfolding in all four quadrants of each two-page spread. Jon Scieszka and Lane Smith's *The Stinky Cheese Man and Other Fairly Stupid Tales* (1992), the best-known English-language children's metafiction, comments on and dismantles the book's form. Little Red Riding Hood and the Wolf leave their stories, Jack moves the endpapers to hide behind them, and the title character's stench melts the edges of the illustrations. Metapictures, a visual manifestation of the metafictional, emerge in Ann Jonas's *Round Trip* (1983), in which each two-page spread can also be read upside-down. As W. J. T. Mitchell (1994) says of metapictures, figure and ground perpetually oscillate, positioning the audience as the subject of the experiment.

However, the earlier appearance of the metafictive and the fragmented upsets the already shaky periodizing definition. Nineteenth-century children arranged myriorama cards, segments of a continuous landscape that yielded multiple combinations, altering both scene and story; seventeenth- and eighteenth-century moveable books for children also invited readers to interact with and influence the narrative (Reid-Walsh 2018a, xvi–xviii, 23–24). In Peter Newell's *Topsys & Turvys* (1902), each page presents a metapicture framed by a couplet, with the first line below the image and right-side up, the second line above and upside-down; turn the book 180 degrees to complete the rhyme and have your mind reread the picture. Metafictional blurring of real and imagined worlds appears in E. Nesbit's "The Town in the Library, in the Town in the Library" (1901), when two children build a town out of books in their family's library and enter the book-town to find a duplicate of their house with a book-town in *its* library. Prefiguring Jorge Luis Borges's "The Library of Babel" (1941), each town contains a duplicate of itself, "like Chinese box puzzles, multiplied by millions and millions for ever and ever" (Nesbit 1901; Rosenberg 2008). Art also bends reality in Winsor McCay's *Little Nemo in Slumberland* of May 2, 1909, when the title character gradually slips from three dimensions into two and then to the stick-figure minimalism of a child's drawing—at which point, he awakens. "Kiseki no mori no monogatari" (Story of the miracle forest; 1949) is the first of many Osamu Tezuka manga to feature its author as a character, a recurring means for introducing "self-conscious humor to the narrative" (Power 2009, 138). Chuck Jones's *Duck Amuck* (1953) reveals Bugs Bunny as the mischievous artist behind all of Daffy Duck's misfortunes, and Crockett Johnson's *Harold and the Purple Crayon* (1955) finds the title character drawing his adventures on an otherwise blank canvas: his only world is the one he creates. From Nesbit's 1901 story to Roger Mello's wordless *Selvagem* (Wild; 2010), children's literature has long blurred the boundary between real and imaginary, which raises the question of where the boundaries of the postmodern lie.

The many continuities between the two might make postmodernism more an extension of modernism—specifically, the modernist avant-garde—than a break from it. Both use collage, experimental design, narrative fragmentation, and a mix of styles to represent disordered contemporary experience. Is Tove Jansson's *Hur gick det sen?* (1952; trans. *The Book about Moomin, Mymble and Little My*, 2004) more modern or more postmodern? In addition to playing with the physical form of the book, its die-cut pages afford the reader windows into both past and future, juxtaposing temporalities and suggesting alternate ways of reading. Though Anthony Browne's *Voices in the Park* (1998)—a rewriting of his *A Walk in the Park* (1977)—has been described as postmodernist (McMillan 2003), the book's visual play conveys a delight in allusiveness that could be both modern and postmodern. Its illustrations cite art by René Magritte, Edward Munch, and Leonardo da Vinci as well as images of Mary Poppins and King Kong. Its decentering of any central narrative could as easily be modern as postmodern: the book offers, in succession, four different accounts of a trip to the park, competing stories that develop a contrast between adults and children, females and males, and upper class and lower class.

If there is a boundary between modern and postmodern, it resides in the historical moment (modernity or postmodernity) to which the work responds, the degree of formal play, and its resistance to metanarratives. Is *Voices in the Park* making visible the class inequalities obscured by Tony Blair's New Labour or distracting us from these very concerns via its proliferation of cultural allusions? The excessiveness of its visual allusiveness—much of which seems only tangentially connected to its social themes—suggests that the book is less invested in a materialist critique of postmodernity and more in a playful escapism, that it is less parody and more pastiche.

Fredric Jameson famously called postmodern pastiche "blank parody, a statue with blind eyeballs" and therefore lacking parody's "satiric impulse" (1991, 17). However, critical opinion lacks consensus on whether postmodernism's playfulness engages with or retreats from postmodernity—a period of global capitalism beginning in the 1960s and dominated by service industries that offer consumerism as a (false) form of agency. Smith's pastiche of styles in *The Stinky Cheese Man* might be "visually arresting" and parodic, its metafictive traits serving a "critical consciousness-raising function" (Cox 1994, 15; Stevenson 1994; Peters 1996, 210). In contrast, *The Grim Grotto* (2004)—Lemony Snicket's "pastiche of *Moby Dick*"—may be "like the white whale . . . presenting a blankness on which readers can project

their longings" (Langbauer 2007, 511). The Harry Potter phenomenon might be a symptom of postmodernity, delivering a pastiche of influences and celebrating consumption (Zipes 2001; Gupta 2003), or it might consciously play with its source material and strive for a political critique (Westman 2002; Nel 2005). The postmodern may be distracting or combative or even offer a bit of both.

Postmodernism's potential to address systemic oppression offers a reason for why its location (national, cultural, social, historical) creates so many variances in its meaning. In Japan, *posutomodan* (postmodern) can also refer to the oppositional impulses of postcolonial studies or cultural studies (Shaoyang 2013). In China, *houxiandai zhuyl* (postmodern) "carries strong connotations of post*revolutionary*" (Dirlik and Xudong 1997, 10n9). The nation's different experience of modernism alters the meaning of postmodernism in other ways: as Arif Dirlik and Zhang Xudong note, since China "experienced modernity as colonialism from the outside and as a coercive state project from the inside," its sense of "postmodernity may allow for the emergence of alternative social and cultural formations that do not so much signal the end of modernity as mark the beginning of imagining alternatives to it" (1997, 17).

Whether or not postmodern art helps realize those imagined alternatives, one of its manifestations—historiographic metafiction—may aid members of disenfranchised communities in developing a self-conscious critique of the material relationships that sustain and perpetuate hierarchies of power. One American example, Walter Dean Myers's *Monster* (1999)—told through screenplay, courtroom transcript, personal journal, and video stills—juxtaposes genres to interrogate the relationship between personal responsibility and the racism endemic to the US criminal justice system. The novel never definitively answers whether its sixteen-year-old Black protagonist is guilty of being an accessory to a robbery that ended in murder, but it does help readers arrive at a more complex and nuanced understanding of whose interests a story serves.

As the screenplay element of Myers's novel indicates, performance underwrites much of what gets labeled postmodern children's literature. In children's theater, interaction between the audience and a play is neither postmodern nor modern; it is merely common, as when, in J. M. Barrie's *Peter Pan* (1904), Peter Pan encourages theatergoers to clap their hands if they believe in fairies. However, when characters in a book break the fourth wall, we designate it postmodern, noting that characters step into a "fourth dimension"—the "space shared between the physical book and the reading/viewing audience" (Goldstone 2008, 118). Tezuka's characters break through their panel borders in many of his books, as do David Wiesner's in *The Three Pigs* (2001) and Jörg Müller's *Das Buch im Buch im Buch* (The book in the book in the book; 2001). Grover seeks the reader's help in Jon Stone and Michael Smollin's *The Monster at the End of This Book!* (1971), as do the characters in Daniel Fehr and Maurizio A. C. Quarello's *Come si legge un libro?* (How do you read a book?; 2018). Delphine Durand's *Bob & Co.* (2006) finds the water, the sun, the earth, the tree, the sky, the emptiness, God, and Bob bursting with ontological and narratological questions while telling a story that explores these questions and the nature of story itself (story is also a character).

Though postmodernism's stylistic elements might challenge readers' expectations of what a book is or should be, a generation raised in postmodernity could experience the allegedly postmodern as merely normal. Habituated to its modes of engagement, contemporary readers may find "fragmentation, non-linearity and playfulness familiar strategies" (Allan 2012, 4). Familiarity with technology—from apps to e-books to video games—could also change young people's relationship with printed texts (Sipe and Pantaleo 2008; Mackey 2008). Players of Niantic's *Pokémon Go* (2016–) seem less likely to worry about a blurred boundary between a fictional world and the real one—for them, a boundary's permeability makes the game more fun. If *postmodern* today, then, marks adults' nostalgia for an imaginary boundary that young people neither perceive nor miss, it nonetheless locates a cluster of formal approaches struggling to diagnose and disentangle the shifting, overlapping structures in which we are enmeshed.

49

Queer
Kerry Mallan

The word *queer* is elusive and confusing; its etymology is uncertain, and academic and popular usage attributes conflicting meanings to the word. It is often used as an umbrella term that refers to a range of "nonnormative" sexualities and genders—gay, lesbian, bisexual, transgender, intersex, and questioning (GLBTIQ). In other contexts, *queer* is a term that resists identity categorizations based on sexual orientation (including heterosexual). As a theoretical strategy, *queer* reveals the social and historical constructions of identity formation and dualistic concepts that govern normative notions of gender and sexuality.

The *OED* suggests that the earliest references to *queer* may have appeared in the sixteenth century. These early examples of *queer* carried negative connotations, such as "vulgar," "bad," "worthless," and "strange." The early nineteenth century, and perhaps earlier, employed *queer* as a verb, meaning to "to put out of order," "to interfere with." The adjectival form also began to emerge during this time to refer to a person's condition as being "not normal," "out of sorts." According to Eve Kosofsky Sedgwick, "the word 'queer' itself means *across*—it comes from the Indo-European root—*twerkw*, which also yields the German *quer* (traverse), Latin *torquere* (to twist), English *athwart* . . . it is relational and strange" (1993, xii). Despite the gaps in the lineage and changes in usage, meaning, and grammatical form, *queer* has evolved to be a universally discursive term—used internationally without translation—that encompasses culturally marginal genders and sexualities.

Early gay, lesbian, and feminist activist movements—including the Swedish Federation for Lesbian, Gay, Bisexual and Transgender Rights (1948); the Stonewall riots in New York (1969); and subsequent Gay Liberation Front movements across the US, UK, and Canada—brought to the fore the need for equal rights for "nonnormative" genders and sexualities. However, it was not until the late 1980s that *queer* began to take on a more political function in Anglo-American contexts. AIDS activist groups in the US such as Queer Nation (1990–93) demanded recognition of the severity of the AIDS crisis and challenged homophobic social attitudes and government policies. Children's fiction about child or adult characters with HIV/AIDS such as M. E. Kerr's *Night Kites* (1987) and Morris Gleitzman's *Two Weeks with the Queen* (1989) attempted to convey a sense of compassion and a counter to homophobia.

Books with child or adolescent characters who harbor, even covertly, same-sex desires emerged in the nineteenth century, whereby the doomed, sacrificed, or dismissed figure of the "erotic child" provided narratives of "childhood sexuality" (Moon 2004; Kincaid 1998). Stockton (2009) offers the notion of the "protogay" or "ghostly gay" child to argue an alternative "sideways growth" in relation to the straight line of heteronormative child-adult development. An early example of protogay characters is found in the homoerotic romances of the "ragged boys" created by Horatio Alger in the popular *Ragged Dick* (1868). Since the 1960s, children's/YA literature in many countries has responded to changing social-political contexts by incorporating gay or lesbian characters and same-sex desire into their narratives. However, some reviewers are critical of these texts for focusing on tragic or negative consequences of being gay or lesbian; for example, the gay protagonist in John Donovan's *I'll Get There. It Better Be Worth the Trip* (1969) experiences shame and guilt about his sexuality, and in Cat Clarke's *Undone* (2013), a gay character kills himself after being outed online. In some contexts, GLBTIQ books have met with hostile public reception and banning—for example, the story of young lesbian love in Nancy Garden's *Annie on My Mind* (1982); same-sex parenting in the case of two male penguins in Richardson, Parnell, and Cole's picture book *And Tango Makes Three* (2005); and Susanne Bösche's *Mette bor hos Morten og Erik* (*Jenny Lives with Eric and Martin*; 1981), about a girl who lives with her father and his male partner (the story met controversy when the English translation of this Danish picture book appeared in UK schools). By contrast, some picture books that challenge sexual and gender stereotypes, such as those by Swedish author-illustrator Pija Lindenbaum, have received praise and public recognition (Kokkola and Österlund 2014). These examples highlight the ongoing challenges of how to imagine "queer" texts for children and what informs them at a particular historical moment.

The reappropriation of *queer*, changing it from an insult to a "linguistic sign of affirmation and resistance" (Butler 1993, 233), was an important precursor to a radical theorization that was to follow—namely, queer theory. Teresa de Lauretis coined the phrase *queer theory* in 1991 as "a working hypothesis for lesbian and gay studies" (de Lauretis 1991, iv). However, *queer* and the theories that support it are in constant formation (Butler 1993). In Uganda, *kuchu* (meaning "sexual and/or gender minority") is used as an umbrella term in much the same way as *queer* in Europe and North America. While *queer* rejects the notion of a community with fixed boundaries, the *kuchu* community is intersectional in that it encompasses racial and regional east African identities as well as sexuality and gender identities (Butler and Falzone 2014). However, both share in the same dilemma of having to rely on an umbrella term that imagines

coherence, without which resistance and personal survival would not be possible.

Despite the broad hegemony of Western knowledge production, there is no global queer theory, as multiple queer international theories reflect alternative local and diverse sociopolitical contexts and histories. Even within Western academic studies, there are conflicts with respect to queer, gay/lesbian, feminist, and transgender theoretical and political concerns (Elliott 2010). Resistance or inability to settle on a clear-cut definition is itself part of the inherent radical potential of queer theory. However, the lack of specificity opens it up to generalization (Warner 1993). An inevitable effect is that *queer* permeates discourses that go beyond GLBTIQ lives, reaching more broadly into Western and some non-Western urban cultures and the marketing of consumer products, including entertainment and fashion. This kind of market fetishization of the word *queer* threatens to dissipate its political valency. Ironically, however, in "Asia" (itself a broad and diverse notion), such privileging by middle-class consumerism has helped keep state censorship at arm's length (Erni 2003). Queer cultural representation extends to child and youth markets. The so-called culture of childhood is an area whereby researchers examine "queerness" in children's cultural texts and practices with respect to young people's sexuality, gay and lesbian parenting, pedophilia, cross-dressing, and transgenderism (see Epstein 2014; Kokkola 2013a; Abate and Kidd 2011; Mallan 2009; Flanagan 2008).

While the uncritical adoption of *queer* in popular culture has certainly domesticated the term to some extent, *queer* retains its conceptually radical challenge to normative structures and discourses. Drawing on feminist, poststructuralist, Foucauldian, and psychoanalytic theories, queer theory began to review and deconstruct categories of gender, sex, and sexuality, arguing the indeterminacy and instability of all sexed and gendered identities. Judith Butler's (1990) concept of "performativity" has provided ways for thinking about the processes by which discourse and language construct identity, the functioning of social norms, and how disruptive performances of gender and sexual identity (e.g., drag and parody) can subvert identity categories and reinforce existing heterosexual structures. Part of queer theory's agenda is to call attention to the power that "heteronormativity" exerts on individuals in naturalizing and privileging normative heterosexuality and upholding the logic of "either/or" (Angelides 2001, 15). Doty (1993, xvi) sees queer as a "binary outlaw" in its refusal to abide binary distinctions between male and female, queer and straight.

Texts for young people have attempted to represent their own binary outlaws who disrupt gender boundaries through the figure of the "tomboy," as in the eponymous character in Gene Kemp's *The Turbulent Term of Tyke Tyler* (1977) or in Céline Sciamma's film *Tomboy* (2011). Texts for younger readers that deploy masquerade and cross-dressing do not necessarily subvert dominant discourses about gender and sexual dualisms but draw attention to binary outlaws, such as Robert the cross-dressing raven in *Ein Schräger Vogel* (*Odd Bird Out*; 2008) by the Austrian author-illustrator Helga Bansch. By contrast, other humorous cross-dressing novels—for instance, *Bill's New Frock* (1989) by Anne Fine—depoliticize gender disruption by offering a closure that returns to the social order of naturalized binaries of male/female. In refusing to take account of the logic of "either/or," bisexuality occupies the position of "both/and." Bisexuality in picture books is often inferred rather than stated, as in Michael Willhoite's *Daddy's Roommate* (1990), but is explicit in David Levithan's YA novel *Boy Meets Boy* (2003). The challenges of being a trans teen are taken up in Ellen Wittlinger's *Parrotfish*

(2007) and Chris Beam's *I Am J* (2011). For younger readers, Jessica Herthel and Jazz Jennings's picture book *I Am Jazz* (2014) and Alex Gino's novel *George* (2015) illustrate the emotional pain trans children experience when they cannot be accepted for who they are. These texts demonstrate the impossibility of any "natural" sexuality and invite readers to question the seemingly unproblematic categories—"male" and "female."

There is no consensus on what makes a "queer" story. Some consider that queer stories are those that include GLBTIQ characters; others contend that some stories (with or without GLBTIQ characters) can be read as having a queer sensibility or "queer effects." Bruhm and Hurley (2004, xiv) suggest that such an effect occurs through "innocence run amok" in Lewis Carroll's *Alice's Adventures in Wonderland* (1865). Wes Anderson's film *Moonrise Kingdom* (2012) is concerned with adolescent heterosexual desire but nevertheless offers a queer or "camp" sensibility (Mallan and McGillis 2019). Children's literature scholars have considered "queerness" in YA fiction about cross-species desire and species ambiguity (Mitchell 2014) and the interplay of queer and camp in children's literature and film (Mallan 2013b; Mallan and McGillis 2005).

Queer fiction for children and young adults remains, like queer theory, a contentious and confused area for many. It also offers pleasures for readers who may gain insights into the lived realities of diverse individual characters, whatever their sexual identity may be. Queer fiction turns identity politics on its head, shifting from *queer* as a noun to a verb, *to queer*. From a queer perspective, the most successful fiction for children makes visible the processes that seek to enforce heteronormative categories and binaries and that foreground subjectivity as multifaceted and shifting, developed more from difference than homogeneity.

50

Race

Katharine Capshaw

A term with a variety of charged meanings, *race* arose in English in the sixteenth century from the French *race* and the Italian *razza* and has been employed as a means of grouping individuals by ethnic, social, or national background. While the term has been applied generally to a range of collective identities, at present the term *race* invokes a categorization attached to imagined physical similarities or to a group's own sense of collective ideals and history. *Race* as a term points both backward toward injurious histories of eugenics and physiognomic pseudoscience (Rivers 1994; Gombrich 1970) and forward toward the term's reclamation and revision within liberationist social movements, like the US civil rights movement of the 1960s and 1970s and postcolonial movements in the Caribbean and Africa.

Within children's literature and culture, representations of race often reflect history's racialist thinking. Hugh Lofting's *The Story of Dr. Doolittle* (1920) and the series that followed are familiar examples of canonical children's books containing race-based stereotypes. One might consider the ways in which obvious racial stereotypes of the "other" emerge in children's literature during periods of white anxiety about social domination, as in the cases of George A. Henty's books that articulate a British imperialist imperative. It is difficult to underestimate the pervasiveness of racist representations of nonwhite characters in children's literature before the mid-twentieth century. Some of the most respected texts in the canon of children's literature

contain representations that offer prejudicial constructions of race, including Frances Hodgson Burnett's *The Secret Garden* (1911), Laura Ingalls Wilder's Little House series, and J. M. Barrie's *Peter Pan* (1904). Contemporary texts representing race can perpetuate conceptualizations that homogenize and belittle, as in the case of Lynne Reid Banks's *The Indian in the Cupboard* (1980). Others offer clumsy and objectionable depictions of racialized historical subjects, as in the case of *A Birthday Cake for George Washington* (2016), which was pulled by its publisher in response to public outcry over the depiction of joyful enslaved people, and *A Fine Dessert* (2015), which remains in print and offers similar depictions of people living happily under slavery. Especially in settler society contexts, children's books can perpetuate implicit racial hierarchies, as in the case of Australian Patricia Wrightson's Song of Wirrun trilogy (1977–81), which foregrounds white hero motifs in a series exploring on Australian Aboriginal identity, or Deborah Savage's *The Flight of the Albatross* (1989), which employs Maori characters as modes of education and enlightenment for a white central character.

Racialized characters have sometimes been used as a vehicle for the transgressive in white-authored children's texts. "Dark" characters invoke fears of violence, allowing white child characters to displace and distance themselves from their own violent impulses, a pattern that surfaces in some depictions of Native Americans, as in Alice Dalgliesh's *The Courage of Sarah Noble* (1954). Characters of color have been associated with libidinal energies and immoderate physical urges, as in the case of pickaninny figures, and sometimes enable white children to imagine themselves as liberated from restrictive social structures by "going native" or otherwise becoming the occasion for white children to test social boundaries. Canonical texts like Heinrich Hoffman's *Der Struwwelpeter* (1845) continue to promote discussion about the valence of racial representation, especially in terms of "The Story of the Inky Boys," in which white children are dipped in ink as a punishment; many note the stereotypical images and concepts in the tale, while others see the story as a satire of the racialized implications of Romantic idealizations of the child (Wesseling 2009). A lively debate appears in contemporary criticism about the role of race in Harry Potter, some claiming the texts as antiracist and others attending to the ascendance of whiteness in the series (Rana 2011).

Voices from within ethnic communities have been decrying the representation of race in children's texts since early in the twentieth century. Antiracist efforts in the field of children's literature came to fruition in the US the 1960s and 1970s and included the organization of the Council on Interracial Books for Children (CIBC) and the publication of Nancy Larrick's landmark article, "The All-White World of Children's Literature" (1965) in the *Saturday Review*. Individual writers have interacted creatively with representations of race and childhood by white writers, whether that be staking a claim to children's traditions that have largely excluded race (as do the representations of black fairies and brownies in W. E. B. Du Bois's *The Brownies' Book* [1920–21] magazine), or recasting and recouping familiar texts (as do Julius Lester and Jerry Pinkney in *Sam and the Tigers* [1996]), or advocating self-publishing as a means to expand the variety of representation of children of color (as does contemporary Canadian American black writer Zetta Elliott). Highlighting the urgent need for nonracist representation, other critics map the history and track the persistence of racist tropes in children's literature, including Karen Sands-O'Connor (2008) on the image of the Caribbean in British texts, Donnarae MacCann and Yulisa Amadu Maddy (2001) on race and Apartheid in South Africa, Beverly Slapin and Doris Seale (2006) and Debbie Reese (2017) on Native experience and

representation, Paula Connolly (2013) on representations of enslavement, and Sarah Park Dahlen on Asian American identity (2016).

Scholars of race in children's literature also attend to the ways that conspicuous biases of the past structure contemporary imaginings of innocence, subjectivity, and otherness. Robin Bernstein's landmark study *Racial Innocence* (2011b) argues that innocence as a value is attached to whiteness and that children's culture smuggles in racialized hierarchies under the cover of narratives of childhood ingenuousness. Philip Nel extends this perspective to the submerged racialization of twentieth-century children's culture, arguing that "the Cat in the Hat, Mickey Mouse, and Bugs Bunny naturalize their minstrel origins" (2017b, 67). Since racialization in the US context has been most frequently associated with blackness, other iterations of racialized identity have become culturally submerged or fused with blackness. The most striking example of the conflation of ideas about blackness to other cultural groups might be Helen Bannerman's *The Story of Little Black Sambo* (1899), which purportedly depicts India but traffics in the visual lexicon of minstrelsy. Throughout the nineteenth and twentieth centuries, ideas about race and Asian and Asian American experience gravitated toward racialized threats of the yellow peril and wartime enemy as well as an othering embrace of the model minority stereotype and valuing of ancient, alien cultures. Midcentury picture books often combined a veneration of folklore, which often depicted racialized heritage as stable and unchanging, with images that drew on caricature, stereotyping, and inauthenticity, as in the case of *Five Chinese Brothers* (1938) and *Tikki Tikki Tembo* (1968).

Racial analogs in children's literature have also proved controversial, as in the use of animals as stand-ins for racial identities. Most famous, perhaps, is Garth Williams's *The Rabbits' Wedding* (1958), which depicts the love between a white and a black bunny and provoked ire among racists in Alabama who read it as endorsing interracial marriage. But in twenty-first-century texts, like Greek writer Eugene Trivizas's *The Last Black Cat* (2001), colors and species of animals remain as stand-ins for racial categories and can perform productive work in destabilizing hierarchies. Fantastic analogs can also be problematic, as Clare Bradford (2007) explains: alien life-forms are figured through biological difference, and humanity is identified with whiteness. In terms of global political contexts, race as a malevolent concept has mobilized fascist movements, and children's literature has responded by offering resistant texts, as Julia Mickenberg studies in *Learning from the Left* (2005) and Julia Benner pursues in *Federkrieg: Kinder- und Jugendliteratur gegen den Nationalsozialismus, 1933–1945* (War of words: Children's and youth literature against national socialism; 2015).

Throughout most of Europe, the post–World War II response to Nazism pushed *race* (or *Rasse*, in German) out of most discourse, inspired by the fear that even using the word affirmed race as a biological "fact," establishing such difference as grounds for discrimination. Seeing *race* as promoting racism, most Europeans avoided the word, which did not remove either race or racism from the continent. Perhaps hinting at the roots of such confusion, postwar Germans were occupied by a segregated US Army, learning that, as Rita Chin notes, "some types of race thinking—namely, discrimination against blacks—were not incompatible with 'democratic forms and values'" (2017, 161). As a result, in West Germany, *race* (*Rasse*) was both a "tarnished category that could no longer be openly invoked" and a category that could be invoked in reference to "Afro-German children of African American GIs and German women" (161). However, European multicultural discourse also can covertly essentialize race by displacing it onto ethnicity, religion, or class. As Gloria

Wekker points out, though such terms are "supposedly softer entities" that "operate on cultural rather than biological terrain," they nonetheless "have been used in such hardened ways that biology and culture have become interchangeable in the stability that is ascribed to the cultures of others" (2016, 22). An example of the tensions in midcentury Europe around the representation of race is German author Erich Kästner's *Die Konferenz der Tiere* (*The Conference of the Animals*; 1949), which aspires to celebrate human variation, while the art (by Walter Trier) visually caricatures the very same differences the text purports to respect.

While the term *race* in the context of children's literature conjures up a variety of cultural tensions and injurious uses, the other main valence of the term emerges through efforts at communal self-articulation. As critics and writers recognize that race as a concept is a social construct and have worked to displace the idea of race from biology, race has been claimed by communities as a way to articulate shared history, culture, and political goals. In the US, children's texts often emerge during periods of cultural nationalism—like the Harlem Renaissance, the Chicano Movement, the Black Arts Movement, and the American Indian Movement—as a means to articulate and inculcate qualities that define "the race." Within these contexts, debates about inclusion and exclusion sometimes blur the line between understanding race as cultural legacy and adhering to the sense that race involves biology, particularly when using blood as a signifier of racial inclusion. The question of whether one is "black enough" or "Indian enough" based on blood or on cultural context surfaces in texts like Virginia Hamilton's *Arilla Sun Down* (1976). For Indigenous peoples, nationhood has been ascendant over the idea of racialized physical markers, with some writers rejecting the conjoining of Indigenous identity with those who self-define as people of color.

Oftentimes, texts invested in racial solidarity reject the idea of childhood as innocent and sheltered, preferring instead to spotlight the child's investment in adult concerns, sometimes with the goal of demonstrating child capability and leadership and sometimes with the intention of rendering child exploitation in order to inspire social change. In terms of race-based political and aesthetic movements, children's literature often enabled women writers to participate, as did the poet Effie Lee Newsome during the Harlem Renaissance or Sonia Sanchez during the Black Arts Movement. While there are a range of approaches to race literature for children, women writers often used children's texts as a means to resist the patriarchal restrictions of race movements and to reshape the race by resisting sexism as well as racism. Race nationalist children's literature sometimes presents a construction of childhood that invokes militarism and violence, as does Nikki Giovanni's *Ego Tripping and Other Poems for Young People* (1973). Even if militarism in service to social revolution is not the goal, many children's texts emerging from race movements figure the child as aware of exploitation and injustice, as does Tomás Rivera's *. . . y no se lo tragó la tierra* (. . . and the earth did not devour him; 1971). Child characters recognize their own implication in racialized systems of economic and social oppression and forge means of political resistance and cultural reinvention.

A particularly vexed discussion in race and children's literature is the question of authenticity—in terms of both definition and advocacy. Bradford calls *authenticity* "an overworked and problematic term in discussions of Indigenous peoples and texts" (2007, 85), an idea that promotes cultural calcification and the location of identity in a past informed by white romanticism and superstition. For black communities in the US, ideas about authenticity have been used to endorse race loyalty, especially during the Black Arts Movement, and critics of

children's literature have grappled with the potential of *authenticity* as a term connected to value. Critics and writers struggle to define "insiders" and "outsiders" in ways that respect the multiplicity of expressions of identity within communities. There is not one monolithic Latinx or Asian identity, for example, and the variety of cultural expressions makes authenticity as a frame increasingly complicated. In service to unsettling the idea of authenticity as necessarily a static frame, scholars have been invested in recovering literary archives and traditions within racialized communities. This recovery work emerges historically, as in Anna Mae Duane's (2007, 2017) scholarship on nineteenth-century black American schooling, and in contemporary contexts, as in the work of Michele Martin (2004) and Rudine Sims Bishop (2007) on African American children's literature. Internationally, recovery and reclamation of the variety of racialized identity appear in the work of Clare Bradford (2001) on Indigenous Australian children's literature and Vivian Yenika-Agbaw (2008) on African children's literature. In addition, as sensitivity to individuals of mixed backgrounds increases, any simplistic use of race as a category dissolves.

Currently, several presses are issuing texts that work to represent the lived experience of children who identify through race or who are categorized through race, including Lee & Low (US), Cinco Puntos (US), Oyate (US), Peepal Tree Press (UK), Groundwood (Canada), Theytus (Canada), Pemmican (Canada), Huia Publishers (New Zealand), Magabala Books (Australia), and Institute for Aboriginal Development Press (Australia). Each year, the Cooperative Children's Book Center at the University of Wisconsin issues statistics on the numbers of books representing children of color and Native children and those authored by members of marginalized communities; its findings consistently note the disproportionate representation of whiteness in children's literature. In response, the We Need Diverse Books campaign has drawn public attention to the need for increased representation of children who identify through race and culture. The situation internationally appears similar to that of the US. For instance, Zetta Elliott (2010) has charted the appearance of black Canadian books since 2000 and found slender publication rates.

Studies of race in children's literature can turn in productive directions—toward the recovery of lost writers as well as the reinvention and reassessment of the canon. Attention to race can problematize discussions of childhood that tilt toward the universal or that assume a white, middle-class subject. An especially exciting site for destabilizing racial representation has been fantasy, in which writers like Nnedi Okorafor and Malorie Blackman have intervened in limiting constructions of racial identity and hierarchy and Jan Mark has drawn attention to whiteness as a structuring social formation. Attention to race as a category can help us attend to the continued presence of white supremacy in children's literature as well as the ways in which writers imagine racialized identity through possibility and reinvention.

51

Realism
Cathryn M. Mercier

Raymond Williams writes that "realism is a difficult word, not only because of the intricacy of the disputes in art and philosophy to which its predominant uses refer, but also because the two words on which it seems to depend, real and reality, have a very complicated linguistic history" prior to the nineteenth century. In the nineteenth century, *realism* was a new word but already had four identifiable meanings, only one of which "describe[d] a method or attitude in art and literature—at first an exceptional accuracy of representation, later a commitment to describing real events and showing things as they actually exist" (Williams 1983b, 259). In literature for children and young adults, each part of this description touches other contested territory in the field.

The eighteenth century's stress on reason and rationality challenged fairy tales and fantasy and made way for the pragmatic and the realistic text. The Romantic era's belief that "fantasy is the proper literature for young children" (Richardson 1994, xiii) might have pushed realism to the side if not for the period's attention to education, literacy, and the growing popularity of the bildungsroman. Despite the rise of British fantasy, the twentieth century's suspicions about the potential dangers of alternative worlds and assumed introduction to the occult again privileged fiction set in the real world. Late twentieth and early twenty-first-century debates about identity call for an accurate representation of race, class, gender, religion, and sexuality in realistic fiction.

Unlike the term *fantasy*, *realism* (or *realistic fiction*) lacks a specific definition to guide its critical discussions of children's and young adult literature. It does not receive its own entry in key reference texts in the field, such as *The Norton Anthology of Children's Literature* (Zipes et al. 2005) and *The Cambridge Guide to Children's Books in English* (Watson 2001). An entry does appear in *The Oxford Encyclopedia of Children's Literature* (2006), where Vanessa Joosen outlines various types of writing aligned with realism. She includes the "everyday-life story" for younger children, the problem novel dominant in the '70s for its attention to issues such as eating disorders and divorce, and texts "with documentary value, describing historical events of social problems with numerous acute details" (2006, 328). *Reading Children's Literature: A Critical Introduction* (Hintz and Tribunella 2013) offers brief histories of realism and addresses the overlap of the modes of realism and fantasy. *The Bloomsbury Introduction to Children's and Young Adult Literature* (Coats 2018) historically and ideologically situates realism in Platonic and Aristotelian concerns about mimesis as well as in today's demand for recognizability in socially conscious fiction.

As Joanne Brown points out, operationalizing a definition of *realism* poses problems if one attempts to measure it against one's perception of reality or "common interpretations" (1999, 329) drawn from lived experience. Definitions of *realism* typically attend to how it is not fantasy, not historical fiction, not narrative nonfiction, and not (necessarily) domestic fiction. Yet such definitions by contrast quickly create the bothersome tautology that realism might be that fiction whose people, places, and happenings *seem* real. Realism as the fiction of the possible and mimetic—as not a reality itself but a self-aware mode whose exemplars adhere to recognizable, shared linguistic codes—aligns with Jonathan Culler's (1975) structuralist understanding of realism in terms of its artificial verisimilitude and attenuates the linguistic constructedness of realism. Such attenuation separates realism from modernism's embrace of experimentation and suspicious rejection of the representational to align it with postmodernism's argument that reality does not have a knowable, exclusive, and essential quality. Given its "ideological core" (Coats 2018), realism implicates the reader in its literary construction and its effect through the intertwining of many "dialectic[s] between social and individual existence" (Berger and Luckmann [1966] 1989, 209).

Narratological interrogations of the polyphonic novel (see Schwenke-Wyile 2003) not only locate agency in the reader's negotiation between ethical dilemmas posited by the text but also engage the reader in negotiating the terms of realism as constructed in and by texts. Readers can traverse the attributes of realism itself through the "hyperrealism" or "ultrarealism" (Joosen 2006, 328) operating in Sonya Hartnett's family drama *Sleeping Dogs* (1995) or Eishes Chayil's *Hush* (2010), in Melvin Brugess's inexorable violence of drug abuse in *Smack* (1997), or in Barry Lyga's gender-reversing story of sexual abuse in *Boy Toy* (2007). Political awakenings further nuance meanings of *realism* in Marjane Satrapi's crossover graphic memoir *Persepolis* (2003), in Louise Erdrich's *The Round House* (2012), and in the transgressive lesbian love story set in Iran in Sara Farizan's *If You Could Be Mine* (2013) and of religious expression in *Does My Head Look Big in This?* (2005) by Randa Abdel-Fattah. Intersections of disability, gender, and race adumbrate the construction of realism in Francisco X. Stork's *Marcelo and the Real World* (2009), and intersections of race, gender, and sexuality texture *Happy Families* (2012) by Tanita S. Davis.

Jerome Bruner emphasizes that realistic narratives operate "as a form not only of representing but of constituting reality" (1992, 5). Bruner's adherence to unity of narrative and the concept of an individual self sits comfortably within conventional practices in children's and young adult literature that offer images of selfhood to young people, yet it sits uncomfortably in examinations of ideologies of identity (McCallum 1999a) or studies of identity as positional or intersectional (Slade 2008). In *Disturbing the Universe: Power and Repression in Adolescent Literature* (2000), Roberta Trites understands of the dialogic work of literature in the complex negotiations between the young adult self and the institutions that determine that self. The social and psychological realism of young adult trailblazers, such as S. E. Hinton's *The Outsiders* (1967), John Donovan's *I'll Get There. It Better Be Worth the Trip* (1969), and Robert Cormier's *The Chocolate War* (1974), center the dialectic between the individual and the social as they present characters enmeshed within a web of social relationships, political discourse, and economic marginalization and often render graphically the violence of such encounters.

Although realistic fiction attends to settings beyond the pastoral, as a mode it struggles with representation of characters across identity categories without qualifying the term itself. "Social" realism, "hyper" realism, and "dark" realism often denote departures from the white heteronormative assumptions of the term, and yet twenty-first-century authors have found ways to reassert realism as relevant to contemporary fiction. In examining black British urban fiction from the 1990s to the 2000s, Modhumita Roy finds "brutalist realism" as a "vivified realism that is active, curious, experimental, and subversive," as it "detail[s] a social ecology far too often elided or ignored in the fiction set in London: the experience of a racialized city and its consequences, especially for young black men . . . [that] capture[es] systemic, embedded injustice" (2016, 96). Although Roy names adult political texts, the young adult narrative voice in Alex Wheatle's *Brixton Rock* (1999) and the

coming-of-age story of Peter Akinti's *Forest Gate* (2009) gesture toward their crossover potential and underscore the presence of brutal realism in works read by young adults.

As Simon Gikandi suggests, modern African writers—such as Chinua Achebe, Franz Fanon, Thomas Mofolo, and Sol Plaatje—demonstrate the need for realism as literary practice that affirmed the colonized writers' lived experience and, simultaneously, became the vehicle through which to resist an imposed language, challenge the colonizers' literary canon, and "provide a counterpoint to the colonial order and its objective claims" (2012, 326). Gikandi concludes that these "writers did not consider romance, realism, and modernism separate categories. Rather, these categories constituted different ways of thinking about time, place, and identity" (312). In a similar vein, Sunyoung Park seeks to understand the fall of realism in Korea, as the very "question of realism . . . carries such theoretical weight concerning the social significance of literature that it cannot be easily dismissed as a thing of the past" (2006, 165). She asserts that while the discussion of realism is bound by Western debates, its historical trajectory in Korean literature enabled the colonized subject to not only represent mimetically Korean society but also resist the colonial legacy to "expose the exploitative social order" in realistic fiction (186). Park concludes that "since the early 1990s, there has been a continuous endeavor to salvage realism . . . [because] it continues to be evoked in Korea as a literature—or the possibility of one—that exposes the uncelebrated sides of shared social conditions in order to inspire aspiration for a better society" (187). A similar exposure and resistance appears in contemporary work of Dominican American Julia Alvarez, Cuban American Ana Veciana-Suarez, and Haitian American Edwidge Danticat, who "document their own experiences and the experience of others through their works of fiction. They chronicle the living conditions, injustices, and oppression that the citizens of their countries were subject to in what is known as a *testimonio* . . . [that] speaks for the individuals in a community as well as for the community as a whole" (Hilton and Nikolajeva 2012, 25).

As children's and young adult literature continues to experiment with not only whose story is told but also how that story is conveyed—for example, in a traditional narrative form, polyphonically, in verse, as a graphic novel—realistic texts will continue to trouble gatekeepers privileging the hopeful narrative, the holistic identity. Perhaps the difficulty in operationalizing a definition of *realism* demonstrates the necessary fluidity of the term itself.

52

Size
Lynne Vallone

The *OED* defines *size* as the "magnitude, bulk, bigness of anything." *Size* may be qualified to denote, describe, or categorize material things—such as nanotechnology—as well as immaterial ones, such as big ideas. In addition, the word *size* relates to the spatial dimension of persons or of items such as books. Although size, like time, may appear to be simply objective and mensural, it is also an experiential phenomenon. Size is both a fact and an epistemology, a measurement and a category of difference used to evaluate persons and things. Although an object or person's size can yield data "by eye" or via tools measuring different aspects (such as height, width, and volume), how the data are organized is a matter of perspective, and how size is experienced is a matter of embodiment and social culture (Vallone 2017). The experience of size is inextricably tied to scale: we understand the adjectives *big* or *small* and their many degrees of superlatives only when an object or body is put in relation to something else. Very often, scale is experienced emotionally. Edmund Burke (1757) theorizes that extremes of size—both large and small—provoke feelings of the sublime. As the go-to measure of both size and value, the human body leads to the creation of "conventions of symmetry and balance on the one hand, and the grotesque and the disproportionate on the other" (Stewart [1984] 1993). Such adjudications play out in children's books in which bodies of exaggerated size are appreciated and found to be beautiful and precious or rejected as ugly and disgusting. Thus notions and negotiations of big and small are integral to the history and development of children's literature (Vallone 2017).

The integration between size and children's literature occurs on two levels: inside and outside of the books themselves. As physical objects, children's books are often sized for small hands. This appealing marketing feature may be traced from John Newbery's publications for children, including *A Little Pretty Pocket-Book* (1744), to Anna Barbauld's *Lessons for Children* (1778–79), the tales of Beatrix Potter (1902–30), and Maurice Sendak's *Nutshell Library* (1962). Size—or more precisely, size difference—is an important concept that is articulated and experienced within children's books through the many gigantic or miniature characters found there. Ogres and thumblings, fantastical beasts, races of tiny and huge beings, giant robots, and ballerina mice populate classic and contemporary global children's literature. Outside of the books, young readers are typically of smaller stature than adults and, even in the case of adolescent readers, less autonomous, wielding less social and political power.

In children's literature, the small character's size functions tropically, reproducing the vulnerability of childhood. Thus Mary Norton's six-inch-tall Borrowers living under the floorboards and dependent on "human beans" for their survival "are essentially voyeurs in a realm of giants, echoing the situation of children in the company of adults" (Griswold 2006, 62). Within the children's literature marketplace, the size difference between adult and child may also reflect an imbalance in which the "big" have greater authority than the "small"—controlling, for the most part, content, publication, and access. Yet challenging this power asymmetry is another hallmark of children's books. Indeed, child characters often defy the expectations that attach to size and age. In J. K. Rowling's Harry Potter series (1997–2007), for example, wizarding youth show themselves to possess powers and insights that are as great as or greater than the adults around them. In a twist that links size to advanced age rather than childhood, Alf Prøysen's Mrs. Pepperpot (1955–70), the shape-shifting old lady who regularly shrinks to the size of a "pepperpot," inhabits the freedom and subversion allowed the miniature—but not the female or the elderly—only when small (Lassén-Seger and Skaret 2014).

Traditional tales establish size conventions as well as subvert them. Tiny characters are weak yet cunning, and giants are brutish and bloodthirsty. In *Gulliver's Travels* (1726), from which Gulliver's first two voyages were later adopted as children's literature, Swift satirizes English religion and politics through the changing scale of Gulliver's environment: he finds the Lilliputians to be small-minded, while the Brobdingnagian king is both noble and wise. Folklore is rife with clever and brave miniatures who demonstrate the motto *multum in parvo*, or "much in little." Tiny heroes such as Charles Perrault's "le petit poucet" (1697) and the Japanese fairy tale hero Issun Bōshi ("One Inch Boy") depart from home, seek their fortunes, and vanquish enormous foes, earning rewards along the way. Offering a different view, some giants are protectors, such as the golem figure in Jewish lore or the enormous metal-eating man in Ted Hughes's *The Iron Man* (1968; published in the US as *The Iron Giant*).

Size difference provides a key site for comedy in the picture-book tall tale and through the scatological humor of many Tom Thumb stories. The ironic play in Swedish author-illustrator Pija Lindenbaum's *Else-Marie and Her Seven Little Daddies* (1991; originally published as *Else-Marie och småpapporna*) uses size difference to make a statement about the nature and acceptance of families. Else-Marie lives a perfectly ordinary and contented life with her mother and seven miniature fathers until the terrifying day her tiny multiple fathers are scheduled to pick her up from her play group, exposing her unconventional family. By setting up the comic situation in which the multiple daddies of extreme size difference are welcomed, Lindenbaum highlights how norms may be challenged and all forms of family celebrated.

Yet children's literature has not been immune from depicting bodily size difference—especially when indexed to race—in offensive ways. Boys' adventure books set in "exotic" locales such as *Bomba the Jungle Boy and the Cannibals; or, Winning against Native Dangers* (Rockwood 1932) showcase colonialist ideologies of the superiority of whites as white youth rescue pygmy Africans. In Roald Dahl's *Charlie and the Chocolate Factory* ([1964] 1973), the tiny, dark-skinned Oompa Loompas are described by Willy Wonka as "'Pygmies . . . imported direct from Africa!'" Although their pygmy identity was edited out of later editions so that the Oompa Loompas become "rosy-white" and no longer hail from Africa but from "Loompaland," their merry prankster slave status marks them as performing racialized miniatures. Even Isabel Allende's magical realist novel for young adults *Bosque de los pigmeos* (*Forest of the Pygmies*; 2005), while idealizing the pygmy culture for its egalitarianism, privileges the "white" teen protagonists (one is from South America) as they often explain Africa to the Africans or decide what is in their best interests.

While one expects to find miniatures and giants in works of fantasy, very small or very big characters from life also play important roles in contemporary children's literature. Historically, persons with medical conditions that retard or advance growth were stigmatized as "freaks." Many recent children's books featuring dwarf, giant, or obese characters counteract these narratives of abnormality through competing arguments about bodily size and identity. Kate Klise and M. Sarah Klise's

picture book *Stand Straight, Ella Kate* (2010) frames the true story of a woman with gigantism as a tale of empowerment as she sees the world with a traveling circus. The dwarf characters in Katherine Marsh's *Jepp, Who Defied the Stars* (2012) and Lisa Graff's *The Thing about Georgie* (2007) find friendship, love, and success unrestricted by their small bodies. YA books such as K. L. Going's *Fat Kid Rules the World* (2003) tackle low self-esteem without targeting size—obesity—as "the problem."

Size also functions didactically and as a moral register within children's literature. After a tomte's miniaturizing spell, the selfish Nils in Selma Lagerlöf's *The Wonderful Adventures of Nils* (1906) undertakes an educational and emotional journey through Sweden on a gander's back. Extreme bodily size makes visible other differences and divisions that exist between people, including those of race, religion, and culture. Visual and verbal representations of size difference encourage the child reader to picture and explore the nature and resolution of prejudice against the "other." In *Les derniers géants* (1992; trans. *The Last Giants*, 1999), François Place revives myths of conquest and empire in order to highlight the costs to those who conquer as well as those who are "discovered." The English anthropologist, who relentlessly pursues a race of peaceful and hospitable giants only to fall in love with their harmonious culture, ultimately destroys them by revealing their existence to the Western world. This profound cautionary tale uses size difference to illustrate the violence of colonialist ideologies perpetrated in the name of science.

We experience and learn about the world, in part, through size and through scale: our bodies inevitably relate to the dimensions of the objects, people, and environment that surround us. The epistemology of size may be especially dramatic and emotional for children. Picture books show the child's perspective through variations in size, typically in conjunction with shape and color. In Francesca Sanna's *The Journey* (2016), the timely, moving, and suspenseful story of a family's forced migration from a war-torn land to a new home is enhanced by the look of radical size difference. The refugee child's fears and fantasies are depicted as an enormous border guard leering over the family and refusing entry as well as by the mother's bountiful flowing hair enveloping the children and providing comfort.

Exceptionally big and small bodies help make ontological observations appropriate for all ages. Through the running dialogue between a three-inch-tall king and a man in despair, Axel Hacke's *Der kleine König Dezember* (*Little King December*; 1993) ruminates on grown-up life's melancholia and its antidotes. The tiny king represents childhood's imagination—which we might understand in psychoanalytic terms as the unconscious (Steedman 1995)—and through his example, he helps the man in despair heal from his alienation. When the shrinking king declares, "In the end, I'm not just a part of a whole. I *am* the whole," he reacquaints the man with childhood's starting point, with the potential of small and its ability to imagine big.

53

Story
Hugh Crago

Almost all of us recognize a story when we encounter one, but often we are hard-pressed to spell out exactly what a story *is*. It seems too simple, too childlike perhaps, to bother with in a scholarly context. We all use the word, but we do not ask what (if anything) it really stands for.

To begin with, we need to discuss *story* in the context of at least two other English words with which it has overlapped and from which it has diverged. These words are *history* and *tale*. *Story* is a shortened form of *estorie*, the Anglo-Norman form of Latin *historia*, which in turn derives from the Greek *histor* (man of learning, man of authority) and thus has to do with knowledge. Yet a history was also a *presentation* of knowledge, since the *histor* stood in the marketplace and proclaimed significant new events to his community (the role taken today by TV newsreaders). In its origins, history was an oral "account of things that happened" (the root meanings of the Chinese characters *Gu-Shi*; compare Latin *res gestae* [things done]). Similarly, the Old English word *talu* (modern *tale*) simply meant "something told." Our modern distinction between fact and fiction was not contained in early usages of either *history* or *story*. From its first appearance in English, *estorie* could refer to both real events and fictional (made up) ones.

Young children learn the difference between *real* and *pretend* from as young as three (White 1954; Crago and Crago 1983), but their limited knowledge of the world means that it is not as clear a distinction as it will be when they grow up—leading to the first of several assumed links between story and children. Many preschoolers expect whatever they find in a story to be true—if not in their own neighborhood, then perhaps somewhere else in the world (Applebee 1978). Yet our comfortable assumption of adult superiority is shakily based when it comes to stories. It was, after all, adult listeners who believed that a Martian invasion of earth was in progress when they listened to a radio adaptation of Wells's *The War of the Worlds* in 1938.

In a society where only a minority was literate, "tales" were generally told aloud—by each of Chaucer's Canterbury pilgrims, for instance. And when, four centuries later, Arthur Mee resoundingly titled one recurring section in his *Children's Encyclopedia* "The Great Stories of The World That Will Be *Told* Forever" (italics mine), he preserved that sense of story as fundamentally oral in its nature. Here is another apparent link between story and childhood, since most preschool children take in stories orally, as did people in preliterate societies. *Told* also suggests a teller, a narrator who is—apparently, at least—in control of a story's content and style, and the issue of who "owns" a story's content and determines the manner of its telling has now become a subject for academic debate (Ellis 1984; Warner 1994a, 2011).

When *story* entered English with the Norman Conquest, its evolving meanings unfolded in parallel with those of the older *tale*. In the late fourteenth century, *Sir Gawain and the Green Knight* (a highly sophisticated verse romance since retold for children), *stori* and *tale* are used as synonyms. Yet during the same period, *tale* acquired the additional meaning of "malicious gossip," and *story* came to embrace "a fabrication" and later (from the seventeenth century) "a lie." (A very similar range of meanings over the spectrum of *truth* is found in Spanish *historia* and Russian *vydumka*.)

With the invention of printing and the gradual spread of literacy, the words *history*, *tale*, and *story* gradually came to have core meanings that reflected educated people's awareness of a significant distinction between "what really happened" (in von Ranke's famous phrase) and what *might* have happened (or what *could never* have happened). As late as the twentieth century, *history* could still be used to title a novel (Wells's *The History of Mr Polly* [1910]), but such usages were self-conscious echoes of much earlier titles (e.g., Fielding's *The History of Tom Jones, a Foundling* [1749]). History is now firmly established as "fact" even though today's historians (and biographers) concede that at best, they can only approximate a truth that is too large, complex, and shifting ever to be definitive.

In the first quarter of the twentieth century, Beatrix Potter preserved a much earlier distinction between *tale* and *story* when she titled her mininovels "tales" and reserved *story* for slighter narratives intended for an even younger age group (*The Story of a Fierce Bad Rabbit* [1906]), but subsequent authors have not followed her, and by the twenty-first century, *tale* has become somewhat archaic. *Story* is the commonly used word for a fictional narrative—though it retains an overlap with *history* in the media, where a *story* is an attention-grabbing short piece that purports to be factual. In literary criticism, *story* was supplanted by *plot* (Wellek and Warren 1949)—on the assumption that an organized sequence of events lies at the heart of every story—and more recently by *narrative*. So what has scholarship contributed to our understanding of this mysterious thing called story?

As Aristotle defined it in his fourth-century BCE *Poetics* (which took most of its examples from Athenian drama), *story* comprises a logically linked series of events within a structure that includes a beginning, a middle, and an end; characters to whom the story happens, and with whom we can identify; and a conclusion that embodies some form of resolution or release. Yet is that structure inherent in the story itself or in the minds of its audience? In 1944, Heider and Simmel made a brief film clip showing circles and triangles moving randomly around a space. The vast majority of those who watched it interpreted the geometric shapes as "characters" in a "story" of conflict and competition. Later, reader-response researchers like Holland (1975) and Radway (1984) would elaborate on the way that readers do not simply respond to meanings inherent in a story but *bring* meanings to it—meanings that may include gendered and ethnically determined assumptions.

Australian illustrator Shaun Tan (whose parents emigrated from Malaysia) exploits the human craving for narrative coherence in his graphic novella *The Arrival* (2006), a wordless depiction of a man arriving in a strange land and struggling to make sense of what he experiences. That both child and adult readers impose a story template on Tan's detailed but ambiguous pictures speaks to our need for the story form itself—as a way of organizing otherwise chaotic and confusing experiences to our evolutionary advantage—an insight explored authoritatively by Brian Boyd (2009).

Critical attempts to define the formal shape of story accelerated as the twentieth century progressed. Vladimir Propp's *Morfologija Skazki* (*The Morphology of the Folktale*; 1928) analyzed the Russian fairy tale as a sequence of events (functions) that always occurred in the same order. To varying degrees, Propp's emphasis has continued in later contributions to structuralism (Frye 1957) and narratology (e.g., Genette [1972] 1980; Labov 1972). Narratologists have focused most of their attention on plot structure, though they also consider narrators and implied and explicit readers (Wall [1991] 1994; Nikolajeva 2014).

As yet, narratology has paid little attention to the *phenomenology* of story. Both story creators and story audiences report feeling "lifted out of themselves" and "drawn along" by a compelling story, immersed in a "hyper-reality" that seems intensely meaningful yet resists the spelling out of that meaning in words (Crago 2014). These features of story, akin to the altered states of dreaming and dissociative trance, have been greatly illuminated by fifty years of neurological research. "Split brain" experiments and brain imaging (Trimble 2007; McGilchrist 2009) have indicated that it is the rational left hemisphere that is concerned with distinguishing fact from fiction, *history* from *story*. For the right hemisphere, which evolved earlier and served the evolutionary function of keeping us safe from danger, that distinction is meaningless; while we are under the spell of a well-told story, we enter into it as if it were true (even though our left hemisphere knows it is not). Coleridge ([1817] 1906) famously called this "willing suspension of disbelief," but it mostly occurs without any conscious decision on our part.

Scholars as different as Lewis (1966) and Bruner (1986) agree with Propp that stories originate in a sense of danger, threat, or trouble. Rationally we know that a piece of fiction poses no real threat to us, but the human right hemisphere is primed to respond to even the *idea* of threat happening to *someone else*. "Mirror neurons" (Cozolino 2002) fire in response to our viewing the distress, fear, or suffering of *others*, whether those others be real or fictional, and anything unknown is a potential threat. Hence mystery as well as danger drives many stories.

When (in the act of reading, viewing movies, or listening to an oral performance) the left hemisphere's rationally based "disbelief" is temporarily suspended, adults and children alike "live" temporarily in the story world and experience that world vividly and dramatically, as they did in infancy (Crago 2014). They "lose themselves" in one or more of its fictional characters and feel with them in their vicissitudes because the right hemisphere, on its own, does not have a separate, observing "self" as the left hemisphere does. Personal associations and meanings become part of readers' experiences of certain stories because the right hemisphere does not distinguish "me" from "not me." All these things point to a potential redefinition of *story* to denote a narrative genre in which right-hemisphere processes and perceptions dominate—a genre once designated by the word *romance* (Beer 1970; Crago 2018), which has now fallen from favor with scholars.

Given the phenomenological evidence of the way readers, listeners, and viewers become immersed in—even addicted to—right hemisphere–dominated narratives, it is hardly surprising that thinkers have always worried about the power of stories to shape behavior for both good and ill. Famously, Plato (in *The Republic*) advised that "poets" (by which he meant writers of fiction as well as poets in our sense) should be banned from his ideal society. In the sixteenth century, Sir Philip Sidney defended *poesie* (which, like Plato and Aristotle, he takes to embrace narrative fiction and drama) on the grounds that it could, as it were, seduce its audience into "vertue" without their realizing it.

But of course, the same argument can easily enough be used to show that the influence of stories may be malign—Wagner's operas and the medieval *Nibelungenlied* seem to have inspired the adolescent Hitler to dreams of world domination and "justified" genocide. Every argument about the influence of stories founders on the evidence that the power stories appear to have over us is ultimately a power we attribute to them, arising from the deep structure of our own personalities and individual histories.

In our evolving world of screens, where enacted dramas replace the written word, moving pictures replace static illustrations, and computer-generated imagery can make the most fantastic things "real," the importance of right hemisphere–dominated narratives may be enhanced, though whether the fundamental shape of story will be permanently altered is another matter. Margaret Mackey ([2002] 2007) has written insightfully on the earlier stages of these developments. When artificial intelligence makes possible conscious "choices" for participants in computer games like *Myst* (echoed somewhat lamely in "gamebooks" like the Choose Your Own Adventure series of the 1980s and 1990s), it may simply be restoring the "conscious, observing self" (McGilchrist 2009) of the left hemisphere to an otherwise right hemisphere–dominated "virtual reality."

54

Taboo

Åse Marie Ommundsen

The word *taboo*—in French, *tabou*—is an adjective, a noun, and a verb and is derived from the Tongan adjective *tabu*, which signifies something that is forbidden. Originally used in Polynesia, Melanesia, and New Zealand, the word denotes actions consecrated to a special use or purpose. A *tabu* may be restricted for the use of a god, a king, priests, or chiefs, while being forbidden for use by others, such as by a particular class—especially women—or by a particular person or persons. *Taboo* can mean "inviolable and sacred" or "forbidden and unlawful," and it is also said of people who are perpetually or temporarily prohibited from carrying out certain actions, from food, or from contact with others (*OED*). The first known use of the word in English dates back to 1777, when British explorer James Cook wrote about his visit to the island Tonga: "When dinner came on table [in Tongataboo] not one of my guests would sit down or eat a bit of anything that was there. Every one was *Tabu*, a word of a very comprehensive meaning which in general signifies forbidden. As everything would very soon be *Tabu*, whoever was found walking about would be *Mated*, that is killed or beat" (quoted in *OED*). What actually is considered taboo varies within different times and cultures and is closely related to social ideas and values.

In everyday language, *taboo* may mean "something we do not speak about," such as sexuality or a family history of alcoholism. Sigmund Freud (1913) postulated that incest and patricide are the only two universal taboos and that they are prerequisites for civilization. However, in the context of children's literature, taboo actions or items can include any subject—such as sexuality and violence—reserved for adult society but considered forbidden for children. The opposite of the taboo is the acceptable, allowed, or usual. While death and dying children were initially common motifs in Nordic children's literature (Alfvén-Eriksson 2000; Skjønsberg 1998), and violence was common in fairy tales for adults, both death and violence later became two of the new taboos in literature exclusively written for children. Around 1900, death became less common as a motif as public health care improved and child death became less common. In the Nordic countries, changing views on childhood and children's culture around 1968 transformed the whole scene, ushering in the gradual acceptance of sex and death in works for the young (Jensen 2017). In contemporary children's books, sexuality, violence, death, and dramatic illustrations may be considered taboo in some cultures but less so in others. Scandinavian children's literature is internationally known for controversial picture books that challenge traditional taboos like sexuality, violence, and death (Evans 2016).

Subjects that later merge as taboo were commonplace in the exemplum—a popular genre from the earliest phase of children's literature, in which a character emerges as either a positive or a negative example for the reader. It may be the poor but kind little girl who sells flowers in order to save her sick mother from death and who at the end is rewarded by a kind helper who saves the poor family. Or it may be the ill-behaved boy who steals from his neighbor in order to buy beer and tobacco and who is ultimately punished (Ommundsen 1998). In many of these stories, the punishment may involve the death of the child character, such as in the classic German series of stories *Der Struwwelpeter* (Shock-headed Peter; 1844). *Der Struwwelpeter* is a parody of cautionary tales—and especially of exemplums—that end with punishment. In one story about the young, fastidious Kasper who does not want to eat his soup, the boy dies after just five days. In another story about a boy who sucks his thumbs despite his mother's warnings, the story ends with both the boy's thumbs being cut off in a bloody scene.

In 1945, Astrid Lindgren's radical child character Pippi provoked a debate about what are acceptable topics for children's literature and what might be harmful to child readers' developing sense of morality (Birkeland, Risa, and Vold 2005). Lindgren's Pippi books challenge both adults' and children's literature's constant need to discipline children to ensure good behavior. As Pippi says, "You understand Teacher, don't you, that when you have a mother who's an angel and a father who is a cannibal king, and when you have sailed on the ocean all your whole life, then you don't know just how to behave in school with all the apples and ibexes" (Lindgren 1950, 60). The autonomous Pippi opposes all the restrictive standards that children, and especially girls, in her time were held to: she lives on her own, and she constantly challenges societal norms and restrictions put on children by adults, including school, the necessity of good hygiene, and so on. Yet she seems to sustain other taboos: in the original Swedish edition (1945) and the Norwegian (1946) and Danish first editions (1946), Pippi's father is a "negro king" (*negerkung/ negerkonge*). In both the English (1954) and the American edition (1950), this is translated to "cannibal king." The words *negro king* and *cannibal king* further indicate both that Pippi might be a less liberating figure for children of color and that taboos change over time. In

order to avoid racist connotations, new editions in the Scandinavian countries use "King of the Southern Sea" (*Sydhavskonge*).

Children's books are an important instrument of socialization in our culture and thus a place to discover society's rapidly changing values and norms. As Theresa Colomer points out, social changes are now so deep and occur at such a high speed that the perception of dominant values seems to be passing through a phase of uncertainty (2010, 45). It is in such a phase of uncertainty that the taboo-breaking tendency is at its strongest, as former norms may become taboo and former taboos can become the new norm (Nikolajeva 1996). One example is Portuguese author Manuel Bacelar's picture book *O Livro do Pedro* (2008). As this was one of the first Portuguese picture books to subvert stereotypical gender roles and normalize homosexual relationships, it was considered taboo breaking upon its publication in Portugal. During the same period in Scandinavia, however, so many picture books were published about homosexual relationships that homosexual characters would not be seen as controversial by the majority.

Views about nudity differ widely in different parts of the world. We may find that within one culture, nudity is a common feature in literature and films for adults but is prohibited in books and films for children. The Norwegian author and illustrator Stian Hole had to change two pictures when his picture book *Garmann's Secret* (2011) was translated for the American market. A picture of Garmann urinating in the forest and a picture of the two main children characters swimming naked in the lake were considered unsuitable for American children. In the American edition, Hole removed the peeing boy and painted a bathing suit on the nude girl. In a Norwegian context, children urinating in the woods and swimming in the nude are considered normal activities and are unlikely to provoke anyone. In 2011, the French picture book on nudity, *Tous à poil* (Franek and Daniau 2011), triggered a great debate. The author and illustrator set out to remove the shame from being naked: "If you think about it, whether you're a baby, a doctor or a baker . . . we all have buttocks, a tummy button, genitals and even moles," they said. An outraged critic said in an interview that "a naked teacher . . . isn't that great for teachers' authority!" French publishers and booksellers responded to the critique with an anticensorship campaign in which they posed in the nude—with strategically placed books.

Another common understanding of taboos in children's literature is the process of dealing with controversial issues or challenging political correctness. As is the case for values and beliefs, controversy, stereotypes, and political correctness also vary across different periods and different cultures. American author Mark Twain's *The Adventures of Huckleberry Finn* (1884) is widely considered to be one of the greatest American works of literature, but it has also been one of the most controversial. Twain wrote the novel after the American Civil War, but the setting he chose for the novel was prewar. Upon its publication, it was still taboo for the white boy, Huck Finn, to become friends with the black man and former slave, Jim. Huck was raised to be racist, but throughout the novel, his attitudes gradually become less racist, and Jim turns out to be a father figure to him. The book is still controversial for both similar and different reasons. The novel's final third seems to forget Huck's moral development, transforming Jim into—as Arnold Rampersad notes—"little more than a plaything . . . for the white boys over whom he once stood morally" (quoted in Nel 2017b). The term *nigger*—a racist slur in the nineteenth century, just as it is today—is repeated 219 times throughout the book, which serves as a reminder of attitudes toward black people both then and now.

Contemporary children's literature may challenge former taboos such as racism, gender stereotyping, homosexuality, mental illness, domestic violence, and abortion and invite the reader to reflect on ethical challenges. The Norwegian author Gro Dahle is a taboo-breaking author, who—together with her husband, Svein Nyhus, and her daughter, Kaia Dahle Nyhus, who are both illustrators—has written several challenging picture books about former taboos such as domestic violence (*Sinna Mann* [2003]), mental illness (*Håret til mamma* [2007]), parental neglect (*Akvarium* [2014]), incest (*Blekkspruten* [2016]), and pornography (*Sesam Sesam* [2017]), highlighting that it is important to talk about these issues with children.

YA fiction straddles the divide between children and adults, and consequently, it is not a surprise that YA tends to challenge taboos in society (Ommundsen 2008b, 2010). In 1990s dystopian YA fiction, motifs such as youth suicide, bullying, and self-harm have become common. American author Suzanne Collins's dystopian trilogy, Hunger Games (2008–10), pushes the boundaries: children in her books kill other children in order to entertain adults. Despite this taboo-busting inclination, or maybe because of it, the Hunger Games series has become an international best seller.

How powerful is the written word? Is a book really capable of harming a child? According to Danish philosopher K. E. Løgstrup (1969), the main character in a children's book must ultimately realize success in order not to extinguish the courage of the child reader. So does this mean that children's literature must follow the common formula for literature in order not to harm its intended audience? In contemporary children's literature, traditional happy endings are more frequently replaced with open endings that invite the reader to engage in his or her own ethical reflections. As American philosopher Martha Nussbaum (1990) points out, literature can play an important role in shaping the reader's morality. Literary texts are never ethically neutral (Ricoeur 1990, 249). Books have an effect on their readers. This is why we read books. Literature will always provide interpretations of the world (Gadamer 1994, 67), and books may be considered to be "the company we keep" (Booth 1988), holding the potential to change the way we think about ourselves and others. Taboos in children's literature will continue to change across different times and cultures, and children's literature will continue to challenge and alter its culture's taboos.

55

Trans

Derritt Mason

In January 2017, the cover of *National Geographic* declared a "gender revolution." Embodying this revolution are "80 young people" from around the world, interviewed by reporters "for a future-facing perspective on gender" (Goldberg 2017, 9). Seven of these young people adorn the cover, expressions defiant, their various identities signposted: intersex nonbinary, transgender male and female, bi-gender, androgynous, male. At the literal center of what this issue describes as "the shifting landscape of gender" is Eli—at age twelve, the youngest and most childlike in appearance of the cover models—a self-identified trans male who stands on a podium, towering over his cohort. The trans child, as produced by *National Geographic*, is a symbolic figurehead for the gender revolution—but one, as the issue goes on to illustrate, who struggles within persistently oppressive and often violent global gender regimes.

In *Trans Kids: Being Gendered in the Twenty-First Century* (2018), Tey Meadow notes that *trans*, an abbreviation of *transgender*, "has historically been used as an umbrella term" (266) for a range of gender identities and expressions. *Trans* may encompass people with nonbinary relationships to gender; "those whose psychological gender is in direct opposition with their chromosomal or biological sex"; individuals who have transitioned between genders through social performance, medical intervention, or a combination thereof; "intersex people; masculine women and feminine men" (266). The *OED* lists two entries for *trans* in addition to its function as an abbreviation: a noun that truncates "translation, transmission, and trans-continental" and the prefix *trans-*, which means "across, through, over, to or on the other side of, beyond, outside of, from one place, person, thing, or state to another." "When used to label a child," Meadow explains, *trans* "most often references a change in social gender categories from one gender to the other" (2018, 266). My focus here will be on how children's literature and culture illuminate the instability and contradictions of the adjective *trans* and invite us to consider *trans-* in its broader sense.

While the *OED* dates the prefix *trans-* back to 1612, *trans* as adjective was not used until 1973, and as Meadow indicates, "we see no references to transgender children prior to the mid-1990s" (2014, 57). Indeed, North American culture has only recently begun imagining the trans child as such, vis-à-vis medical and sociological discourse, literature, film, and television. Thinking *trans* in relation to childhood raises concerns about agency; the child, as Claudia Castañeda points out, "is always already seen as incomplete . . . its gender is not fully mature, and the child is also seen as not fully capable of knowing its own gender" (2014, 59). Do children possess the bodily autonomy to self-determine and self-fashion as trans, to request hormone therapy and/or surgery? How are adults implicated in consenting to medical procedures? As Meadow asks, "Is it possible, and what would it mean, to make the 'wrong' decisions?" (2014, 57). Moreover, can children's and young adult literature engage these issues without rehearsing reductive "problem novel" themes, which would reduce trans characters to "martyr-target-victims" (Rofes 2004)? When is the trans child, in Castañeda's words, "a new site of bodily subjection *to* normalizing gender regimes" and when are they "a site of possibility for new, nonnormative, or resistant transgender subjectivities" (2014, 61)?

Whereas initial young adult novels with trans characters—such as Julie Anne Peters's *Luna* (2004)—tended to recapitulate narratives of victimization and oppression familiar to readers of early gay adolescent fiction (see Jenkins and Cart 2018), a recent surge of titles featuring trans and genderfluid youth (and, notably, written by queer and trans-identified authors) deal thoughtfully with questions of gender identity and relationality, toying with and often subverting formal and generic conventions. James St. James's *Freak Show* (2007) campily sends up problem-novel tropes of the bullied loner, alcoholic parent, and closeted jock love interest to tell the story of a "self-proclaimed Superfreak" (212) in a conservative high school. Vivek Shraya's *God Loves Hair* (2014) is something of a trans-form: part picture book, part bildungsroman, and part memoir, Shraya's stories tackle the complex interconnectivity of race, religion, sexuality, and gender. Kai Cheng Thom's *Fierce Femmes and Notorious Liars: A Dangerous Trans Girl's Confabulous Memoir* (2016) takes a similar, unruly trans-genre approach, fusing fairy tales, fantasy, poetry, and the coming-of-age story to craft a strikingly original transition narrative.

Contemporary trans visibility, however, raises some temporal questions. Although Meadow signals that the trans child is "a relatively new social form" (2014, 7), Jules Gill-Peterson's remarkable *Histories of the Transgender Child* (2018) illustrates, through early twentieth-century medical archives, how trans children have existed long prior to the invention of *transgender*. Children's literature, too, has spent centuries imagining what we might call in contemporary parlance genderfluid, genderqueer, or trans children. See Hellfire Hotchkiss, from Mark Twain's unfinished novel of the same name, a girl described as "the only genuwyne male man" in her town ([1897] 1989, 121), and Tip, the gender-shifting protagonist of L. Frank Baum's *The Marvelous*

Land of Oz (1904). Victoria Flanagan (2008), moreover, has written on the forms and functions of cross-dressing in children's literature and film, and Michelle Ann Abate has documented the lengthy cultural history of the tomboy, which includes familiar figures like the protagonist of *Harriet the Spy* (1964) and Jo March of Alcott's *Little Women* (1868–69). Additionally, Nat Hurley (2014) illustrates how the evocative titular figure from Hans Christian Andersen's "The Little Mermaid" (1837) appeals to a number of trans constituencies, including children, and compellingly, Susan Honeyman suggests that the symbolically potent figure of the child as "genderless ideal" (2013, 169) stretches back to the Romantic era and beyond—think of John Locke's tabula rasa metaphor from 1693, which offers the child as a blank slate awaiting inscription ([1693] 1989, 265). Given the complexity and range of historical modes of gender identification and representation, *trans* presents a narrative contradiction: Does trans literature for young people follow the emergence of the trans child, or does trans lit precede this "new" social category? How have trans lit and the trans child produced one another? What does the circulation of *trans* as critical keyword enable, and what might it potentially erase?

Thus *trans* also contains a linguistic problem: What language, if any, can adequately capture the diversity of gender (anti-)identity in childhood across history and geography? Do *queer*, *trans*, and the notoriously problematic *transgender umbrella* (Singer 2014) suffice? What about terms like *gender creative* (Ehrensaft 2016) or *gender-fluid*—the latter added to the *OED* in 2016, at which point Merriam-Webster began including *cisgender*, *genderqueer*, and "Mx.," a gender-neutral title (Gutierrez-Morfin 2016)? Can *trans* properly account for "X," the "fabulous child" of Louis Gould's (1978) groundbreaking story; the amorphic, body-swapping protagonist in David Levithan's *Every Day* (2012); the

young intersex characters in Alyssa Brugman's *Alex as Well* (2013) and I. W. Gregorio's *None of the Above* (2015); or Mandy, profiled in *National Geographic*, who identifies as the Samoan third gender "Fa'afafine" (Goldberg 2017, 62–63)? As critical keyword, *trans* both dramatizes and pushes the limits of language that describes embodied gender identity.

This leads us to a spatial problem: as Susan Stryker and Paisley Currah indicate, *trans* is colonial and Eurocentric, and its usage risks obscuring non-Western and Indigenous gender paradigms and stymying trans-national thinking (2014, 8). As general editors of *Transgender Studies Quarterly*, Stryker and Currah have dedicated themselves to decolonizing *trans*. A special issue on this topic examines, among other subjects, trans childhood in 1950s and '60s Peru (Cornejo) and trans/two-spirit restoration among the Stó:lõ people of British Columbia, Canada (Wesley). Within the field of children's literature in English, there is a dearth of writing on trans childhoods from global and decolonial perspectives; this is likely due to the challenges of locating such literature across geographic and linguistic barriers. Film, however, has been steadily providing international stories about genderqueer childhoods: see *Ma vie en rose* (Belgium/France; 1997); *The Blossoming of Maximo Oliveros* (Philippines; 2005); *XXY* (Argentina/Spain/France; 2007); and *Tomboy* (France; 2011).

In a North American context, we are witnessing incrementally heightened visibility of trans characters in texts for children, including picture books for young readers (see Bittner, Ingres, and Stamper 2016 for an overview). Given the relative absence of international texts and scholarship on the topic, however, I am reminded of a 1999 essay by Jody Norton. Responding to the invisibility of trans children in literature, Norton advocates for "transreading" as a strategy to "intervene in the reproductive cycle of transphobia," which "may involve as simple a move as locating a male identity in a female body" or "may constitute itself as a much subtler imaginative enactment of a much wider range of identities" (299). What, I wonder, might "transreading" look like today? Without reducing trans children to the figural, typically white, "genderless ideal" child or the objects of anthropological curiosity, and while still recognizing the material violence inflicted on children as a consequence of global gender regimes, I wonder, Can we see *trans* as an invitation—or provocation—to think "across, through, over, beyond, and outside of" existing paradigms of gender *and/in* children's literature scholarship? This could mean thinking more deeply and broadly about trans-forms and trans-genres; it might mean cultivating a "transnational literacy" where children's literature is concerned, as Clare Bradford (2011, via Gayatri Spivak) encourages us to do; it could also entail thinking the *trans* in translation, as does Mingming Yuan in an analysis of Peter Pan's "disguised" gender in Chinese translations during the New Culture Movement of the 1920s (2016, 26). Transreading today will likely entail a bit of willfulness and a touch of disobedience where scholarly conventions are concerned. This is not inappropriate: as the *OED* tells us about *trans*, "in Old French the inherited form was in *tres-*, as *trespasser*"—to trespass.

56

Translation
Emer O'Sullivan

The *OED* offers a range of definitions for the noun *translation*, whose origin lies in the Latin verb meaning "to transfer." The first is "transference; removal or conveyance from one person, place, or condition to another," a meaning that, after having been dormant for some time, regained currency following the anthropological turn in translation studies, which regards translation not as a product but as a process that can be extended to include people, travel, and migration. This is the sense in which Salman Rushdie uses the term to describe his situation as a British Indian writer: "The word 'translation' comes, etymologically, from the Latin for 'bearing across.' Having been borne across the world, we are translated men" (1991, 16). The more commonly applied meaning of *translation* as "the action or process of turning from one language into another; also, the product of this; a version in a different language" (*OED*) follows later. The term *translation* is not itself contested in children's literature, but the appreciation of translation as an expression of internationalism, and especially the actual practice of translating, are.

Children's literature has, since its inception in the eighteenth century, been a site of intense translational activity, transcending linguistic and cultural borders since books and magazines specifically intended for young readers were produced. *Emil and the Detectives, The Story of Babar, Pippi Longstocking*, and many other modern classics of children's literature would be unknown to readers of English if they had not been translated. The Harry Potter series has found its way into more than seventy languages, including Latin, Scots, and most recently, Mongolian, thanks to the efforts of translators. Today children's literature is the most translated segment in many literary markets from China (Tan 2017) to Galicia (Millán-Varela 1999), to name but two examples. Although many children's literatures are aware of the debt their own development owes to texts imported via translation, most histories of children's literature nonetheless only include books originally written by members of their nation, region, or language.

Debate over how children's literature should be translated reflects the central tension between the ideal of preserving the artistic and cultural integrity of the source text (in seeing the authority reside in the original) and adapting the text to the abilities of the child audience (in allowing the authority to reside in an imagined child reader). Göte Klingberg (1986), one of the first children's literature scholars to seriously address the issue of translation, argues that the integrity of the original work should be violated as little as possible and systematically lists the culture- and language-specific references that might occur, regarding them as one of the main sources for "deviations" from the source text in translation. Riitta Oittinen's (2000) child-centered theory, on the other hand, concentrates exclusively on the child reader, disputing any authority for the text; she programmatically speaks of "translating for children" rather than "translating children's literature." Since these pioneering works, translation research in children's literature studies now reflects these tensions, manifesting an increased awareness of the fact that to talk of children's literature as a singular entity is to disregard the huge variety of texts encompassed by this term and the different ages of their readers, all of which has to be taken into account when discussing their translation.

Following Rousseau's dictum that children must be shielded from anything that may be culturally unfamiliar, translators and publishers sometimes underestimate young readers. Cognitive and linguistic developmental issues and the actual receptive ability of child readers to tolerate or understand foreign elements are at the heart of children's literature translation, always "a balancing act between adapting foreign elements to the child reader's level of comprehension, and to what is deemed appropriate, and preserving the differences that constitute a translated foreign text's potential for the enrichment of the target culture" (O'Sullivan 2013, 453). What children actually understand and how well they can and do cope with the culturally unfamiliar is the great black box of translating for children. Gillian Lathey (2006, 12) has rightly observed that a greater emphasis on empirical research into reader response would better inform current speculation. In this zone of conflicting aims, editors and translators make their own decisions determined by their assessment of child readers' capabilities and by the prevailing cultural and ideological norms of the target culture, which may go as far as to include institutionalized censorship (Thomson-Wohlgemuth 2009). Translation for children is therefore heavily informed by the image of childhood in any given culture at a given time.

Children's literature in translation has often been seen as a window through which children can access foreign cultures. However, a sense of the foreign origin of a text may be eradicated when a translation is heavily adapted to the target culture, or "domesticated" (Venuti 1995), hence offering a distorted window. The notion of translated children's literature as a window has featured largely in discussions of the internationalism of children's literature, which can be traced back to Paul

Hazard's famous utopian vision of the power of children's books: "Each of them is a messenger that goes beyond mountains and rivers, beyond the seas, to the very ends of the world in search of new friendships. Every country gives and every country receives—innumerable are the exchanges—and so it comes about that in our first impressionable years the universal republic of childhood is born" ([1932] 1944, 146). The discourse on international exchange in children's literature, which often owes more to wishful thinking than to observation of the actual exchange, harbors a number of paradoxes and contradictions (O'Sullivan 2016), especially relating to the imbalance of exchange between countries and languages.

The dynamics of the literary field, the status of the language and of children's literature, the traditions of cultural exchange, and commercial factors all determine the direction of textual flows. Emergent literatures depend on translations from other languages to enrich their language and literature, while literatures in dominant languages often regard themselves as more self-sufficient and therefore import less. The proportion of translation in children's literatures ranges from 1 percent to 80 percent of the annual book production, with the Scandinavian countries heading the league table in Europe; the Netherlands, Italy, and Germany in the midfield; and Britain and the US—the greatest exporters—bringing up the rear with somewhere between 2.5 and 4 percent and 1 and 2 percent, respectively (O'Sullivan 2013, 458). In many countries, the origins of up to 80 percent of translated books are Britain and the US, and literatures from numerous countries struggle to find their way into the dominant world market. Organizations such as Baobab Books (Switzerland) and Forlaget Hjulet (Denmark) work to make books from Asia, Africa, and Latin America available to young Western readers.

How a children's book is translated is linked to its cultural status, and this aspect offers a real-life dramatization of the translation studies debate between the integrity of a text versus the needs of an audience. In her study of English narrative fiction for girls translated into Dutch, Mieke Desmet reveals how the differential status between formula fiction and canonized texts effects translation: while translations of award-winning novels demonstrate a tendency to preserve as much as possible of the aesthetic quality of the source text, translations of formula fiction reveal a primary concern for the enjoyment of the reader and his or her understanding of the text and therefore adapt their content strongly to the target culture (Desmet 2007). As a large proportion of translated books today belong to (globalized) series, the undifferentiated notion that all translations are interculturally enriching cannot be sustained.

While one approach toward translation sees it providing texts that may open new perspectives and encourage intercultural tolerance, other, more critical stances fear cultural erasure. Many children's literatures struggling to establish a presence in their own domestic market do not join the chorus heralding translation as unqualified cultural enrichment. Some Arab scholars who find that the amount of translations presented to Arab children is too high warn that they are threatened by a cultural invasion from the West and that "the waves of translated books filling the markets in the Arab world prevent the spread of local children's literature" (Mdallel 2003). And recent reports in Hong Kong's *South China Morning Post* claim that Chinese publishers had received orders that the number of foreign picture books being printed in the booming children's book market should be cut back to support local production and that publishers would have to sell the rights to domestic children's books abroad if they want to continue importing foreign titles (Beech 2017).

TRANSLATION EMER O'SULLIVAN

In 2017, Baobab published a crowd-funded German translation of a picture book by Tatia Nadareišvili from Georgia (Eurasia) about a young boy who cannot sleep and tries to copy the different positions of sleeping animals on land, sea, and air. The ornately lettered Georgian text was integrated into the illustrations in the original edition, and these are retained in the bilingual German version, *Schlaf gut* (Sleep well), with the translated text below (Nadareišvili 2017). Individual words in both languages stand out in different colors, visualizing the concept of translation for children and showing that even if they cannot decipher the Georgian word, they can see that it corresponds to the word highlighted in their language. A postscript by translator Rachel Gratzfeld tells young readers about this special script with its three alphabets, which was recently added to UNESCO's list of the Intangible Cultural Heritage of Humanity. This imaginative and beautifully executed and produced book is a genuine embodiment of the idea of translated children's books opening up new worlds for young readers.

57

Transnational

Evelyn Arizpe

According to the *OED*, definitions of the adjectival form of *transnational* cluster around the idea of extending beyond national frontiers or political boundaries into a social space that is multinational or global. The term has close connections to other concepts that "challenge the stable and fixed (hegemonic) concept of the national" (Higbee and Hwee Lim 2010, 10), such as *multicultural* or *cosmopolitan*. Like its cognates, *transnational* stems from movements that incline toward making nation states irrelevant, yet the etymology remains rooted in the geopolitical notion of "nation," an indication of the difficulties faced by attempts to ignore prescribed geopolitical boundaries and the securities afforded by "imagined communities" (Anderson 1983). The term first appeared in English in 1921, entering the lexicon through economics and then seeping into other disciplines. Since then, its various derivatives (*transnationality*, *transnationalism*) have become so snarled up in political and scholarly discussion in a variety of fields that scholars have had to defend the value of continuing to use the term—if only as a conceptual form that implies an understanding of nation as "a thing contested, interrupted, and always shot through with contradiction" (Briggs, McCormick, and Way 2008, 627).

Initially used in the context of the economy, law, and business, the "*transnational* turn" within social studies in the 1960s led to the inclusion of the term within cultural studies and anthropology. The rise of big corporations and globalization in the following decades created definitions of the term "from above," while "on the ground," the "unprecedented flows of people and cultural artifacts" created definitions "from below" (Iriye and Saunier 2009, 1047). Theoretical paradigms emerging from these disciplines, and especially from postcolonial studies (such as the seminal work of Arjun Appadurai and Gayatri Spivak), attempted to understand what this meant for the humans who were participating in events that transcended national frontiers. These events initially referred to governance, but the term has become familiar in the description of social and religious movements as well as the arts (cinema, music, performance, and literature). Literary scholars have added to the debates about definition but also about whether the *transnational* is "something inherently progressive" or whether, in an Anglo-global world, it ends up supporting the imperialist nationalisms it seeks to subvert (Huggan 2011).

From the middle of the twentieth century, one of the strongly held assumptions about childhood in the liberal, global North continues to be that *transnational* experiences are beneficial: they are learning experiences that have the potential to diminish ethnocentrism and increase intercultural understandings. It would follow that children's literature that transcends national boundaries is therefore an ideal vehicle for these experiences when they cannot take place in real life: it introduces readers to characters from other countries and cultures, inviting them vicariously to experience different lives and thus helping transcend mental divisions between "us" and "them" This belief inspired Jella Lepman's founding of the International Board of Books for Young People (IBBY) in 1953 and the International Youth Library in Munich in 1949. There is a sense that *internationalism* is understood here as building bridges not only between nations but also between different ethnic or religious groups. This belief continues to propel children's literature initiatives such as the International Children's Digital Library that attempt to cross national frontiers and benefit readers across the globe. The fact that none of these initiatives (so far) has used *transnational* as a descriptive keyword may be because it still carries the connotation of wealth and ease of travel (globe-trotting) as distinct from the hardships and distress of forced displacement (diaspora).

This utopian vision of what internationalism or *transnational*ism can achieve through children's literature carries various risks. First, it risks the loss of literary aesthetics in favor of the didactic impulse. Second, it upholds a Romantic notion of "the child" who can transcend social and political structures, a notion that harks back to what Paul Hazard, writing in 1932, described as the "universal republic of childhood." Third, it fails to consider that although for some, a transnational childhood comes with the benefits of bilingualism and cosmopolitanism, for others, it signifies vulnerabilities brought about by forced displacement. Finally, it has ignored the pragmatics of the publishing industry (O'Sullivan 2004, 22; Bradford 2011).

Surprisingly, despite the debates and critical analyses around terms such as *multicultural*, *nationalism*, or *diversity* within children's literature, few scholars in this field have critically addressed the term *transnational*. To date, only Clare Bradford has engaged directly with it, with a focus on transnationalism in colonial texts and with reference to globalization and book publishing, defining *transnational* as the "duality in the lives of individuals and groups and to textual manifestations of this duality" (Bradford 2011, 23). Bradford's emphasis is on *negotiation*: "Transnational identities are formed when individuals and groups negotiate between and across cultures and languages" (23).

These sites of negotiation occur in four main spaces of children's literature: the creative space of writing for children, the texts, publishing and distribution, and the readers' engagement and response. It has become common to come across authors who see themselves as belonging to two or more cultures and who are described as transnational; for example, the *World of Words* blog (Kyung Sung and Sakoi 2016) from Arizona University has dedicated various entries to "transnational Asian authors" such as Linda Sue Park, the first Korean American author (born in the US to Korean immigrants) to win the Newbery Award with *A Single Shard* (2001), a novel about a potter in twelfth-century Korea. Two of her other novels are also transnational because they involve the crossing of borders, political and cultural: *Long Walk to Water* (2010) is about a Sudanese boy who is given asylum in New York, and *Project Mulberry* (2005) deals with the difficulties of incorporating a Korean tradition into an American high school project.

Can we assume that books by transnational authors are transnational by default? On the other side of the coin, can a "monocultural" author write a transnational book? This question refers us to the debates about authenticity in children's literature. Australian author Morris Gleitzman sets the first part of *Boy Overboard* (2003) in Afghanistan (a country that, by his own admission, the author had never visited) and describes the experience of a young boy fleeing with his family from the Taliban. Rather than depending on the author, is transnational a quality that is embedded in an authentic portrayal of the duality or multiplicity of character identities? Must it have a plot that involves moving across nations, such as the many books that retell the transnational experience through stories about migrants and refugees, from Beverly Naidoo's *The Other Side of Truth* (2002), to Shaun Tan's *The Arrival* (2006), to José Manuel Mateo and Javier Martínez Pedro's *Migrar* (2011)? In what ways are these texts meaningful to readers who have not experienced a transnational childhood?

In terms of publishing and marketing, it is questionable whether a text duly becomes transnational once it is published in different languages and is read by readers across the globe. Or is the Harry Potter series (Rowling 1997–2007) transnational because it has been published in over seventy languages even when it is so British-centered? Ironically, it is the so-called transnational corporations that have perpetuated the lopsided distribution of children's books (Palgrave 2009, 126) so that books in or translated from English swamp the production of other countries, and there is little reciprocal buying and translating. The response in some countries has been a call for a national children's literature, resulting in more deeply entrenched nationalisms. At the same time, the industry has come under attack for lacking texts that represent ethnic minorities, languages, and cultures (predominantly in postimperial countries).

Given that the above examples and the questions they raise point to the power relations at the core of both transnationalism and the study of children's literature, it is perhaps within this scholarship that the manifestation of these power relations can be highlighted, such as in the hegemonic Western assumption adults make about books that offer apparently benign invitations to celebrate heritage but in fact construct nationalist ideologies. This scholarship can also examine current and historical sites of negotiation—especially the intersections of culture, language, and identity—along with postcolonial and critical race and gender theories that interrogate "universal" categories applied to childhood.

Bradford suggests scholars should respond to Spivak's call for a transnational literacy that "would alert us to the politics of textuality—who is powerful, who is not," leading to a "respectful acknowledgement of difference" (2011, 33). For example, it can provide a perspective on elements that straddle difference, as Nina Christensen shows in her analysis of Norwegian Stian

Hole's Garmann trilogy, which "include elements that can be anchored in a specific national context" but also "set in a *transnational* reality" (2013, 193). Transnational literacy can also provide tools to explore the dynamics of belonging or exclusion, as in the case of Macarena García González's (2017) contrasting study between the cultural construction of narratives of transnational adoption and migration in Spanish children's literature, where she not only examines the metaphor of "nation as family" in the texts but also embeds the study in the current context of immigration in Spain.

Mavis Reimer picks up on a crucial point when she asks whether young readers are "being shaped and shaping themselves as transnational or global subjects by wide reading across the picture books" or whether the transnational child subject "is in fact, under construction elsewhere, in the critical discourses surrounding the books" (2014, 3). This question begs both textual and empirical research. In 2000, Meek noted that there was a lack of "reports and substantial analyses of children reading translated books that have different renderings of common experiences" (2000, xvi), and this is still the case to date. So far, only a handful of studies report on how readers with transnational experiences negotiate meaning and create spaces for dual or multiple identities within texts and/or literacy practices (e.g., Arizpe, Colomer, and Martínez-Roldán 2014; Scherer 2015). Given that the reality created by shared global references seems set to expand through young people's access to digital texts and practices, scholarship has still to examine in what ways and to what extent cyberspace really is transnational.

58

Trauma
Lydia Kokkola

The word *trauma* originally comes from medicine, where it describes a physical wound caused by something external to the body, such as a physical blow. Other derivations of the Greek word *trauma* refer to piercing, and in the nineteenth century, the association with psychological injury began to dominate (Macareavey 2016, 154). In children's literature, trauma is primarily associated with psychological wounds. Even when physical trauma is central to the plot, the narrative tends to focus on the mental anguish incurred. Both the car crash that temporarily disables Pollyanna in Eleanor Porter's *Pollyanna* (1913) and Katy's fall from the swing in Susan Coolidge's *What Katy Did* (1872) focus on the mental rehabilitation of the eponymous heroines, which is rewarded with physical recovery. The association of the word *trauma* with *piercing* captures another feature of trauma in children's literature: it represents a breach of a border that was assumed to be impervious. Cutting through the skin violates the border between the body and the world. In literature for young readers, this rupture exposes the inner self to society, and the character's pain dominates the narrative thereafter.

Trauma fractures time. A traumatic event divides a person's life into "before" and "after," and it is partly for this reason that trauma plays such a central role in fiction for adolescents. In *From Mythic to Linear* (1991), Maria Nikolajeva shows how literature for young children is dominated by *kairos* (circular time), whereas fiction for adolescents is marked by the onset of *chronos* (linear time). In these primarily character-driven novels, the departure from childhood and entry into adulthood is portrayed as a rupture: Christopher Robin must leave the Hundred Acre Wood. Trauma represents the end of childhood and the onset of adulthood—the main narrative pattern of fiction for adolescents, as Roberta Seelinger Trites establishes in *Disturbing the Universe* (2000) and develops in *Twenty-First-Century Feminisms in Children's and Adolescent Literature* (2018). Trites identifies death and sex as the pivotal tropes for expressing a traumatic entry into adulthood. While the connection between death and trauma reflects real life, the connection between sex and trauma is culturally specific. Trites's assertion that sex is regarded as an encroachment on adulthood for which the teenager must be punished is certainly true of anglophone literature but less true in other contexts. Even fairly early YA fiction by Swedish author Gunnel Beckman (1910–2003) reflects this pattern. Annika, the eighteen-year-old narrator of Beckman's novel *Tillträde till festen* (*Admission to the Feast*; [1969] 1971), reflects—in a letter to her female friends—on the adulthood that her terminal leukemia will deny her. Female bonding is also central in Beckman's books about Mia, the sexually active teenage protagonist of *Tre veckor över tiden* (*Mia Alone*; 1973) and *Våren då allting hände* (*That Early Spring*; 1974). In *Mia Alone*, published the year before abortion became legal in Sweden, Mia discovers she is pregnant, and although it eventually results in a miscarriage, the novel does not render pregnancy as punishment for being sexually active but focuses on the impact young motherhood would have on her life plans. The sequel focuses on sisterly bonds between women. Neither book portrays sex as a traumatic entry into adulthood.

Although the content of trauma can be culturally specific, the existence of trauma is wedded to the end of childhood. As Eric Tribunella points out, trauma often figures as a catalyst for maturation: the melancholia that arises from the traumatic encounter enables the mature adult to remain in contact with his or her child self because the memory of loss is "repetitive or intrusive" (2010, 134). Traumatic events are never resolved but remain touchstones in survivors' interpretations of the present. Tribunella's point is that by positing trauma as an entry point into adulthood, the world of childhood can "haunt" the adult. Tribunella is not endorsing this melancholic incorporation of traumatic experiences into selfhood; he demonstrates that the results can be disturbing as well as sophisticatedly advantageous. His examples include scenes of homoerotic desire in classic school stories such as Fredrick Farrah's *Erik, or Little by Little* (1858) and John Knowles's *A Separate Peace* (1959) coupled with deaths that form a disturbingly permeable interface between queerness and trauma (Tribunella 2010, 4–11). The melancholic nature of this association does not allow for growth; instead, it haunts the characters' futures.

Not all forms of trauma haunt the future: adolescent characters are often expected to work through their grief at a demanding pace. The title of Tribunella's study alludes to "Mourning and Melancholia" ([1922] 2005), in which Sigmund Freud distinguishes between lasting melancholia and the healthy process of mourning. The work of mourning—*trauerarbeit* in German—enables individuals to move past trauma, whereas melancholic individuals keep the trauma alive. Freud proposes that talking through trauma with a therapist would enable patients to begin the work of mourning and so leave melancholia behind. Examples of *trauerarbeit* include Rosa Guy's Harlem trilogy—*The Friends* (1973), *Ruby* (1976), and *Edith Jackson* (1978)— in which the protagonists move on from the loss of their mother and create new lives for themselves. Less benign examples abound, to the extent that talking through the traumatic experience may be presented as a demand. In Laurie Halse Anderson's prizewinning novel *Speak* (1999), rape so traumatizes Melinda that she finds herself almost incapable of speech. Her formerly good grades plummet; she self-mutilates and hides in a closet. Her only form of self-expression is her art, and the novel ends when Melinda begins to tell her art teacher about the rape. The novel posits this as the first step on the road to recovery: by speaking, Melinda may begin the work of mourning and recover from her trauma.

Recovery from trauma cannot be timetabled. Yet since children represent adult hopes for the future, YA fiction depicting trauma may insist on recovery at an unrealistic pace. If these books are to reach adolescent readers who have been subjected to similar experiences, they must resist publishers' preference for optimistic resolution. As Kimberley Reynolds observes, writing for teens also needs "to acknowledge disturbing experiences and overwhelming feelings of despair, anger, and frustration" (2007, 89). Requiring victims to speak about their traumatic experiences can further disempower them. In a Foucaldian analysis of *Speak*, Chris McGee observes that Melinda's decision to tell her teacher is an act of confession: "When the confessor confesses, she is not simply confessing a secret but admitting that she must confess, that this is the person to whom she must confess, and that every secret must be turned into discourse. Power desires that everything is seen and made visible and, in disciplinary terms, that the individual knows there is no place outside of scrutiny" (2009, 185). The insistence on speaking is not wholly benign: it is also a means by which adult power is asserted over the young victim.

If individual trauma literature is associated with the end of childhood, "national trauma" literature shows how collective pain lingers. I use the term *national* loosely to describe not only nation states but also ethnic groups who may even be formed as a result of trauma. The Aboriginal peoples of Australia, for instance, are composed of many different nations. The collective term came into being in the context of colonization. The traumas of genocide, forced separation of children from parents, and violation of spiritual sites forge a collective sense of Aboriginal nationhood even as they speak to the price paid for that collective sense of identity. In the YA dystopian novel *The Marrow Thieves* by Métis Canadian author Cherie Dimaline, Indigenous people are hunted for their bone marrow in a world collapsing under the pressure of global warming. Picture books such as Daisy Utemorrah and Pat Torres's *Do Not Go around the Edges* (1990) make these traumas accessible to younger children. This picture book places the written words describing Utemorrah's life in the danger zone—"around the edges" of the photos and artwork. Her family and her culture are placed in the center, although how much young readers can understand will depend on their previous knowledge and the support they receive from the adult reading alongside them. Utemorrah's agency in her adult life is acknowledged without an insistence on recovery: the loss of cultural heritage cannot be resolved or put right.

The Holocaust is one of the most frequently represented national traumas in books for young readers. Most of the picture books and novels accessible to children under ten focus on experiences of Jews in hiding and kindly adults who care for the children. There are also picture books, such as Margaret Wild and Julie Vivas's *Let the Celebrations Begin!* (1991), that are set in a concentration camp but insist on a hopeful ending. Indeed, much Holocaust fiction for children tempers the imparting of historical knowledge via devices that protect child readers from knowing more than they wish to know (Kokkola 2013b) to the extent that Zohar Shavit (2005) has accused German children's literature of deliberately evading culpability.

In Korea, picture books depicting the national trauma of the "comfort women" are less protective of the child reader. These girls and young women, primarily from Korea, were forced to serve the Japanese army as sex slaves during World War II. Repeatedly raped and subjected to other forms of physical and psychological torture, many died from their injuries or committed suicide. The few who returned home endured further humiliations in a society that until recently was ill-equipped to openly discuss such intimate acts of violence. In the last few years, picture books accessible to young readers incorporate paratexts emphasizing the historical truthfulness of the events and do not shy from depicting the horrors. The victim in Yoon Duk Kwon's *The Flower Granny* (2010) describes how the soldiers "lined up . . . after one left, another one entered the room. . . . It was hard to count how many soldiers entered this room [and raped me]" and recalls seeing that "a thirteen-year-old girl's bottom was suffused with blood" (quoted in Sung 2012, 27). Depicting this degree of trauma in a format that is accessible to young children is unusual, even in the context of national trauma literature for children. It is departs from Holocaust literature in depicting the continued impact of these horrific experiences on the women. Soonyi, the protagonist of Jung Mo Yoon's *The Season of Balsamina* (2008), is known as "Granny Hedgehog" because she remains so prickly (Sung 2012). The impossibility of individual recovery is woven into the national trauma, creating the "haunting" effect Tribunella identifies in relation to melancholia and queerness. The trauma becomes part of the country's present, not just its past.

National trauma fiction differs from other trauma literature not only in the way it reaches out to a younger readership but also because it forms part of a political movement aimed at creating national unity. Child-friendly formats do not necessarily mean that the books are intended to be read by or to children; the format also makes the material more shocking by juxtaposing the "innocent" child reader implicated in the text with a brutal historical past. Moreover, their individual child characters represent the collective trauma inflicted on the particular group. In contrast, novels that individualize the traumatic event insist that the characters begin the work of mourning needed for recovery to move on from the rupture.

59

Voice

Mike Cadden

The first mention of *voice* as metaphor appeared in 1587, when Golding De Mornay wrote that "there is . . . a dubble Speech; the one in the mynd . . . the other the sounding image thereof . . . vttered by our mouth" (*OED*). The *Dictionary of Narratology* defines *voice* as "the set of signs characterizing the narrator and, more generally, the narrating instance, and governing the relations between narrating and narrative text as well as between narrating and narrated" (Prince 1987, 104). In defining what constitutes literature for children or young people, voice is typically regarded as a key determinant, especially when used to distinguish an adult voice of authority from an implied (receptive) child listener.

What makes a book a children's book, says Barbara Wall, "is not what is said, but the way it is said, and to whom it is said" ([1991] 1994). She underscores the significance of power relations by focusing on the "overt authorial narrator," the patronizing avuncular voice—popular in nineteenth-century children's fiction—the one that speaks "as 'I,' 'your author,' [or] 'dear reader.'" Although that particular authorial affectation has long been out of fashion, it has since become a target for parody. Daniel Handler's sardonic adoption of that voice in his enormously successful thirteen-part Series of Unfortunate Events (1999–2006)—authored by the fictional Lemony Snicket—has been a particularly successful franchise. But it is an anomaly. More typically, as Jacqueline Rose famously argued in 1984,

children's literature is "impossible." Because of the distance between the adult author's construction of an implied child reader and actual children, no literary genre has as great a "rupture" between the writer and the implied and real reader as children's literature (Rose 1984). Power relations are at the core of the problem—power that comes both with age differentials and narrative authority. Maria Nikolajeva summarizes the problem: "The profound difference in life experience as well as linguistic skills create an inevitable discrepancy between the (adult) narrative voice and both the focalized child character's and the young reader's levels of comprehension" (2002; Hunt 1991). For children's literature scholars working in feminism and postcolonialism (Kertzer 1996; Romines 1995; McGillis 1998–99; Nodelman 1992), the power differential is at the center of their critique. As an alternate approach to the problem of narrative authority, scholars such as Uli Knoepflmacher, Mitzi Myers, and Sandra Beckett turn their attention to crossover literature, defined as something that works for two audiences—"a dialogic mix of older and younger voices" appealing to both children and adults (Knoepflmacher and Myers 1997, vii).

As the eighteenth-century idea of a child in need of enlightenment and the innocent nineteenth-century child in need of protection faded into history, a late twentieth-century emphasis on crossover fiction and child agency and an awareness of multiple voices speaking began to figure more distinctly in children's literature. In *Voices in the Park* (1998)—a revisioning of his *A Walk in the Park* (1977)—Anthony Browne disturbs the conventional authority of the narrator by creating a story composed of four separate "voices," each with its own characteristic typeface and style of illustration, each character engaging dialogically with the others in a verbal fugue. Four different characters tell their own stories in their own voices: the angry, upper-class mother and her repressed son, the dispirited lower-class father and his upbeat, joyful daughter. Around the turn to the twenty-first century, children's literature was marked by its welcoming of multiple voices—by signaling not just differences in race, class, gender, and age but also temporal changes. Christopher Paul Curtis's *The Watsons Go to Birmingham, 1963* (1995) relies on the linguistic register of the dialogue to subtly indicate that the events of the novel occurred thirty years earlier.

Although attention to changing narrative voices in children's fiction tends to be the focus in critical discussions, the changing voices in children's poetry are equally significant. The instructive, devotional voice of Isaac Watts in the eighteenth-century *Divine Songs* (1715), offering moral advice in verse, gave way to the new and refreshing speaking voice of the child in Robert Louis Stevenson's *A Child's Garden of Verses* (1885). The late twentieth century saw the rise of the verse novel, its attraction to young adult readers being its immediate, intimate, and personal voice. The genre veers toward the dramatic and usually employs the soliloquy in free-verse form. Multiple voices are also invoked to tell the whole story without the use of other forms of narration. Though Karen Hesse's *Out of the Dust* (1997) was very successful (and felt new and interesting when it was first published), the verse novels that subsequently flooded the anglophone market rarely succeeded as well, largely because they could never adequately address the question, Why verse? By way of contrast, the wordless picture book demonstrated how visual storytelling might transcend the linguistic limits of voice. Regis Faller's Polo books (2002–) and JonArno Lawson's *Sidewalk Flowers* (2015) have turned out to be wonderfully successful cases in point.

Narrative voice's power to direct readers' sympathies (and antipathies) locates this keyword at the center of a debate between artistic and ethical concerns.

While writers who take a rhetorical view express ethical qualms about what one might write (Paterson 1981; Byars 1982; Hunter 1976), those who take a more aesthetic view argue that the writer must not censor (Walsh 1973). Some make the case that children's writers focus on ethics more than writers for other audiences (Mills 1997; Cadden 2000a). Indeed, Rod McGillis (1998–99) even wonders whether writers for children "steal the voices of others in the very act of providing a medium for those voices?" To remedy that problem, some critics espouse strategies for defensive or resistant reading or celebrate books that present multiple voices (McCallum 1999b; Cadden 2000b; Trites 2000). As John Stephens (1992) suggests, the "most important concept for children to grasp about literary fictions is always that of narrative point of view, since this has the function of constructing subject positions and inscribing ideological assumptions."

Acknowledgments

Thanks to all of our contributors for sharing their expertise via the keywords essay, one of the most demanding critical genres, requiring a balance of etymologies, literary and cultural histories, and representative examples from different countries and traditions—all succinctly organized in about eight paragraphs. Your hard work makes this book possible.

For inspiring the second edition of *Keywords for Children's Literature*, thanks to the Norwegian Institute for Children's Books and its director, Kristin Ørjasæter, for hosting the August 2012 Oslo conference Nordic Children's Literature—a New Research Question? (Nordisk barnelitteratur—et nytt kunstforskningsspørsmål?). Thanks to Glenn Hendler, whose presentation at the 2007 Futures of American Studies Institute inspired the first edition. Indeed, thanks to both him and Bruce Burgett for the model they provide in their *Keywords for American Cultural Studies* (now in its third edition).

For offering a critique of the first edition, thanks to the participants in the international roundtable discussion on *Keywords for Children's Literature* at the August 2013 International Research Society for Children's Literature conference in Maastricht, including panelists Nina Alonso, Francesca Orestano, Emer O'Sullivan, and everyone in the audience.

For helping the book speak to literary traditions outside of the editors' knowledge, thanks to the Keywords for Children's Literature 2.0 International Advisory Board: John Agard (poet and playwright, UK), Nina Alonso (independent scholar, Luxembourg), Clémentine Beauvais (University of York, UK), Sandra Beckett (Brock University, Canada), Robin Bernstein (Harvard University, US), Clare Bradford (Deakin University, Australia), Natalia Cecire (University of Sussex, UK), Ute Dettmar (Frankfurt University, Germany), Victoria Flanagan (Macquarie University, Australia), Richard Flynn (Georgia Southern University, US), Nina Goga (Bergen University College, Norway), Mick Gowar (Anglia Ruskin University, UK), Marah Gubar (MIT, US), Erica Hateley (independent scholar, UK), Olga Holownia (British Library, UK), Andrea Immel (Cotsen Collection, Princeton University, US), Vanessa Joosen (University of Antwerp, Belgium), Lydia Kokkola (Luleå University of Technology, Sweden), Lourdes López-Ropero (University of Alicante, Spain), Nadia Mansour (Aarhus University, Denmark), Michelle Martin (University of Washington, US), Claudia Mendes (Federal University of Rio de Janeiro, Brazil), Julia Mickenberg (University of Texas at Austin, US), Pamela Mordecai (poet, Canada), Francesca Orestano (State University of Milan, Italy), Emer O'Sullivan (Leuphana University of Lüneburg, Germany), Marek Oziewicz (University of Minnesota, US), Mavis Reimer (University of Winnipeg, Canada), Kimberley Reynolds (Newcastle University, UK), David Rudd (University of Roehampton, UK), Lara Saguisag (CUNY, US), Roger Sutton (editor of *Horn Book*, US), Ebony Elizabeth Thomas (Penn State, US), Lynne Vallone (Rutgers University, US), Sara Van den Bossche (Tilburg University, Netherlands), and Boel Westin (Stockholm University, Sweden).

For providing both research and organizational assistance, thanks to Roxana Loza and Corinne Matthews. And for preliminary work on the bibliography, thanks to Reuben Plance.

For their work on and support of this book, thanks to Eric Zinner, Dolma Ombadykow, and Lisha Nadkarni of New York University Press.

For guiding the manuscript through the copyediting phase, thanks to Elvis Ramirez of Scribe Inc.

For his support and guidance on the second edition, thanks to our agent Stephen Barbara of InkWell Management. For his help on the first edition, thanks to the late George Nicholson of Sterling Lord Literistic.

For lending a spouse to the cause, thanks to Karin Westman, Geoff Bubbers, and Jørgen Michaelsen.

Finally, thanks to readers of the first edition of this book. Your use of and responses to the 2011 version of *Keywords for Children's Literature* makes this new version possible.

References

Abate, Michelle Ann. 2008. *Tomboys: A Literary and Cultural History*. Philadelphia: Temple University Press.

———. 2010. *Raising Your Kids Right: Children's Literature and American Political Conservatism*. New Brunswick, NJ: Rutgers University Press.

Abate, Michelle Ann, and Gwen Athene Tarbox, eds. 2017. *Graphic Novels for Children and Young Adults: A Collection of Critical Essays*. Jackson: University Press of Mississippi.

Abate, Michelle Ann, and Kenneth Kidd, eds. 2011. *Over the Rainbow: Queer Children's and Young Adult Literature*. Ann Arbor: University of Michigan Press.

Abbott, Jacob. 1855. *The Harper Establishment; or, How the Story Books Are Made*. New York: Harper & Brothers.

ABC News. 2017. "Aladdin: Disney Reveals the Cast for the Live Action Remake." July 16, 2017. www.abc.net.

Abdel-Fattah, Randa. 2005. *Does My Head Look Big in This?* Sydney: Pan Macmillan.

Abel, Marco. 2007. *Violent Affect: Literature, Cinema, and Critique after Representation*. Lincoln: University of Nebraska Press.

Abrams, M. H. 1993. "Genre." In *A Glossary of Literary Terms*, 75–78. 6th ed. New York: Harcourt.

Achebe, Chinua. (1977) 1988. *The Drum*. Nairobi: Heinemann.

Adams, Gillian. 1986. "The First Children's Literature? The Case for Sumer." *Children's Literature* 14:1–30.

———. 1998. "Medieval Children's Literature: Its Possibility and Actuality." *Children's Literature* 26:1–24.

Adichie, Chimamanda Ngozi. 2009. "The Danger of a Single Story." TED Talk, July 2009. www.ted.com.

Adorno, Theodor. (1970) 2004. *Aesthetic Theory*. Translated by Robert Hullot-Kentor. London: Continuum.

Ahenakew, Freda. 1988. *How the Mouse Got Brown Teeth: A Cree Story for Children*. Illustrated by George Littlechild. Saskatoon: Fifth House.

Ahern, Stephen. 2016. *Affect and Abolition in the Anglo-Atlantic, 1770–1830*. London: Routledge.

Åhlberg, Lars-Olof. 2003. "The Invention of Modern Aesthetics: From Leibniz to Kant." *Historični Seminar* 4 (2001–3): 133–53.

Ahmed, Sara. (2004) 2014. *The Cultural Politics of Emotion*. Edinburgh: Edinburgh University Press.

Aisawi, Sabah A. 2013. "Perspectives on Nature in Contemporary Arabic Picturebooks." In *Looking Out and Looking In: National Identity in Picturebooks of the New Millennium*, edited by Åse Marie Ommundsen, 29–44. Oslo: Novus Press.

Akinti, Peter. 2009. *Forest Gate*. London: Jonathan Cape.

Akpan, Ntieyong Udo. 1966. *Ini Abasi and the Sacred Ram*. London: Longman.

Alabed, Bana. 2017. *Dear World: A Syrian Girl's Story of War and Plea for Peace*. New York: Simon & Schuster.

Alexander, Lloyd. 1987. "The Perilous Realms: A Colloquy." Edited by Betty Levin. In *Innocence and Experience: Essays & Conversations on Children's Literature*, edited by Barbara Harrison and Gregory Maguire. New York: Lothrop, Lee, and Shepard.

Alcott, Louisa May. (1868–69) 1998. *Little Women*. New York: Grosset and Dunlap.

———. (1868–69). 2004. *Little Women, or Meg, Jo, Beth and Amy: Authoritative Text, Backgrounds and Contexts, Criticism*. Edited by Anne K. Phillips and Gregory Eiselein. New York: W. W. Norton.

———. (1870) 2008. *An Old-Fashioned Girl*. Project Gutenberg. Accessed July 11, 2008. www.gutenberg.org.

———. 2012. *Jack and Jill*. Carlisle, MA: Applewood.

Aldrich, Thomas Bailey. (1869) 1996. *The Story of a Bad Boy*. Lebanon, NH: University Press of New England.

Alexie, Sherman. 2007. *The Absolutely True Diary of a Part-Time Indian*. New York: Little, Brown.

Alfvén-Eriksson, Anne-Marie. 2000. "Døden i børnelitteraturen. Om døden som motiv, tema og tabu." *BUM* 18, nos. 3–4: 73–78.

Alger, Horatio. (1868) 1962. *Ragged Dick*. New York: Collier.

Allan, Cherie. 2012. *Playing with Picturebooks: Postmodernism and the Postmodernesque*. London: Palgrave Macmillan.

Allende, Isabel. 2005. *Forest of the Pygmies*. Translated by Margaret Sayers Peden. New York: HarperCollins.

Almond, David. 1998. *Skellig*. New York: Dell Yearling.

Alston, Ann. 2008. *The Family in English Children's Literature*. New York: Routledge.

Andersen, Hans Christian. 1837. *Eventyr fortalte for Børn*. Copenhagen: C. A. Reitzel.

———. 1974. *The Complete Fairy Tales and Stories*. Translated by Erik Christian Haugaard. Garden City, NY: Anchor Books.

———. 2004. *Fairy Tales*. Edited by Jackie Wullschläger. Translated by Tiina Nunnally. London: Penguin Books.

Anderson, Benedict. 1983. *Imagined Communities*. London: Verso.

Anderson, Laurie Halse. 1999. *Speak*. London: Hodder Books.

———. 2010. *Wintergirls*. New York: Penguin.

Anderson, M. T. 2002. *Feed*. Somerville, MA: Candlewick Press.

Anderson, Wes, dir. 2012. *Moonrise Kingdom*. Indian Paintbrush.

Andersson, Maria. 2016. "The New Woman as a Boy: Female Masculinity in Ellen Idström's *Tvillingsystrarna*." *Scandinavian Studies* 88, no. 3 (Fall): 295–318.

Anelli, Melissa, and Emerson Spartz. 2005. "The Leaky Cauldron and Mugglenet Interview with Joanne Kathleen Rowling." *The Leaky Cauldron*, July 16, 2005. www.the-leaky-cauldron.org.

Angelides, Steven. 2001. *A History of Bisexuality*. Chicago: University of Chicago Press.

Anstey, F. 1882. *Vice Versa; or, A Lesson to Fathers*. New York: D. Appleton.

Antony, Steve. 2015. *Green Lizards vs. Red Rectangles*. London: Hodder.

Antrobus, John S., ed. 1970. *Cognition and Affect*. Boston: Little, Brown.

Appadurai, Arjun. 1986. "Introduction: Commodities and the Politics of Value." In *The Social Life of Things: Commodities in Cultural Perspective*, 3–63. New York: Cambridge University Press.

Appel Charlotte, and Ning de Coninck-Smith, eds. 2013–15. *Dansk skolehistorie*. Vols. 1–5. Aarhus: Aarhus Universitetsforlag.

Applebaum, Noga. 2010. *Representations of Technology in Science Fiction for Young People*. Abingdon: Routledge.

Applebee, Arthur N. 1978. *The Child's Concept of Story, Ages Two to Seventeen*. Chicago: University of Chicago Press.

Applegate, Katherine. 2012. *The One and Only Ivan*. New York: HarperCollins.

Appleyard, J. A. 1990. *Becoming a Reader: The Experience of Fiction from Childhood to Adulthood*. Cambridge: Cambridge University Press.

Arac, Jonathan. 1997. *Huck Finn as Idol and Target: The Functions of Criticism in Our Time*. Madison: University of Wisconsin Press.

Ariès, Philippe. 1960. *L'enfant et la vie familiale sous l'ancien régime*. Paris: Plon.

———. 1962. *Centuries of Childhood: A Social History of Family Life*. Translated by Robert Baldick. New York: Vintage.

Arizpe, Evelyn, Teresa Colomer, and Carmen Martínez-Roldán. 2014. *Visual Journeys through Wordless Narratives: An International Inquiry with Immigrant Children and* The Arrival. London: Bloomsbury Academic.

Ashcroft, Bill. 2001. *Post-colonial Transformation*. London: Routledge.

Ashcroft, Bill, Gareth Griffiths, and Helen Tiffin. 1989. *The Empire Writes Back: Theory and Practice in Post-colonial Literatures*. London: Routledge.

Ashford, Daisy. 1919. *The Young Visiters; or, Mr. Salteena's Plan*. London: Chatto & Windus.

Attebery, Brian. 1992. *Strategies of Fantasy*. Bloomington: Indiana University Press.

———. 2014. *Stories about Stories: Fantasy and the Remaking of Myth*. Oxford: Oxford University Press.

Atia, Nadia, and Jeremy Davies. 2010. "Nostalgia and the Shape of History." *Memory Studies* 3, no. 3: 181–86.

Augustine. (ca. 1470) 1961. *The City of God against the Pagans*. 7 vols. Edited by George E. McCracken. London: Heinemann.

Austen, Jane. (1813) 2014. *Pride and Prejudice*. Harmondsworth: Penguin.

Austin, Linda M. 2003. "Children of Childhood: Nostalgia and the Romantic Legacy." *Studies in Romanticism* 42, no. 1 (Spring): 75–98.

———. 2007. *Nostalgia in Transition, 1780–1917*. Charlottesville: University of Virginia Press.

Avery, Gillian. 1995. "The Beginning of Children's Reading to c. 1700." In *Children's Literature: An illustrated History*, edited by Peter Hunt, 1–25. New York: Oxford University Press.

Babbitt, Natalie. (1975) 2010. *Tuck Everlasting*. New York: Square Fish.

Bacchilega, Cristina. 2004. "Genre and Gender in the Cultural Reproduction of India as 'Wonder Tale.'" In *Fairy Tales and Feminism: New Approaches*, edited by Donald Haase, 179–95. Detroit: Wayne State University Press.

Bacelar, Manuel. 2008. *O livro do Pedro*. Edições Afrontamento.

Baden-Powell, Robert. 1908. *Scouting for Boys*. London: Horace Cox.

Bader, Barbara. 1976. *The American Picturebook: From Noah's Ark to the Beast Within*. New York: Macmillan.

Bai, Limin. 2005. *Shaping the Ideal Child: Children and Their*

REFERENCES

Primers in Late Imperial China. Hong Kong: Chinese University of Hong Kong Press.

Bak, Meredith. 2018. "Material Culture (Fairy-Tale Things: Studying Fairy Tales from a Material Culture Perspective)." In *The Routledge Companion to Media and Fairy-Tale Cultures*, edited by Pauline Greenhill, Jill Terry Rudy, Naomi Hamer, and Lauren Bosc, 328–36. New York: Routledge.

Baker, Jennifer. 2016. "Review: *When We Was Fierce*." *Crazy-QuiltedI* (blog), July 2016. https://campbele.wordpress.com.

Baker, Steve. 1993. *Picturing the Beast: Animals, Identity, and Representation*. Manchester: Manchester University Press.

Bakhtin, Mikhail. 1981. "Forms of Time and Chronotope in the Novel." In *The Dialogic Imagination: Four Essays*, edited by Michael Holquist, translated by Caryl Emerson and Michael Holquist, 84–259. Austin: University of Texas Press.

———. 1984. *Rabelais and His World*. Bloomington: Indiana University Press.

Baldacchino, Christine. 2014. *Morris Micklewhite and the Tangerine Dress*. Illustrated by Isabelle Malenfant. Toronto: Groundwood.

Ballantyne, R. M. (1857) 2015. *The Coral Island*. Richmond, VA: Valancourt Books.

Bang, Molly. (1991) 2000. *Picture This: How Pictures Work*. New York: SeaStar Books.

Banks, James A., and Cherry A. McGee Banks, eds. 2009. *Multicultural Education: Issues and Perspectives*. Hoboken, NJ: John Wiley & Sons.

Banks, Lynne Reid. 1980. *The Indian in the Cupboard*. Garden City, NY: Doubleday.

Bannerman, Helen. 1899. *The Story of Little Black Sambo*. London: Grant Richards.

Bansch, Helga. 2008. *Odd Bird Out*. Translated by Monika Smith. Wellington: Gecko Press.

Baring-Gould, William Stuart, and R. Hart-Davis, eds. 1969. *Lure of the Limerick*. London: Hart Davis.

Barnes, Clare, Jr. 1950. *Home Sweet Zoo*. Garden City, NY: Doubleday.

Barrie, J. M. (1905) 1998. *Peter Pan; or, The Boy Who Wouldn't Grow Up*. London: Bloomsbury.

———. 1991. *Peter and Wendy*. In *Peter Pan in Kensington Gardens and Peter and Wendy*, edited by Peter Hollindale, 67–226. Oxford: Oxford University Press.

Baum, L. Frank. (1900) 1997. *The Wonderful Wizard of Oz*. Edited and with an introduction and notes by Susan Wolstenholme. Oxford: Oxford University Press.

———. (1904) 1969. *The Marvelous Land of Oz*. New York: Dover.

Bauman, Zygmunt. 2000. *Liquid Modernity*. Cambridge: Polity.

Baumgarten, Alexander G. (1750–58) 1986. *Aesthetica*. Hildesheim: G. Olms.

Beam, Chris. 2011. *I Am J*. New York: Little, Brown.

Beaty, Bart. 2005. *Fredric Wertham and the Critique of Mass Culture*. Jackson: University Press of Mississippi.

Beaty, Bart, and Benjamin Woo. 2016. *The Greatest Comic Book of All Time: Symbolic Capital and the Field of American Comic Books*. London: Palgrave Macmillan.

Beauchamp, Miles, Wendy Chung, Alijandra Mogilner, and Svetlana Zakinova, with Harpreet Mall. 2015. *Disabled Literature: A Critical Examination of the Portrayal of Individuals with Disabilities in Selected Works of Modern and Contemporary American Literature*. Boca Raton, FL: Brownwalker Press.

Beauvais, Clémentine. 2015. *The Mighty Child: Time and Power in Children's Literature*. Amsterdam: John Benjamins.

Bechdel, Alison. 2006. *Fun Home: A Family Tragicomic*. New York: Houghton Mifflin.

Bechtel, Louise Seaman. n.d. Untitled memoir. Ms. 136, 4–5. Papers of Louise Seaman Bechtel, Baldwin Library of Historical Children's Literature, University of Florida.

Beckett, Sandra L. 1995. "From the Art of Rewriting to the Art of Crosswriting Child and Adult: The Secret of Michel Tournier's Dual Readership." In *Voices from Far Away: Current Trends in International Children's Literature Research*, vol. 24, edited by Maria Nikolajeva, 9–34. Stockholm: Centrum för barnkulturforskning.

———. 1996–97. "Crosswriting Child and Adult: Henri Bosco's *L'Enfant et la rivière*." *Children's Literature Association Quarterly* 21, no. 4 (Winter): 189–98.

———. 1997. *De grands romanciers écrivent pour les enfants*. Montreal: Presses de l'Université de Montréal.

———. 1999. *Transcending Boundaries: Writing for a Dual Audience of Children and Adults*. New York: Garland.

———. 2001. "Livres pour tous: Le flou des frontières entre fiction pour enfants et fiction pour adultes." *Tangence* 67:9–22.

———. 2003. "Romans pour tous?" In *Perspectives contemporaines du roman pour la jeunesse, Actes du colloque organisé les 1ᵉʳ et 2 décembre 2000 par l'Institut International Charles Perrault*, edited by Virginie Douglas, 57–73. Paris: L'Harmattan.

———. 2006. "Crossover Books." In *The Oxford Encyclopedia of Children's Literature*, vol. 1, edited by Jack Zipes, 369–70. New York: Oxford University Press.

———. 2009a. *Crossover Fiction: Global and Historical Perspectives*. New York: Routledge.

———. 2009b. "J.-M. G. Le Clézio et la cross-fiction." *Nous voulons lire!* 179 (April): 5–13.

——. 2011a. "Crossover Classics: Classics for All Ages." In *Brave New World: Old and New Classics of Children's Literature*, edited by Elena Paruolo, 31–44. Oxford: Peter Lang.

——. 2011b. "Crossover Literature." In *Keywords for Children's Literature*, edited by Philip Nel and Lissa Paul, 58–61. New York: New York University Press.

——. 2012. *Crossover Picturebooks: A Genre for All Ages*. New York: Routledge.

——. 2018. "Crossover Picturebooks." In *The Routledge Companion to Picturebooks*, edited by Bettina Kümmerling-Meibauer, 209–19. New York: Routledge.

Beckett, Sandra L., and Maria Nikolajeva, eds. 2006. *Beyond Babar: The European Tradition in Children's Literature*. Lanham, MD: Scarecrow Press.

Beckman, Gunnel. (1969) 1971. *Admission to the Feast*. Translated by Joan Tate. New York: Holt, Rinehart & Winston.

——. 1971. *Nineteen Is Too Young to Die*. London: Macmillan.

——. (1973) 1978. *Mia Alone*. Translated by Joan Tate. New York: Dell.

——. (1974) 1977. *That Early Spring*. Translated by Joan Tate. New York: Viking.

Beech, Hannah. 2017. "Children's Books and China's Crackdown on Western Ideology." *New Yorker*, March 16, 2017. www.newyorker.com.

Beer, Gillian. 1970. *The Romance*. Critical Idiom Series. London: Methuen.

Bell, Cece. 2014. *El Deafo*. New York: Abrams Books.

Benary-Isbert, Margot. (1959) 1963. *The Long Way Home*. Translated by Richard and Clara Winston. New York: Scholastic.

Benjamin, Walter. 1969. *Illuminations: Essays and Reflections*. Edited with an introduction by Hannah Arendt. Translated by Harry Zohn. New York: Schocken Books.

Benner, Julia. 2015. *Federkrieg: Kinder- und Jugendliteratur gegen den Nationalsozialismus 1933–1945* [War of words: Children's and youth literature against national socialism 1933–1945]. Göttingen: Wallstein Verlag.

Bennett, Tony. 2005. "Home." In *New Keywords: A Revised Vocabulary of Culture and Society*, edited by Tony Bennett, Lawrence Grossberg, and Meaghan Morris, 162–64. Oxford: Blackwell.

Bennett, Tony, Lawrence Grossberg, and Meaghan Morris, eds. 2005. *New Keywords: A Revised Vocabulary of Culture and Society*. Oxford: Blackwell.

Ben-Sasson, Haim Hillel. 1971. *Jewish Society through the Ages*. New York: Schocken Books.

Benton, Michael. (1995) 2005. "Readers, Texts, Contexts: Reader-Response Criticism." In *Understanding Children's Literature*, edited by Peter Hunt, 86–102. London: Routledge.

Benton-Benai, Edward. 1988. *The Mishomis Book: The Voice of the Ojibway*. Hayward, WI: Indian Country Communications.

Berger, John. 1980. "Why Look at Animals?" In *About Looking*, 1–28. New York: Pantheon.

Berger, Peter L., and Thomas Luckmann. (1966) 1989. *The Social Construction of Reality: A Treatise in the Sociology of Knowledge*. New York: Anchor.

Berggren, Arne. 1997. *Fisken* [The fish]. Oslo: Aschehoug.

Bergstrom, Brian. 2014. "Avonlea as 'World': Japanese *Anne of Green Gables* Tourism as Embodied Fandom." *Japan Forum* 26, no. 2: 224.

Berliner, Alain, dir. 1997. *Ma vie en rose*. Sony Pictures Classics.

Bernstein, Robin. 2011a. "The Queerness of Harriet the Spy." In *Over the Rainbow: Queer Children's Literature*, edited by Kenneth B. Kidd and Michelle A. Abate, 111–20. Ann Arbor: University of Michigan Press.

——. 2011b. *Racial Innocence: Performing American Childhood from Slavery to Civil Rights*. New York: New York University Press.

——. 2013. "Toys Are Good for Us: Why We Should Embrace the Historical Integration of Children's Literature, Material Culture, and Play." *Children's Literature Association Quarterly* 38, no. 4: 458.

Best American Books. 1893. *The Critic* 19 (June 3, 1893): 589.

Betjeman, John. (1960) 1989. *Summoned by Bells*. London: John Murray.

Bettelheim, Bruno. 1976. *The Uses of Enchantment: The Meaning and Importance of Fairy Tales*. New York: Alfred A. Knopf.

Bhabha, Homi K. 1994. *The Location of Culture*. London: Routledge.

Bial, Henry, ed. 2007. *The Performance Studies Reader*. 2nd ed. London: Routledge.

Bien-Lietz, Malgorzata. 1998. "Nonsens i nordisk barnelitteratur etter 1945." PhD diss., Adam Mickiewicz University.

Billing, Andrew. 2013 "Political Anthropology and Its Animal Others in Rousseau's 'Discours sur l'inégalité.'" *French Forum* 38, nos. 1-2 (Winter/Spring): 1–17.

Birdsall, Jeanne. 2005. *The Penderwicks: A Summer Tale of Two Sisters, Two Rabbits, and a Very Interesting Boy*. New York: Random House.

Birkeland, Tone, Gunvor Risa, and Karin Beate Vold. 2005. *Norsk barnelitteraturhistorie*. Oslo: Det Norske Samlaget.

Bishop, Claire Huchet. 1938. *Five Chinese Brothers*. Illustrated by Kurt Wiese. New York: Coward-McCann.

Bishop, Gavin. 1999. *The House That Jack Built*. Auckland: Scholastic.

Bishop, Rudine Sims. 2003. "Reframing the Debate about

Cultural Authenticity." In *Stories Matter: The Complexity of Cultural Authenticity in Children's Literature,* edited by Dana L. Fox and Kathy G. Short, 25–37. Urbana, IL: National Council of Teachers of English.

———. 2007. *Free within Ourselves: The Development of African American Children's Literature.* Westport, CT: Greenwood.

Bittner, Rob, Jennifer Ingres, and Christine Stamper. 2016. "Queer and Trans-Themed Books for Young Readers: A Critical Review." *Discourse: Studies in the Cultural Politics of Education* 37, no. 6: 948–64.

Black, Gavin. 1975. *The Golden Cockatrice.* London: Fontana.

Blackford, Holly Virginia. 2004. *Out of This World: Why Literature Matters to Girls.* New York: Teachers College Press.

Blake, Quentin. 1995. *La vie de la page.* Paris: Gallimard Jeunesse.

———. *Tell Me a Picture.* (2001) 2002. London: Frances Lincoln Children's Books.

Blake, William. (1789) 1982. "The Divine Image." In *The Complete Poetry and Prose of William Blake,* rev. ed., edited by David V. Erdman, 12–13. Berkeley: University of California Press.

———. (1793) 1982. "VISIONS of the Daughters of Albion." In *The Complete Poetry and Prose of William Blake,* rev. ed., edited by David V. Erdman, 45–51. Berkeley: University of California Press.

Block, Francesca Lia. 1989–2005. Dangerous Angels series, comprising *Weetzie Bat, Witch Baby, Cherokee Bat and the Goat Guys, Missing Angel Juan, Baby Be-Bop, Necklace of Kisses,* and *Pink Smog.* New York: HarperCollins.

Blum, Virginia. 1995. *Hide and Seek: The Child between Psychoanalysis and Fiction.* Champaign: University of Illinois Press.

Boehmer, Elleke. 1995. *Colonial and Postcolonial Literature: Migrant Metaphors.* Oxford: Oxford University Press.

Boehrer, Bruce Thomas. 2002. *Shakespeare among the Animals: Nature and Society in the Drama of Early Modern England.* New York: Palgrave Macmillan.

———. 2010. *Animal Characters: Nonhuman Beings in Early Modern Literature.* Haney Foundation Series. Philadelphia: University of Pennsylvania Press.

Boethius, Ulf, ed. 1998. *Modernity, Modernism and Children's Literature.* Stockholm: Stockholm University Press.

Bogost, Ian. 2016. *Play Anything: The Pleasure of Limits, the Uses of Boredom, and the Secret of Games.* New York: Basic Books.

Boileau, Nicolas. 1893. "Lettre à Brossette, 10 novembre 1699." In *Les aventures de Télémaque,* by François Fénelon. Paris: Hachette. www.gutenberg.org.

Bolter, Jay David, and Richard Gruisin. 1999. *Remediation: Understanding New Media.* Cambridge, MA: MIT Press.

Bone, Ian. 2004. *Sleep Rough Tonight.* Camberwell: Penguin.

Booth, Wayne C. 1974. *A Rhetoric of Irony.* Chicago: University of Chicago Press.

———. 1988. *The Company We Keep: An Ethics of Fiction.* Berkeley: University of California Press.

———. 1991. *The Rhetoric of Fiction.* London: Penguin.

Borges, Jorge Luis. (1941) 1998. "The Library of Babel." In *Collected Fictions,* translated by Andrew Hurley, 112–18. New York: Viking.

Bösche, Susanne. 1983. *Jenny Lives with Eric and Martin.* Translated by L. Mackay. London: Gay Men's Press. Originally published as *Mette bor hos Morten og Erik* (Copenhagen: Fremad, 1981).

Botelho, Maria José, and Masha Kabakow Rudman. 2009. *Critical Multicultural Analysis of Children's Literature: Mirrors, Windows, and Doors.* New York: Routledge.

Bottigheimer, Ruth B. 1978. *Grimm's Bad Girls & Bold Boys: The Moral & Social Vision of the Tales.* New Haven, CT: Yale University Press.

———. 2009. *Fairy Tales: A New History.* Albany: State University of New York Press.

Bourdieu, Pierre. (1979) 1998. *Distinction: A Social Critique of the Judgment of Taste.* Translated by Richard Nice. Cambridge, MA: Harvard University Press.

Boyd, Brian. 2009. *On the Origin of Stories: Evolution, Cognition and Fiction.* Cambridge, MA: Harvard University Press.

Boym, Svetlana. 2001. *The Future of Nostalgia.* New York: Basic Books.

Bradbury, Malcolm, and James MacFarlane. 1976. *Modernism 1890–1930.* Harmondsworth: Penguin.

Bradford, Clare. 2001. *Reading Race: Aboriginality in Australian Children's Literature.* Carlton South: Melbourne University Publishing.

———. 2006. "Multiculturalism and Children's Books." In *The Oxford Encyclopedia of Children's Literature,* vol. 3, edited by Jack Zipes, 113–18. New York: Oxford University Press.

———. 2007. *Unsettling Narratives: Postcolonial Readings of Children's Literature.* Waterloo: Wilfrid Laurier University Press.

———. 2011. "Children's Literature in a Global Age: Transnational and Local Identities." *Nordic Journal of ChildLit Aesthetics* 2:20–34.

Bradford, Clare, Robyn McCallum, Kerry Mallan, and John Stephens. 2008. *New World Orders in Contemporary Children's Literature.* Basingstoke: Palgrave Macmillan.

Brennan, Teresa. 2004. *The Transmission of Affect.* Ithaca, NY: Cornell University Press.

Briggs, Jimmie. 2005. *Innocents Lost: When Child Soldiers Go to War*. New York: Basic Books.

Briggs, Julia. 2005. "'Delightful Task!': Women, Children and Reading in the Mid-eighteenth Century." In *Culturing the Child: 1640–1914*, edited by Donelle Ruwe, 67–82. Lanham, MD: Scarecrow Press.

Briggs, Laura, Gladys McCormick, and J. T. Way. 2008. "Transnationalism: A Category of Analysis." *American Quarterly* 60, no. 3: 625–48.

Briggs, Raymond. 1978. *The Snowman*. New York: Random House.

Bristow, Joseph. 1991. *Empire Boys: Adventures in a Man's World*. New York: HarperCollins Academic.

Brites, Andreia. 2015. "O Crossover como ponte universal." Interview with Sandra L. Beckett. *Blimunda* 38 (July): 67–78.

Brocklebank, Lisa. 2000. "Disney's 'Mulan'—the 'True' Deconstructed Heroine?" *Marvels & Tales* 14, no. 2: 268–83.

Brooker, Will. 2004. *Alice's Adventures: Lewis Carroll in Popular Culture*. New York: Continuum.

Brooks, Wanda, and Jonda C. McNair. 2009. "'But This Story of Mine Is Not Unique': A Review of Research on African American Children's Literature." *Review of Educational Research* 79, no. 1: 125–62.

Broomé, Agnes, and Nichola Smalley. 2014. "A Farewell to Age Restrictions? The Rise of Crossover Fiction in Swedish." *Swedish Book Review*. www.swedishbookreview.com.

Brown, Gillian. 2001. *The Consent of the Governed: The Lockean Legacy in Early American Culture*. Cambridge, MA: Harvard University Press.

Brown, Jayna. 2008. *Babylon Girls: Black Women Performers and the Shaping of the Modern*. Durham, NC: Duke University Press.

Brown, Joanne. 1999. "Interrogating the 'Real' in Young Adult Realism." *New Advocate* 12, no. 4: 345–57.

Brown, Margaret Wise. 1947. *Goodnight Moon*. Illustrated by Clement Hurd. New York: Harper & Brothers.

Browne, Anthony. 1977. *A Walk in the Park*. London: Hamilton.

———. 1992. *Zoo*. London: Julia MacRae Books.

———. (1998) 1999. *Voices in the Park*. London: Picture Corgi.

Bruce, Mary Grant. 1910–42. Billabong series, comprising *A Little Bush Maid, Mates at Billabong, Norah of Billabong, From Billabong to London, Jim and Wally, Captain Jim, Back to Billabong, Billabong's Daughter, Billabong Adventurers, Bill of Billabong, Wings Above Billabong, Billabong Gold, Son of Billabong,* and *Billabong Riders*. Melbourne: Ward Lock.

Bruder, Helen P., and Tristanne J. Connolly. 2010. *Queer Blake*. New York: Palgrave Macmillan.

Brugman, Alyssa. 2013. *Alex as Well*. New York: Square Fish.

Bruhm, Steven, and Natasha Hurley, eds. 2004. *Curiouser: On the Queerness of Children*. Minneapolis: University of Minnesota Press.

Bruhn, Jørgen. 2016. *The Intermediality of Narrative Literature: Medialities Matter*. London: Palgrave Macmillan.

Bruner, Jerome. 1986. *Actual Minds, Possible Worlds*. Cambridge, MA: Harvard University Press.

———. 1992. "The Narrative Construction of Reality." *Critical Inquiry* 18, no. 1: 1–21.

Buchanan, Andrea J., and Miriam Peskowitz. 2007. *The Daring Book for Girls*. New York: HarperCollins.

Buitrago, Jairo. 2015. *Two White Rabbits*. Illustrated by Rafael Yockteng. Translated by Elisa Amado. Ronto: Groundwood / House of Anansi.

Bunge, Marcia J., ed. 2001. *The Child in Christian Thought*. Grand Rapids: William B. Eerdmans.

Bunyan, John. 1678. *The Pilgrim's Progress*. London: Nath, Ponder.

———. 1686. *A Book for Boys and Girls; or, Country Rhimes for Children*. London: Printed for NP.

Burgess, Melvin. 1997. *Smack*. New York: Holt.

Burgett, Bruce, and Glenn Hendler, eds. 2014. *Keywords for American Cultural Studies*. 2nd ed. New York: New York University Press.

Burke, Edmund. (1757) 1958. *A Philosophical Enquiry into the Origin of Our Ideas of the Sublime and Beautiful*. Edited by J. T. Boulton. London: Routledge.

Burke, Michael. 2011. *Literary Reading, Cognition and Emotion: An Exploration of the Oceanic Mind*. London: Routledge.

Burke, Michael, and Emily T. Troscianko, eds. 2017. *Cognitive Literary Science: Dialogues between Literature and Cognition*. Oxford: Oxford University Press.

Burn, Andrew. 2004. "Potterliteracy: Cross-Media Narratives, Cultures and Grammars." *Papers: Explorations in Children's Literature* 14, no. 2: 5–17.

Burnett, Frances Hodgson. (1886) 2009. *Little Lord Fauntleroy*. Project Gutenberg. Accessed January 10, 2009. www.gutenberg.org.

———. (1911) 1951. *The Secret Garden*. Harmondsworth: Penguin-Puffin Books.

Burton, Robert. (1621) 1886. *The Anatomy of Melancholy*. London: Nimmo.

Busch, Wilhelm. (1865) 1925. *Max und Moritz*. Munich: Braun und Schneider.

Butler, Judith. 1988. "Performative Acts and Gender Constitution: An Essay in Phenomenology and Feminist Theory." *Theatre Journal* 40, no. 4: 519–31.

———. 1990. *Gender Trouble: Feminism and the Subversion of Identity*. New York: Routledge.

———. 1993. *Bodies That Matter: On the Discursive Limits of Sex*. New York: Routledge.

Butler, Melanie, and Paul Falzone. 2014. "'Born This Way': Media and Youth Identities in Uganda's Kuchu Community." In *Queer Youth and Media Cultures*, edited by Christopher Pullen, 224–38. Houndmills: Palgrave Macmillan.

Butts, Dennis. 2003. "'Tis a Hundred Years Since: G. A. Henty's *With Clive in India* and Philip Pullman's *The Tin Princess*." In *The Presence of the Past in Children's Literature*, edited by Ann Lawson Lucas, 81–87. Westport, CT: Praeger.

Byars, Betsy. 1982. "Writing for Children." *Signal* 37 (January): 3–10.

Cadden, Mike. 2000a. "The Irony of Narration in the Young Adult Novel." *Children's Literature Association Quarterly* 25, no. 3: 146–54.

———. 2000b. "Speaking to Both Children and Genre: Le Guin's Ethics of Audience." *Lion and the Unicorn* 24, no. 1 (January): 128–42.

———, ed. 2011. *Telling Children's Stories: Narrative Theory and Children's Literature*. Lincoln: University of Nebraska Press.

Cai, Mingshui. 2008. "Transactional Theory and the Study of Multicultural Literature." *Language Arts* 85, no. 3: 212–20.

Calvert, Karin. 1992. *Children in the House: The Material Culture of Early Childhood, 1600–1900*. Boston: Northeastern University Press.

Cammaerts, Emile. 1925. *The Poetry of Nonsense*. New York: Dutton.

Campbell, Eddie. 2001. *Alec: How to Be an Artist*. Paddington, Australia: Eddie Campbell Comics.

Campbell, Edith. 2016. "Review: When We Was Fierce." *CrazyQuiltedI* (blog), July 2016. https://campbele.wordpress.com.

Campbell, Joseph. 1949. *The Hero with a Thousand Faces*. New York: Pantheon.

Campbell, Maria. 1995. *Stories of the Road Allowance People*. Penticton: Theytus.

Campbell, Nicola I. 2008. *Shin-chi's Canoe*. Illustrated by Kim LeFave. Toronto: Groundwood / House of Anansi.

Campe, Joachim Heinrich. (1799) 1917. *Robinson der Jüngere. Ein Lesebuch für Kinder*. Munich: G. W. Dietrich.

Capshaw, Katharine. 2014. *Civil Rights Childhood: Picturing Liberation in African American Picture Books*. Minneapolis: University of Minnesota Press.

Capshaw, Katharine, and Anna Mae Duane, eds. 2017. *Who Writes for Black Children? African American Children's Literature before 1900*. Minneapolis: University of Minnesota Press.

Caputi, Jane. 2004. *Goddesses and Monsters: Women, Myth, Power, and Popular Culture*. Madison: University of Wisconsin Press.

Carle, Eric. 1969. *The Very Hungry Caterpillar*. New York: World.

Carlson, Nancy. 1992. *Arnie and the New Kid*. New York: Puffin.

Carpenter, Carole H. 1996. "Enlisting Children's Literature in the Goals of Multiculturalism." *Mosaic: A Journal for the Interdisciplinary Study of Literature* 29, no. 3: 53–74.

Carpenter, Humphrey. 1985. *Secret Gardens: A Study of the Golden Age of Children's Literature*. Boston: Houghton Mifflin.

Carroll, John T. 2008. "'What Then Will This Child Become?': Perspectives on Children in the Gospel of Luke." In *The Child in the Bible*, edited by Marcia J. Bunge, Terence E. Fretheim, and Beverly Roberts Gaventa, 177–94. Grand Rapids: William B. Eerdmans.

Carroll, Lewis. 1990. *The Annotated Alice: The Definitive Edition of Alice's Adventures in Wonderland (1865) & Through the Looking Glass (1872)*. Edited by Martin Gardner. New York: Norton.

Carruthers, Mary, and Jan M. Ziolkowski, eds. 2002. *The Medieval Craft of Memory: An Anthology of Texts and Pictures*. Philadelphia: University of Pennsylvania Press.

Carter, Forrest. 1976. *The Education of Little Tree*. New York: Delacorte Press.

Casement, William. 1987. "Literature and Didacticism: Examining Some Popularly Held Ideas." *Journal of Aesthetic Education* 21, no. 1: 101–11.

Castañeda, Claudia. 2014. "Childhood." *Transgender Studies Quarterly* 1, nos. 1–2: 59–61.

Cech, John. 1986. "Touchstones and the Phoenix: New Directions, New Dimensions." *Children's Literature Association Quarterly* 10, no. 4: 177.

Centre for Literacy in Primary Education (CLPE). 2018. "Reflecting Realities: Survey of Ethnic Representation within UK Children's Literature 2017." CLPE, July 2018. https://clpe.org.uk.

Cerny, Lothar. 1992. "Reader Participation and Rationalism in Fielding's *Tom Jones*." *Connotations* 2, no. 2: 137–62.

Chagall, Irene, dir. 2014. *Let's Get the Rhythm: The Life and Times of Miss Mary Mack*. New York: Women Make Movies.

Chakrabarty, Dipesh. 1992. "Postcoloniality and the Artifice of History: Who Speaks for 'Indian' Pasts?" *Representations* 32 (Winter): 1–26.

Chan, Kara. 2015. "Children and Consumer Culture." In *The Routledge International Handbook of Children, Adolescents and Media*, edited by Dafna Lemish, 141–47. New York: Routledge.

Chang, Ta-Chun. 1996. *Wild Child*. In *Wild Kids: Two Novels about Growing Up*. Translated by M. Berry. New York: Columbia University Press.

Charlip, Remy, and Jerry Joyner. 1975. *Thirteen*. New York: Parents Magazine Press.

Chayil, Eishes. 2010. *Hush*. New York: Bloomsbury.

Chen, Chih-Yuan. 2004. *Guji Guji*. La Jolla, CA: Kane/Miller.

Chen, Minjie. 2009. "From Victory to Victimization: The Sino-Japanese War (1937–1945) as Depicted in Chinese Youth Literature." *Bookbird* 47, no. 2: 27–35.

———. 2016. *The Sino-Japanese War and Youth Literature: Friends and Foes on the Battlefield*. London: Routledge.

Chen, Suh Shan, and Ming Cherng Duh. 2013. "Subjectivity without Identity: Huang Chunming's Fiction in Postcolonial Vein." In *Subjectivity in Asian Children's Literature and Film: Global Theories and Implications*, edited by John Stephens, 197–212. New York: Routledge.

Cherniavsky, Eva. 2007. "Body." In *Keywords for American Cultural Studies*, edited by Glenn Hendler and Bruce Burgett. https://keywords.nyupress.org.

Cherubini, Eugenio. 1911. *Pinocchio in Africa*. Translated by Angelo Patri. Illustrated by Charles Copeland. Boston: Ginn.

Chin, Rita. 2017. *The Crisis of Multiculturalism in Europe: A History*. Princeton, NJ: Princeton University Press.

Christensen, Nina. 2013. "Contemporary Picturebooks in the Nordic Countries: Concepts of Literature and Childhood." In *Looking Out and Looking In: National Identity in Picturebooks of the New Millennium*, edited by Åse Marie Ommundsen, 183–94. Oslo: Novus Forlag.

———. 2017. "Imagining Equality: The Emergence of the Ideas of Tolerance, Universalism, and Human Rights in Danish Magazines for Children, 1750–1800." In *Imagining Sameness and Difference in Children's Literature*, edited by Emer O'Sullivan and Andrea Immel, 111–27. London: Palgrave Macmillan.

Christie, Agatha. 1939. *Ten Little Niggers*. London: Colliers. Later published as *And Then There Were None* (New York: William Morrow, 2011).

Clark, Beverly Lyon. 1996. *Regendering the School Story: Sassy Sissies and Tattling Tomboys*. New York: Routledge.

———. 2003. *Kiddie Lit: The Cultural Construction of Children's Literature in America*. Baltimore: Johns Hopkins University Press.

Clark, Gillian. 1994. "The Fathers and the Children." In *The Church and Childhood*, edited by Diana Wood, 1–27. Oxford: Blackwell.

Clarke, Cat. 2013. *Undone*. London: Quercus.

Clough, Patricia Ticineto, with Jean Halley, eds. 2007. *The Affective Turn: Theorizing the Social*. Durham, NC: Duke University Press.

Clute, John, and John Grant, eds. 1997. *The Encyclopedia of Fantasy*. London: Orbit.

Coats, Karen. 2010. "Fantasy." In *The Routledge Companion to Children's Literature*, edited by David Rudd, 75–86. London: Routledge.

———. 2018. *The Bloomsbury Introduction to Children's and Young Adult Literature*. London: Bloomsbury Academic.

Cobley, Paul. 2001. s.v. "Genre" in "Glossary." In *Narrative*. London: Routledge.

Coetzee, J. M. (1993) 2001. "What Is a Classic?" In *Stranger Shores: Literary Essays*, 1–17. New York: Viking Penguin.

Cogan, Thomas. 1813. *A Treatise on the Passions and Affections of the Mind, Philosophical, Ethical, and Theological*. London: Printed for T. Cadell and W. Davies.

Cohoon, Lorinda B. 2006. *Serialized Citizenships: Periodicals, Books, and American Boys, 1840–1911*. Lanham, MD: Scarecrow Press.

Cole, Babette. 1987. *Princess Smartypants*. London: Hamish Hamilton Children's Books.

Cole, Henry [Felix Summerly, pseud.]. 1843. *Beauty and the Beast*. In *Home Treasury of Books, Toys, etc. Purposed to Cultivate the Affection, Fancy, Imagination and Taste of Children*, 3–23. London: Joseph Cundall.

Colebrook, Claire. 2004. *Irony*. New York: Routledge.

Coleridge, Samuel Taylor. (1817) 1906. *Biographia Literaria*. London: Dent.

Collins, Jessanne. 2013. "Girl Powder: A Cultural History of Love's Baby Soft." *The Awl* (blog), March 5, 2013. https://theawl.com.

Collins, Suzanne. 2008. *The Hunger Games*. New York: Scholastic Press.

———. 2009. *Catching Fire*. New York: Scholastic Press.

———. 2010. *Mockingjay*. New York: Scholastic Press.

Collins, Wilkie. 1858. "Doctor Dulcamara, M.P." *Household Words* 19:49–52. www.web40571.clarahost.co.uk.

Collodi, Carlo. (1883) 1996. *The Adventures of Pinocchio*. Translated by Anne Lawson Lucas. Oxford: Oxford World Classics.

Colomer, Teresa. 2010. "Picturebooks and Changing Values at the Turn of the Century." In *New Directions in Picturebook Research*, edited by Teresa Colomer, Bettina Kümmerling-Meibauer, and Cecilia Silva-Díaz, 41–54. London: Routledge.

Colón, Cristóbal. 1893. *The Journal of Christopher Columbus (during His First Voyage), and Documents Relating to the Voyages of John Cabot and Gaspar Corte Real*. Translated by Clements R. Markham. London: Printed for the Hakluyt Society.

Colston, Herbert L., and Raymond W. Gibbs Jr. 2007. "A Brief History of Irony." In *Irony in Language and Thought: A Cognitive Science Reader*, edited by Raymond W. Gibbs and Herbert L. Colston, 3–21. New York: Erlbaum.

Comenius, Johann Amos. 1658. *Orbis sensualium pictus*. Nuremberg: Typis & sumptibus Michaelis Endteri.

Connolly, Paula. 2013. *Slavery in American Children's Literature, 1790–2010*. Iowa City: University of Iowa Press.

Conrad, Rachel. 2013a. "'And Stay, a Minute More, Alone': Time and Subjectivities in Gwendolyn Brooks' *Bronzeville Boys and Girls*." *Children's Literature Association Quarterly* 38, no. 4 (Winter): 379–98.

——. 2013b. "'We Are Masters at Childhood': Time and Agency in Poetry by, for, and about Children." *Jeunesse* 5, no. 2 (Winter): 124–50.

Cook, Barry, and Tony Bancroft, dirs. 1998. *Mulan*. Walt Disney Pictures.

Cook, D. T. 2008. "The Missing Child in Consumption Theory." *Journal of Consumer Culture* 8, no. 2: 219–43.

Cook, James. 1967. "Entries of 15 and 25 June 1777." In *Journals of Captain James Cook*, vol. 3, pp. 129, 146. Cambridge: Hakluyt Society at the University Press.

Coolidge, Susan. (1872) 2006. *What Katy Did*. New York: Dover.

Cooper, Susan. 1981. "Escaping into Ourselves." In *Celebrating Children's Books*, edited by Betsy Hearne and Marilyn Kaye, 14–23. New York: Lothrop.

——. 2017. "A Catch of the Breath." Lecture, J. R. R. Tolkien Lecture on Fantasy Literature, Pembroke College, Oxford, April 27, 2017. Unpublished video. https://tolkienlecture.org.

Cooperative Children's Book Center (CCBC). 2017. "Publishing Statistics on Children's Books about People of Color and First/Native Nations by People of Color and First/Native Nations Authors and Illustrators." CCBC, May 2017. https://ccbc.education.wisc.edu.

Cormier, Robert. 1974. *The Chocolate War*. New York: Pantheon.

Cornejo, Giancarlo. 2014. "For a Queer Pedagogy of Friendship." *Transgender Studies Quarterly* 1, no. 3: 352–67.

Corsaro, William. 2017. *The Sociology of Childhood*. Los Angeles: Sage.

Cosslett, Tess. 2006. *Talking Animals in British Children's Fiction, 1786–1914*. Aldershot: Ashgate.

Coulter, Natalie. 2014. *Tweening the Girl: The Crystallization of the Tween Market*. New York: Peter Lang.

Coveney, Peter. 1967. *The Image of Childhood*. Harmondsworth: Penguin.

Cox, Cynthia. 1994. "'Postmodern Fairy Tales' in Contemporary Literature." *Children's Folklore Review* 16, no. 2: 13–19.

Cozolino, Louis. 2002. *The Neuroscience of Psychotherapy*. New York: Norton.

Crago, Hugh. 2014. *Entranced by Story: Brain, Tale and Teller, from Infancy to Old Age*. London: Routledge.

——. 2018. "With a Tale He Cometh to You: A Phenomenological Journey to the Centre of Story." *Journal of the Fantastic in the Arts* 29, no. 3: 422–44.

Crago, Maureen, and Hugh Crago. 1983. *Prelude to Literacy: A Preschool Child's Encounter with Picture and Story*. Carbondale: Southern Illinois University Press.

Craik, Dinah Mulock. 2009. *The Little Lame Prince and His Travelling Cloak*. Wildside Press.

Crain, Patricia. 2000. *The Story of A: The Alphabetization of America from the New England Primer to the Scarlet Letter*. Palo Alto, CA: Stanford University Press.

——. 2016. *Reading Children: Literacy, Property, and the Dilemmas of Childhood in Nineteenth-Century America*. Philadelphia: University of Pennsylvania Press.

Crampton, Patricia. 1983. *An Introduction to the History and Work of IBBY*. International Board on Books for Young People. http://www.literature.at.

Creech, Sharon. 1994. *Walk Two Moons*. New York: Scholastic.

Creusere, Marlena A. 2007. "A Developmental Test of Theoretical Perspectives on the Understanding of Verbal Irony: Children's Recognition of Allusion and Pragmatic Insincerity." In *Irony in Language and Thought: A Cognitive Science Reader*, edited by Raymond W. Gibbs and Herbert L. Colston, 409–24. New York: Erlbaum.

Crompton, Richmal. (1922) 1983. *Just William*. London: Macmillan.

Cross, Julie. 2011. *Humor in Contemporary Junior Fiction*. New York: Routledge.

Cruikshank, George. 1854. *George Cruikshank's Magazine*, no. 2 (February 1854). Edited by Frank E. Smedley [Frank Fairlegh]. London: D. Bogue.

Cullen, Countee. (1925) 2013. "Heritage." In *Countee Cullen: Collected Poems*, edited by Major Jackson. New York: Library of America.

Culler, Jonathan. 1975. *Structuralist Poetics: Structuralism, Linguistics and the Study of Literature*. Ithaca, NY: Cornell University Press.

Cultural Survival. n.d. "The Issues." Accessed December 8, 2018. www.culturalsurvival.org.

Cummins, June. 2011. "Marketing." In *Keywords for Children's Literature*, edited by Philip Nel and Lissa Paul, 146–50. New York: New York University Press.

Cunningham, Hugh. 1995. *Children and Childhood in Western Society since 1500*. London: Longman.

Curry, Alice. 2013. *Environmental Crisis in Young Adult Fiction: A Poetics of Earth*. New York: Palgrave Macmillan.

Curtis, Christopher Paul. 1995. *The Watsons Go to Birmingham, 1963*. New York: Random House Children's Books.

Dahl, Roald. (1964) 1973. *Charlie and the Chocolate Factory*. New York: Alfred A. Knopf.

———. (1988) 1990. *Matilda*. Illustrated by Quentin Blake. New York: Puffin.

Dahle, Gro, and Kaia Dahle Nyhus. 2017. *Sesam Sesam*. Oslo: Cappelen Damm.

Dahle, Gro, and Svein Nyhus. 2003. *Sinna Mann*. Oslo: Cappelen Damm.

———. 2007. *Håret til mamma*. Oslo: Cappelen.

———. 2014. *Akvarium*. Oslo: Cappelen Damm.

———. 2016. *Blekkspruten*. Oslo: Cappelen Damm.

Dahlen, Sarah Park. 2016. "Alvin Ho: Not Allergic to Playing Indian, Feathers, and Other Stereotypical Things." In *The Early Reader in Children's Literature and Culture*, edited by Jennifer Miskec and Annette Wannamaker, 158–70. New York: Routledge.

Damasio, Antonio. 2000. *The Feeling of What Happens: Body and Emotion in the Making of Consciousness*. London: Routledge.

Darr, Yael. 2017. "Nation Building and Children's Literary Canons: The Israeli Test Case." In *Constitution and Canon Change in Children's Literature*, edited by Bettina Kümmerling-Meibauer and Anja Müller, 23–38. New York: Routledge.

Darton, F. J. Harvey. (1932, 1958) 1970. *Children's Books in England: Five Centuries of Social Life*. Cambridge: Cambridge University Press.

Daubert, Hannelore. 2007. "Thoughtful and Grave: Changing Images of the Family in Postwar European Children's Literature." *Bookbird* 45, no. 2: 6–14.

Davidson, Jenny. 2009. *Breeding: A Partial History of the Eighteenth Century*. New York: Columbia University Press.

Davidson, Michael. 2008. *Concerto for the Left Hand: Disability and the Defamiliar Body*. Ann Arbor: University of Michigan Press.

Davies, Bronwyn. 1989. *Frogs and Snails and Feminist Tales*. Sydney: Allen & Unwin.

Davis, Lennard. 1995. *Enforcing Normalcy: Disability, Deafness and the Body*. London: Verso.

Davis, Robert A. 2011. "Brilliance of a Fire: Innocence, Experience and the Theory of Childhood." *Journal of Philosophy of Education* 45, no. 2 (May): 379–97.

Davis, Tanita S. 2012. *Happy Families*. New York: Knopf.

Dawson, Melanie. 2005. *Laboring to Play: Home Entertainment and the Spectacle of Middle-Class Cultural Life, 1850–1920*. Tuscaloosa: University of Alabama Press.

Day, Sara K. 2014. "Pure Passion: The *Twilight* Saga, 'Abstinence Porn,' and Adolescent Women's Fan Fiction." *Children's Literature Association Quarterly* 39, no. 1: 28–48.

de Brunhoff, Jean. (1931) 1961. *The Story of Babar: The Little Elephant*. New York: Random House.

de Brunhoff, Laurent, and Phyllis Rose. 2003. *Babar's Museum of Art*. New York: Abrams Books for Young Readers.

Defoe, Daniel. 1719. *The Life and Strange Surprizing Adventures of Robinson Crusoe, of York, Mariner*. London: W. Taylor.

———. (1719) 1994. *Robinson Crusoe*. Edited by Michael Shinagel. New York: Norton.

———. 1726. *Mere Nature Delineated; or, A Body Without a Soul*. London: Printed for T. Warner, at the Black Boy, in Pater-Noster-Row.

De Genlis, Mme [Stéphanie Félicité]. 1779–80. *Théâtre à l'usage des jeunes personnes*. Paris: Lambert & Baudouin.

de Lauretis, Teresa. 1991. "Queer Theory: Lesbian and Gay Sexualities." *differences: A Journal of Feminist Cultural Studies* 3, no. 2: iii–xviii.

Deleuze, Gilles, and Félix Guattari. 1987. *A Thousand Plateaus: Capitalism and Schizophrenia*. Translated by Brian Massumi. Minneapolis: University of Minnesota Press.

DeNicolo, Christina P., and Maria E. Franquiz. 2006. "'Do I Have to Say It?': Critical Encounters with Multicultural Children's Literature." *Language Arts* 84, no. 2: 157–70.

dePaola, Tomie. 1979. *Oliver Button Is a Sissy*. Orlando: Voyager Books.

Derrida, Jacques. 2002. "The Animal That Therefore I Am (More to Follow)." Translated by David Wills. *Critical Enquiry* 28:369–418.

———. 2008. *The Animal That Therefore I Am*. New York: Fordham University Press.

De Saint Exupéry, Antoine. 2015. *The Little Prince*. Translated by Ros Schwartz. London: Picador.

Desmet, Mieke K. T. 2007. *Babysitting the Reader: Translating English Narrative Fiction for Girls into Dutch, 1946–1995*. Berlin: P. Lang.

Desta, Yohana. 2016. "The Year Disney Started to Take Diversity Seriously." *Vanity Fair*, November 23, 2016. www.vanityfair.com.

Dettmar, Ute. 2002. *Das Drama der Familienkindheit: Der Anteil des Kinderschauspiels am Familiendrama des späten 18. und frühen 19. Jahrhunderts*. Munich: W. Fink.

de Vigan, Delphine. (2007) 2010. *No and Me*. Translated by G. Miller. Toronto: Random House–Anchor Canada.

Devitt, Amy. 2004. *Writing Genres*. Carbondale: Southern Illinois UP.

Dews, Shelley, Ellen Winner, Joan Kaplan, Elizabeth Rosenblatt, Malia Hunt, Karen Lim, Angela McGovern, Alison Qualter, and Bonnie Smarsh. 1996. "Children's Understanding of the Meaning and Functions of Verbal Irony." *Child Development*, no. 67: 3071–85.

Dickens, Charles. (1848) 1970. *Dombey and Son*. Harmondsworth: Penguin.

Dickinson, Peter. 1988. *Eva*. London: Victor Gollancz.

Dickson, Gary. 2009. "*Rites de Passage*: The Children's Crusade and Medieval Childhood." *Journal of the History of Childhood and Youth* 2, no. 3 (Fall): 315–32.

Dijk, Lutz van. 1995. *Damned Strong Love: The True Story of Willi G. and Stefan K.* Translated by Elizabeth D. Crawford. New York: Henry Holt.

Dimaline, Cherie. 2017. *The Marrow Thieves*. Toronto: DCB.

Dirks, Nicholas. 2005. "Postcolonialism." In *New Keywords: A Revised Vocabulary of Culture and Society*, edited by Tony Bennett, Lawrence Grossberg, and Meaghan Morris, 267–69. Malden, MA: Blackwell.

Dirlik, Arif, and Zhang Xudong. 1997. "Introduction: Postmodernism and China." *boundary 2* 24, no. 3 (Fall): 1–18.

Dixon, Bob. 1977. *Catching Them Young: Sex, Race and Class in Children's Fiction*. London: Pluto Press.

Docter, Pete, dir. 2015. *Inside Out*. Pixar.

Dodge, Mary Maples. (1865) 2003. *Hans Brinker, or The Silver Skates*. New York: Dover.

Donovan, John. 1969. *I'll Get There. It Better Be Worth the Trip*. New York: Harper & Row.

Doonan, Jane. 1993. *Looking at Pictures in Picture Books*. Stroud: Thimble Press.

Doty, Alexander. 1993. *Making Things Perfectly Queer: Interpreting Mass Culture*. Minneapolis: University of Minnesota Press.

Douglas, Allen, and Fedwa Malti-Douglas. 1999. "An Arab Girl Draws Trouble." In *Girls, Boys, Books, Toys: Gender in Children's Literature and Culture*, edited by Beverly Lyon Clark and Margaret R. Higonnet, 210–26. Baltimore: Johns Hopkins University Press.

Draper, Sharon M. 2006. *Copper Sun*. New York: Atheneum Books for Young Readers.

———. 2010. *Out of My Mind*. New York: Atheneum Books for Young Readers.

Driscoll, Catherine. 2002. *Girls: Feminine Adolescence in Popular Culture and Cultural Theory*. New York: Columbia University Press.

Druker, Elina, and Bettina Kümmerling-Meibauer, eds. 2015. *Children's Literature and the Avant-Garde*. Amsterdam: John Benjamins.

Duane, Anna Mae. 2007. "Examination Days: The New York African Free School Collection." New-York Historical Society. www.nyhistory.org.

———. 2010. "'Like a Motherless Child': Racial Education at the New York African Free School and in *My Bondage and My Freedom*." *American Literature* 82, no. 3: 461–88.

Dubois, Claude K. 2012. *Akim Court*. Paris: L'école des loisirs.

Du Bois, W. E. B. 1920–21. *The Brownies' Book: A Monthly Magazine for the Children of the Sun*. January 1920–December 1921.

Dubrow, Heather. 1982. *Genre*. London: Methuen.

Dudek, Debra. 2006a. "Dogboys and Lost Things; or Anchoring a Floating Signifier: Race and Critical Multiculturalism." *Ariel* 37, no. 4: 1–20.

———. 2006b. "Of Murmels and Snigs: Detention-Centre Narratives in Australian Literature for Children." *Overland* 185:38–42.

———. 2006c. "Under the Wire: Detainee Activism in Australian Children's Literature." *Papers* 16, no. 2: 17–22.

Dudek, Debra, and Wenche Ommundsen. 2007. "Building Cultural Citizenship: Multiculturalism and Children's Literature." Special issue, *Papers* 17, no. 2: 3–6.

Dumas, Alexandre. 1844. *Les trois mousquetaires*. Paris: Baudry.

Dumas, William. 2013. *Piism Finds Her Miskanow*. Illustrated by Leonard Paul. Winnipeg: Portage and Main Press.

Dunne, Anna Mae, and Katharine Capshaw Smith, eds. 2017. *Who Writes for Black Children? African American Children's Literature before 1900*. Minneapolis: University of Minnesota Press.

Durand, Delphine. 2006. *Bob & Co.* London: Tate. Originally published as *Bob & Cie* (Rodez: Éditions du Rouergue, 2004).

Dusinberre, Juliet. 1987. *Alice to the Lighthouse: Children's Books and Radical Experiments in Art*. Basingstoke: Macmillan.

Duyvis, Corinne. 2015. "Own Voices." *Corinne Duyvis Sci-Fi and Fantasy in MG & YA* (blog), September 2015. www.corinneduyvis.net.

——— (@corinneduyvis). 2017. "It's all gotten kind of complicated and messy and I don't want to be seen as like, trying to overtake the conversation." Twitter, July 10, 2017. https://twitter.com/corinneduyvis/status/884438074721263617.

Dwan, Allan, dir. 1937. *Heidi*. Twentieth Century Fox.

Dyer, Jennifer R., Marilyn Shatz, and Henry M. Wellman. 2000. "Young Children's Storybooks as a Source of Mental State Information." *Child Development* 15, no. 1: 17–37.

Eagleton, Terry. 2000. *The Idea of Culture*. Oxford: Blackwell.

Eastman, P. D. 1960. *Are You My Mother?* New York: Random House.

Echterling, Clare. 2016. "How to Save the World and Other Lessons from Children's Environmental Literature." *Children's Literature in Education* 47, no. 4: 283–99.

Eddy, Jacalyn. 2006. *Bookwomen: Creating an Empire in Children's Book Publishing, 1919–1939*. Madison: University of Wisconsin Press.

Edelman, Lee. 2004. *No Future: Queer Theory and the Death Drive*. Durham, NC: Duke University Press.

Edgeworth, Maria. 1796. *The Parent's Assistant; Or, Stories for Children*. London: J. Johnson in St. Paul's Church-Yard.

———. 1827. "Little Plays for Children." In *The Parent's Assistant*, vol. 7. London: R. Hunter / Baldwin, Cradock, and Joy.

Edgeworth, Maria, and Richard Lovell Edgeworth. (1798) 1855. *Practical Education*. New York: Harper & Brothers.

Edward, Summer. 2018. "Caribbean Children's Literature, Where's Our Diversity Jedi?" Anansesem, October 25, 2018. www.anansesem.com.

Edwards, Brent Hayes. 2014. "Diaspora." In *Keywords for American Cultural Studies*, 2nd ed., edited by Bruce Burgett and Glenn Hendler, 76–78. New York: New York University Press.

Egan, R. Danielle, and Gail Hawkes. 2010. *Theorizing the Sexual Child in Modernity*. New York: Palgrave Macmillan.

Ehrenberg, Pamela. 2017. *Queen of the Hanukkah Dosas*. Illustrated by Anjan Sarkar. New York: Farrar, Strauss and Giroux Books for Young Readers.

Ehrensaft, Diane. 2016. *The Gender Creative Child: Pathways for Nurturing and Supporting Children Who Live Outside Gender Boxes*. New York: The Experiment.

Eisner, Will. (1978) 2000. *A Contract with God and Other Tenement Stories*. New York: DC Comics.

Ekman, Paul, and Wallace V. Friesen. 1986. "A New Pancultural Facial Expression of Emotion." *Motivation and Emotion* 10:159–68.

Eliot, T. S. (1944) 1975. "What Is a Classic?" In *Selected Prose of T. S. Eliot*, edited and introduced by Frank Kermode, 115–31. New York: Harcourt Brace Jovanovich.

Elliot, Patricia. 2010. *Debates in Transgender, Queer, and Feminist Theory: Contested Sites*. Surrey: Ashgate.

Elliott, Anthony. 2015. *Identity Troubles: An Introduction*. London: Routledge.

Elliott, Zetta. 2010. "Black Canadian Children's Literature: The Stats." *Fledgling* (blog), April 5, 2010. https://zettaelliott.wordpress.com.

Ellis, Deborah. 2000. *The Breadwinner*. Toronto: Groundwood Books.

Ellis, John M. 1984. *One Fairy Story Too Many: The Brothers Grimm and Their Tales*. Chicago: University of Chicago Press.

Ellis, Sarah. 2006. *Odd Man Out*. Toronto: Groundwood.

Enciso, Patrica.1997. "Negotiating the Meaning of Difference: Talking Back to Multicultural Literature." In *Reading across Cultures: Teaching Literature in a Diverse Society*, edited by Theresa Rogers and Anna Soter, 13–41. New York: Teacher's College Press.

Ende, Michael. 1979. *Die unendliche Geschichte*. Stuttgart: Thienemann.

Enright, Elizabeth. 1941, 1942, 1944, 1951. The Melendy Quartet, comprising *The Saturdays*, *The Four-Story Mistake*, *Then There Were Five*, and *Spiderweb for Two: A Melendy Maze*. New York: Holt.

Epstein, B. J. 2014. "'The Case of the Missing Bisexuals': Bisexuality in Books for Young Readers." *Journal of Bisexuality* 14, no. 1: 110–25.

Epstein, Rebecca, Jamilia J. Blake, and Thalia González. 2017. *Girlhood Interrupted: The Erasure of Black Girls' Childhood*. Washington, DC: Center on Poverty and Inequality. Georgetown Law.

Erard, Michael. 2018. "What Dutch Children's Books Can Teach Adults." *New York Times*, July 15, 2018.

Erdrich, Louise. 1999. *The Birchbark House*. New York: Hyperion.

———. 2012. *The Round House*. New York: Harper.

Erni, John Nguyet. 2003. "Run Queer Asia Run." *Journal of Homosexuality* 45, nos. 2–4: 381–84.

Estes, Eleanor. 1941. *The Moffats*. New York: Harcourt Brace.

Evans, Janet. 2016. *Challenging and Controversial Picturebooks: Creative and Critical Responses to Visual Texts*. London: Routledge.

Ewers, Hans-Heino. 1989. *Kindheit als poetische Daseinsform. Studien zur Entstehung der romantischen Kindheitsutopie im 18. Jahrhundert: Herder, Jean Paul, Novalis und Tieck*. Munich: Fink.

———. 2001. "Kinderliteratur als Medium der Entdeckung von Kindheit." In *Kinder. Kindheit. Lebensgeschichte*, edited by Imbke Behnken and Jürgen Zinecker, 47–62. Seelze-Velber: Kallmeyer.

———. 2009. *Fundamental Concepts of Children's Literature Research*. New York: Routledge.

Ewert, Marcus. 2008. *10,000 Dresses*. Illustrated by Rex Ray. London: Seven Stories Press.

Ezell, Margaret. 2014. "Handwriting and the Book." In *The Cambridge Companion to History of the Book*, edited by Leslie Howsom, 90–106. Cambridge: Cambridge University Press.

Falconer, Rachel. 2004. "Crossover Literature." In *International Companion Encyclopedia of Children's Literature*, vol. 1, 2nd ed., edited by Peter Hunt, 556–75. London: Routledge.

———. 2009. *The Crossover Novel: Contemporary Children's Fiction and Its Adult Readership*. New York: Routledge.

Faller, Régis. 2006. *The Adventures of Polo*. New York: Roaring Brook Press. Originally published as *Le voyage de Polo* (Paris: Bayard Jeunesse, 2002).

———. 2015. *3 Aventures de Pollo*. Paris. Bayard Jeunesse.

Fallon, Claire. 2017. "YA Author Accused of Lying about Credentials and His Native Heritage." *Huffington Post*, August 31, 2017.

Farizan, Sara. 2013. *If You Could Be Mine*. Chapel Hill, NC: Algonquin.

Farquhar, Mary Ann. 1999. *Children's Literature in China: From Lu Xun to Mao Zedong*. Abingdon: Taylor & Francis.

Farrar, Frederic William. 1858. *Eric, or, Little by Little: A Tale of Roslyn School*. Adam and Charles Black, North Bridge. Available: https://www.gutenberg.org/ebooks/23126.

Fehr, Daniel, and Maurizio A. C. Quarello. 2018. *Come si legge un libro?* Rome: Orecchio Acerbo.

Feingold, Ruth. 2015. "Mapping the Interior: Place, Self, and Nation in the *Dreamhunter Duet*." In *Space and Place in Children's Literature, 1789 to the Present*, edited by Maria Sachiko Cecire, Hannah Field, Kavita Mudan Finn, and Malini Roy, 129–46. London: Routledge.

Fénelon, François de Salignac de la Mothe. (1699) 1785. *The Adventures of Telemachus, the Son of Ulysses: In English Verse, from the French of Monsieur Fenelon*. Translated by Samuel Leacroft. London: J. Nichols.

Fernyhough, Charles. 2008. *The Baby in the Mirror: A Child's World from Birth to Three*. London: Granta.

Fetterley, Judith. 1978. *The Resisting Reader: A Feminist Approach to American Fiction*. Bloomington: Indiana University Press.

Field, Corinne T. 2014. *The Struggle for Equal Adulthood: Gender, Race, and the Fight for Citizenship in Antebellum America*. Chapel Hill: University of North Carolina Press.

Fielding, Henry. 1749. *Tom Jones*. London: Printed for A. Millar.

Fielding, Sarah. 1749. *The Governess, or The Little Female Academy*. London: A. Millar.

Fine, Anne. 1989. *Bill's New Frock*. London: Methuen.

Fish, Stanley. 1980. *Is There a Text in This Class? The Authority of Interpretive Communities*. Cambridge, MA: Harvard University Press.

Fisher, Margery. 1986. *The Bright Face of Danger*. London: Hodder & Stoughton.

Flanagan, Victoria. 2008. *Into the Closet: Cross-Dressing and the Gendered Body in Children's Literature and Film*. London: Routledge.

———. 2014. *Technology and Identity in Young Adult Fiction: The Posthuman Subject*. London: Macmillan.

———. 2017. "Girls Online. The Representation of Adolescent Female Sexuality in the Digital Age." In *Gender(ed) Identities: Critical Rereadings of Gender in Children's and Young Adult Literature*, edited by Tricia Clasen and Holy Hassel, 28–41. London: Routledge.

Flood, Alison. 2014. "French Booksellers Pose Naked to Support Children's Book on Nudity." *Guardian*, February 26, 2014. www.theguardian.com.

Flynn, Richard. 1997. "The Intersection of Children's Literature and Childhood Studies." *Children's Literature Association Quarterly* 22, no. 3: 142–43.

———. 2002. "'Affirmative Acts': Language, Childhood, and Power in June Jordan's Cross-Writing." *Children's Literature* 30:159–85.

———. 2016. "What Are We Talking about When We Talk about Agency?" *Jeunesse: Young People, Texts, Cultures* 8, no. 1: 254–65.

Folguiera, Ana. 2009. *En algún lugar de China*. Illustrated by Emilio Amade. Barcelona: Syballius.

Foltz, Richard. 2006. *Animals in Islamic Traditions and Muslim Cultures*. London: One World.

Ford, Paul Leicester. (1777) 1899. *The New England Primer: A Reprint of the Earliest Known Edition; with Many Facsimiles and Reproductions; and an Historical Introduction*. New York: Dodd, Mead.

Forest, Danielle E., Kasey L. Garrison, and Sue C. Kimmel. 2015. "'The University for the Poor': Portrayals of Class in Translated Children's Literature." *Teachers College Record* 117, no. 2: n2.

Forrester, Kathleen. 2016. "Kinship and Queer Perversions of *Six-Dinner Sid* and *Else-Marie and Her Seven Little Daddies*." *Jeunesse: Young People, Texts, Cultures* 8, no. 2: 119–41.

Foster, Shirley, and Judy Simons. 1995. *What Katy Read: Feminist Re-readings of 'Classic' Stories for Girls*. Iowa City: University of Iowa Press.

Foucault, Michel. 1980. *Power/Knowledge: Selected Interviews and Other Writings, 1972–1977*. Translated by Colin Gordon. New York: Pantheon.

Fox, Dana L., and Kathy G. Short, eds. 2003. *Stories Matter: The Complexity of Cultural Authenticity in Children's Literature*. Urbana, IL: National Council of Teachers of English.

Fox, Mem. 2017. *I'm Australian Too*. Sydney: Scholastic.

Fox, Paula. 1995. *The Eagle Kite*. New York: Dell.

Franek, Claire, and Marc Daniau. 2011. *Tous à poil*. Rodez: Éditions du Rouergue.

Frank, Anne. 1947. *Het achterhuis: Dagboekbrieven van 14 juni
1942 tot 1 augustus 1944*. Amsterdam: Contact.

Franks, Beth. 2001. "Gutting the Golden Goose: Disability in
Grimms' Fairy Tales." In *Embodied Rhetorics: Disability in
Language and Culture*, edited by James Wilson and Cynthia
Lewiecki-Wilson, 244–58. Carbondale: Southern Illinois
University Press.

Freud, Sigmund. 1913. *Totem und Tabu: Einige Übereinstim-
mungen im Seelenleben der Wilden und der Neurotiker*. Leipzig:
H. Heller & Cie.

———. (1919) 1955. "The 'Uncanny.'" Translated by Alix
Strachey. In *The Standard Edition of the Complete Psycho-
logical Works of Sigmund Freud*, vol. 17, edited by James
Strachey with Anna Freud, assisted by Alix Strachey and
Alan Tyson, 218–52. London: Hogarth.

———. (1922) 2005. *On Murder, Mourning and Melancholia*. London: Penguin UK.

Frevert, Ute. 2014. *Learning How to Feel: Children's Literature
and Emotional Socialization, 1870–1970*. Oxford: Oxford
University Press.

Fried, Michael. 1980. *Absorption and Theatricality: Painting and
Beholder in the Age of Diderot*. Chicago: University of Chicago Press.

Frissen, Valerie, Sybille Lammes, Michiel de Lange, Jos de Mul,
and Joost Raessens. 2012. "Homo ludens 2.0: Play, Media, and Identity. Playful Identities." In *The Ludification
of Digital Media Cultures*, edited by Valerie Frissen, Sybille
Lammes, Michiel de Lange, Jos de Mul, and Joost Raessens,
9–50. Amsterdam: Amsterdam University Press.

Frith, Simon. 2005. "Youth." In *New Keywords: A Revised
Vocabulary of Culture and Society*, edited by Tony Bennett,
Lawrence Grossberg, and Meaghan Morris, 380–82. Ox-
ford: Blackwell.

Frow, Jonathan. 2005. *Genre*. New York: Routledge.

Frye, Northrop. 1957. *Anatomy of Criticism: Four Essays*. Princeton, NJ: Princeton University Press.

Fuchs, Cynthia J. 1999. "Girling Popular Culture: Proving
What I've Got to Prove: Pop Culture, Sex and the New Girl
Power." Paper presented at the Modern Language Associa-
tion Conference, Chicago, December 1999.

Fudge, Erica. 2008. *Pets*. Stocksfield, UK: Acumen.

Funke, Cornelia. 2007. *Tintentod*. Hamburg: Dressler. Translated by Anthea Bell as *Inkdeath* (Frome: Chicken House,
2008).

Fussell, Betty. 2016. *Eat, Live, Love, Die: Selected Essays*. Berkeley, CA: Counterpoint.

Gaarder, Jostein. (1991) 1994. *Sophie's World*. Translated by
Paulette Møller. London: Phoenix.

Gabilliet, Jean-Paul. (2005) 2010. *Of Comics and Men: A Cul-
tural History of American Comic Books*. Translated by Bart
Beaty and Nick Nguyen. Jackson: University Press of
Mississippi.

Gadamer, Hans-Georg. 1994. *Literature and Philosophy in Dialogue: Essays in German Literary Theory*. New York: State
University of New York Press.

Gaiman, Neil. 2002. *Coraline*. London: Bloomsbury.

García, Santiago. (2010) 2015. *On the Graphic Novel*. Translated
by Bruce Campbell. Jackson: University Press of Mississippi.

García González, Macarena. 2017. *Origin Narratives: The Stories
We Tell Children about International Adoption and Immigration*. London: Routledge.

García González, Macarena, and Elisabeth Wesseling. 2013.
"The Stories We Adopt by: Tracing 'The Red Thread' in Contemporary Adoption Narratives." *Lion and the Unicorn* 37,
no. 2: 31–61.

Garden, Nancy. 1982. *Annie on My Mind*. New York: Farrar,
Strauss and Giroux.

Gardner, Jared. 2012. *Projections: Comics and the History of
Twenty-First-Century Storytelling*. Palo Alto, CA: Stanford
University Press.

Garland-Thomson, Rosemarie. 1997. *Extraordinary Bodies: Figuring Physical Disability in American Culture and Literature*.
New York: Columbia University Press.

Gates, Henry Louis, Jr. 1988. *The Signifying Monkey: A Theory
of African-American Literary Criticism*. Oxford: Oxford University Press.

———. 2003. "Authenticity, or The Lesson of Little Tree." In
*Stories Matter: The Complexity of Cultural Authenticity in
Children's Literature*, edited by Dana L. Fox and Kathy G.
Short, 135–42. Urbana, IL: National Council of Teachers of
English.

Gaunt, Kyra D. 2006. *The Games Black Girls Play: Learning the
Ropes from Double-Dutch to Hip-Hop*. New York: New York
University Press.

Gay, Roxane. 2018. "Can I Enjoy the Art but Denounce
the Artist?" *Marie Claire* (blog), February 6, 2018. www
.marieclaire.com.

Gearino, Dan. 2017. *Comic Shop: The Retail Mavericks Who
Gave Us a New Geek Culture*. Athens: Swallow Press / Ohio
University Press.

Gee, James Paul. 2003. *What Video Games Have to Teach Us
about Learning and Literacy*. New York: Palgrave Macmillan.

Genette, Gérard. (1972) 1980. *Narrative Discourse*. Oxford:
Blackwell.

George, Jean Craighead. (1959) 1962. *My Side of the Mountain*. London: Bodley Head.

———. 1972. *Julie of the Wolves*. New York: Harper & Row.

George, Rosemary Marangoly. 1996. *The Politics of Home: Postcolonial Relocations and Twentieth-Century Fiction*. Cambridge: Cambridge University Press.

Gibney, Shannon. 2018. *Dream Country*. New York: Dutton Books for Young Readers.

Gikandi, Simon. 2012. "Realism, Romance and the Problem of African Literary History." *Modern Language Quarterly* 73, no. 3 (September): 309–28.

Gill-Peterson, Jules. 2018. *Histories of the Transgender Child*. Minneapolis: University of Minnesota Press.

Gino, Alex. 2015. *George*. New York: Scholastic Press.

Giovanni, Nikki. 1973. *Ego Tripping and Other Poems for Young People*. New York: Lawrence Hill.

Giroux, Henry A. 2000. *Stealing Innocence: Youth, Corporate Power, and the Politics of Culture*. New York: Palgrave Macmillan.

Gitelman, Lisa. 2014. *Paper Knowledge: Toward a Media History of Documents*. Durham, NC: Duke University Press.

Gleitzman, Morris. 1989. *Two Weeks with the Queen*. Sydney: Pan Books.

———. 2003. *Boy Overboard*. London: Puffin.

Glenwright, Melanie, and Penny Pexman. 2003. "Children's Perception of the Social Functions of Verbal Irony." *Discourse Processes* 36:147–65.

Godwin, William [William Scolfield, pseud.]. 1802. Preface to *Bible Stories, Memorable Acts of the Ancient Patriarchs, Judges and Kings, Extracted from Their Original Historians, for the Use of Children*. London: R. Phillips.

Goff, Phillip Atiba, Matthew Christian Jackson, Brooke Allison Lewis Di Leone, Carmen Marie Culotta, and Natalie Ann DiTomasso. 2014. "The Essence of Innocence: Consequences of Dehumanizing Black Children." *Journal of Personality and Social Psychology* 106, no. 4: 526–45.

Goffman, Erving. (1963) 1986. *Stigma: Notes on the Management of Spoiled Identity*. New York: Touchstone.

Going, K. L. 2003. *Fat Kid Rules the World*. New York: Puffin Books.

Goldberg, Susan. 2017. "What If All Could Thrive?" *National Geographic* 231, no. 1: 9.

Golding, William. 1954. *Lord of the Flies*. London: Faber.

Goldman, Michael. 2000. *On Drama: Boundaries of Genre, Borders of Self*. Ann Arbor: Univeristy of Michigan Press.

Goldstone, Bette. 2008. "The Paradox of Space in Postmodern Picturebooks." In *Postmodern Picturebooks: Play, Parody, Self-Referentiality*, edited by Lawrence R. Sipe and Sylvia Pantaleo, 117–29. New York: Taylor & Francis.

Gombert, Jean E. 1992. *Metalinguistic Development*. New York: Harvester Wheatsheaf.

Gombrich, E. H. 1970. "The Mask and the Face: The Perception of Physiognomic Likeness in Life and in Art." In *Art, Perception, and Reality*, 1–46. Baltimore: Johns Hopkins University Press.

Gonick, Marnina, and Susan Gannon, eds. 2014. *Becoming Girl: Collective Biography and the Production of Girlhood*. Toronto: Women's Press.

Gonzalez, Maya Christina. 2014. *Call Me Tree / Llámame árbol*. New York: Lee & Low Books.

González, Rigoberto. 2009. *The Mariposa Club*. New York: Alyson Books.

Gordon, Ian. 1998. *Comic Strips and Consumer Culture, 1890–1945*. Washington, DC: Smithsonian Institution Press.

Goscinny, René. 2011. *Nicholas*. Illustrated by Jean-Jacques Sempé. Translated by Anthea Bell. New York: Phaidon. Originally published as *Le petit Nicholas* (Paris: Gallimard, 1960).

Goswami, Supriya. 2012. *Colonial India in Children's Literature*. New York: Routledge.

Gould, Lois. (1978) 2008. "X: A Fabulous Child's Story." In *Tales for Little Rebels: A Collection of Radical Children's Literature*, edited by Julia L. Mickenberg and Philip Nel, 233–42. New York: New York University Press.

Graff, Lisa. 2006. *The Thing about Georgie*. New York: Harper Trophy.

Grahame, Kenneth. (1908) 1984. *The Wind in the Willows*. Harmondsworth: Penguin-Puffin Books.

Graves, Robert. 1960. *The Penny Fiddle*. Garden City, NY: Doubleday.

Gravett, Paul. 2004. *Manga: Sixty Years of Japanese Comics*. London: Laurence King.

Greder, Armin. 2007. *The Island*. Sydney: Allen & Unwin.

Greenblatt, Stephen J. 1976. "Learning to Curse: Aspects of Linguistics Colonialism in the Sixteenth Century." In *First Images of America: The Impact of the New World on the Old*, edited by Fredi Chiappelli, 561–80. Berkeley: University of California Press.

Gregg, Melissa, and Gregory J. Seigworth, eds. 2010. *The Affect Theory Reader*. Durham, NC: Duke University Press.

Gregorio, I. W. 2015. *None of the Above*. New York: Balzer + Bray.

Grenby, M. O. 2006. "Tame Fairies Make Good Teachers: The Popularity of Early British Fairy Tales." *The Lion and the Unicorn* 30, no. 1: 1–24.

———. 2008. *Children's Literature*. Edinburgh: Edinburgh University Press.

———. 2009. "The Origins of Children's Literature." In *The Cambridge Companion to Children's Literature*, edited by Matthew Grenby and Andrea Immel, 3–18. Cambridge: Cambridge University Press.

———. 2011. *The Child Reader, 1700–1840*. Cambridge: Cambridge University Press.

Grendler, Paul. 1989. *Schooling in Renaissance Italy*. Baltimore: Johns Hopkins University Press.

Greven, Philip. (1990) 1992. *Spare the Child: The Religious Roots of Punishment and the Psychological Impact of Physical Abuse*. New York: Vintage Books.

Grimm, Jacob, and Wilhelm Grimm. (1812–57) 1990. *Household Tales*. Hoboken, NJ: BiblioBytes.

Grishakova, Marina, and Marie-Laure Ryan, eds. 2010. *Intermediality and Storytelling*. Berlin: De Gruyter.

Griswold, Jerry. 1996. "Children's Literature in the USA: A Historical Overview." In *International Companion Encyclopedia of Children's Literature*, edited by Peter Hunt, 860–70. London: Routledge.

———. 1997. "The Disappearance of Children's Literature (or Children's Literature as Nostalgia) in the United States in the late Twentieth Century." In *Reflections of Change: Children's Literature Since 1945*, edited by Sandra L. Beckett, 35–41. Westport, CT: Greenwood.

———. 2006. *Feeling like a Kid: Childhood and Children's Literature*. Baltimore: Johns Hopkins University Press.

Groensteen, Thierry. (2000) 2009. "Why Are Comics Still in Search of Cultural Legitimization?" In *A Comics Studies Reader*, edited by Jeet Heer and Kent Worcester, 3–11. Jackson: University Press of Mississippi.

Grosvenor, Ian. 2002. "'Unpacking My Library': Children's Literature in the Writings of Walter Benjamin." *Paedagogica Historica* 38, no. 1: 97–111.

Grosvenor, Kali. 1970. *Poems by Kali*. New York: Doubleday.

Grundy, Isobel. 2009. "Women and Print: Readers, Writers and the Market." In *Cambridge History of the Book in Britain*, vol. 5, edited by Michael F. Suarez and Michael L. Turner, 146–60. Cambridge: Cambridge University Press.

Grzegorczyk, Blanka. 2014. *Discourses of Postcolonialism in Contemporary British Children's Literature*. New York: Routledge.

Gubar, Marah. 2009. *Artful Dodgers: Reconceiving the Golden Age of Children's Literature*. New York: Oxford University Press.

———. 2011. "*Peter Pan* as Children's Theatre: The Issue of Audience." In *The Oxford Handbook of Children's Literature*, edited by Julia L. Mickenberg and Lynne Vallone, 475–95. Oxford: Oxford University Press.

———. 2012. "Introduction: Children and Theatre." *Lion and the Unicorn* 36, no. 2 (April): v–xiv.

———. 2013. "Risky Business: Talking about Children in Children's Literature Criticism." *Children's Literature Association Quarterly* 38, no. 4: 450–57.

———. 2016a. "The Cult of the Child Revisited: Making Fun of Fauntleroy." In *Late Victorian into Modern*, edited by Laura Marcus, Michèle Mendelssohn, and Kirsten E. Shepherd-Barr, 398–441. Oxford: Oxford University Press.

———. 2016b. "The Hermeneutics of Recuperation: What a Kinship-Model Approach to Children's Agency Could Do for Children's Literature and Children's Literature Studies." *Jeunesse: Young People, Texts, Cultures* 8, no. 1: 291–310.

———. 2020. "Urchins, Unite: *Newsies* as an Antidote to *Annie*." In *Children, Childhood, and Musical Theater*, edited by James Leve and Donelle Ruwe, 138–63. New York: Routledge.

Guillory, John. 1993. *Cultural Capital: The Problem of Literary Canon Formation*. Chicago: University of Chicago Press.

Gupta, Suman. 2003. *Re-reading Harry Potter*. New York: Palgrave Macmillan.

Gupta, Suman, with Cheng Xiao. 2009. "Harry Potter Goes to China." In *Children's Literature: Approaches and Territories*, edited by Janet Maybin and Nicola J. Watson, 338–52. New York: Palgrave Macmillan.

Gutierrez, Anna Katrina. 2017. *Mixed Magic—Global-Local Dialogues in Fairy Tales for Young Readers*. Amsterdam: John Benjamins.

Gutierrez-Morfin, Noel. 2016. "'Gender-Fluid' among Recent Additions to Oxford English Dictionary." *NBC News*, September 16, 2016. www.nbcnews.com.

Guy, Rosa. 1973. *The Friends*. New York: Holt, Rinehart and Winston.

———. 1976. *Ruby*. New York: Viking.

———. 1978. *Edith Jackson*. New York: Viking.

Haase, Donald. 1999. "Yours, Mine, or Ours? Perrault, the Brothers Grimm, and the Ownership of Fairy Tales." In *The Classic Fairy Tales*, edited by Maria Tatar, 353–64. New York: Norton.

———. 2004. "Feminist Fairy-Tale Scholarship." In *Fairy Tales and Feminism: New Approaches*, edited by Donald Haase, 1–36. Detroit: Wayne State University Press.

———. 2008. "Fairy Tale." In *The Greenwood Encyclopedia of Fairy Tales*, vol. 1, edited by Donald Haase, 322–25. Westport, CT: Greenwood.

Hacke, Axel. (1993) 2002. *Little King December*. Translated by Rosemary Davidson. London: Bloomsbury.

Haddon, Mark. 2003. *The Curious Incident of the Dog in the Night-Time*. London: Jonathan Cape.

Hajdu, David. 2008. *The Ten-Cent Plague: The Great Comic-Book Scare and How It Changed America*. New York: Farrar, Straus and Giroux.

Hage, Ghassan. 2003. *Against Paranoid Nationalism: Searching for Hope in a Shrinking Society*. Annandale: Pluto Press.

Haggard, H. Rider. (1885) 2002. *King Solomon's Mines*. Orchard Park, NY: Broadview.

Hair, Nicole L., Jamie. L. Hanson, Barbara L. Wolfe, and Seth D. Pollak. 2015. "Association of Child Poverty, Brain Development, and Academic Achievement." *JAMA Pediatrics* 169, no. 9 (July): 822–29.

Halberstam, Judith. 2011. *The Queer Art of Failure*. Durham, NC: Duke University Press.

Hall, Stuart, and Paul du Gay. 1996. *Questions of Cultural Identity*. London: Sage.

Hallberg, Kristin. 1982. "Litteraturvetenskapen och bilderboksforskningen." *Tidskrift för litteraturvetenskap* 3, no. 4: 163–68.

Hamer, Naomi. 2017. "The Design and Development of the Picture Book for Mobile and Interactive Platforms: 'You Get to BE Harold's Purple Crayon.'" In *More Words about Pictures: Current Research on Picture Books and Visual/Verbal Texts for Young People*, edited by Naomi Hamer, Perry Nodelman, and Mavis Reimer. New York: Routledge: 63–80.

———. 2018. "Children's Museums and Fairy-Tale Cultures and Media." In *The Routledge Companion to Media and Fairy-Tale Cultures*, edited by Pauline Greenhill, Jill Terry Rudy, Naomi Hamer, and Lauren Bosc, 435–42. London: Routledge.

Hamer, Naomi, Perry Nodelman, and Mavis Reimer, eds. 2017. *More Words about Pictures: Current Research on Picture Books and Visual/Verbal Texts for Young People*. New York: Routledge.

Hamilton, Virginia. 1974. *M.C. Higgins, the Great*. New York: Dell-Laurel Leaf Books.

———. (1976) 1995. *Arilla Sun Down*. New York: Scholastic.

Handler, Daniel. 2014. *A Series of Unfortunate Events*. Book Collection Pack Set. London: Egmont.

Hanson, Karl, Diana Volonakis, and Mohammed Al-Rozzi. 2015. "Child Labour, Working Children and Children's Rights." In *Routledge International Handbook of Children's Rights Studies*, edited by Wouter Vandenhole, Ellen Desmet, Didier Reynaert, and Sara Lembrechts, 316–30. New York: Routledge.

Haraway, Donna. 1985. "A Manifesto for Cyborgs: Science, Technology, and Socialist Feminism in the 1980s." *Socialist Review* 15, no. 2: 65–107.

———. 2003. *The Companion Species Manifesto: Dogs, People, and Significant Otherness*. Chicago: Prickly Paradigm Press.

Harris, Alexandra. 2010. *Romantic Moderns: English Writers, Artists and the Imagination from Virginia Woolf to John Piper*. London: Thames and Hudson.

Harris, Violet J. 2003. "The Complexity of Debates about Multicultural Literature and Cultural Authenticity." In *Stories Matter: The Complexity of Cultural Authenticity in Children's Litearture*, edited by L. Dana Fox and Kathy Short, 116–39. Urbana, IL: National Council of Teachers of English.

———. 2006a. "Continuing Dilemmas, Debates, and Delights in Multicultural Literature for Children." *New Advocate* 9, no. 2: 107–22.

———. 2006b. "Review of *Brown Gold: Milestones of African-American Children's Picture Books, 1845–2002*, by Michele Martin." *Lion and the Unicorn* 30, no. 2: 274–79.

Hartnett, Sonya. 1995. *Sleeping Dogs*. New York: Viking.

Harvey, Robert C. 2001. "The Graphic Novel, Will Eisner, and Other Pioneers." *The Comics Journal* 233 (May): 103–6.

———. 2009. "How Comics Came to Be: Through the Juncture of Word and Image from Magazine Gag Cartoons to Newspaper Strips, Tools for Critical Appreciation plus Rare Seldom Witnessed Historical Facts." In *A Comics Studies Reader*, edited by Jeet Heer and Kent Worcester, 25–45. Jackson: University Press of Mississippi.

Hassan, Ihab. 1977. "Prometheus as Performer: Toward a Post-humanist Culture?" *Georgia Review* 31, no. 4: 830–50.

Hatfield, Charles. 2005. *Alternative Comics: An Emerging Literature*. Jackson: University Press of Mississippi.

———. 2011. "Redrawing the Comic Strip Child: Charles M. Schulz's *Peanuts* as Cross-Writing." In *The Oxford Handbook of Children's Literature*, edited by Julia L. Mickenberg and Lynne Vallone, 165–87. Oxford: Oxford University Press.

Haughton, Hugh, ed. 1988. *The Chatto Book of Nonsense*. London: Chatto & Windus.

Hazard, Paul. 1932. *Les livres, les enfants et les hommes*. Paris: Flammarion. Translated by Marguerite Mitchell as *Books, Children and Men* (Boston: Horn Book, 1944).

Heider, F., and M. Simmel. 1944. "An Experimental Study in Apparent Behavior." *American Journal of Psychology* 57:243–59.

Heine, Steven J., Darrin R. Lehman, Hazel Rose Markus, and Shinobu Kitayama. 1999. "Is There a Universal Need for Positive Self-Regard?" *Psychological Review* 106:766–94.

Hemmings, Robert. 2007. "A Taste of Nostalgia: Children's Books from the Golden Age—Carroll, Grahame, and Milne." *Children's Literature* 35:54–79.

Herthel, Jessica, and Jazz Jennings. 2014. *I Am Jazz*. New York: Dial Books for Young Readers.

Hesse, Karen. (1997) 1999. *Out of the Dust*. New York: Scholastic.

Heyman, Michael. 2007. *The Tenth Rasa: An Anthology of Indian Nonsense*. Edited by Michael Heyman, with Sumanyu Satpathy and Anushka Ravishankar. New Delhi: Penguin.

Heywood, Colin. 2001. *A History of Childhood: Children and Childhood in the West from Medieval to Modern Times*. Cambridge: Polity.

Heywood, Sophie. 2015. "*Pippi Longstocking*, Juvenile Delinquent? Hachette, Self-Censorship and the Moral Reconstruction of Postwar France." *Itinéraires*, no. 2. https://journals.openedition.org.

Higbee, Will, and Song Hwee Lim. 2010. "Concepts of Transnational Cinema: Towards a Critical Transnationalism in Film Studies." *Transnational Cinemas* 1, no. 1: 7–21.

Higonnet, Anne. 1998. *Pictures of Innocence: The History and Crisis of Ideal Childhood*. New York: Thames and Hudson.

Higonnet, Margot. 2000. "A Pride of Pleasures." *Children's Literature* 28:30–37.

Hill, Anthony. 1994. *The Burnt Stick*. Ringwood: Penguin Viking.

Hilton, Mary, and Maria Nikolajeva, eds. 2012. *Contemporary Adolescent Literature and Culture: The Emergent Adult*. Burlington, VT: Ashgate.

Hine, Lewis W. 1936. *Men at Work*. New York: Macmillan.

Hinton, S. E. 1967. *The Outsiders*. New York: Viking.

Hintz, Carrie, and Eric L. Tribunella. 2013. *Reading Children's Literature: A Critical Introduction*. Boston: Bedford / St. Martin's.

Ho, Laina. 1997. "Chinese Children's Literature—Then and Now." *New Review of Children's Literature and Librarianship* 3, no. 1: 127–37.

———. 2004. "China." In *International Companion Encyclopedia of Children's Literature*, 2nd ed., edited by Peter Hunt, 1029–38. London: Routledge.

Ho, Minfong. 1990. *Rice without Rain*. New York: Lothrop, Lee and Shephard.

Hoban, Russell. (1967) 1993. *The Mouse and His Child*. Harmondsworth: Puffin.

Hobson, Christopher Z. 2000. *Blake and Homosexuality*. New York: Palgrave Macmillan.

Hockney, Jenny, and Allison James. 2003. *Social Identities across the Life Course*. New York: Palgrave Macmillan.

Hodgkin, Katherine. 2016. "Childhood and Loss in Early Modern Life Writing." *Parergon* 33, no. 2: 115–34.

Hofer, Johannes. 1688. *Dissertatio medica de Nostalgia, oder Heimwehe*. Basel: Typis Jacobi Bertschii.

Hoffman, Heinrich. 1844. *Der Struwwelpeter* [Shockheaded Peter]. Frankfurt: Heinrich Corbet.

Hoffmann, E. T. A. (1816) 2016. *The Nutcracker and the Mouse King*. Translated by Joachim Neugroschel. London: Penguin.

Hogan, Patrick Com. 2011. *What Literature Teaches Us about Emotions*. Cambridge: Cambridge University Press.

———. 2012. *Affective Narratology: The Emotional Structure of Stories*. Lincoln: University of Nebraska Press.

Hole, Stian. 2011. *Garmann's Secret*. Grand Rapids: Eerdmans Books for Young Readers.

Holland, Dorothy, Willian S. Lachicotte Jr., Debra Skinner, and Carole Cain. 2001. *Identity and Agency in Cultural Worlds*. Cambridge, MA: Harvard University Press.

Holland, Norman. 1975. *5 Readers Reading*. New Haven, CT: Yale University Press.

Hollindale, Peter. 1988. *Ideology and the Children's Book*. Stroud: Thimble Press.

———. 1997. *Signs of Childness in Children's Books*. Stroud: Thimble Press.

Homans, Margaret. 2013. *The Imprint of Another Life: Adoption Narratives and Human Possibility*. Ann Arbor: University of Michigan Press.

Honeyman, Susan. 2013. "Trans(cending) gender through Childhood." In *The Children's Table: Childhood Studies and the Humanities*, edited by Anna Mae Duane, 167–82. Athens: University of Georgia Press.

Honwana, Alcinda. 2012. *The Time of Youth: Work, Social Change, and Politics in Africa*. Sterling, VA: Kumarian Press.

Horne, Jackie. 2001. "Punishment as Performance in Catherine Sinclair's *Holiday House*." *Children's Literature Association Quarterly* 26, no. 1: 22–32.

Horning, K. T. 2016. "When Whiteness Dominates Reviews." *Reading while White* (blog), July 2016. https://readingwhilewhite.blogspot.com.

Horsley, Richard A. 2001. *Hearing the Whole Story: The Politics of Plot in Mark's Gospel*. Louisville, KY: Westminster John Knox Press.

Howe, LeAnne. 1999. "Tribalography: The Power of Native Stories." *Journal of Dramatic Theory and Criticism* 14, no. 1 (Fall): 117–25.

Høyrup, Helene. 2017. "Towards a Connective Ethnography of Children's Literature and Digital Media: The New Media Encounter." In *More Words about Pictures: Current Research on Picture Books and Visual/Verbal Texts for Young People*, edited by Naomi Hamer, Perry Nodelman, and Mavis Reimer, 81–99. New York: Routledge.

Hubler, Angela. 2010. "Faith and Hope in the Feminist Political Novel for Children: A Materialist Feminist Analysis." *Lion and the Unicorn* 34, no. 1 (January): 57–75.

Huggan Graham. 2011. "The Trouble with World Literature." In *A Companion to Comparative Literature*, edited by Ali Behdad and Dominic Thomas, 490–505. London: Wiley-Blackwell.

———. 2013. "Introduction." In *The Oxford Handbook of Postcolonial Studies*, edited by Graham Huggan, 1–26. Oxford: Oxford University Press.

Hughes, Emily. 2013. *Wild*. London: Flying Eye Books.

Hughes, Richard. (1931) 1972. *The Spider's Palace and Other Stories*. Harmondsworth: Puffin.

Hughes, Ted. 1968. *The Iron Man: A Children's Story in Five Nights*. London: Faber.

———. (1968) 1999. *The Iron Giant*. New York: Alfred A. Knopf.

———. 2005. Edward James Hughes Papers. British Library Archives and Manuscripts. MS 88918: December 18, 1890–March 20, 2005.

Hughes, Thomas. (1857) 1999. *Tom Brown's Schooldays*. New York: Oxford University Press.

Hugo, Victor. (1831) 2002. *The Hunchback of Notre Dame*. New York: Modern Library.

Huizinga, Johan. (1938) 1971. *Homo Ludens: A Study of the Play-Element in Culture*. Boston: Beacon Press.

Huld, Palle. 1929. *A Boy Scout around the World: A Boy Scout Adventure*. Translated by Eleanor Hard. New York: Coward-McCann.

Hulme, Peter. 1995. "Including America." *Ariel* 26, no. 1: 117–20.

Hunt, Peter. 1991. *Criticism, Theory, and Children's Literature*. Oxford: Blackwell.

———. 1996. "Passing on the Past: The Problem of Books That Are for Children and That Were for Children." *Children's Literature Association Quarterly* 21, no. 4: 200–202.

———. 2001. *Children's Literature*. London: Blackwell.

Hunter, Mollie. 1976. *Talent Is Not Enough*. New York: Harper & Row.

Hurley, Nat. 2011. "The Perversions of Children's Literature." *Jeunesse* 3, no. 2: 118–32.

———. 2014. "The Little Transgender Mermaid: A Shape-Shifting Tale." In *Seriality and Texts for Young People: The Compulsion to Repeat*, edited by Mavis Reimer, Nyala Ali, Deanna England, and Melanie Dennis Unrau, 258–80. New York: Palgrave Macmillan.

Hürlimann, Bettina. 1968. *Europäische Kinderbücher in drei Jahrhunderten Broschiert* [Three centuries of children's books in Europe]. Cleveland: World Publishing Company.

Hutcheon, Linda. 1989. *The Politics of Postmodernism*. London: Routledge.

———. 1994. *Irony's Edge: The Theory and Politics of Irony*. London: Routledge.

———. 2006. *A Theory of Adaptation*. New York: Routledge.

Hutchins, Pat. 1968. *Rosie's Walk*. New York: Macmillan.

Idström, Ellen. 1893. *Tvillingsystrarna: Berättelse för unga flickor*. Stockholm: P. A. Huldbergs.

Iggulden, Conn, and Hal Iggulden. 2006. *The Dangerous Book for Boys*. London: HarperCollins.

Immel, Andrea. 2010. "Children's Books and School-Books." In *Oxford Companion to the Book*, edited by Michael J. Suarez and H. R. Woudhuysen, 736–49. New York: Oxford University Press.

Inness, Sherrie A. 1997. "Is Nancy Drew Queer? Popular Reading Strategies of the Lesbian Reader." *Women's Studies: An Inter-Disciplinary Journal* 26, nos. 3–4: 343–72.

International Board on Books for Young People (IBBY). n.d. "How It All Began." IBBY. Accessed September 22, 2018. www.ibby.org.

International Diaspora Engagement Alliance (IdEA). n.d. "What Is a Diaspora?" Accessed March 23, 2018. www.diasporaalliance.org.

Ionesco, Eugène. (1968) 1978. *Story Number 1*. Illustrated by Étienne Delessert. Translated by Calvin K. Towle. New York: Harlin Quist.

———. (1970) 1978. *Story Number 2*. Illustrated by Étienne Delessert. Translated by Calvin K. Towle. New York: Harlin Quist.

———. 1971. *Story Number 3*. Illustrated by Philippe Corentin. Translated by Ciba Vaughan. New York: Harlin Quist.

———. 1973. *Story Number 4*. Illustrated by Jean-Michel Nicollet. Translated by Ciba Vaughan. New York: Harlin Quist.

Iriye, Akira, and Pierre-Yves Saunier. 2009. *The Palgrave Dictionary of Transnational History*. Basingstoke: Palgrave Macmillan.

Isaacs, Anne. 2006. *Pancakes for Supper*. Illustrated by Mark Teague. New York: Scholastic.

Iser, Wolfgang. 1974. *The Implied Reader: Patterns of Communication in Prose Fiction from Bunyan to Beckett*. Baltimore: Johns Hopkins University Press.

Ito, Kinko. 2005. "A History of Manga in the Context of Japanese Culture and Society." *Journal of Popular Culture* 38, no. 3: 456–75.

Jacobs, Alan. 2008. *Original Sin: A Cultural History*. New York: HarperOne.

James, Allison, and Adrian L. James. 2008. *Key Concepts in Childhood Studies*. Sage Key Concepts. Los Angeles: Sage.

James, Henry. (1883–84) 1900. *A Little Tour in France*. Rev. ed. Illustrated by Joseph Pennell. Boston: Houghton.

———. (1889) 1990. "The Future of the Novel." In *Children's Literature: The Development of Criticism*, edited by Peter Hunt, 71–89. London: Routledge.

Jameson, Fredric. 1991. *Postmodernism; or, The Cultural Logic of Late Capitalism*. Durham, NC: Duke University Press.

Janiewski, Dolories. 1995. "Gendering, Racializing and Classifying: Settler Colonization in the United States, 1590–1990." In *Unsettling Settler Societies: Articulations of Gender, Race, Ethnicity and Class*, edited by Daiva Stasiulis and Nira Yuval-Davis, 132–60. London: Sage.

Jansson, Tove. 2004. *The Book about Moomin, Mymble and Little My*. Translated by Sophie Hannah. London: Sort of Books. Originally published as *Hur gick det sen? Boken om Mumlan, Mummintrollet och lilla My* (Stockholm: Geber, 1952).

———. (1970) 2011. *Moominvalley in November*. Translated by Kingsley Hart. London: Puffin.

Jaques, Zoe. 2015. *Children's Literature and the Posthuman*. London: Routledge.

Jary, David, and Julia Jary. 1995. *Collins Dictionary of Sociology*. 2nd ed. Glasgow: HarperCollins.

Jenkins, Christine A., and Michael Cart. 2018. *Representing the Rainbow in Young Adult Literature: LGBTQ+ Content since 1969*. Lanham, MD: Rowman & Littlefield.

Jenkins, Elwyn. 2006. *National Character in South African English Children's Literature*. New York: Routledge.

Jenkins, Henry. 1998. *The Children's Culture Reader*. New York: New York University Press.

———. 2006. *Convergence Culture: Where Old and New Media Collide*. New York: New York University Press.

Jenkins, Henry, Mizuko Ito, and danah boyd. 2015. *Participatory Culture in a Networked Era: A Conversation on Youth, Learning, Commerce and Politics*. Boston: Polity.

Jensen, Helle Strandgaard. 2017. *From Superman to Social Realism: Children's Media and Scandinavian Childhood*. Amsterdam: John Benjamins.

Jiang, Ji-li. 1997. *Red Scarf Girl*. New York: HarperCollins.

Jiménez García, Marilisa. 2014. "Pura Belpre Lights the Storyteller's Candle: Reframing the Legacy of a Legend and What It Means for the Fields of Latino/a Studies and Children's Literature." *Centro Journal* 26, no. 1: 110.

Johannisson, Karin. 2001. *Nostalgia. En känslas historia*. Stockholm: Bonnier Essä.

Johansen, Stine Liv. 2018. "News Kids Can Use—to Play With." In *Youth and News in a Digital Media Environment: Nordic-Baltic Perspectives*, edited by Yvonne Andersson, Ulf Dalquist, and Jonas Ohlsson, 125–31. Gothenburg, Sweden: Nordicom.

Johanson, Kristine. 2016. "On the Possibility of Early Modern Nostalgias." *Parergon* 33, no. 2: 1–15.

Johnson, Crockett. 1955. *Harold and the Purple Crayon*. New York: Harper & Brothers.

Johnson, Ingrid, Joyce Bainbridge, and Farha Shariff. 2007. "Exploring Issues of National Identity, Ideology and Diversity in Contemporary Canadian Picture Books." *Papers* 17, no. 2: 75–83.

Johnson, Samuel. 1750. "The Modern Form of Romances Preferable to the Ancient. The Necessity of Characters Morally Good." Johnsonessays.com. www.johnsonessays.com.

Johnson, Walter A. 2013. "Bookrolls as Media." In *Comparative Textual Media*, edited by Katherine Hayles and Jessica Pressman, 101–24. Minneapolis: University of Minnesota Press.

Johnston, Annie Fellows. 1895. *The Little Colonel*. Boston: L. C. Page.

Jonas, Ann. (1983) 1990. *Round Trip*. New York: Mulberry.

Jones, Chuck, dir. 1953. *Duck Amuck*. Warner Bros.

Jones, Gerard. 2002. *Killing Monsters: Why Children Need Fantasy, Super Heroes, and Make-Believe Violence*. New York: Basic.

Jones, Steve. 2007. *Coral: A Pessimist in Paradise*. London: Little, Brown.

Joosen, Vanessa. 2006. "Realism." In *Oxford Encyclopedia of Children's Literature*, vol. 3, edited by Jack Zipes, 328. New York: Oxford University Press.

———. 2014. "Canonisation and Adaptation in the Early Dutch and English Translations of the Brothers Grimm's *Kinder- und Hausmärchen*." In *Neverending Stories: Adaptation, Canonisation and Ideology in Children's Literature*, edited by Sylvie Geerts and Sara Van den Bossche, 89–107. Gent: Academia Press.

Joosen, Vanessa, and Gillian Lathey, eds. 2014. *Grimms' Tales around the Globe: The Dynamics of Their International Reception*. Detroit: Wayne State University Press.

Jordan, Anne Devereaux. 1974. "ChLA Notes." *Children's Literature* 3:249–50.

Jordan, Benjamin René. 2016. *Modern Manhood and the Boy Scouts of America: Citizenship, Race, and the Environment, 1910–1930*. Chapel Hill: University of North Carolina Press.

Joseph, Michael Scott. 1997. "A Pre-modernist Reading of 'The Drum': Chinua Achebe and the Theme of the Eternal Return." *Ariel: A Review of International English Literature* 28:149–66.

———. 1998. "Myth of the Golden Age: Journey Tales in African Children's Literature." In *Critical Perspectives on*

Postcolonial African Children's and Young Adult Literature, edited by Meena Khorana, 117–30. Westport, CT: Greenwood.

Joy, Louise. 2019. *Literature's Children: The Critical Child and the Art of Idealization*. London: Bloomsbury.

Juster, Norton. (1961) 1989. *The Phantom Tollbooth*. New York: Alfred A. Knopf.

Kahane, Reuven. 1997. *The Origins of Postmodern Youth: Informal Youth Movements in a Comparative Perspective*. Berlin: De Gruyter.

Kamenetsky, Christa. 1992. *The Brothers Grimm and Their Critics: Folktales and the Quest for Meaning*. Athens: Ohio University Press.

Kant, Immanuel. (1790) 1987. *Critique of Judgment*. Translated by Werner S. Pluhar. Indianapolis: Hackett.

Karoff, Helle Skovbjerg. 2013. "Play Practices and Play Moods." *International Journal of Play* 2, no. 2: 76–86.

Kästner, Erich. 1931. *Emil and the Detectives*. Translated by Margaret Goldsmith. London: Jonathan Cape. Originally published as *Emil und die Detektive* (Berlin: Cecilie Dressler, 1929).

———. (1949) 2017. *Die Konferenz der Tiere*. Hamburg, Germany: Dressler Verlag GmbH.

Kaye, Geraldine. (1984) 1986. *Comfort Herself*. London: Methuen.

Kaye, Nick. 2000. "Intermedia and Location." *Degrés* 101:b1–b17.

Keats, John. 1818. "On the Aims of Poetry: Letter to J. H. Reynolds, 3 February 1818." Poetry Foundation, October 13, 2009. www.poetryfoundation.org.

Keen, Suzanne. 2007. *Empathy and the Novel*. Oxford: Oxford University Press.

Keith, Lois. 2001. *Take Up Thy Bed and Walk: Death, Disability and Cure in Classic Fiction for Girls*. London: Routledge.

Kelen, Christopher, and Björn Sundmark. 2013. *The Nation in Children's Literature: Nations of Childhood*. New York: Routledge.

Kelleter, Frank. 2012. "Toto, I Think We're in Oz Again (and Again and Again): Remakes and Popular Seriality." In *Film Remakes, Adaptations and Fan Productions: Remake/Remodel*, edited by Kathleen Loock and Constantin Verevis, 19–44. Basingstoke: Palgrave Macmillan.

Kemp, Gene. 1977. *The Turbulent Term of Tyke Tyler*. London: Faber & Faber.

Kérchy, Anna. 2016. *Alice in Transmedia Wonderland: Curiouser and Curiouser New Forms of a Children's Classic*. Jefferson, NC: McFarland.

Kermode, Frank. 1954. Introduction to *The Tempest*, by William Shakespeare, xi–xxiii. London: Metheuen.

———. 1975. *The Classic: Literary Images of Permanence and Change*. London: Faber & Faber.

Kernis, Michael H., and Brian M. Goldman. 2006. "A Multicomponent Conceptualization of Authenticity: Theory and Research." *Advances in Experimental Social Psychology* 38:283–357.

Kerr, M. E. 1987. *Night Kites*. New York: Harper.

Kertzer, Adrienne. 1996. "Reclaiming Her Maternal Pre-text: Little Red Riding Hood's Mother and Three Young Adult Novels." *Children's Literature Association Quarterly* 21, no. 1: 20–27.

Keyser, Elizabeth Lennox, ed. 1999. *Little Women: A Family Romance*. New York: Twayne.

Khorana, Meena. 1998. *Critical Perspectives on Postcolonial African Children's and Young Adult Literature*. Westport, CT: Greenwood.

Kidd, Kenneth B. 2002. "Children's Culture, Children's Studies, and the Ethnographic Imaginary." *Children's Literature Association Quarterly* 27, no. 3: 146–55.

———. 2004. *Making American Boys: Boyology and the Feral Tale*. Minneapolis: University of Minnesota Press.

———. 2006. "How to Make a Children's Classic: The Middlebrow Projects of Louise Seaman Bechtel and Morton Schindel." *Journal of Children's Literature Studies* 3, no. 2: 51–79.

———. 2007. "Prizing Children's Literature: The Case of Newbery Gold." *Children's Literature* 35:166–90.

———. 2011a. "The Child, the Scholar, and the Children's Literature Archive." *Lion and the Unicorn* 35, no. 1 (January): 1–23.

———. 2011b. "Classic." In *Keywords for Children's Literature*, edited by Philip Nel and Lissa Paul, 52–58. New York: New York University Press.

———. 2011c. *Freud in Oz: At the Intersections of Psychoanalysis and Children's Literature*. Minneapolis: University of Minnesota Press.

Kidd, Kenneth, Lucy Pearson, and Sarah Pyke. 2016. "Serendipity and Children's Literature Research in the Library." *International Research in Children's Literature* 9, no. 2: 162–78.

Kidd, Kenneth, and Joe Sutliff Sanders, eds. 2017. *Prizing Children's Literature: The Cultural Politics of Children's Book Awards*. Abingdon: Taylor & Francis.

Kilcup, Karen L., and Angela Sorby, eds. 2013. *Over the River and through the Wood: An Anthology of Nineteenth-Century American Children's Poetry*. Baltimore: Johns Hopkins University Press.

Kilodavis, Cheryl. (2009) 2010. *My Princess Boy*. New York: Aladdin.

Kincaid, James. 1992. *Child-Loving: The Erotic Child and Victorian Culture*. New York: Routledge.

———. 1998. *Erotic Innocence: The Culture of Child Molesting*. Durham, NC: Duke University Press.

Kinchin, Juliet, Aidan O'Connor, and Tanya Harrod, eds. 2012. *Century of the Child: Growing by Design 1900–2000*. New York: Museum of Modern Art.

King, Martin Luther, Jr. (1956) 1991. "Facing the Challenge of a New Age." In *A Testament of Hope: The Essential Writings of Martin Luther King, Jr.*, edited by James Melvin Washington, 135–44. San Francisco: HarperCollins.

King, Thomas, and William Kent Monkman. 1992. *A Coyote Columbus Story*. Toronto: Douglas & McIntyre.

Kingsley, Charles. 1856. *The Heroes; or Greek Fairy Tales for My Children*. Cambridge: Palgrave Macmillan.

King-Smith, Dick. 1983. *The Sheep-Pig*. London: Gollancz.

Kinsella, Sharon. 2000. *Adult Manga: Culture and Power in Contemporary Japanese Society*. Honolulu: University of Hawai'i Press.

Kipling, Rudyard. (1894, 1895) 1961. *The Jungle Books*. New York: Signet Classics.

Kirkus Reviews. 2016. "Review of *When We Was Fierce*, by E. E. Charlton-Trujillo." July 2016. www.kirkusreviews.com.

Kleckner, Kathy, Marianne Martens, and Dorothy Stoltz. 2014. "Up for Debate: Are Ebooks Better Than Print Books?" *School Library Journal*, August 2014. www.slj.com.

Kline, Daniel T., ed. 2003. *Medieval Literature for Children*. New York: Routledge.

Kline, Stephen. (1993) 1995. *Out of the Garden: Toys, TV and Children's Culture in the Age of Marketing*. London: Verso.

Klingberg, Göte. 1986. *Children's Fiction in the Hands of the Translators*. Lund: Leerup.

———. 2008. *Facets of Children's Literature Research: Collected and Revised Writings*. Stockholm: Svenska barnboksinstitutet.

Klise, Kate. 2010. *Stand Straight, Ella Kate: The True Story of a Real Giant*. Illustrated by M. Sarah Klise. New York: Dial Books.

Knoepflmacher, U. C. 2005. "The Hansel and Gretel Syndrome: Survivorship Fantasies and Parental Desertion." *Children's Literature* 33:171–84.

Knoepflmacher, U. C., and Mitzi Myers. 1997. "'Cross-Writing' and the Reconceptualization of Children's Literary Studies." *Children's Literature* 25:vii–xvii.

Knowles, John. 1959. *A Separate Peace*. London: Secker and Warburg.

Koball, Heather, and Yang Jiang. 2018. *Basic Facts about Low-Income Children: Children under 18 Years, 2016*. New York: National Center for Children in Poverty, Columbia University Mailman School of Public Health. www.nccp.org.

Koertge, Ron. 2011. *Stoner & Spaz*. Somerville, MA: Candlewick Press.

Kokkola, Lydia. 2013a. *Fictions of Adolescent Carnality: Sexy Sinners and Delinquent Deviants*. Amsterdam: John Benjamins.

———. 2013b. *Representing the Holocaust in Children's Literature*. New York: Routledge.

Kokkola, Lydia, and Mia Österlund. 2014. "Celebrating the Margins: Families and Gender in the Work of the Swedish Picturebook Artist Pija Lindenbaum." *Bookbird* 52, no. 1: 77–82.

Kong, Lily, and Lily Tay. 1998. "Exalting the Past: Nostalgia and the Construction of Heritage in Children's Literature." *Area* 30, no. 2: 133–43.

Konigsburg, E. L. 1967. *From the Mixed-Up Files of Mrs. Basil E. Frankweiler*. New York: Atheneum.

Korczak, Janusz. 2004. *King Matt the First*. Translated by Richard Lourie. Chapel Hill, NC: Algonquin Books.

Korneliussen, Niviaq. 2014. *Homo Sapienne*. Nuuk: Milik.

Kreilkamp, Ivan. 2005. "Petted Things: *Wuthering Heights* and the Animal." *Yale Journal of Criticism* 18, no. 1: 81–110.

Kristeva, Julia. 1986. "Word, Dialogue and Novel." In *The Kristeva Reader*, edited by Toril Moi, 34–61. New York: Columbia University Press.

Kümmerling-Meibauer, Bettina. 1999. "Metalinguistic Awareness and the Child's Developing Sense of Irony." *Lion and the Unicorn* 23, no. 2: 157–83.

———. 2003. *Kinderliteratur, Kanonbildung und literarische Wertung*. Stuttgart: Metzler.

———. 2008. "Crosswriting und Mehrfachadressiertheit: Anmerkungen in der Kinderliteratur." In *Am Rande bemerkt: Anmerkungspraktiken in literarischen Texten*, edited by Bernhard Metz and Sabrine Zubarik, 277–95. Berlin: Kulturverlag Kadmos.

———. 2012. "Emotional Connection: Representation of Emotions in Young Adult Literature." In *Contemporary Adolescent Literature and Culture: The Emergent Adult*, edited by Mary Hilton and Maria Nikolajeva, 127–38. New York: Ashgate.

Kümmerling-Meibauer, Bettina, and Anja Müller. 2017. "Canon Studies and Children's Literature." In *Canon Constitution and Canon Change in Children's Literature*, edited by Bettina Kümmerling-Meibauer and Anja Müller, 1–14. London: Routledge.

Kunzle, David. 1973. *The History of the Comic Strip*. Vol. 1, *The Early Comic Strip: Narrative Strips and Picture Stories in the*

European Broadsheet from c. 1450 to 1825. Berkeley: University of California Press.

———. 1990. *The History of the Comic Strip*. Vol. 2, *The Nineteenth Century*. Berkeley: University of California Press.

Kusugak, Michael. 1990. *Baseball Bats for Christmas*. Toronto: Annick Press.

Kutzer, M. Daphne. 2000. *Empire's Children: Empire and Imperialism in Classic British Children's Books*. New York: Garland.

Kwon, Yoon Duk. 2010. *The Flower Granny*. Paju: Sakyejul.

Kyung Sung, Yoo, and Junko Sakoi. 2016. "Transnational Authors' Cultural Backgrounds and Further Reading." *World of Words* (blog), October 31, 2016. https://wowlit.org.

Labov, William. 1972. *Language in the Inner City*. Oxford: Blackwell.

Lagerlöf, Selma. (1906–7a) 2014. *Nils Holgersson's Wonderful Journey through Sweden*. Translated by Peter Graves. London: Norvik Press.

———. (1906–7b) 1947. *The Wonderful Adventures of Nils*. Translated by Velma Howard. New York: Grosset and Dunlap.

Lancy, David F. 2015. *The Anthropology of Childhood: Cherubs, Chattel, Changelings*. 2nd ed. Cambridge: Cambridge University Press.

Lang, Walter, dir. (1939) 1998. *The Little Princess*. Twentieth Century Fox.

Langbauer, Laurie. 2007. "The Ethics and Practice of Lemony Snicket: Adolescence and Generation X." *PMLA* 122, no. 2: 502–21.

Lankshear, Colin, and Michele Knobel, eds. 2007. *A New Literacies Sampler*. New York: Peter Lang.

Larbalestier, Justine. 2009. *Liar*. New York: Bloomsbury.

Larrick, Nancy. 1965. "The All-White World of Children's Books." *Saturday Review of Literature* 48, no. 37: 63–65, 84–85.

Larsen, Reif. 2009. *The Selected Works of T.S. Spivet*. New York: Penguin.

Lassén-Seger, Maria, and Anne Skaret, eds. 2014. *Empowering Transformations. Mrs. Pepperpot Revisited*. Newcastle upon Tyne: Cambridge Scholars.

Lathey, Gillian, ed. 2006. *The Translation of Children's Literature: A Reader*. Topics in Translation 31. Clevedon: Multilingual Matters.

Latimer, Bonnie. 2009. "Leaving Little to the Imagination: The Mechanics of Didacticism in Two Children's Adaptations of Samuel Richardson's Novels." *Lion and the Unicorn* 33:167–88.

Latour, Bruno. 1993. *We Have Never Been Modern*. Translated by Catherine Porter. Cambridge, MA: Harvard University Press.

Lawson, JonArno. 2015. *Sidewalk Flowers*. Illustrated by Sydney Smith. Toronto: Groundwood.

Lea, Tess, and Catherine Driscoll. 2012. *Evaluation of the Smith Family's Girls at the Centre Program Centralian Middle School, Alice Springs*. Sydney: Department of Gender and Cultural Studies, University of Sydney. https://pdfs.semanticscholar.org.

Lear, Edward. 1846. *A Book of Nonsense*. London: McLean.

———. 1871. *Nonsense Songs, Stories, Botany, and Alphabets*. London: R. J. Bush.

———. 1872. *More Nonsense, Pictures, Rhymes, Botany, Etc.* London: R. J. Bush.

———. 1877. *Laughable Lyrics: A Fourth Book of Nonsense Poems, Songs, Botany, Music, Etc.* London: Bush.

Leavitt, Martine. 2003. *Tom Finder*. Calgary: Red Deer Press.

———. 2015. *Calvin*. Toronto: Groundwood.

Lee, Hye-Kyung. 2009. "Between Fan Culture and Copyright Infringement: Manga Scanlation." *Media Culture Society* 31, no. 6: 1011–22.

Lee, Sung-Ae. 2014. "Fairy-Tale Scripts and Intercultural Conceptual Blending in Modern Korean Film and Television Drama." In *Grimms' Tales around the Globe: The Dynamics of Their International Reception*, edited by Vanessa Joosen and Gillian Lathey, 275–93. Detroit: Wayne State University Press.

Leerssen, Joep. 2007. *Imagology: History and Method*. Amsterdam: Rodopi.

Le Guin, Ursula K. 1973. *From Elfland to Poughkeepsie*. Portland, OR: Pendragon Press.

Lent, John A., ed. 1999. *Pulp Demons: International Dimensions of the Postwar Anti-comics Campaign*. Madison, NJ: Fairleigh Dickinson University Press.

———. 2009. "The Comics Debates Internationally." In *A Comics Studies Reader*, edited by Jeet Heer and Kent Worcester, 69–76. Jackson: University Press of Mississippi.

Lerer, Seth. 2008. *Children's Literature: A Reader's History, from Aesop to Harry Potter*. Chicago: University of Chicago Press.

———. 2012. "Devotion and Defacement: Reading Children's Marginalia." *Representations* 118, no. 1 (Spring): 126–53.

Lesnik-Oberstein, Karín. 1994. *Children's Literature: Criticism and the Fictional Child*. Oxford: Oxford University Press.

———. 1998. *Children in Culture: Approaches to Childhood*. Basingstoke: Macmillan.

Lester, Jasmine Z. 2014. "Homonormativity in Children's Literature: An Intersectional Analysis of Queer-Themed Picture Books." *Journal of LGBT Youth* 11, no. 3: 244–75.

Lester, Julius. 1996. *Sam and the Tigers: A Retelling of "Little Black Sambo."* Illustrated by Jerry Pinkney. New York: Picture Puffin Books.

Levi, Dorothy Hoffman. 1989. *A Very Special Friend*. Illustrated by Ethel Gold. Washington, DC: Kendall Green Press.

Levine, Judith. 2002. *Harmful to Minors: The Perils of Protecting Children from Sex*. Minneapolis: University of Minnesota Press.

Levithan, David. 2003. *Boy Meet Boy*. New York: Alfred A. Knopf.

———. 2012. *Every Day*. New York: Knopf Books for Young Readers.

Lewis, C. S. 1952. "On Three Ways of Writing for Children." In *Only Connect: Readings on Children's Literature*, edited by Sheila Egoff, G. T. Stubbs, and L. F. Ashley, 207–20. Oxford: Oxford University Press.

———. 1966. "On Stories." In *Of Other Worlds: Essays and Stories*, edited by W. Hooper, 3–21. London: Bles.

Lewis, David. 2001. *Reading Contemporary Picture Books: Picturing Text*. London: Routledge Falmer.

Lewis, Magda. 1988. "Are Indians Nicer Now? What Children Learn from Books about Native North Americans." In *How Much Truth Do We Tell the Children? The Politics of Children's Literature*, edited by Betty Bacon, 135–56. Minneapolis: MEP.

Lieberman, Marcia. 1972. "'Some Day My Prince Will Come': Female Acculturation through the Fairy Tale." *College English* 34:383–95.

Lierop-Debrauwer, Helma van, and Neel Bastiaansen-Harks. 2005. *Over grenzen: De adolescentenroman in het literatuuronderwijs*. Delft: Eburon.

Liljeström, Rita. 1972. "Det dolda mönstret i ungdomsböcker" [The concealed pattern in books for young people]. In *Könsdiskriminering förr och nu: Litteratursociologiska och historiska studier*, edited by Karin Westman Berg, 46–54. Stockholm: Prisma.

Lin, Grace. 2007. *The Red Thread: An Adoption Fairy Tale*. Morton Grove, IL: Albert Whitman.

———. 2012. "Rethinking Tikki Tikki Tembo." *GraceLinBlog* (blog), April 2012. www.gracelinblog.com.

———. 2017. "The Problem with Celebrating Tikki Tikki Tembo." *GraceLinBlog* (blog), May 2017. www.gracelinblog.com.

Lindenbaum, Pija. 1990. *Else-Marie och småpapporna*. Stockholm: Bonniers.

———. 1991. *Else-Marie and Her Seven Little Daddies*. Adapted by Gabrielle Charbonnet. New York: Henry Holt.

Lindgren, Astrid. 1950. *Pippi Longstocking*. Translated by Florence Lamborn Johnson. Illustrated by Louis S. Glanzman. New York: Viking. Originally published as *Pippi Långstrump* (Stockholm: Rabén & Sjögren, 1945).

———. 1959. *Pippi in the South Seas*. Translated by Gerry Bothmer. New York: Viking.

———. 2015. *The Best of Pippi Longstocking*. Oxford: Oxford University Press.

Lionni, Leo. (1959) 1995. *Little Blue and Little Yellow*. New York: HarperCollins.

Lippit, Akira. 2000. *Electric Animal: Toward a Rhetoric of Wildlife*. Minneapolis: University of Minnesota Press.

Lissitzky, El. (1922) 2000. *About Two Squares: A Suprematist Tale about Two Squares in Six Constructions*. Translated by Patricia Railing. Berlin: Skythen.

Liu, Alan. 2007. "Imagining the New Media Encounter." In *Digital Literary Studies*, edited by Ray Siemens and Susan Schreibman, 3–25. London: Blackwell.

Lloyd, Rosemary. 1998. "Twenty Thousand Leagues below Modernism." In *Modernity, Modernism and Children's Literature*, edited by Ulf Boethius, 51–74. Stockholm: Stockholm University Press.

Locke, John. (1688) 1960. *Two Treatises of Government*. Edited by Peter Laslett. Cambridge: Cambridge University Press.

———. (1690) 1964. *An Essay concerning Human Understanding*. New York: Meridian.

———. (1693) 1989. *Some Thoughts concerning Education*. Edited with introduction, notes, and critical apparatus by John W. Yolton and Jean S. Yolton. Oxford: Clarendon.

Lofting, Hugh. (1920) 1923. *The Story of Doctor Dolittle*. Toronto: McClelland & Stewart.

Logan, Mawuena Kossi. 1999. *Narrating Africa: George Henty and the Fiction of Empire*. New York: Routledge.

Løgstrup, K. E. 1969. "Moral og børnebøger." In *Børne- og ungdomsbøger. Problemer og analyser*, edited by Sven Møller Kristensen and Preben Ramløv, 19–26. Copenhagen: Gyldendal.

Lomeña Cantos, Andrés. 2013. "Entrevista con Sandra Beckett sobre literatura crossover e infantil." *Heterocosmicas*, August 20, 2013. http://heterocosmicas.blogspot.com.

London, Jack. 1903. *The Call of the Wild*. New York: Macmillan.

Lorde, Audre. (1984) 2007. *Sister Outsider: Essays and Speeches*. Berkeley, CA: Crossing Press.

Loud Crow Interactive. 2012. *Goodnight Moon*. App for iPad.

Louv, Richard. 2005. *Last Child in the Woods: Saving Our Children from Nature-Deficit Disorder*. Chapel Hill, NC: Algonquin Books.

Low, Jason. 2016. "Where Is the Diversity in Publishing?" *Lee and Low Books: The Open Book* (blog), January 26, 2016. https://blog.leeandlow.com.

Lucashenko, Melissa. 2000. "Black on Black." *Meanjin* 59, no. 3: 112–18.

Lundblad, Michael. 2009. "From Animal Studies to Animality Studies." *PMLA* 124, no. 2 (March): 496–502.

Lundin, Anne. 2004. *Constructing the Canon of Children's Literature: Beyond Library Walls and Ivory Towers*. New York: Routledge.

Lundqvist, Jesper. 2012. *Kivi & Monsterhund* [Kivi & Monster Dog]. Illustrated by Bettina Johansson. Stockholm: Olika förlag.

Lurie, Alison. 1990. *Don't Tell the Grown-Ups: Subversive Children's Literature*. Boston: Little, Brown.

Lyga, Barry. 2007. *Boy Toy*. Boston: Houghton.

Lynn, Ruth Nadelman. 2005. *Fantasy Literature for Children and Young Adults: A Comprehensive Guide*. 5th ed. Westport, CT: Libraries Unlimited.

Macareavey, Naomi. 2016. "Reading Conversion Narratives as Literature of Trauma: Radical Religion, the Wars of the Three Kingdoms and the Cromwellian Re-conquest of Ireland." In *Region, Religion and English Renaissance Literature*, edited by David Coleman, 163–80. London: Routledge.

Macaulay, David. 1990. *Black and White*. Boston: Houghton Mifflin.

MacCann, Donnarae. (1998) 2001. *White Supremacy in Children's Literature: Characterizations of African Americans, 1830–1900*. New York: Routledge.

———. 2001. "Editor's Introduction: Racism and Antiracism: Forty Years of Theories and Debates." *Lion and the Unicorn* 25, no. 3: 337–52.

MacCann, Donnarae, and Yulisa Amadu Maddy. 2001. *Apartheid and Racism in South African Children's Literature*. New York: Routledge.

MacCann, Donnarae, and Gloria Woodard, eds. (1972) 1985. *The Black American in Books for Children: Readings in Racism*. 2nd ed. Metuchen, NJ: Scarecrow Press.

Macdonald, George. (1893) 1973. "The Fantastic Imagination." In *The Gifts of the Child Christ: Fairy Tales and Stories for The Childlike*, edited by Glenn Edward Sadler, 23–29. Grand Rapids: William B. Eerdmans.

Mackey, Margaret. (2002) 2007. *Literacies across Media: Playing the Text*. London: Routledge.

———. 2007. *Mapping Recreational Literacies: Contemporary Adults at Play*. New York: Peter Lang.

———. 2008. "Postmodern Picture Books and the Material Conditions of Reading." In *Postmodern Picturebooks*, edited by L. R. Sipe and S. Pantaleo, 103–16. New York: Routledge.

———. 2011. *Narrative Pleasures: Young Adults Interpret Book, Film, and Video Game*. Houndmills: Palgrave Macmillan.

MacRae, Cathi Dunn. 1998. *Presenting Young Adult Fantasy Fiction*. New York: Twayne.

Mahne, Nicole: 2007. *Transmediale Erzähltheorie*. Göttingen: V&R.

Mahy, Margaret. 1990. *The Seven Chinese Brothers*. Illustrated by Jean Tseng and Mou-sien Tseng. New York: Scholastic.

Makdisi, Saree. 2003. *William Blake and the Impossible History of the 1790s*. Chicago: University of Chicago Press.

Malan, Robin. 1998. *The Sound of New Wings*. Cape Town: Maskew Miller Longman.

Malcolm, Noel. 1998. *The Origins of English Nonsense*. London: HarperCollins.

Mallan, Kerry. 2009. *Gender Dilemmas in Children's Fiction*. Basingstoke: Palgrave Macmillan.

———. 2013a. "Empathy: Narrative Empathy and Children's Literature." In *(Re)imagining the World: Children's Literature's Response to Changing Times*, edited by Yan Wu, Kerry Mallan, and Roderick McGillis, 105–14. Berlin: Springer.

———. 2013b. *Secrets, Lies and Children's Fiction*. Houndmills: Palgrave Macmillan.

Mallan, Kerry, and Roderick McGillis. 2005. "Between a Frock and a Hard Place: Camp Aesthetics and Children's Culture." *Canadian Review of American Studies* 35, no. 1: 1–19.

———. 2019. "Escape to Moonrise Kingdom: Let's Go Camping!" In *Queer as Camp: Essays on Summer, Style, and Sexuality*, edited by Kenneth B. Kidd and Derritt Mason, 211–22. New York: Fordham University Press.

Malot, Hector. (1878) 1888. *Sans famille*. Paris: Dentu.

———. 1893. *En famille*. Paris: E. Flammarion.

Mansbach, Adam. 2011. *Go the Fuck to Sleep*. Illustrated by Ricardo Cortés. New York: Akashic Books.

Maracle, Lee. 2002. *Will's Garden*. Penticton: Theytus Books.

Marcellino, Fred. 1996. *The Story of Little Babaji*. New York: HarperCollins.

Marcus, Leonard S. 2007. *Golden Legacy: The Story of Golden Books*. New York: Random House.

———. 2008. *Minders of Make-Believe Idealists, Entrepreneurs, and the Shaping of American Children's Literature*. New York: Houghton Mifflin Harcourt.

Mark, Jan. 2004. *Useful Idiots*. London: Random House.

Markoosie. 1970. *Harpoon of the Hunter*. Kingston: McGill–Queen's University Press.

Marraffa, Massimo. 2011. "Theory of Mind." Internet Encyclopedia of Philosophy, November 11, 2011. www.iep.utm.edu.

Marsh, Katherine. 2012. *Jepp, Who Defied the Stars*. New York: Hyperion.

Marshall, Elizabeth. 2004. "Stripping for the Wolf: Rethinking Representations of Gender in Children's Literature." *Reading Research Quarterly* 39, no. 3: 256–70.

———. 2018. *Graphic Girlhoods: Visualizing Education and Violence*. New York: Routledge.

Martí, José. 1889. *La Edad de Oro: Publicación mensual de recreo e instrucción dedicada a los niños de América*. New York.

Martin, Michele H. 2004. *Brown Gold: Milestones of African American Children's Picture Books, 1845–2002*. New York: Routledge.

Martinez, Victor. 1996. *Parrot in the Oven: Mi Vida*. New York: HarperCollins.

Martínez-Roldán, Carmen M. 2013. "The Representation of Latinos and the Use of Spanish: A Critical Content Analysis of *Skippyjon Jones*." *Journal of Children's Literature* 39, no. 1: 5–14.

Martín Gaite, Carmen. 1990. *Caperucita en Manhattan*. Madrid: Siruela.

Marxveldt, Cissy van [Setske de Haan]. (1919) 2010. *De H.B.S. tijd van Joop ter Heul* [Joop ter Heul's high school years]. Kampen: West Friesland, 2010.

Massumi, Brian. 1995. "The Autonomy of Affect." *Cultural Critique* 31:83–109.

———. 2015. *Politics of Affect*. Cambridge: Polity.

Mateo, José, and Javier Martínez Pedro. 2011. *Migrar*. Mexico City: Ediciones Tecolote.

May, Jill P. 1995. *Children's Literature & Critical Theory*. New York: Oxford University Press.

Mazzucato, Valentina, and Djamila Schans. 2011. "Transnational Families and the Well-Being of Children: Theoretical and Methodological Perspectives." *Journal of Marriage and Family* 73, no. 4: 704–12.

McCabe, Janice, Emily Fairchild, Liz Grauerholz, Bernice A. Pescosolido, and Daniel Tope. 2011. "Gender in Twentieth-Century Children's Books: Patterns of Disparity in Titles and Central Characters." *Gender and Society* 25, no. 2: 197–226.

McCallum, Robyn. 1991. "The Embrace: Narrative Voice and Children's Books." *Canadian Children's Literature* 63:24–40.

———. 1997. "Cultural Solipsism, National Identities and the Discourse of Multiculturalism in Australian Picture Books." *Ariel* 28, no. 1: 101–16.

———. 1999a. *Ideologies of Identity in Adolescent Fiction: The Dialogic Construction of Subjectivity*. New York: Taylor & Francis.

———. 1999b. *Voices of the Other: Children's Literature and the Postcolonial Context*. New York: Garland.

McCarthy, Catharine, Martha Brady, and Kelly Hallman. 2016. *Investing When It Counts: Reviewing the Evidence and Charting a Course of Research and Action for Very Young Adolescents*. New York: Population Council. www.popcouncil.org.

McCay, Winsor. 1997. *The Best of Little Nemo in Slumberland*. Edited and with an introduction by Richard Marschall. New York: Stewart, Tabori & Chang.

McCloud, Scott. 1993. *Understanding Comics*. Northampton, MA: Kitchen Sink Press.

McCooey, David, and Emma Hayes. 2017. "The Liminal Poetics of *The Wind in the Willows*." *Children's Literature* 45:45–68.

McCormick, Patricia. 2006. *Sold*. New York: Hyperion.

McDermott, Gerald. 1972. *Anansi the Spider: A Tale from the Ashanti*. New York: Henry Holt.

———. 2001. *Raven: A Trickster Tale from the Pacific Northwest*. San Diego: Perfection Learning.

———. 2011. *Monkey: A Trickster Tale from India*. Boston: HMH Books for Young Readers.

McDonald, Grantley. 2016. *Biblical Criticism in Early Modern Europe: Erasmus, the Johannine Comma and Trinitarian Debate*. Cambridge: Cambridge University Press.

McDonald, Meme, and Boori Monty Pryor. 2002. *Njunjul the Sun*. Sydney: Allen & Unwin.

McGavran, James Holt, Jr., and Jennifer Smith Daniel. 2012. "Introduction." In *Time of Beauty, Time of Fear: The Romantic Legacy in the Literature of Childhood*, edited by McGavran, xi–xxv. Iowa City: University of Iowa Press.

McGee, Chris. 2009. "Why Won't Melinda Just Talk about What Happened? Speak and the Confessional Voice." *Children's Literature Association Quarterly* 34, no. 2: 172–87.

McGilchrist, Iain. 2009. *The Master and His Emissary: The Divided Brain and the Making of the Western World*. New Haven, CT: Yale University Press.

McGillis, Roderick. 1998–99. "The Delights of Impossibility: No Children, No Books, Only Theory." *Children's Literature Association Quarterly* 23, no. 4 (Winter): 202–8.

———. 1999. *Voices of the Other: Children's Literature and the Postcolonial Context*. New York: Garland.

McGovern, Cammie. 2014. *Say What You Will*. New York: HarperTeen.

McKee, David. 1978. *Tusk Tusk*. London: Andersen Press.

McKibben, Bill. 1990. *The End of Nature*. New York: Viking Penguin.

McLeod, John. 2015. *Life Lines: Writing Transcultural Adoption*. London: Bloomsbury.

McMillan, Cheryl. 2003. "Playing with Frames: Spatial Images in Children's Fiction." In *Children's Literature and the Fin de Siècle*, edited by Roderick McGillis, 121–28. Westport, CT: Praeger.

Mdallel, Sabeur. 2003. "Translating Children's Literature in the Arab World: The State of the Art." *Traduction pour les enfants* 48, nos. 1–2: 298–306.

Meadow, Tey. 2014. "Child." *Transgender Studies Quarterly* 1, nos. 1–2: 57–59.

———. 2018. *Trans Kids: Being Gendered in the Twenty-First Century*. Berkeley: University of California Press.

Mee, Arthur. 1923. *The Children's Encyclopedia*. 20 vols. London: Educational Book Company.

Meek, Margaret, ed. 2000. *Children's Literature and National Identity*. Stoke-on-Trent: Trentham Books.

Mello, Roger. 2010. *Selvagem*. São Paulo: Global.

Melville, Herman. 1851. *Moby Dick; or, The Whale*. New York: Harper & Brothers.

Mendlesohn, Farah. 2005. *Diana Wynne Jones: Children's Literature and the Fantastic Tradition*. London: Routledge.

———. 2008. *Rhetorics of Fantasy*. Middletown, CN: Wesleyan University Press.

Menon, Radhika. 2006. "Questioning Cultural Stereotypes through Children's Books." Tulika Books for Children, October 2006. www.tulikabooks.com.

Meyer, Urs, Roberto Simanowski, and Christoph Zeller, eds. 2006. *Transmedialität. Zur Ästhetik paraliterarischer Verfahren*. Göttingen: Wallstein.

Mickenberg, Julia. 2006. *Learning from the Left: Children's Literature, the Cold War, and Radical Politics in the United States*. New York: Oxford University Press.

Mickenberg, Julia, and Philip Nel. 2008. *Tales for Little Rebels: A Collection of Radical Children's Literature*. New York: New York University Press.

Mikkelsen, Nina. 2001. "Little Black Sambo Revisited." Review of *Pictus Orbis Sambo: A Publishing History, Checklist, and Price Guide for the Story of Little Black Sambo (1899–1999)*, by Phyllis Settecase Barton. *Children's Literature* 29:260–66.

Millán-Varela, María del Carmen. 1999. "(G)alicia in Wonderland: Some Insights." *Fragmentos*, no. 16 (January–June): 97–117.

Miller, Ann. 2007. *Reading Bande Dessinée: Critical Approaches to French-Language Comic Strip*. Chicago: Intellect Books.

Miller, J. Hillis. 1992. *Illustration*. Cambridge, MA: Harvard University Press.

Mills, Alice. 2007. "Australian Children's Literature." In *A Companion to Australian Literature to 1900*, edited by Nicholas Birns and Rebecca McNeer, 417–28. Rochester, NY: Camden House.

Mills, Claudia. 1997. "The Ethics of the Author/Audience Relationship in Children's Fiction." *Children's Literature Association Quarterly* 22, no. 4: 181–87.

Mills, Mara. 2012. "What Should We Call Reading?" *Flow: A Critical Forum on Media and Culture* 17, no. 3. www.flowjournal.org.

Milne, A. A. (1924) 1952. *When We Were Very Young*. New York: Dell.

———. (1928) 1989. *The House at Pooh Corner*. London: Mammoth.

———. 1957. *The World of Pooh*. The Complete *Winnie-the-Pooh* (1926) and *The House at Pooh Corner* (1928). New York: E. P. Dutton.

———. 1988. *Winnie-the-Pooh*. New York: Dutton Books.

Mintz, Steven. 2004. *Huck's Raft: A History of American Childhood*. Cambridge, MA: Harvard University Press.

———. 2015. *The Prime of Life: A History of Modern Adulthood*. Cambridge, MA: Belknap Press.

Mitchell, Claudia, and Jacqueline Reid-Walsh. 2002. *Researching Children's Popular Culture: The Cultural Spaces of Childhood*. New York: Routledge.

———. 2008. "How to Study Girl Culture." In *Girl Culture: An Encyclopedia*, vol. 1, edited by Claudia Mitchell and Jacqueline Reid-Walsh, 17–24. Westport, CT: Greenwood.

Mitchell, David, and Sharon Snyder. 2000. *Narrative Prosthesis: Disability and the Dependencies of Discourse*. Ann Arbor: University of Michigan Press.

Mitchell, Jennifer. 2014. "'A Girl. A Machine. A Freak': A Consideration of Contemporary Queer Composites." *Bookbird* 52, no. 1: 51–62.

Mitchell, Lucy Sprague. 1921. *Here and Now Storybook*. New York: Dutton.

Mitchell, Sally. 1995. *The New Girl: Girls' Culture in England, 1880–1915*. New York: Columbia University Press.

Mitchell, W. J. T. 1994. *Picture Theory: Essays on Verbal and Visual Representation*. Chicago: University of Chicago Press.

Miyazaki, Hayao, dir. 1997. *Princess Mononoke*. Studio Ghibli.

———. 2008. *Ponyo on the Cliff by the Sea*. Studio Ghibli.

Moebius, William. 1986. "Introduction to Picture Book Codes." *Word & Image: A Journal of Verbal/Visual Enquiry* 2, no. 2: 141–58.

———. 1994. "Informing Adult Readers: Symbolic Experience in Children's Literature." In *Reading World Literature: Theory, History, Practice*, edited by Sarah Lawall, 309–27. Austin: University of Texas Press.

———. 1999. "Making the Front Page: Views of Women, Women's Views in the Picturebook." In *Girls, Boys, Books, Toys: Feminist Theory and Children's Culture*, edited by Margaret R. Higonnet and Beverly Lyon Clark, 112–29. Baltimore: Johns Hopkins University Press.

———. Forthcoming. "Introduction: Aura and Prestige: The Literary and the Picture Book." In *Aesthetics and Memory in the Picture Book*.

Mohr, Richard D. (1996) 2004. "The Pedophilia of Everyday Life." In *Curiouser: On the Queerness of Children*, edited by

Steven Bruhm and Natasha Hurley, 17–30. Minneapolis: University of Minnesota Press.

Moissard, Boris. 2005. "Écrire pour tous les âges." *Littérature de jeunesse, incertaines frontiers: Colloque de Cérisy la Salle (juin 2004)*, edited by Isabelle Nières-Chevrel, 28–33. Paris: Gallimard Jeunesse.

Montessori, Maria. 1919. "Children's Imagination by Means of Fairy Tales: Address to the Child Study Society." In *Times Educational Supplement*. London. Reprinted in *AMI Communications*, no. 2, 1975. Quoted by Glenn Goodfellow in https://montessori-nw.org, March 4, 2014.

Montgomery, L. M. (1908) 2017. *Anne of Green Gables*. London: Virago.

——. 1937. *Jane of Lantern Hill*. Toronto: McClelland & Stewart.

——. 1997. *The Annotated Anne of Green Gables*. Edited by Wendy E. Barry, Margaret Anne Doody, and Mary E. Doody Jones. Oxford: Oxford University Press.

Moon, Michael. 2004. "'The Gentle Boy from the Dangerous Classes': Pederasty, Domesticity, and Capitalism in Horatio Alger." In *Curiouser: On the Queerness of Children*, edited by Steven Bruhm and Natasha Hurley, 31–56. Minneapolis: University of Minnesota Press.

Moore, Anne Carroll. 1938. "The Three Owls' Notebook." *Horn Book* 14 (January–February): 31–33.

Moore-Mallinos, Jennifer. 2008. *My Friend Has Down Syndrome*. Illustrated by Marta Fabrega. Hauppauge, NY: Barron's.

Morey, Anne, ed. 2012. *Genre, Reception, and Adaptation in the "Twilight" Series*. Burlington, VT: Ashgate.

Morgenstern, John. 2001. "The Rise of Children's Literature Reconsidered." *Children's Literature Association Quarterly* 26, no. 2: 64–73.

——. 2015. "The Mother of Boys' Adventure Fiction: Reassessing Catherine Parr Traill's *Canadian Crusoes* and R.M. Ballantyne's *The Coral Island*." *Lion and the Unicorn* 39, no. 3 (September): 294–310.

Mori, Kyoko. 1994. *Shizuko's Daughter*. New York: Fawcett.

Morley, David. 2000. *Home Territories: Media, Mobility and Identity*. London: Routledge.

——. 2005. "Audience." In *New Keywords: A Revised Vocabulary of Cultures and Society*, edited by Tony Bennett, Lawrence Grossberg, and Meaghan Morris, 8–10. Malden, MA: Blackwell.

Morris, Wesley. 2015. "The Year We Obsessed over Identity." *New York Times Magazine*, October 6, 2015. www.nytimes.com.

Moruzi, Kristine, and Michelle J. Smith. 2013. "'A Great Strange World': Reading the Girls' School Story." In *Girls' School Stories, 1749–1929*, edited by Kristine Moruzi and Michelle J. Smith, xiii–xxxii. Abingdon: Taylor & Francis.

Moruzi, Kristine, Michelle J. Smith, and Elizabeth Bullen, eds. 2017. *Affect, Emotion, and Children's Literature: Representation and Socialisation in Texts for Children and Young Adults*. Abingdon: Routledge.

Mosel, Arlene. 1968. *Tikki Tikki Tembo*. Illustrated by Blair Lent. New York: Holt.

Mott, Frank Luther. 1938. *A History of American Magazines, 1850–1865*. Vol. 2. Cambridge, MA: Harvard University Press.

Mouritsen, Flemming, and Jens Qvortrup. 2003. "Introduction." In *Childhood and Children's Culture*, edited by Flemming Mouritsen and Jens Qvortrup, 7–13. Odense: University Press of Southern Denmark.

Mukherjee, Ankhi. 2014. *What Is a Classic? Postcolonial Rewriting and Invention of the Canon*. Palo Alto, CA: Stanford University Press.

Müller, Jörg. 2001. *Das Buch im Buch im Buch im Buch*. Frankfurt: Verlag Sauerländer.

Müller, Jürgen E. 1996. *Intermedialität. Formen moderner kultureller Kommunikation*. Münster: Nodus.

Müller, Sonja. 2009. *Die Gründerjahre der Internationalen Forschungsgesellschaft für Kinder- und Jugendliteratur. Diskussionen und Projekte 1970–1978* [The early years of IRSCL—International Research Society for Children's Literature: Discussions and projects from 1970 to 1978]. Frankfurt: International Research Society for Children's Literature.

Munsch, Robert. 1980. *The Paper Bag Princess*. Illustrated by Michael Martchenko. Toronto: Annick Press.

Münz, Rainer, and Rainer Ohliger, eds. 2003a. *Diasporas and Ethnic Migrants: Germany, Israel and Russia in Comparative Perspective*. New York: Routledge.

——. 2003b. *Israel and Post-Soviet Successor States in Comparative Perspective*. London: Frank Cass.

Murai, Mayako. 2014. "Before and after the 'Grimm Boom.'" In *Grimms' Tales around the Globe: The Dynamics of Their International Reception*, edited by Vanessa Joosen and Gillian Lathey, 153–76. Detroit: Wayne State University Press.

——. 2018. "Happily Ever after for the Old in Japanese Fairy Tales." In *Connecting Childhood and Old Age in Popular Media*, edited by Vanessa Joosen, 43–60. Jackson: University of Mississippi Press.

Murfin, Ross. (1831) 2000. s.v. "Genre" in "Glossary of Critical and Literary Terms." In *Frankenstein*, written by Mary Shelley and edited by Johanna M. Smith. 2nd ed. Boston: St. Martin's.

Murray, Kirsty. 2003. *Bridie's Fire*. Children of the Wind Series Book 1. Sydney: Allen & Unwin.

———. 2004. *Becoming Billy Dare*. Children of the Wind Series Book 2. Sydney: Allen & Unwin.

———. 2005. *A Prayer for Blue Delaney*. Children of the Wind Series Book 3. Sydney: Allen & Unwin.

———. 2006. *The Secret Life of Maeve Lee Kwong*. Children of the Wind Series Book 3. Sydney: Allen & Unwin.

Myers, Christopher. 2014. "The Apartheid of Children's Literature." *New York Times*, March 16, 2014.

Myers, Walter Dean. 1999. *Monster*. Illustrated by Christopher Myers. New York: HarperCollins.

———. 2014. "Where Are the People of Color in Children's Books?" *New York Times*, March 16, 2014.

Nadareišvili, Tatia. 2017. *Schlaf gut: Ein Bilderbuch aus Georgien*. Translated by Rachel Gratzfeld. Basel: Baobab Books.

Naidoo, Beverly. 2002. *The Other Side of Truth*. London: Puffin.

Nakagawa, Rieko, and Yuriko Yamawaki. 2002. *Guri and Gura*. Translated by Peter Howlett and Richard McNamara. Boston: Tuttle.

Nakassis, Constantine, and Jesse Snedeker. 2002. "Beyond Sarcasm: Intonation and Context as Relational Cues in Children's Recognition of Irony." In *Proceedings of the Twenty-Sixth Boston University Conference on Language Development*, edited by Barbara Skarabela, Stanley Fish, and Anna Do, 429–40. Somerville, MA: Cascadilla Press.

Natov, Roni. 2001. "Harry Potter and the Extraordinariness of the Ordinary." *Lion and the Unicorn* 25:310–27.

———. 2003. *The Poetics of Childhood*. London: Routledge.

Nayar, Pramod. 2013. *Posthumanism*. Cambridge: Polity.

Needle, Jan. 1981. *Wild Wood*. London: Deutsch.

Nel, Philip. 2005. "Is There a Text in This Advertising Campaign? Literature, Marketing, and Harry Potter." *Lion and the Unicorn* 29, no. 2: 236–67.

———. 2010. "Obamafiction for Children: Imagining the Forty-Fourth US President." *Children's Literature Association Quarterly* 35, no. 4: 334–56.

———. 2017a. "Refugee Stories for Young Readers." *Public Books*, March 23, 2017.

———. 2017b. *Was the Cat in the Hat Black? The Hidden Racism in Children's Literature and the Need for Diverse Books*. New York: Oxford University Press.

———. 2018. "Introduction: Migration, Refugees, and Diaspora in Children's Literature." *Children's Literature Association Quarterly* 43, no. 4: 357–61.

Nelson, Blake. 2006. *Paranoid Park*. New York: Penguin-Speak.

Nelson, Claudia. 2003. "The Unheimlich Maneuver: Uncanny Domesticity in the Urban Waif Tale." In *Youth Cultures: Texts, Images, and Identities*, edited by Kerry Mallan and Sharyn Pearce, 109–21. Westport, CT: Praeger.

———. 2004. "That Other Eden: Adult Education and Youthful Sexuality in *The Pearl*, 1979–1880." In *Sexual Pedagogies: Sex Education in Britain, Australia, and America, 1879–2000*, edited by Claudia Nelson and Michelle H. Martin, 15–32. New York: Palgrave.

Nelson, Claudia, and Roberta Morris, eds. (2014) 2016. *Representing Children in Chinese and U.S. Children's Literature*. London: Routledge.

Nesbit, E. 1901. *Nine Unlikely Tales for Children*. London: T. Fisher Unwin.

———. 1975. *The Story of the Amulet*. Harmondsworth: Puffin.

Newbery, John. 1744. *A Little Pretty Pocket-Book*. London: Newbery and Carnan.

———. 1764. *The Renowned History of Giles Gingerbread, a Little Boy, Who Lived upon Learning*. London: John Newbery.

———. 1765. *The History of Little Goody Two-Shoes*. London: John Newbery.

Newell, Peter. (1902) 1964. *Topsys & Turvys*. New York: Dover.

The New England Primer. 1727. Boston: S. Kneeland and T. Green.

Newton, Michael. 2002. "Bodies without Souls: The Case of Peter the Wild Boy." In *At the Borders of the Human: Beasts, Bodies and Natural Philosophy in the Early Modern Period*, edited by Erica Fudge, Ruth Gilbert, and Susan Wiseman, 196–214. New York: Palgrave Macmillan.

Nichols, Grace. 1984. *The Fat Black Woman's Poems*. London: Virago.

Nieto, Sonia M. 2002. "Profoundly Multicultural Questions." *Educational Leadership* 60, no. 4: 6–10.

Nikolajeva, Maria. 1991. *From Mythic to Linear: Time in Children's Literature*. Lanham, MD: Scarecrow Press.

———. 1996. *Children's Literature Comes of Age: Toward a New Aesthetic*. New York: Garland.

———. 2002. *The Rhetoric of Character in Children's Literature*. Lanham, MD: Scarecrow Press.

———. 2005. *Aesthetic Approaches to Children's Literature: An Introduction*. Lanham, MD: Scarecrow Press.

———. 2010. *Power, Voice and Subjectivity in Literature for Young Readers*. London: Routledge.

———. 2011. "Translation and Crosscultural Reception." In *Handbook of Research on Children's and Young Adult Literature*, edited by Shelby A. Wolf, Karen Coats, Christine Jenkins, and Patricia A. Enciso, 404–27. New York: Routledge.

———. 2014. *Reading for Learning: Cognitive Approaches to Children's Literature*. Amsterdam: John Benjamins.

Nikolajeva, Maria, and Carole Scott. 2000. *How Picturebooks Work*. New York: Routledge.

Nilsen, Alleen Pace. 1971. "Women in Children's Literature." *College English* 32, no. 8: 918–26.

Noakes, Vivien. 2001. "Introduction." In *Edward Lear: The Complete Verse and Other Nonsense*, edited by Vivien Noakes, xix–xxxiv. London: Penguin.

Nodelman, Perry. 1985. "Introduction: Matthew Arnold, a Teddy Bear, and a List of Touchstones." In *Touchstones: Reflections on the Best in Children's Literature*, vol. 1, pp. 1–12. West Lafayette, IN: ChLA.

———. 1988. *Words about Pictures: The Narrative Art of Children's Picture Books*. Athens: University of Georgia Press.

———. 1992. "The Other: Orientalism, Colonialism, and Children's Literature." *Children's Literature Association Quarterly* 17, no. 1 (Spring): 29–35.

———. 2000a. "Pleasure and Genre: Speculations on the Characteristics of Children's Fiction." *Children's Literature* 28:1–14.

———. 2000b. "The Urge to Sameness." *Children's Literature* 28:38–43.

———. 2008. *The Hidden Adult: Defining Children's Literature*. Baltimore: Johns Hopkins University Press.

Nodelman, Perry, and Mavis Reimer. 2003. *The Pleasures of Children's Literature*. 3rd ed. Boston: Allyn and Bacon.

Norton, Jody. 1999. "Transchildren and the Discipline of Children's Literature." *Lion and the Unicorn* 23, no. 3 (September): 415–36.

———. (1999) 2011. "Transchildren and the Discipline of Children's Literature." In *Over the Rainbow: Queer Children's and Young Adult Literature*, edited by Michelle Ann Abate and Kenneth Kidd, 293–313. Ann Arbor: University of Michigan Press.

Norton, Mary. (1952) 1990. *The Borrowers*. New York: Odyssey / Harcourt Brace.

Nuccio, Matteo. 2008. "Se la letteratura per ragazzi piace agli adulti. E viceversa." *Il Venerdì di Repubblica*, November 28, 2008, 114–17.

Nussbaum, Martha C. 1990. *Love's Knowledge: Essays on Philosophy and Literature*. New York: Oxford University Press.

———. 2003. *Upheavals of Thought: The Intelligence of Emotions*. Cambridge: Cambridge University Press.

Nyberg, Amy Kiste. 1998. *Seal of Approval: The History of the Comics Code*. Jackson: University Press of Mississippi.

Oatley, Keith. 2002. "Emotions and the Story Worlds of Fiction." In *Narrative Impact: Social and Cognitive Foundations*, edited by Melanie C. Green, Jeffrey J. Strange, and Timothy C. Brock, 39–69. Mahwah, NJ: Lawrence Erlbaum & Associates.

Odaga, Asenath Bole. 1989. *The Diamond Ring*. Kisumu: Lake Publishers.

O'Dell, Scott. (1960) 1961. *Island of the Blue Dolphins*. London: Constable.

Odira. 2010. *Pakruok*. Performed at Osiri Beach, Homa Bay, Kenya, July 13, 2010. Translated by Adrian Onyando.

Oittinen, Riitta. 2000. *Translating for Children*. New York: Garland.

Okami, Paul, Richard Olmstead, and Paul R. Abramson. 1997. "Sexual Experiences in Early Childhood: 18-Year Longitudinal Data from the UCLA Family Lifestyles Project." *Journal of Sex Research* 34, no. 4 (December): 339–47.

Older, Daniel José. 2014. "Diversity Is Not Enough: Race, Power, Publishing." BuzzFeed, April 17, 2014.

O'Malley, Andrew. 2008. "Island Homemaking: Catharine Parr Traill's *Canadian Crusoes* and the Robinsonade Tradition." In *Home Words: Discourses of Children's Literature in Canada*, edited by Mavis Reimer, 67–86. Waterloo: Wilfrid Laurier University Press.

———. 2012. *Children's Literature, Popular Culture, and Robinson Crusoe*. London: Palgrave Macmillan.

Ommundsen, Åse Marie. 1998. *Djevelfrø og englebarn: Synet på barn i kristne barneblader i perioden 1875–1910* [Devil seeds and little angels: The view upon children in religious children's magazines between 1875 and 1910]. Oslo: University of Oslo Press.

———. 2006. "All-alder-litteratur. Litteratur for alle eller ingen." In *Kartet og terrenget. Linjer og dykk i barne-og ungdomslitteraturen*, edited by Kari Sverdrup and Jon Ewo, 50–71. Oslo: Pax.

———. 2008a. "Fiction for All Ages? 'All-Ages-Literature' as a New Trend in Late Modern Norwegian Children's Literature." In *An Invitation to Explore: New International Perspectives in Children's Literature*, edited by N. D. Laura Atkins, Michele Gill, and Liz Thiel, 100–114. Lichfield: Pied Piper.

———. 2008b. "Liquid Limitlessness and Hope: Two Tendencies in Late Modern Norwegian Young Adult Fiction." *Bookbird* 46, no. 3: 38–44.

———. 2010. *Litterære grenseoverskridelser. Når grensene mellom barne- og voksenlitteraturen viskes ut* [Literary boundary crossings: Erasing the borders between literature for children and adults]. Oslo: University of Oslo Press.

———. 2011. "La *crossover* littérature scandinave." *La Revue des livres pour enfants* 257 (February): 128–34.

———. 2015. "Who Are These Picturebooks For? Controversial Picturebooks and the Question of Audience." In *Challenging and Controversial Picturebooks: Creative and Critical Responses to Visual Texts*, edited by Janet Evans, 71–93. New York: Routledge.

O'Neill, Louise. 2018. *The Surface Breaks: A Reimagining of the Little Mermaid*. London: Scholastic.

op de Beeck, Nathalie. 2010. *Suspended Animation: Children's Picture Books and the Fairy Tale of Modernity*. Minneapolis: University of Minnesota Press.

Opie, Iona, and Peter Opie. 1959. *The Lore and Language of Schoolchildren*. New York: Oxford University Press.

Ord, Priscilla, ed. 1981. "Special Section on Children's Folklore." *Children's Literature Association Quarterly* 6, no. 2: 11–34.

Origen, Erich, and Dan Golan. 2008. *Goodnight Bush*. Boston: Little, Brown.

Ortiz, Simon. 1977. *The People Shall Continue*. San Francisco: Children's Book Press.

Osgood, Samuel. 1865. "Books for Our Children." *Atlantic Monthly* 16 (December): 724–36.

O'Sullivan, Emer. 2004. "Internationalism, the Universal Child and the World of Children's Literature." In *International Companion Encyclopedia of Children's Literature*, edited by Peter Hunt, 13–25. London: Routledge.

———. 2005. *Comparative Children's Literature*. Translated by Anthea Bell. London: Routledge.

———. 2011. "Comparative Children's Literature." *PMLA* 126, no. 1 (January): 189–96.

———. 2013. "Children's Literature and Translation Studies." In *The Routledge Handbook of Translation Studies*, edited by Carmen Millán-Varela and Bartrina Francesca, 451–63. London: Routledge.

———. 2016. "Discourses of Internationalism in Children's Literature." In *Child Governance and Autonomy in Children's Literature: Where Children Rule*, edited by Christopher Kelen and Björn Sundmark, 30–42. New York: Routledge.

Panszczyk, Anna. 2016. "The 'Becoming' of Pinocchio: The Liminal Nature of Collodi's Boy-Toy." *Children's Literature* 44:192–218.

Paris, Leslie. 2008. *Children's Nature: The Rise of the American Summer Camp*. New York: New York University Press.

Park, Linda Sue. 2001. *A Single Shard*. New York: Clarion Books.

———. 2005. *Project Mulberry*. Boston: Houghton Mifflin Harcourt.

———. 2010. *Long Walk to Water*. New York: Clarion Books.

Park, Robert E. 1928. "Human Migration and the Marginal Man." *American Journal of Sociology* 33, no. 6 (May): 881–93.

Park, Sunyoung. 2006. "The Colonial Origin of Korean Realism and Its Contemporary Manifestation." *positions* 14, no. 1: 165–92.

Parkes, Christopher. 2006. "Treasure Island and the Romance of the British Civil Service." *Children's Literature Association Quarterly* 31, no. 4: 332–45.

Parkinson, Siobhán. 1999. *Breaking the Wishbone*. Dublin: O'Brien Press.

Parmalee, Maurice. 1916. *Poverty and Social Progress*. New York: Macmillan.

Partridge, Eric. 1979. *Origins: A Short Etymological Dictionary of Modern English*. New York: MacMillan.

Paterson, Katherine. 1981. *Gates of Excellence: On Reading and Writing Books for Children*. New York: Elsevier / Nelson Books.

Paul, Lissa. 1998. *Reading Otherways*. Portland: Calendar Islands.

———. 2005. "Sex and the Children's Book." *Lion and the Unicorn* 29:222–35.

———. 2009. "Learning to be Literate." In *The Cambridge Companion to Children's Literature*, edited by M. O. Grenby and Andrea Immel, 127–42. Cambridge: Cambridge University Press.

———. 2011. *The Children's Book Business: Lessons from the Long Eighteenth Century*. New York: Routledge.

Paz, Marcela. 2006. *Papelucho*. Translated by Lina Craddock, Ailsa Shaw, and Jean Paul Beuchat. Bilingual Spanish-English ed. Santiago: SM Ediciones. Originally published as *Papelucho* (Santiago: Editorial Rapa-Nui, 1947).

Pearce, Philippa. (1958) 1976. *Tom's Midnight Garden*. Harmondsworth: Penguin-Puffin Books.

Pearce, Sharyn. 2003. "Messages from the Inside? Multiculturalism in Contemporary Australian Children's Literature." *Lion and the Unicorn* 27, no. 2: 235–50.

Pearson, Lucy. 2013. *The Making of Modern Children's Literature in Britain: Publishing and Criticism in the 1960s and 1970s*. London: Routledge.

Pendlebury, David. 1974. Afterword to *The Walled Garden of Truth*, by Hakim Sanai, translated and abridged by David Pendlebury, 53–74. London: Octagon Press.

Perreau, Bruno. 2014. *The Politics of Adoption: Gender and the Making of French Citizenship*. Translated by Deke Dusinberre. Cambridge, MA: MIT Press. Originally published as *Penser l'adoption: Éthique et philosophie morale* (Paris: Presses Universitaires de France, 2012).

Perrot, Jean. 1991. *Art baroque, art d'enfance*. Nancy: Presses Universitaires de Nancy.

Pescosolido, Bernice A., Elizabeth Grauerholz, and Melissa A. Milkie. 1997. "Culture and Conflict: The Portrayal of Blacks in US Children's Picture Books through the Mid-and-Late-Twentieth Century." *American Sociological Review* 62, no. 3: 443–64.

Peters, Henk. 1996. "Postmodernist Poetics in Children's Literature." In *AUETSA 96, I–II: Southern African Studies*, edited by Hermann Wittenberg and Loes Nas, 207–11. Bellville: University of Western Cape Press.

Peters, Julie Anne. 2004. *Luna*. Boston: Little, Brown.

Pexman, Penny, and Melanie Glenwright. 2007. "How Do Typically Developing Children Grasp the Meaning of Verbal Irony?" *Journal of Neurolinguistics* 20:178–96.

Pfister, Marc. 1992. *The Rainbow Fish*. Zürich: NordSüd Verlag.

Philbrick, Rodman. 2001. *Freak the Mighty*. New York: Blue Sky.

Pinsent, Pat. 2005. "Language, Genres and Issues: the Socially Committed Novel." In *Modern Children's Literature: An Introduction*, edited by Kimberley Reynolds, 191–208. New York: Macmillan.

Piper, Andrew. 2012. *Book Was There: Reading in Electronic Times*. Chicago: University of Chicago Press.

Place, François. 1999. *The Last Giants*. Translated by William Rodarmor. London: Chrysalis Children's Books. Originally published as *Les derniers géants* (Tournai: Casterman, 1992).

Plato. 1966. *The Republic*. Cambridge: Cambridge University Press.

Poe, Edgar A. 1850. "The Poetic Principle." *Home Journal* 238, no. 36 (August): 1–6.

Poindexter, Cynthia Cannon. 1999. "Promises in the Plague: Passage of the Ryan White Comprehensive AIDS Resources Emergency Act as a Case Study for Legislative Action." *Health & Social Work* 24, no. 1 (February): 35–41.

Poland, Owen. 2016. "Cao Wenxuan Becomes First Chinese Writer to Receive Anderson Award." China Global Television Network. YouTube, August 21, 2016. www.youtube.com/watch?v=26VbpjYbsfg.

Polkinghome, Donald. 2004. *Practice and the Human Sciences: The Case for a Judgement-Based Practice of Care*. New York: State University of New York Press.

Poole, Robert P. 2011. "What Became of the Taíno?" *Smithsonian Magazine*, October 2011.

Porter, Eleanor H. (1913) 1946. *Pollyanna: The Glad Book*. London: Harrap.

Porter, James. 1997. "Foreword." In *The Body and Physical Difference: Discourses of Disability*, edited by David Mitchell and Sharon Snyder, xiii–xiv. Ann Arbor: University of Michigan Press.

Postman, Neil. 1994. *The Disappearance of Childhood*. New York: Delacorte.

Potter, Beatrix. 1902. *The Tale of Peter Rabbit*. London: Penguin.

Power, Natsu Onoda. 2009. *God of Comics: Osamu Tezuka and the Creation of Post–World War II Manga*. Jackson: University Press of Mississippi.

Prelutsky, Jack. 1984. *New Kid on the Block*. New York: Greenwillow.

Prince, Gerald. 1987. *Dictionary of Narratology*. Lincoln: University of Nebraska Press.

Propp, Vladimir. (1928) 1968. *Morphology of the Folktale*. 2nd ed. Revised and edited by Louis A. Wagner. Translated by Laurence Scott. Austin: University of Texas Press.

Puenzo, Lucía, dir. 2007. *XXY*. Historia Cinematográficas Cinemania.

Pullman, Philip. 1995a. *The Golden Compass*. London: Yearling.

———. 1995b. *Northern Lights*. London: Scholastic.

———. 1997. *The Subtle Knife*. London: Scholastic.

———. 2000. *The Amber Spyglass*. London: Scholastic.

Quart, Alissa. 2003. *Branded: The Buying and Selling of Teenagers*. London: Random House.

Quenchua, Douglas. 2014. "Is E-reading to Your Toddler Story Time, or Simply Screen Time?" *New York Times*, October 11, 2014.

Radway, Janice A. 1984. *Reading the Romance: Women, Patriarchy and Popular Literature*. Chapel Hill: University of North Carolina Press.

———. 1997. *A Feeling for Books: The Book-of-the-Month Club, Literary Taste, and Middle-Class Desire*. Chapel Hill: University of North Carolina Press.

Rajewsky, Irina O. 2002. *Intermedialität*. Tübingen: Francke.

———. 2010. "Border Talks: The Problematic Status of Media Borders in the Current Debate about Intermediality." In *Media Borders, Multimodality and Intermediality*, edited by Lars Elleström, 51–68. Basingstoke: Palgrave Macmillan.

Rana, Marion. 2011. "'The Less You Lot Have ter Do with These Foreigners, the Happier Yeh'll Be': Cultural and National Otherness in J.K. Rowling's *Harry Potter* Series." *International Research in Children's Literature* 4, no. 1: 45–58.

Rand, Erica. 1995. *Barbie's Queer Accessories*. Durham, NC: Duke University Press.

Ransome, Arthur. 1930. *Swallows and Amazons*. London: Cape.

———. 1937. *We Didn't Mean to Go to Sea*. London: Cape.

Raskin, Ellen. 1966. *Nothing Ever Happens on My Block*. New York: Atheneum.

Rasmussen, Bonnie. 1987. "Irony in Picture Books: Some Examples." *Orana* 23, no. 4 (November): 180–86.

Ratelle, Amy. 2014. *Animality and Children's Literature and Film*. New York: Palgrave Macmillan.

Raud, Piret. 2009. *Härra Linnu lugu* [Mister Bird's story]. Tallinn: Tammerraamat.

Ray, Sukumar, and Satyajit Ray. 1997. *Select Nonsense of Sukumar Ray*. Translated by Sukanta Chaudhuri. New Delhi: Oxford University Press.

———. 2007. "Article Twenty-One." In *The Tenth Rasa: An Anthology of Indian Nonsense*, edited by Michael Heyman, with Sumanyu Satpathy and Anushka Ravishankar, 14. New Delhi: Penguin.

Ray, Sukumar. 2018. *Hajabarala*. Createspace Independent Publishing Platform.

Reese, Debbie. 2017. "John Smelcer's Stealing Indians as a Finalist for the PEN Center USA 2017?" American Indians in Children's Literature, August 2017. https://americanindiansinchildrensliterature.blogspot.com.

———. 2018. "Winners of 2018 American Indian Library Association's Youth Literature Award!" American Indians in Children's Literature, February 2018. https://americanindiansinchildrensliterature.blogspot.com.

Reeve, Philip. 2001–6. *Mortal Engines Quartet*. New York: Scholastic Press.

Reid-Walsh, Jacqueline. 2012. "Activity and Agency in Historical 'Playable Media.'" *Journal of Children and Media* 6, no. 2: 164–81.

———. 2016. "Modding as Making: Religious Flap Books Created by Eighteenth and Nineteenth Century Anglo American Girls." In *Girlhood Studies and the Politics of Place: Contemporary Paradigms for Research*, edited by Claudia Mitchell and Carrie Rentschler, 195–211. New York: Berghahn.

———. 2018a. *Interactive Books: Playful Media before Pop-Ups*. New York: Routledge.

———. 2018b. "Review of *When We Were Alone* by David A. Robertson and Julie Flett." *Book 2.0* 8, nos. 1–2: 149–52.

Reimer, Mavis. 2014. "Transnational Literary Studies, National Child Subjects." *Barnelitterært Forskningstidsskrift* 5, no. 1. doi:10.3402/blft.v5.25170.

Renaud, Catherine. 2007. *Les "incroyabilicieux" mondes de Ponti: Une etude du double lectorat dans l'oeuvre de Claude Ponti*. Uppsala: Uppsala University Press.

Repp, Charles. 2012. "What's Wrong with Didacticism?" *British Journal of Aesthetics* 52, no. 3 (July): 271–86.

Rey, H. A. 1941. *Curious George*. Boston: Houghton Mifflin.

Reynolds, Jason, and Brendan Kiely. 2015. *All American Boys*. New York: Atheneum.

Reynolds, Kimberley. 2007. *Radical Children's Literature: Future Visions and Aesthetic Transformations in Juvenile Fiction*. Basingstoke: Palgrave Macmillan.

———. 2008. "Families Forever? Changing Families in Children's Fiction." In *The Cambridge Companion to Children's Literature*, edited by M. O. Grenby and Andrea Immel, 193–208. Cambridge: Cambridge University Press.

———. 2016. *Left Out: The Forgotten Tradition of Radical Publishing for Children in Britain: 1910–1949*. Oxford: Oxford University Press.

Richardson, Alan. 1990. "Colonialism, Race, and Lyric Irony in Blake's 'The Little Black Boy.'" *Papers on Language and Literature* 26, no. 2 (Spring): 233–48.

———. 1994. *Literature, Education, and Romanticism: Reading as Social Practice, 1780–1832*. Cambridge: Cambridge University Press.

Richardson, Bill. 2000. *After Hamelin*. Toronto: Annick Press.

Richardson, Justin, Peter Parnell, and Henry Cole. 2005. *And Tango Makes Three*. New York: Simon & Schuster.

Richardson, Michael. 2016. *Gestures of Testimony: Torture, Trauma, and Affect in Literature*. London: Bloomsbury.

Richardson, Robert. 1875. *The Boys of Springdale*. Edinburgh: William Oliphant.

Richardson, Samuel. 1740. *Pamela*. London: Printed for C. Rivington and J. Osborn.

Ricoeur, Paul. 1990. *Time and Narrative*. Chicago: University of Chicago Press.

———. 2004. *Memory, History, Forgetting*. Translated by Kathleen Blamey and David Pellauer. Chicago: University of Chicago Press.

Ringgold, Faith. 1991. *Tar Beach*. New York: Crown.

Rippl, Gabriele, ed. 2015. *Handbook of Intermediality: Literature —Image—Sound—Music*. Berlin: De Gruyter.

Ritvo, Harriet. 1986. "Pride and Pedigree: The Evolution of the Victorian Dog Fancy." *Victorian Studies* 29, no. 2: 227–53.

Rivera, Tomás. 1971. *. . . y no se lo tragó la tierra* [. . . and the earth did not devour him]. Berkeley, CA: Quinto Sol.

Rivers, Christopher. 1994. *Face Value: Phyisognomical Thought and the Legible Body in Marivaux, Lavater, Balzac, Gautier, and Zola*. Madison: University of Wisconsin Press.

Robertson, David, and Julie Frett. 2016. *When We Are Alone*. Winnipeg: Portage and Main Press.

Robinson, Joanna. 2016. "How Pacific Islanders Helped Disney's *Moana* Finds Its Way." *Vanity Fair*, November 16, 2016.

Robson, Catherine. 2001. *Men in Wonderland: The Lost Girlhood of the Victorian Gentleman*. Princeton, NJ: Princeton University Press.

Robson, Eleanor. 2007. "The Clay Tablet Book in Sumer, Assyria, and Babylonia." In *A Companion to the History of the Book*, edited by Simon Eliot and Jonathan Rose, 67–83. Malden, MA: Blackwell.

Rochman, Hazel. 2003. "Beyond Political Correctness." In *Stories Matter: The Complexity of Cultural Authenticity in Children's Literature*, edited by Dana L. Fox and Kathy G. Short, 101–15. Urbana, IL: National Council of Teachers of English.

Rockwood, Roy. 1932. *Bomba the Jungle Boy and the Cannibals; or, Winning against Native Dangers*. New York: Cupples and Lion.

Rodgers, Mary. (1972) 2009. *Freaky Friday*. New York: Bowen.

Roemer, Cornelia. 2007. "The Papyrus Roll in Egypt, Greece, and Rome." In *A Companion to the History of the Book*, edited by Simon Eliot and Jonathan Rose, 84–94. Malden, MA: Blackwell.

Rofes, Eric. 2004. "Martyr-Target-Victim: Interrogating Narratives of Persecution and Suffering among Queer Youth." In *Youth and Sexualities: Pleasure, Subversion and Insubordination In and Out of Schools*, edited by Mary Louise Rasmussen, Eric Rofes, and Susan Talburt, 41–62. New York: Palgrave Macmillan.

Roffman, Deborah M. 2001. *Sex and Sensibility: The Thinking Parent's Guide to Talking Sense about Sex*. New York: Da Capo.

Romano, Aja. 2015. "J.K. Rowling's Take on Hermione Being Black Has Been a Long Time Coming." Daily Dot, December 21, 2015. www.dailydot.com.

Romines, Ann. 1995. "Preempting the Patriarch: The Problem of Pa's Stories in *Little House in the Big Woods*." *Children's Literature Association Quarterly* 20, no. 1: 15–18.

Rose, Jacqueline. 1984. *The Case of Peter Pan, or The Impossibility of Children's Fiction*. London: Macmillan.

Rosen, Judith. 1997. "Breaking the Age Barrier." *Publishers Weekly*, September 8, 1997, 28–31.

Rosenberg, Teya. 2008. "Transforming the Quotidian: Borges, Nesbit, and Threads of Influence." Paper presented at the Children's Literature Association Annual Conference, Illinois State University, Normal, IL, June 14, 2008.

Rosenwein, Barbara H., and Riccardo Cristiani. 2018. *What Is the History of Emotions?* Cambridge: Polity.

Rosoff, Meg. 2004. *How I Live Now*. London: Penguin.

Rossetti, Christina. (1872) 1968. *Sing-Song: A Nursery Rhyme Book*. Illustrated by Arthur Hughes. New York: Dover.

Rothschild, Nathalie. 2012. "Sweden's New Gender-Neutral Pronoun: *Hen*." Slate, April 11, 2012. www.slate.com.

Rousseau, Jean-Jacques. (1762) 1911. *Emile*. Translated by Barbara Foxley. London: Dent.

Rowling, J. K. 1997. *Harry Potter and the Philosopher's Stone*. London: Bloomsbury.

———. 1998. *Harry Potter and the Chamber of Secrets*. London: Bloomsbury.

———. 1999. *Harry Potter and the Prisoner of Azkaban*. London: Bloomsbury.

———. 2000. *Harry Potter and the Goblet of Fire*. London: Bloomsbury.

———. 2003. *Harry Potter and the Order of the Phoenix*. London: Bloomsbury.

———. 2005. *Harry Potter and the Half-Blood Prince*. London: Bloomsbury.

———. 2007. *Harry Potter and the Deathly Hallows*. London: Bloomsbury.

Roy, Modhumita. 2016. "Bruatlised Lives and Brutalist Realism: Black British Urban Fiction (1990s–2000s)." In *Cambridge Companion to British Black and Asian Literature*, edited by Deidre Osborne, 95–109. Cambridge: Cambridge University Press.

Royal Commission on Bilingualism and Biculturalism. 1965. *Preliminary Report*. Ottawa: Queen's Printer.

Rubin, Joan Shelley. 1992. *The Making of Middlebrow Culture*. Chapel Hill: University of North Carolina Press.

Rudd, David. 2004. "Theorising and Theories: The Conditions of Possibility of Children's Literature." In *International Companion Encyclopedia of Children's Literature*, 2nd ed., edited by Peter Hunt, 30–43. London: Routledge.

———. 2010. "Children's Literature and the Return to Rose." *Children's Literature Association Quarterly* 35, no. 3: 290–310.

———. 2013. *Reading the Child in Children's Literature: An Heretical Approach*. New York: Palgrave Macmillan.

Rudman, Masha Kabakow. 2006. "Multiculturalism." In *The Oxford Encyclopedia of Children's Literature*, vol. 3, edited by Jack Zipes, 111–13. New York: Oxford University Press.

Rushdie, Salman. 1990. *Haroun and the Sea of Stories*. London: Granta.

———. 1991. *Imaginary Homelands: Essays and Criticism 1981–1991*. London: Granta.

Rushton, Rosie. 2009. *Love, Lies and Lizzie*. London: Piccadilly Press.

Ruwe, Donelle, ed. 2005. *Culturing the Child, 1690–1914: Essays in Memory of Mitzi Myers*. Lanham, MD: Scarecrow Press.

Rybczynski, Witold. 1986. *Home: A Short History of an Idea*. New York: Viking.

Saguisag, Lara. 2018. *Incorrigibles and Innocents: Constructing Childhood and Citizenship in Progressive Era Comics*. New Brunswick, NJ: Rutgers University Press.

Said, Edward. 1978. *Orientalism*. New York: Pantheon.

———. 1993. *Culture and Imperialism*. New York: Vintage.

Saint Amour, Paul. 2018. "Weak Theory, Weak Modernism." *Modernism and Modernity* 3, no. 3 (August). https://modernismmodernity.org.

Sainte-Beuve, Charles-Augustin. 1881. "Qu'est-ce qu'un classique?" In *Causeries du Lundi*, 3rd ed. vol 3, pp. 38–55. Paris: Garnier Frères.

Salinger, J. D. 1951. *The Catcher in the Rye*. Boston: Little, Brown.

Sammond, Nicholas. 2015. *Birth of an Industry: Blackface Minstrelsy and the Rise of American Animation*. Durham, NC: Duke University Press.

Sánchez-Eppler, Karen. 2008. "Practicing for Print: The Hale Family's Manuscript Libraries." *Journal of the History of Childhood and Youth* 1, no. 2: 188–209.

———. 2011a. "Childhood." In *Keywords for Children's Literature*, edited by Philp Nel and Lissa Paul, 35–41. New York: New York University Press.

———. 2011b. "Marks of Possession: Methods for an Impossible Subject." *PMLA* 126, no. 1: 151–59.

Sanders, Chris, and Dean DeBois, dirs. 2010. *How to Train Your Dragon*. Dreamworks.

Sanders, Dori. 1990. *Clover*. New York: Random House.

Sanders, Joe Sutliff. 2015. "Almost Astronauts and the Pursuit of Reliability in Children's Nonfiction." *Children's Literature in Education* 46, no. 4: 378–93.

Sands-O'Connor, Karen. 2003. "Smashing Birds in the Wilderness: British Racial and Cultural Integration from Insider and Outsider Perspectives." *Papers* 13, no. 3: 43–50.

———. 2008. *Soon Come Home to This Island: West Indians in British Children's Literature*. New York: Routledge.

Sanna, Francesca. 2016. *The Journey*. London: Flying Eye Books.

Sarmiento, Thomas Xavier. 2014. "The Empire Sings Back: Glee's Queer Materialization of Filipina/o America." *MELUS* 39, no. 2: 211–34.

Sartre, Jean-Paul. (1946) 2004. "Existentialism Is a Humanism." Translated by Philip Mairet. In *Reading for Philosophical Inquiry: A Brief Introduction*, edited by Lee Archie and John G. Archie, 278–302. Open-source textbook. https://philosophy.lander.edu.

Satrapi, Marjane. 2003. *Persepolis*. New York: Pantheon.

Saxton, Ruth O., ed. 1998. *The Girl: Constructions of the Girl in Contemporary Fiction by Women*. New York: St. Martin's.

Sayers, Francis Clarke, and Charles M. Weisenberg. 1965. "Walt Disney Accused." *Horn Book*. Accessed October 1, 2016. www.hbook.com.

Schachner, Judy. 2003. *Skippyjon Jones*. New York: Dutton.

Schechner, Richard. 2013. *Performance Studies: An Introduction*. 3rd ed. New York: Routledge.

Scheffler, H. W. 1985. "Filiation and Affiliation." *Man* 20, no. 1: 1–21.

Scherer, Lexie. 2015. "British Ethnic Minority Children's Meaning-Making of Transnational Belonging/s in the Primary School." *Transnational Social Review* 5, no. 2: 131–44.

Schiller, Friedrich. (1793) 2016. *On the Aesthetic Education of Man*. New York: Penguin Books.

Schmidt, Annie M. G. (1971) 2010. *Pluk van de Petteflet*. Amsterdam: Querido.

———. 2011. *Tow-Truck Pluck*. London: Pushkin Children's Books.

Schmidt-Wullfen, Wulf. 2012. *Ten Little Niggers: Racial Discrimination in Children's Books*. London: Lit Verlag.

Schmiesing, Ann. 2014. *Disability, Deformity and Disease in the Grimms' Fairy Tales*. Detroit: Wayne State University Press.

Schneider, Ana-Karina. 2014. "International Contexts (Europe): The Romanian Context; Between Realism and Postmodernism." In *The 1980s: A Decade of Contemporary British Fiction*, edited by Emily Horton and Philip Tew, 203–23. London: Bloomsbury.

Schodt, Frederik L. (1983) 1986. *Manga! Manga! The World of Japanese Comics*. Rev. ed. Tokyo: Kodansha International.

Schoenberg, Nara. 2016. "Slavery in Children's Books: What Works?" *Chicago Tribune*, February 15, 2016.

Schore, Allan N. 1994. *Affect Regulation and the Origin of the Self: The Neurobiology of Emotional Development*. Hillsdale, NJ: Lawrence Erlbaum Associates.

Schwartz, Elaine G. 1995. "Crossing Borders/Shifting Paradigms: Multiculturalism and Children's Literature." *Harvard Educational Review* 65, no. 4: 634–51.

Schwebel, Sara L. 2016. "The Limits of Agency for Children's Literature Scholars." *Jeunesse* 8, no. 1: 278–90.

Schwenke-Wyile, Andrea. 2003. "The Value of Singularity in First- and Restricted Third-Person Engaging Narration." *Children's Literature* 31:116–41.

Schwimmer, Eric, John R. Clammer, and Sylvie Poirier, eds. 2004. *Figured Worlds: Ontological Obstacles in Intercultural Relations*. Toronto: University of Toronto Press.

Schwyzer, Philip. 2016. "Late Losses and the Temporality of Early Modern Nostalgia." *Parergon* 33, no. 2: 97–113.

Sciamma, Céline, dir. 2011. *Tomboy*. Arte France Cinema.

Scieszka, Jon, and Lane Smith. 1992. *The Stinky Cheese Man and Other Fairly Stupid Tales*. New York: Viking Penguin.

Sealander, Judith. 2003. *The Failed Century of the Child: Governing America's Young in the Twentieth Century*. New York: Cambridge University Press.

Sedgwick, Eve Kosofsky. 1993. *Tendencies*. Durham, NC: Duke University Press.

———. 2003. *Touching Feeling: Affect, Pedagogy, Performativity*. Durham, NC: Duke University Press.

Sedgwick, Eve Kosofsky, and Adam Frank. 1995. "Shame in the Cybernetic Fold: Reading Silvan Tomkins." *Critical Inquiry* 21, no. 2: 496–522.

Seed, Patricia. 2001. *American Pentimento: The Invention of Indians and the Pursuit of Riches*. Minneapolis: University of Minnesota Press.

Ségur, Sophie, Comtesse de. 1858. *Les malheurs de Sophie*. Project Gutenberg. Accessed December 23, 2016. www.gutenberg.org.

Seibert, Ernst. 2007. "Jugendliteratur in transkultureller Sicht. Anmerkungen zu Kanonfragen einer Literatur mit verminderter Halbwertszeit." In *Der Kanon—Perspektiven, Erweiterungen und Revisionen*, edited by Jürgen Struger, 461–73. Vienna: Praesens.

Seiter, Ellen. 1993. *Sold Separately: Children and Parents in Consumer Culture*. New Brunswick, NJ: Rutgers University Press.

Selick, Henry, dir. 2009. *Coraline*. Laika.

Selznick, Brian. 2007. *The Invention of Hugo Cabret*. New York: Scholastic.

———. 2008. "Caldecott Medal Acceptance." The Invention of Hugo Cabret, December 20, 2011. www.theinventionofhugocabret.com.

Sendak, Maurice. 1963. *Where the Wild Things Are*. New York: Harper & Row.

———. 1970. *In the Night Kitchen*. New York: Harper & Row.

———. 1993. *We Are All in the Dumps with Jack and Guy*. New York: HarperCollins.

Sewell, Anna. (1887) 2009. *Black Beauty*. Harmondsworth: Puffin.

Sewell, Elizabeth. 1952. *The Field of Nonsense*. London: Chatto & Windus.

Shakespeare, William. 1985. *The Tempest*. Edited by Frank Kermode. London: Methuen.

Shaoyang, Lin. 2013. "Japanese Postmodern Philosophy's Turn to Historicity." *Journal of Japanese Philosophy* 1:111–35.

Shavit, Zohar. 1986. *The Poetics of Children's Literature*. Athens: University of Georgia Press.

———. 1999. "The Concept of Childhood and Children's Folktales: Test Case—'Little Red Riding Hood.'" In *The Classic Fairy Tales*, edited by Maria Tatar, 317–32. New York: Norton.

———. 2005. *A Past without a Shadow: Constructing the Past in German Books for Children*. New York: Routledge.

Shelley, Mary. (1818) 1969. *Frankenstein, or The Modern Prometheus*. Edited by M. K. Joseph. New York: Oxford University Press.

Shen, Lisa Chu. 2019. "Femininity and Gender in Contemporary Chinese School Stories: The Case of *Tomboy Dai An*." *Children's Literature in Education* 50, no. 3 (September): 278–96.

Shortsleeve, Kevin. 2007. "The Politics of Nonsense: Civil Unrest, Otherness and National Mythology in Nonsense Literature." PhD diss., University of Oxford.

Shraya, Vivek. 2014. *God Loves Hair*. Vancouver: Arsenal Pulp Press.

———. 2016. *The Boy & the Bindi*. Illustrated by Rajni Perera. Vancouver: Arsenal Press.

Shriver, Maria. 2001. *What's Wrong with Timmy?* Illustrated by Sandra Speidel. Boston: Little, Brown.

Sicart, Miguel. 2014. *Play Matters*. Cambridge, MA: MIT Press.

Silver, Carole G. 2008. "Animal Bride, Animal Groom." In *The Greenwood Encyclopedia of Fairy Tales*, vol. 1, edited by Donald Haase, 40–42. Wesport, CT: Greenwood.

Silverstein, Shel. 1974. *Where the Sidewalk Ends*. New York: Harper & Row.

Sima, Jessica. 2017. *Not Quite Narwhal*. New York: Simon & Schuster.

Simpson, Leanne Betasamosake. 2014a. "Land as Pedagogy: Nishnaabeg Intelligence and Rebellious Transformation." *Decolonization: Indigeneity, Education, and Society* 3, no. 3: 1–25.

———. 2014b. "Not Murdered, Not Missing: Rebelling against Colonial Gender Violence." *Leanne Betasamosake Simpson* (blog), March 5, 2014. www.leannesimpson.ca.

Sims, Rudine. 1982. *Shadow and Substance: Afro-American Experience in Contemporary Children's Fiction*. Urbana, IL: National Council of Teachers of English.

Sinclair, Catherine. 1838. *Holiday House*. Roehampton Digital Collection. Accessed December 24, 2016. http://urweb.roehampton.ac.uk.

Singer, Isaac Bashevis. 1978. "Nobel Banquet Speech." Nobelprize.org. Accessed April 17, 2020. http://nobelprize.org.

Singer, T. Benjamin. 2014. "Umbrella." *Transgender Studies Quarterly* 1, nos. 1–2: 259–61.

Sipe, Lawrence R. 1998. "How Picture Books Work: A Semiotically Framed Theory of Text-Picture Relationships." *Children's Literature in Education* 29, no. 2: 97–108.

Sipe, Lawrence R., and Sylvia Pantaleo, eds. 2008. *Postmodern Picturebooks: Play, Parody, and Self-Referentiality*. New York: Routledge.

SIU Department of Africana Studies. 2018. "About the Sankofa Bird." Accessed March 23, 2018. http://cola.siu.edu.

Skarmeta, Antonio, and Alfonso Ruano. 2000. *The Composition*. Translated by Elisa Amado. Toronto: Groundwood.

Skjønsberg, Kari. 1998. "Døden i eldre norsk barnelitteratur. Var døden tabu?" *Bokvennen* 10, no. 1: 58–64.

Slade, Bonnie L. 2008. "Intersectionality." In *International Encyclopedia of the Social Sciences*, 2nd ed., edited by William A. Darity Jr., 114–16. Detroit: Macmillan Reference.

Slapin, Beverly. 2013. "Skippyjon Jones: Transforming a Racist Stereotype into an Industry." *De Colores: The Raza Experience in Books for Children* (blog), April 2013. http://decoloresreviews.blogspot.com.

Slapin, Beverly, and Doris Seale. 2006. *A Broken Flute: The Native Experience in Books for Children*. Lanham, MD: AltaMira Press.

Slemon, Stephen. 1987. "Monuments of Empire: Allegory/Counter-discourse/Post-colonial Writing." *Kunapipi* 9, no. 3: 1–16.

Slettan, Svein. 2013. "Ski Tracks in the Wilderness: Nature and Nation in Norwegian Young Adult Books from the 1930s." In *The Nation in Children's Literature*, edited by Christopher Kelen and Björn Sundmark, 23–37. New York: Routledge.

Slovic, Paul, Daniel Västfjäll, Arvid Erlandsson, and Robin Gregory. 2017. "Iconic Photographs and the Ebb and Flow of Empathetic Response to Humanitarian Disasters." *Proceedings of the National Academy of Sciences* 114, no. 4 (January): 640–44.

Small, David. 1988. *Imogene's Antlers*. New York: Dragonfly Books.

Smelcer, John E. 2016. *Stealing Indians*. Fredonia, NY: Leapfrog Press.

Smith, Cynthia Leitich. 2000. *Jingle Dancer*. New York: Morrow Junior Books.

Smith, Jacob. 2010. "The Books That Sing: Children's Phonograph Records, 1890–1930." *Journal of Children and Media* 4, no. 1: 90–108.

Smith, Katharine Capshaw. 2004. *Children's Literature of the Harlem Renaissance*. Bloomington: Indiana University Press.

Smith, Lane. 2010. *It's a Book*. New York: Roaring Brook Press.

Smith, William Jay. 1990. *Laughing Time: Collected Nonsense*. New York: Farrar, Straus and Giroux.

Smolderen, Thierry. (2000) 2014. *The Origins of Comics: From William Hogarth to Winsor McCay*. Translated by Bart Beaty and Nick Nguyen. Jackson: University Press of Mississippi.

Snell, Heather R. 2016. "Shifting Places." *Jeunesse: Young People, Texts, Cultures* 8, no. 1 (August): 1–19.

Snicket, Lemony. 1999. *The Bad Beginning*. New York: HarperCollins.

Solito, Auraeus, dir. 2007. *The Blossoming of Maximo Oliveros*. Cinemalaya.

Solomon, Andrew. 2012. "Theme from the Book: Identity." Far from the Tree. Accessed April 17, 2020. www.farfromthetree.com.

Sorby, Angela. 2005. *Schoolroom Poets: Childhood, Performance, and the Place of American Poetry, 1865–1917*. Durham, NH: University of New Hampshire Press.

———. 2017. "Conjuring Readers: Antebellum African American Children's Poetry." In *Who Writes for Black Children? African American Children's Literature before 1900*, edited by Katharine Capshaw and Anna Mae Duane, 3–21. Minneapolis: University of Minnesota Press.

Sorby, Angela, and Karen L. Kilcup, eds. 2014. *Over the River and through the Wood: An Anthology of Nineteenth-Century American Children's Poetry*. Baltimore: Johns Hopkins University Press.

Spinoza, Baruch. (1677) 1992. *The Ethics; Treatise on the Emendation of the Intellect; Selected Letters*. Translated by Samuel Shirley. Indianapolis: Hackett.

Spivak, Gayatri. 1985. "Can the Subaltern Speak? Speculations on Widow Sacrifice." In *Colonial Discourse and Postcolonial Theory: A Reader*, edited by Patrick Williams and Laura Chrisman, 66–111. Hemel Hempstead: Harvester Wheatsheaf.

Spufford, Margaret. 1985. *Small Books and Pleasant Histories: Popular Fiction and Its Readership in Seventeenth-Century England*. Cambridge: Cambridge University Press.

Spyri, Johanna. (1881) 1995. *Heidi: Heidi's Lehr- und Wanderjahre*. Würzberg: Arena.

———. 1881. *Heidis Lehr- und Wanderjahre*. Project Gutenberg. Accessed December 23, 2016. www.gutenberg.org.

Stanton, Andrew, dir. 2003. *Finding Nemo*. Pixar.

Starobinski, Jean. 1966. "The Idea of Nostalgia." Translated by Will Kemp. *Diogenes* 54:81–103.

St. Clair, William. 2007. *The Reading Nation in the Romantic Period*. Cambridge: Cambridge University Press.

Stearns, Peter N. 2009. *Childhood in World History*. New York: Routledge.

Stedman, Jane W. 1996. *W. S. Gilbert: A Classic Victorian and His Theatre*. Oxford: Oxford University Press.

Steedman, Carolyn. 1995. *Strange Dislocations: Childhood and the Idea of Human Interiority, 1780–1930*. Cambridge, MA: Harvard University Press.

Steen, John. 2018. *Affect, Psychoanalysis, and American Poetry: This Feeling of Exaltation*. London: Bloomsbury Academic.

Stein, Gertrude. (1939) 1993. *The World Is Round*. New York: Barefoot Books.

Stein, Nancy L., Marc W. Hernandez, and Tom Trabasso. 2008. "Advances in Modelling Emotion and Thought: The Importance of Developmental, Online, and Multilevel Analyses." In *Handbook of Emotions*, 3rd ed., edited by Michael Lewis, Jeannette M. Haviland-Jones, and Lisa Feldman Barrett, 574–86. New York: Guilford Press.

Stephens, John. 1990. "Advocating Multiculturalism:

Migrants in Australian Children's Literature after 1972." *Children's Literature Association Quarterly* 15, no. 4: 180–85.

———. 1992. *Language and Ideology in Children's Fiction*. London: Longman.

———. 1996. "Multiculturalism in Recent Australian Children's Fiction: (Re-)constructing Selves through Personal and National Histories." In *Other Worlds, Other Lives*, vol. 3, edited by Myrna Machet, Sandra Olen, and Thomas van der Walt, 1–19. Pretoria: University of South Africa Press.

———. 2000. "Continuity, Fissure, or Dysfunction? From Settler Society to Multicultural Society in Australian Fiction." In *Voices of the Other: Children's Literature and the Postcolonial Context*, edited by Roderick McGillis, 55–70. New York: Garland.

———, ed. 2002. *Ways of Being Male: Representing Masculinities in Children's Literature and Film*. London: Routledge.

———. 2015. "Affective Strategies, Emotion Schemas, and Empathic Endings: Selkie Girls and a Critical Odyssey." *Papers: Explorations into Children's Literature* 23, no. 1: 1–16.

Stephens, John, and Robyn McCallum. 1998. *Retelling Stories, Framing Culture*. New York: Garland.

Stephens, John, and Rolf Romøren. 2002. "Representing Masculinities in Norwegian and Australian Young Adult Fiction: A Comparative Study." In *Ways of Being Male: Representing Masculinities in Children's Television and Film*, edited by John Stephens, 216–33. New York: Routledge.

Stevens, Paul. 1984. "Milton and the Icastic Imagination." *Milton Studies* 20:43–71.

Stevenson, Deborah. 1994. "'If You Read This Last Sentence, It Won't Tell You Anything': Postmodernism, Self-Referentiality, and *The Stinky Cheese Man*." *Children's Literature Association Quarterly* 19, no. 1: 32–34.

———. 1997. "Sentiment and Significance: The Impossibility of Recovery in the Children's Literature Canon, or, The Drowning of *The Water-Babies*." *Lion and the Unicorn* 21, no. 1: 112–30.

Stevenson, Edward-Prime. (1891) 2016. *Left to Themselves*. Richmond, VA: Valancourt Books.

Stevenson, Robert Louis. (1883) 1998. *Treasure Island*. Oxford: Oxford University Press.

———. 1885. *A Child's Garden of Verses*. London: Longman, Green.

Stewart, Susan. 1979. *Nonsense: Aspects of Intertextuality in Folklore and Literature*. Baltimore: Johns Hopkins University Press.

———. (1984) 1993. *On Longing: Narratives of the Miniature, the Gigantic, the Souvenir, the Collection*. Durham, NC: Duke University Press.

St. James, James. 2007. *Freak Show*. New York: Speak.

Stockton, Kathryn Bond. 2009. *The Queer Child, or Growing Sideways in the Twentieth Century*. Durham, NC: Duke University Press.

Stoler, Ann Laura. 1995. *Race and the Education of Desire: Foucault's History of Sexuality and the Colonial Order of Things*. Durham, NC: Duke University Press.

Stone, Jon. (1971) 1999. *The Monster at the End of This Book*. Illustrated by Michael Smollin. New York: Golden Books.

Stonequist, Everett V. 1935. "The Problem of the Marginal Man." *American Journal of Sociology* 41, no. 1 (July): 1–12.

Storey, John. 2005. "Postmodernism." In *New Keywords: A Revised Vocabulary of Culture and Society*, edited by Tony Bennett, Lawrence Grossberg, and Meaghan Morris, 269–72. Malden, MA Blackwell.

Stork, Francisco X. 2009. *Marcelo and the Real World*. New York: Scholastic.

Storytoy. 2017. My Very Hungry Caterpillar AR. App for iPad.

Stott, John. 1982. "'It's Not What You Expect': Teaching Irony to Third Graders." *Children's Literature in Education* 13:153–63.

Stowe, Harriet Beecher. (1852) 2002. *Uncle Tom's Cabin*. Oxford: Oxford University Press.

Strachey, Edward. 1888. "Nonsense as a Fine Art." *Quarterly Review* 167 (July–October): 335–65.

Stryker, Susan, and Paisley Currah. 2014. "Introduction." *Transgender Studies Quarterly* 1, no. 12: 1–18.

Stuve-Bodeen, Stephanie. 1998. *We'll Paint the Octopus Red*. Illustrated by Pam DeVito Woodbine. Bethesda, MD: Woodbine House.

Suarez, Michael S. 2009. "Towards a Bibliometric Analysis of the Surviving Record, 1701–1800." In *The Cambridge History of the Book in Britain*, vol. 5, edited by S. J. Suarez, F. Michael, and Michael L. Turner, 37–65. Cambridge: Cambridge University Press.

Suhr-Sytsma, Mandy. 2014. "Spirits from Another Realm, Activists in Their Own Right: The Figure of the Yankton/Romantic Child in Zitkala-Sa's Work." *Children's Literature* 42:136–68.

Sullivan, Tara. 2013. *Golden Boy*. New York: G. P. Putnam's Sons.

———. 2016. *The Bitter Side of Sweet*. New York: G. P. Putnam's Sons.

Sunderland, Jane. 2004. *Gendered Discourses*. Basingstoke: Palgrave Macmillan.

Sung, Yoo Kyung. 2012. "Hearing the Voices of Comfort Women: Confronting Historical Trauma in Korean Children's Literature." *Bookbird: A Journal of International Children's Literature* 50, no. 1: 20–30.

Sutherland, Robert. 1985. "Hidden Persuaders: Political Ideologies in Literature for Children." *Children's Literature in Education* 16, no. 3: 143–57.

Sutton-Smith, Brian. 1997. *The Ambiguity of Play*. Cambridge, MA: Harvard University Press.

Svendsen, Kester. 1956. *Milton and Science*. Cambridge, MA: Harvard University Press.

Svensson, Sonja. 1999. "Dødsspolare, skuggmän och förlorade fäder." In *Forankring og fornying*, edited by Eli Flatekval, 107–21. Oslo: Cappelen Akademisk.

Swift, Jonathan. (1726) 1967. *Gulliver's Travels*. New York: Penguin.

Tabbert, Reinbert. 1999. Personal communication with William Moebius, Paris.

Taher, Walid. 2009. *Al-Nuqtah al-Sawda* [The black dot]. Madinat Nasr, al-Qahirah: Dar al-Shruruq.

Taketani, Etsuko. 1999. "Spectacular Child Bodies: The Sexual Politics of Cross-Dressing and Calisthenics in the Writings of Eliza Leslie and Catharine Beecher." *Lion and the Unicorn* 23, no. 3: 355–72.

Talley, Lee. 2011. "Young Adult." In *Keywords for Children's Literature*, edited by Philip Nel and Lissa Paul, 228–32. New York: New York UP.

Tan, Shaun. 2006. *The Arrival*. Melbourne: Lothian.

———. 2010. *The Lost Thing*. Sydney: Lothian Books.

Tan, Teri. 2017. "Children's Books in China 2017: An Overview of the Children's Book Market in China." *Publishers Weekly*, March 17, 2017. www.publishersweekly.com.

Tapscott, Don. 1997. *Growing Up Digital: The Rise of the Net Generation*. New York: McGraw Hill.

Tatar, Maria, ed. 1999. *The Classic Fairy Tales*. New York: Norton.

———. 2003. *The Hard Facts of the Grimms' Fairy Tales*. 2nd ed. Princeton, NJ: Princeton University Press.

———, ed. 2017. *The Classic Fairy Tales*. 2nd ed. New York: Norton.

Taylor, Jane, and Ann Taylor. (1806) 1807. *Rhymes for the Nursery*. London: Darton and Harvey.

Terada, Rei. 2001. *Feeling in Theory: Emotion after the "Death of the Subject."* Cambridge, MA: Harvard University Press.

Tezuka, Osamu. (1949) 1993. "Kiseki no mori no monogatari" [Story of the miracle forest]. In *Mori no yonkenshi*, 121–216. Toyko: Kôdansha.

Thacker, Deborah. 2000. "Disdain or Ignorance? Literary Theory and the Absence of Children's Literature." *Lion and the Unicorn* 26, no. 1: 1–17.

Thiel, Elizabeth. 2008. *The Fantasy of Family: Nineteenth-Century Children's Literature and the Myth of the Domestic Ideal*. Children's Literature and Culture. New York: Routledge.

Thom, Kai Cheng. 2016. *Fierce Femmes and Notorious Liars: A Dangerous Trans Girl's Confabulous Memoir*. Montreal: Metonymy Press.

Thomas, Angie. 2017. *The Hate U Give*. New York: Balzer and Bray.

Thomas, Ebony Elizabeth. 2019. *The Dark Fantastic: Race and the Imagination from Harry Potter to the Hunger Games*. New York: New York University Press.

Thomas, Joseph T. 2007. *Poetry's Playground: The Culture of Contemporary American Children's Poetry*. Detroit: Wayne State University Press.

Thomas, Keith. 1983. *Man and the Natural World: Changing Attitudes in England 1500–1800*. London: Allen Lane.

Thompson, Kay. 1955. *Eloise*. Illustrated by Hilary Knight. New York: Simon & Schuster.

Thomson-Wohlgemuth, Gaby. 2009. *Translation under State Control: Books for Young People in the German Democratic Republic*. New York: Routledge.

Thongthiraj, Rahpee. 2006. "Negotiated Identities and Female Personal Space in Thai American Adolescent Literature." *Lion and the Unicorn* 30:234–49.

Thor, Annika. 2014. *Flickan från långt borta*. Illustrated by Maria Jönsson. Stockholm: Bonnier Carlsen.

Thunberg, Greta. 2019. *No One Is Too Small to Make a Difference*. London: Penguin Random House UK.

Tiffin, Jessica. 2008. "Lewis Carroll." In *The Greenwood Encyclopedia of Fairy Tales*, vol. 1, edited by Donald Haase, 161–62. Westport, CT: Greenwood.

Tigges, Wim. 1987. "The Limerick: The Sonnet of Nonsense?" In *Explorations in the Field of Nonsense*, edited by Wim Tigges, 118–33. Amsterdam: Rodopi.

———. 1988. *An Anatomy of Literary Nonsense*. Amsterdam: Rodopi.

Tilley, Carol L. 2012. "Seducing the Innocent: Fredric Wertham and the Falsifications That Helped Condemn Comics." *Information & Culture* 47, no. 4: 383–413.

———. 2015. "Children's Print Culture: Tradition and Innovation." In *The Routledge International Handbook of Children, Adolescents and Media*, edited by Dafna Lemish, 87–94. New York: Routledge.

Tobin, Joseph, ed. 2004. *Pikachu's Global Adventure: The Rise and Fall of Pokémon*. Durham, NC: Duke University Press.

Todd, Dennis. 1995. *Imagining Monsters: Miscreations of the Self in Eighteenth-Century England*. Chicago: University of Chicago Press.

Todorov, Tzvetan. 1975. *The Fantastic: A Structural Approach to a Literary Genre*. Ithaca, NY: Cornell University Press.

———. 1990. *Genres in Discourse*. Translated by Catherine Porter. London: Cambridge University Press.

Tolkien, J. R. R. 1947. "On Fairy-Stories." In *Essays Presented to Charles Williams*, edited by C. S. Lewis, 38–89. London: Oxford University Press.

Tomkins, Silvan. 1984. "Affect Theory." In *Approaches to Emotion*, edited by Klaus R. Scherer and Paul Ekman, 163–95. Hillside, NJ: Psychology Press.

———. 1995. *Exploring Affect: The Selected Writings of Silvan S. Tomkins*. Cambridge: Cambridge University Press.

———. 1961. *Affect, Imagery, Consciousness*. New York: Springer.

———. 2008. *Affect, Imagery, Consciousness: The Complete Edition*. New York: Springer.

Tosenberger, Catherine. 2008. "Homosexuality at the Online Hogwarts: Harry Potter Slash FanFiction." *Children's Literature* 36:185–207.

———. 2014. "Mature Poets Steal: Children's Literature and the Unpublishability of Fanfiction." *Children's Literature Association Quarterly* 39, no. 1: 4–27.

Townsend, John Rowe. 1971. *A Sense of Story: Essays on Contemporary Writers for Children*. London: Longman Young Books.

———. (1971) 1990. "Standards of Criticism for Children's Literature." In *Children's Literature: Critical Concepts in Literary and Cultural Studies*, edited by Peter Hunt, 86–97. London: Routledge.

Traavik, Ingjerd. 2012. *På liv og død: Tabu i bildeboka: Analyser og refleksjoner*. Oslo: Gyldendal Akademisk.

Tribunella, Eric L. 2010. *Melancholia and Maturation: The Use of Trauma in American Children's Literature*. Knoxville: University of Tennessee Press.

Trimble, Michael R. 2007. *The Soul in the Brain: The Cerebral Basis of Language, Art and Belief*. Baltimore: Johns Hopkins University Press.

Trimmer, Sarah. 1791. *The Fabulous Histories: Designed for the Instruction of Children, Respecting Their Treatment of Animals*. London: T. Bensley.

———. 1802a. *The Guardian of Education, a Periodical work; consisting of a practical essay on Christian education founded immediately on the Scriptures and the Sacred Offices of the Church of England: Memoirs of Modern Philosophers, and Extracts from their Writings; Extracts from Sermons and Other books relating to Religious Education; and a copious Examination of Modern Systems of Education, Children's Books, and Books for Young Persons/ Conducted by Mrs. Trimmer*. Vol. 1. London: J. Hatchard.

———. (1802b) 1976. "Observations on the Changes Which Have Taken Place in Books for Children and Young Persons." In *A Peculiar Gift: Nineteenth Century Writings on Books for Children*, edited by Lance Salway, 19–22. London: Kestrel.

———. 1803. *The Guardian of Education*. Vol. 2. London: J. Harchard.

———. 1804. *The Guardian of Education*. Vol. 3. London: J. Harchard.

———. 1805. *The Guardian of Education*. Vol. 4. London: F. C. and J. Rivington; J. Hatchard.

Trites, Roberta S. 2000. *Disturbing the Universe: Power and Repression in Adolescent Literature*. Iowa City: University of Iowa Press.

———. 2014. *Literary Conceptualizations of Growth: Metaphors and Cognition in Adolescent Literature*. Amsterdam: John Benjamins.

———. 2018. *Twenty-First-Century Feminisms in Children's and Adolescent Literature*. Jackson: University Press of Mississippi.

Trivizas, Eugene. 2001. *I teleftaia mavri gata*. Athens: Ellinika Grammata. Translated by Sandy Zervas as *The Last Black Cat* (London: Egmont Books, 2005).

Tuck, Eve, and K. Wayne Yang. 2014. "Unbecoming Claims: Pedagogies of Refusal in Qualitative Research." *Qualitative Inquiry* 20, no. 6: 811–18.

Tucker, Kathy. 2003. *The Seven Chinese Sisters*. Illustrated by Grace Lin. Morton Grove, IL: Albert Whitman.

Tucker, Nicholas. 1997. "Fairy Tales and Their Early Oponents: In Defence of Mrs Trimmer." In *Opening the Nursery Door: Reading, Writing and Childhood 1600–1900*, edited by Mary Hilton, Morag Styles, and Victor Watson, 104–16. London: Routledge.

Turchi, Peter. 2004. *Maps of the Imagination: The Writer as Cartographer*. San Antonio, TX: Trinity University Press.

Turner, Edith. 1990. "The Literary Roots of Victor Turner's Anthropology." In *Victor Turner and the Construction of Cultural Criticism*, edited by Kathleen Ashley, 163–69. Bloomington: Indiana University Press.

Turner, Ethel. (1894) 2003. *Seven Little Australians*. Caberwell: Penguin Group Australia.

Turner, Victor. 1969. *The Ritual Process*. Chicago: Aldine.

———. (1982) 1992. *From Ritual to Theatre: The Human Seriousness of Play*. New York: Performing Arts Journal Publications.

Tuttle, Carolyn. 1999. *Hard at Work in Factories and Mines: The Economics of Child Labor during the British Industrial Revolution*. Oxford: Westview Press.

Twain, Mark. (1876) 1976. *The Adventures of Tom Sawyer*. In *The Unabridged Mark Twain*, vol. 1, edited by Lawrence Teacher, 436–85. Philadelphia: Running Press.

———. 1884. *The Adventures of Huckleberry Finn*. London: Chatto & Windus.

———. (1897) 1989. "Hellfire Hotchkiss." In *Huck Finn and Tom Sawyer among the Indians and Other Unfinished Stories*, 109–33. Berkeley: University of California Press.

UNICEF. n.d. "UN Convention on the Rights of the Child in Child-Friendly Language." Poster. Accessed April 2020. https://sites.unicef.org.

———. 2019. "Under-Five Mortality." September 2019. https://data.unicef.org.

United Nations Permanent Forum on Indigenous Issues. 2007. "Indigenous People, Indigenous Voices." May 2007. www.un.org.

Utemorrah, Daisy, and Pat Torres. 1990. *Do Not Go Around the Edges*. Broome: Magabala.

Uther, Hans-Jörg. 2004. *The Types of International Folktales: A Classification and Bibliography Based on the System of Antti Aarne and Stith Thompson*. Helsinki: Suomalainen Tiedeakatemia, Academia Scientiarum Fennica.

Vail, Rachel. (2012) 2015. *Piggy Bunny*. Illustrated by Jeremy Tankard. New York: Feiwel & Friends.

Valk, Ülo. 2008. "Myth." In *The Greenwood Encyclopedia of Fairy Tales*, vol. 1, edited by Donald Haase, 652–56. Wesport, CT: Greenwood.

Vallone, Lynne. 2017. *Big and Small: A Cultural History of Extraordinary Bodies*. New Haven, CT: Yale University Press.

Van Allsburg, Chris. 1984. *The Mysteries of Harris Burdick*. Boston: Houghton Mifflin.

———. 1995. *Bad Day at Riverbend*. Boston: Houghton Mifflin.

Van der Linden, Sophie. 2000. *Claude Ponti*. Paris: Éditions Être.

van Loon, Hendrik Willem. 1921. *The Story of Mankind*. New York: Boni and Liveright.

Van Sant, Gus, dir. 2007. *Paranoid Park*. IFC Films.

Vargas, Deborah R., Nancy Raquel Mirabal, and Lawrence La Fountain-Stokes, eds. 2017. *Keywords for Latino/a Studies*. New York: New York University Press.

Vattimo, Gianni. (1985) 2008. *Art's Claim to Truth*. New York: Columbia University Press.

Velthuijs, Max. 2014. *Frog Is Frog*. London: Anderson Press.

Venuti, Lawrence. 1995. *The Translator's Invisibility: A History of Translation*. London: Routledge.

Vermeule, Blakey. 2010. *Why Do We Care about Literary Characters?* Baltimore: Johns Hopkins University Press.

Vermeulen, Pieter. 2015. *Contemporary Literature and the End of the Novel*. Basingstoke: Palgrave Macmillan.

Vey, Shauna. 2015. *Childhood and Nineteenth-Century American Theatre: The Work of the Marsh Troupe of Juvenile Actors*. Carbondale: Southern Illinois University Press.

Voipio, Myry. 2013. "Light, Love and Desire: The New Wave of Finnish Girls' Literature." *Girlhood Studies: An Interdisciplinary Journal* 6, no. 2 (Winter): 119–35.

Wakely-Mulroney, Katherine, and Louise Joy. 2017. *The Aesthetics of Children's Poetry: A Study of Children's Verse in English*. London: Routledge.

Walkerdine, Valerie. 1997. *Daddy's Girl: Young Girls and Popular Culture*. Cambridge, MA: Harvard University Press.

Wall, Barbara. (1991) 1994. *The Narrator's Voice: The Dilemma of Children's Fiction*. Houndmills: Macmillan.

Walsh, Jill Paton. 1973. "The Writer's Responsibility." *Children's Literature in Education* 10:30–36.

Walsh, Sue. 2011. "Irony and the Child." In *Children in Culture, Revisited*, edited by Karin Lesnik-Oberstein, 126–46. New York: Palgrave Macmillan.

———. 2016. "Gender and Irony: Children's Literature and Its Criticism." *Asian Women* 32, no. 2: 91–110.

Walshaw, Margaret. 2007. *Working with Foucault in Education*. Rotterdam: Sense.

Wang, Yinglin. 2011. *The Three Character Classic: A Bilingual Reader of China's ABCs*. Translated by Phebe Xu Gray. Paramus, NJ: Homa & Sekey Books.

Wang, Zhenghua. 2016. "Gender-Specific Textbook Targets Primary School Boys." *China Daily*, October 31, 2016. www.chinadaily.com.cn.

Wannamaker, Annette. 2008. *Boys in Children's Literature and Popular Culture: Masculinity, Abjection, and the Fictional Child*. New York: Routledge.

Wargo, Jon M. 2017. "At the Risk of 'Feeling Brown' in Gay YA: Machismo, Mariposas, and the Drag of Identity." In *Affect, Emotion, and Children's Literature: Representation and Socialisation in Texts for Children and Young Adults*, edited by Kristine Moruzi, Michelle J. Smith, and Elizabeth Bullen, 175–91. New York: Routledge.

Warner, Marina. 1994a. *From the Beast to the Blonde: On Fairy Tales and their Tellers*. London: Vintage.

———. 1994b. *Managing Monsters: Six Myths of Our Time—the 1994 Reith Lectures*. London: Vintage.

———. 2005. *Only Make Believe: Ways of Playing*. Catalog of the exhibition at Compton Verney, Warwickshire, March 25–June 5, 2005. Compton Verney: Compton Verney House Trust.

———. 2011. *Stranger Magic: Charmed States & the Arabian Nights*. London: Chatto & Windus.

Warner, Michael. 1993. *Fear of a Queer Planet: Queer Politics and Social Theory*. Minneapolis: University of Minnesota Press.

Warner, Sylvia Townsend. 1926. *Lolly Willowes*. New York: Viking.

Watson, Victor, ed. 2001. *The Cambridge Guide to Children's Books in English*. Cambridge: Cambridge University Press.

Watts, Isaac. (1715) 1789. *Divine Songs Attempted in Easie Language for the Use of Children*. London: H. & G. Mozley.

Weaver, Matthew. 2010. "Angela Merkel: German Multiculturalism Has 'Utterly Failed.'" *The Guardian*, October 17, 2010. www.theguardian.com.

Wegelius, Jakob. (2014) 2017. *The Murderer's Ape*. Translated by Peter Graves. London: Pushkin Children's Books.

Weikle-Mills, Courtney. 2011. "'My Book and Heart Shall Never Part': Reading Printing, and Circulation in the New England Primer." In *The Oxford Handbook of Children's Literature*, edited by Lynne Vallone and Julia Mickenberg, 411–31. Oxford: Oxford University Press.

Weinreich, Torben. 2000. *Children's Literature: Art or Pedagogy?* Frederiksberg: Roskilde University Press.

Weitzman, Lenore, Deborah Eifler, Elizabeth Hokada, and Catherine Ross. 1972. "Sex-Role Socialization in Picture Books for Preschool Children." *American Journal of Sociology* 77, no. 6: 1125–50.

Wekker, Gloria. 2016. *White Innocence: Paradoxes of Colonialism and Race*. Durham, NC: Duke University Press.

Wellek, René, and Austin Warren. (1949) 1963. *Theory of Literature*. 3rd ed. London: Peregrine.

Wells, Carolyn, ed. 1902. *A Nonsense Anthology*. New York: Scribner.

Wendell, Susan. 1996. *The Rejected Body: Feminist Philosophical Reflections on Disability*. New York: Routledge.

We Need Diverse Books. 2006. "Mission Statement." We Need Diverse Books. https://diversebooks.org.

Wesley, Saylesh. 2014. "Twin-Spirited Women: Sts'iyóye smestíyexw slhá:li." *Transgender Studies Quarterly* 1, no. 3: 338–51.

Wesseling, Elisabeth. 2009. "Blacker Than Black: Contextualising the Issue of White Supremacy in Heinrich Hoffmann's 'The Story of the Inky Boys.'" *International Research in Children's Literature* 2, no. 1 (July): 49–64.

Westerfeld, Scott. 2005–7. *Uglies*. New York: Simon Pulse.

Westman, Karin. 2002. "Spectres of Thatcherism: Contemporary British Culture in J.K. Rowling's Harry Potter Series." In *The Ivory Tower and Harry Potter: Perspectives on a Literary Phenomenon*, edited by Lana Whited, 305–28. Columbia: University of Missouri Press.

———. 2007. "Children's Literature and Modernism: The Space Between." *Children's Literature Association Quarterly* 32, no. 4: 283–86.

Wheatle, Alan. 1999. *Brixton Rock*. London: BlackAmber Books.

White, Dorothy. 1954. *Books before Five*. Wellington: New Zealand Council for Educational Research / Whitcombe and Tombs.

White, E. B. 1952. *Charlotte's Web*. Illustrated by Garth Williams. New York: HarperCollins.

Wiesner, David. 2001. *The Three Pigs*. New York: Clarion Books.

Wiggin, Kate Douglas. 1896. *Marm Lisa*. Project Gutenberg. Accessed July 10, 2008. www.gutenberg.org.

Wild, Margaret, and Julie Vivas. 1991. *Let the Celebrations Begin!* London: Bodley Head.

Wilk, Christopher, ed. 2006. *Modernism 1914–1939: Designing a New World*. London: V&A.

Wilkending, Gisela, with Silke Kirch, eds. 2003. *Mädchenlitteratur der Kaiserzeit: Zwischen weiblicher Identifizierung und Grenzüberschreitung*. Stuttgart: Metzler.

Willems, Mo. 2010. *We Are in a Book!* An Elephant & Piggie Book. New York: Hyperion.

Willhoite, Michael. 1990. *Daddy's Roommate*. Boston: Alyson.

Williams, Raymond. 1976. *Keywords: A Vocabulary of Culture and Society*. New York: Oxford University Press.

———. 1983a. *Culture & Society: 1780–1950*. New York: Columbia University Press.

———. 1983b. *Keywords: A Vocabulary of Culture and Society*. Rev. ed. New York: Oxford University Press.

Willingham, Bill. 2002–15. *Fables*. New York: DC/Vertigo.

Willis, Jeanne. 2000. *Susan Laughs*. Illustrated by Tony Ross. New York: Henry Holt.

Wimsatt, W. K., and Monroe C. Beardsley. (1954) 1970. "The Affective Fallacy." In *The Verbal Icon: Studies in the Meaning of Poetry*, by W. K. Wimsatt, 3–18. London: Methuen.

Winner, Ellen. 1988. *The Point of Words: Children's Understanding of Metaphor and Irony*. Cambridge, MA: Harvard University Press.

Winsnes, Hanna. 1852. *Aftenerne paa Egelund*. Christiania: Wulfsberg.

Wittlinger, Ellen. 2007. *Parrotfish*. New York: Simon & Schuster.

Wolf, Doris. 2017. "Changing Minds and Hearts: Felt Theory and the Carceral Child in Indigenous Canadian Residential School Picture Books." In *Affect, Emotion, and Children's Literature: Representation and Socialisation in Texts for Children and Young Adults*, edited by Kristine Moruzi, Michelle J. Smith, and Elizabeth Bullen, 146–58. New York: Routledge.

Wolf, Werner. 2005. "Intermediality." In *Routledge Encyclopedia of Narrative Theory*, edited by David Herman, Manfred Jahn, and Marie-Laure Ryan, 252–56. New York: Routledge.

WoMANtís RANDom. 2016. *Gummiband-Familien / Rubberband Families*. Berlin: Worte und Meer.

Woodson, Jacqueline. 2003. "Who Can Tell My Story?" In *Stories Matter: The Complexity of Cultural Authenticity in*

Children's Literature, edited by Dana L. Fox and Kathy G. Short, 41–45. Urbana, IL: National Council of Teachers of English.

———. 2014. *Brown Girl Dreaming*. New York: Penguin.

Woolf, Virginia. (1939) 1985. "A Sketch of the Past." In *Moments of Being*. 2nd ed., edited by Jeanne Schulkind, 61–159. New York: Harcourt Brace Jovanovich.

Woollvin, Bethan. 2017. *Rapunzel*. London: Pan Macmillan.

Wordsworth, William. (1802) 1983. "TO A YOUNG LADY, Who had been reproached for taking long Walks in the Country." In *Poems, in Two Volumes, and Other Poems, 1800–1807*, edited by Jared Curtis, 231. Ithaca, NY: Cornell University Press.

———. (1805) 1997. *The Five Book Prelude*. Edited by Duncan Wu. Oxford: Blackwell.

———. (1807) 1983. "Ode: Intimations of Immortality from Recollections of Early Childhood." In *Poems, in Two Volumes, and Other Poems, 1800–1807*, edited by Jared Curtis, 269–77. Ithaca, NY: Cornell University Press.

———. (1850) 1979. *The Prelude*. In *The Prelude 1799, 1805, 1850*, edited by Jonathan Wordsworth, M. H. Abrams, and Stephen Gill. New York: Norton.

Wulf, Andrea. 2015. *The Invention of Nature: The Adventures of Alexander von Humboldt, the Lost Hero of Science*. London: John Murray.

Wyile, Andrea Schwenke. 1999. "Expanding the View of First-Person Narration." *Children's Literature in Education* 30, no. 3: 185–202.

Xie, Shaobo. 2000. "Rethinking the Identity of Cultural Otherness: The Discourse of Difference as an Unfinished Project." In *Voices of the Other: Children's Literature and the Postcolonial Context*, edited by R. McGillis, 1–13. New York: Routledge.

Yang, Hongying. 2008. *Ma Xiaotiao* series, English translations comprising *Four Troublemakers, Teacher's Pet, Pesky Monkeys, Best Mom Ever, Best Friends, Super Cool Uncle, Pet Parade*, and *Class Genius*. New York: HarperCollins.

———. 2010. *Jia Xiaozi Dai An* [Tomboy Dai An]. Beijing: Zuojia chubanshe.

Yanping, Liao. 2006. *El hilo rojo: Cuento popular chino*. Barcelona: Maguregui Ediciones.

Yee, Paul. 1989. *Tales from Gold Mountain*. Toronto: Groundwood.

Yenika-Agbaw, Vivian. 2008. *Representing Africa in Children's Literature: Old and New Ways of Seeing*. New York: Routledge.

———. 2013. "Black Cinderella: Multicultural Literature and School Curriculum." *Pedagogy, Culture & Society* 22, no. 2: 233–50.

Yik, Michelle. 2010. "How Unique Is Chinese Emotion?" In *The Oxford Handbook of Chinese Psychology*, edited by Michael Harris Bond, 205–20. Oxford: Oxford University Press.

Yokota, Junko. 1993. "Issues in Selecting Multicultural Children's Literature." *Language Arts* 70, no. 3: 156–67.

———. 2009. "Asian Americans in Literature for Children and Young Adults." *Teacher Librarian* 36, no. 3: 15–19.

Yolen, Jane. 1990. *The Devil's Arithmetic*. New York: Puffin Books.

Yoon, Jung Mo. 2008. *The Season of Balsamina*. Paju: Purunnamu.

Yousafzai, Malala, and Patricia McCormick. 2014. *I Am Malala: How One Girl Stood Up for Education and Changed the World*. New York: Little, Brown.

Yuan, Mingming. 2016. "Translating Gender in Children's Literature in China during the 1920s: A Case Study of Peter Pan." *International Journal of Comparative Literature and Translation Studies* 4, no. 3: 26–31.

Yun, Kouga. 2006. *Loveless*. Vol. 1. Translated by Ray Yoshimoto. Los Angeles: TokyoPop.

Zevin, Gabrielle. 2012. *All These Things I've Done*. New York: Square Fish.

Zipes, Jack. 2001. *Sticks and Stones: The Troublesome Success of Children's Literature from Slovenly Peter to Harry Potter*. New York: Routledge.

———. 2002. *Breaking the Magic Spell: Radical Theories of Folk and Fairy Tales*. Rev. ed. Lexington: University of Kentucky Press.

———. 2006. "Fairy Tales and Folk Tales." In *The Oxford Encyclopedia of Children's Literature*, vol. 2, edited by Jack Zipes, 45–54. Oxford: Oxford University Press.

———. 2012. *The Irresistible Fairy Tale: The Cultural and Social History of a Genre*. Princeton, NJ: Princeton University Press.

Zipes, Jack, Lissa Paul, Lynne Vallone, Peter Hunt, and Gillian Avery, eds. 2005. *The Norton Anthology of Children's Literature: The Traditions in English*. New York: Norton.

Zolkover, Adam. 2008. "Corporealizing Fairy Tales: The Body, the Bawdy, and the Carnivalesque in the Comic Book *Fables*." *Marvels and Tales* 22, no 1: 38–51.

Zuidervaart, Lambert. 1991. *Adorno's Aesthetic Theory: The Redemption of Illusion*. Cambridge, MA: MIT Press.

Zunshine, Lisa. 2001. *Why We Read Fiction: Theory of Mind and the Novel*. Columbus: Ohio State University Press.

About the Contributors

Evelyn Arizpe is Professor of Children's Literature at the University of Glasgow and Leader of the Erasmus Mundus Joint Master's Degree program, Children's Literature, Media and Culture. She is the co-author (with Morag Styles) of *Children Reading Picturebooks: Interpreting Visual Texts* (2003/2016) and *Visual Journeys through Wordless Narratives* (2014; with Carmen Martínez-Roldán and Teresa Colomer). She is the co-editor of *Children as Readers in Children's Literature: The Power of Text and the Importance of Reading* (2016) and *Young People Reading: Empirical Research across International Contexts* (2018). Her current research is on "Children's Literature in Critical Contexts of Displacement: Exploring How Story and Arts-Based Practices Create 'Safe Spaces' for Displaced Children and Young People."

Deirdre Baker is Assistant Professor of English Literature at the University of Toronto, where she teaches children's literature. She reviews and writes regularly for the *Horn Book Magazine* and has published various articles on children's literature; she has been the children's book reviewer for the *Toronto Star* since 1998. She is the author of the children's novel *Becca at Sea* (2007) and *Becca Fair and Foul* (2018). She is the co-author with Ken Setterington of *A Guide to Canadian Children's Books* (2005).

Clémentine Beauvais is Senior Lecturer in English in Education at the University of York. She has worked on children's literature theory and the history and cultural sociology of child giftedness and is now working on literary translation in education, looking at the uses of literary translation in the classroom for purposes of language learning and literary education. She is the author of *The Mighty Child: Time and Power in Children's Literature* (2015) and the co-editor, with Maria Nikolajeva, of *The Edinburgh Companion to Children's Literature* (2017). She is also a writer and a literary translator of children's and young adult literature.

Sandra L. Beckett is Professor Emeritus at Brock University, where she taught in the Department of Modern Languages, Literatures and Cultures. She is a member of the Royal Society of Canada, a Chevalier in the Order of the Palmes Académiques and in the Order of La Pléiade, and a former president of the International Research Society for Children's Literature. Her most recent books include *Revisioning Red Riding Hood around the World: An Anthology of International Retellings* (2014), *Crossover Picturebooks: A Genre for All Ages* (2012), and *Crossover Fiction: Global and Historical Perspectives* (2009). Her current projects include a book on the contemporary illustration of *Alice's Adventures in Wonderland*.

Robin Bernstein is the author of *Racial Innocence: Performing American Childhood from Slavery to Civil Rights* (2011), which won five book awards, including prizes from the Children's Literature Association, the Society for the History of Children and Youth, and the International Research Society for Children's Literature. She is Dillon Professor of American History and Professor of African and African American Studies and of Studies of Women, Gender, and Sexuality at Harvard University.

Colleen Glenney Boggs is Professor of English at Dartmouth College. She is the author of *Transnationalism and American Literature: Literary Translation, 1773–1892* (2007), *Animalia Americana: Animal Representations and Biopolitical Subjectivity* (2013), and *Patriotism by Proxy: The Civil War Draft and the Cultural Formation of Citizen-Soldiers, 1863–1865* (2020) and the editor of *MLA Options for Teaching the Literatures of the American Civil War* (2016). She is the recipient of fellowships from the Mellon Foundation, the American Philosophical Society, and the National Endowment for the Humanities.

Clare Bradford is Emeritus Professor at Deakin University. Her books include *Reading Race: Aboriginality in Australian Children's Literature* (2001), which won the Children's Literature Association Book Award and the International Research Society Book Award; *Unsettling Narratives: Postcolonial Readings of Children's Literature* (2007); *New World Orders in Contemporary Children's Literature: Utopian Transformations* (2009; with Mallan, Stephens, and McCallum); and *The Middle Ages in Children's Literature* (2015), which won the Children's Literature Association Book Award.

Mike Cadden is Professor of English and Director of Childhood Studies at Missouri Western State University, where he teaches courses in children's and young adult literature. He is the author of *Ursula K. Le Guin beyond Genre* (2005) and editor of *Telling Children's Stories: Narrative Theory and Children's Literature* (2010). He is also one of the editors of *Teaching Young Adult Literature* (2020), a volume in MLA's Teaching Options series.

Katharine Capshaw is Professor of English and Affiliate in Africana Studies at the University of Connecticut. She is the co-editor of *Who Writes for Black Children? African American Children's Literature before 1900* (2017) and the author of *Civil Rights Childhood: Picturing Liberation in African American Photobooks* (2014) and *Children's Literature of the Harlem Renaissance* (2004). She is working on a book on black children's theater of the 1970s.

Nina Christensen is Professor in Children's Literature and Head of the Centre for Children's Literature and Media at Aarhus University. She is the author of three books on children's literature (in Danish) and a number of articles, especially on picture books, the history of children's literature, and children's literature and concepts of childhood. Recent articles in English include "Follow the Child, Follow the Book" (2017; with Charlotte Appel) and "Picturebooks and Representations of Childhood" (2018).

Beverly Lyon Clark is Professor of English and Women's and Gender Studies at Wheaton College. She is the author of *Kiddie Lit: The Cultural Construction of Children's Literature in America* (2003) and *The Afterlife of "Little Women"* (2014), and she has edited or co-edited works by or about Louisa May Alcott, Mark Twain, Flannery O'Connor, Carson McCullers, and Evelyn Sharp.

Karen Coats is Professor in the Faculty of Education and Director of the Centre for Research in Children's Literature at the University of Cambridge. Her most recent books include *The Bloomsbury Introduction to Children's and Young Adult Literature* (2017) and, with Mike Cadden and Roberta Seelinger Trites, the co-edited volume *Teaching Young Adult Literature* (forthcoming).

Hugh Crago is an independent scholar and practicing psychotherapist who has also taught literature, life-span human development, and counseling at several universities in Australia. He is the author of eight books, including *Prelude to Literacy* (1983; with Maureen Crago) and

Entranced by Story (2014). In preparation are *The Landscape of Wonder* and *Self and Story in the Preschool Years*.

Patricia Crain is Professor of English at New York University and the author of *The Story of A: The Alphabetization of America from* The New England Primer *to* The Scarlet Letter (2000) and *Reading Children: Literacy, Property, and the Dilemmas of Nineteenth-Century Childhood* (2016). Her recent work explores the emergence of child readers as galvanizing cultural and literary figures in the nineteenth century, the genealogy of the key cultural concept of literacy in the late nineteenth century, and the related (historical and current) moral panics concerning children and reading.

Sarah Park Dahlen is Associate Professor in the Master of Library and Information Science Program at St. Catherine University and a member of the American Library Association, Children's Literature Association, International Research Society for Children's Literature, and the Association for Asian American Studies. She cofounded and co-edits *Research on Diversity in Youth Literature* (2017–), co-edited *Children's Literature Association Quarterly*'s special issue on orphanhood and adoption in children's literature (2015), and co-edited the book *Diversity in Youth Literature: Opening Doors through Reading* (2013).

Ute Dettmar is Professor of Children's Literature at the Institut für Jugendbuchforschung (Department for Children's and Young Adult Literature Research) at Goethe University in Frankfurt, Germany. Dettmar's research is mainly on children's literature, seriality and transmedia storytelling, and popular culture. She is cofounder and co-editor of Metzler Verlag's book series Studien zu Kinder- und Jugendliteratur und -medien (Studies on Children's Literature and Media). Her major publications include *Das Drama der Familienkindheit. Der Anteil des Kinderschauspiels am Familiendrama des 18. und 19. Jahrhunderts* (2002); *Spielarten der Populärkultur. Kinder- und Jugendliteratur und -medien im Feld des Populären*, edited with Ingrid Tomkowiak (2018); and *Märchen im Medienwechsel. Zur Geschichte und Gegenwart des Märchenfilms*, edited with Claudia Pecher and Ron Schlesinger (2018).

Debra Dudek is Associate Professor in the English Program at Edith Cowan University. Debra is on the executive board of the International Research Society for Children's Literature and on the editorial board of *Bookbird: A Journal of International Children's Literature*. She is the author of *The Beloved Does Not Bite: Moral Vampires and the Humans Who Love Them* (2017). Her essays have appeared in *Children's Literature Association Quarterly*, *Papers*, *Jeunesse*, *Children's Literature in Education*, *Ariel*, *Canadian Review of Comparative Literature*, *Seriality and Young People's Texts* (2014), and *Affect, Emotion, and Children's Literature: Representation and Socialisation in Texts for Children and Young Adults* (2017).

Richard Flynn is Professor of English at Georgia Southern University. Recent work on Marilyn Nelson and Jaqueline Woodson appears in *Lion and the Unicorn*, and he has an essay titled "Elizabeth Bishop's Sanity: Childhood Trauma, Psychoanalysis, and Sentimentality" in *Elizabeth Bishop and the Literary Archive* (2020), edited by Bethany Hicok.

Marah Gubar is Associate Professor of Literature at MIT and the author of *Artful Dodgers: Reconceiving the Golden Age of Children's Literature* (2009). Her essays on youth literature and culture have appeared in journals such as *PMLA*, *American Quarterly*, and *Children's Literature* and in venues such as *Public Books* and the *Los Angeles Review of Books*.

Kelly Hager is Professor of English and Women's and Gender Studies at Simmons University, where she teaches Victorian literature, children's literature, and the history of feminism. She is the author of *Dickens and the Rise of Divorce* (2010) and co-edited, with Talia Schaffer, a special issue of *Victorian Review*: "Extending Families." Her work has appeared in *The Blackwell Encyclopedia of Victorian Literature, BRANCH: Britain, Representation and Nineteenth-Century History, The Oxford Handbook of Children's Literature, Victorian Literature and Culture, Children's Literature Association Quarterly*, and *ELH*.

Naomi Hamer is Assistant Professor in the Department of English at Ryerson University. Her current research and publications examine the cross-media adaptation of children's literature with a focus on picture books, mobile apps, and children's museums. She is the co-editor of *More Words about Pictures: Current Research on Picture Books and Visual/Verbal Texts for Young People* (2017; with Nodelman and Reimer) and *The Routledge Companion of Fairy-Tale Cultures and Media* (2018; with Greenhill, Rudy, and Bosc). Her current research project ("Curating the Story Museum: Transmedia Practices, Participatory Exhibits, and Youth Citizenship") has been awarded a SSHRC Insight Development Grant.

Charles Hatfield is Associate Professor of English at California State University, Northridge, and the author of *Alternative Comics* (2005) and *Hand of Fire: The Comics Art of Jack Kirby* (2011), co-editor of *The Superhero Reader* (2013) and *Comic Studies: A Guidebook* (2020), and curator of *Comic Book Apocalypse: The Graphic World of Jack Kirby* (2015). His essays have appeared in myriad books and periodicals. He has chaired the International Comic Arts Forum and the MLA Forum on Comics and Graphic Narratives and cofounded the Comics Studies Society.

Michael Heyman is Professor of English at Berklee College of Music. His scholarship has appeared in the *Children's Literature Association Quarterly*; the *Horn Book Magazine*; *Lion and the Unicorn*, where he was also a four-time judge for the *Lion and the Unicorn* Award for Excellence in North American Poetry; and IBBY's *Bookbird*, where he was a guest editor for the nonsense literature special issue (2015). He is the head editor of *The Tenth Rasa: An Anthology of Indian Nonsense* (2007). His poems and stories for children can be found in *The Puffin Book of Bedtime Stories* (2005), *The Moustache Maharishi and Other Unlikely Stories* (2007), *This Book Makes No Sense: Nonsense Poems and Worse* (2012), and *Poetry International* (2019).

Peter Hollindale is Former Reader in English and Educational Studies at the University of York. His publications include *Ideology and the Children's Book* (1988), *Signs of Childness in Children's Books* (1997), and editions of both the prose and dramatic texts of *Peter Pan*.

Peter Hunt is Professor Emeritus in English and Children's Literature at Cardiff University. He has lectured on children's literature at over 160 universities in twenty-three countries and is the author or editor of around thirty-five books and over five hundred other publications on the subject. His latest books are *Children's Literature: 50 Frequently Asked Questions* (2019) and *The Making of the 'Alice' Books* (2020). In 2003, he was awarded the Brothers Grimm Award for services to children's literature from the International Institute for Children's Literature.

Zoe Jaques is the author of *Children's Literature and the Posthuman* (2015) and co-author of *Lewis Carroll's* Alice's Adventures in Wonderland *and* Through the Looking-Glass: *A Publishing History* (2013). She is also one of the general editors of the forthcoming *Cambridge History of Children's Literature in English* (2022). She has received research fellowships from the Houghton Library at Harvard University, the Baldwin Library at the University of Florida, Kent State University, and the Harry Ransom Center, University of Texas at Austin.

Stine Liv Johansen is Associate Professor at the Centre for Children's Literature and Media at Aarhus University. She studies children's media use in different contexts, most recently practices related to children's use of YouTube. She is the head of the Danish Media Council for Children and Youth.

Vanessa Joosen is Associate Professor of English Literature and Children's Literature at the University of Antwerp. Her publications include the monographs *Critical and Creative Perspectives on Fairy Tales* (2011) and *Adulthood in Children's Literature* (2018) and the edited volumes *Grimm's Tales around the Globe* (2014; with Gillian Lathey) and *Connecting Childhood and Old Age in Popular Media* (2018).

Michael Joseph is the editor of *Gravesiana: The Journal of the Robert Graves Society*. Recent publications include "'Like Snow in a Dark Night': Exile and Displacement in the Poetics of Robert Graves" in *Book 2.0* (2018) and "The Winding Road to *Illo Tempore*: Fairy Tale Poems" in *The Companion to Fairy-Tale Cultures and Media* (2018). He is the author of several illustrated books for children, including *The Real Story of Puss in Boots* (2007), *La Nouvelle Chatte, or The New White Cat* (2013), and *Puss in Boots on Mars* (2017). From 1998 to 2020, he was the Rare Books Librarian at Rutgers University.

Louise Joy is Vice-Principal of Homerton College, Cambridge, where she is Fellow and Director of Studies in English. She is the author of *Eighteenth-Century Literary Affections* (2020) and *Literature's Children: The Critical Child and the Art of Idealization* (2019). She has co-edited two volumes of essays: *Poetry and Childhood* (2010) and *The Aesthetics of Children's Poetry: A Study of Children's Verse in English* (2018). With Eugene Giddens and Zoe Jaques, she is co-editing the first two volumes of *The Cambridge History of Children's Literature* (2022).

Kenneth Kidd is Professor of English at the University of Florida and the author of *Theory for Beginners, or Children's Literature Otherwise* (2020), *Freud in Oz* (2011), and *Making American Boys* (2004). He is a co-editor of *Queer as Camp: Essays in Summer, Style, and Sexuality* (2019), *Prizing Children's Literature: The Cultural Politics of Children's Book Awards* (2017), *Over the Rainbow* (2004), and *Wild Things* (2004). He is also the co-editor of the third volume of *Cambridge History of Children's Literature*, now in preparation, and with Elizabeth Marshall, he co-edits Routledge's Children's Literature and Culture series, the oldest-running monograph series in the field.

Lydia Kokkola works at the University of Oulu, where her main responsibilities involve educating future teachers of English. Her most recent publications concern adolescents reading in English as a foreign language. In the past, she has worked on Holocaust fiction for youth and fictional portrayals of adolescent sexuality. Together with Roxanne Harde, she has edited several issues of *Bookbird*, a volume on Pollyanna, and most recently, the IRSCL award-winning collection *The Embodied Child* (2017). Together with Sara van den Bossche, she has edited a special issue of the *Children's Literature Association Quarterly* (2019) on cognitive approaches to children's literature and is currently working on a special issue of *Barnboken* on diversity in the Nordic countries.

Bettina Kümmerling-Meibauer is Professor in the German Department at the University of Tübingen. She had been a guest professor at the University of Växjö/Kalmar, Sweden, and the University of Vienna, Austria. Her recent publications include *Maps and Mapping in Children's Literature* (2017; co-edited with Nina Goga), *Canon Constitution and Canon Change in Children's Literature* (2017; co-edited with Anja Müller), and *The Routledge Companion to Picturebooks* (2018).

JonArno Lawson, a writer who has published many books for children and adults, received the Lion and the Unicorn Award for Excellence in North American Poetry four times. Paradoxically, he is probably best known for his wordless picture book *Sidewalk Flowers* (2015). More recent publications are *Leap!* (2017), *But It's So Silly: A Cross-Cultural Collage of Nonsense, Play, and Poetry* (2017), *Over the Rooftops Under the Moon* (2019), *The Playgrounds of Babel* (2019), and *Over the Shop* (2021). He lives in Toronto, Ontario, with his wife and three children.

Kerry Mallan is Emeritus Professor at Queensland University of Technology, Australia. She is the author and co-editor of several books on children's literature, including: *Gender Dilemmas in Children's Fiction, Secrets, Lies and Children's Fiction*, and *Contemporary Children's Literature and Film* (co-edited with Clare Bradford). She co-authored *New World Orders in Contemporary Children's Literature: Utopian Transformations* (with Clare Bradford, John Stephens & Robyn McCallum).

Nicole Markotić is Professor of English at the University of Windsor. She teaches creative writing, children's literature, and disability studies. She has published a YA novel, *Rough Patch* (2017); four books of poetry; two novels; and a critical book, *Disability in Film and Literature* (2016). She is currently completing a poetry book and doing research on representations of disability in children's literature.

Elizabeth Marshall is Associate Professor of Education at Simon Fraser University. She is the co-editor of *Rethinking Popular Culture and Media* (2016), author of *Graphic Girlhoods: Visualizing Education and Violence* (2018), and co-author of *Witnessing Girlhood: Toward an Intersectional Tradition of Life Writing* (2019).

Michelle Martin is the Beverly Cleary Endowed Professor for Children and Youth Services in the Information School at the University of Washington, where she teaches graduate courses in children's and young adult literature and youth services. She is the author of *Brown Gold: Milestones of African-American Children's Picture Books, 1845–2002* (2004) and *Sexual Pedagogies: Sex Education in Britain, Australia, and America, 1879–2000* (co-edited with Claudia Nelson, 2004). With Dr. Rachelle D. Washington, she is the founder and codirector of Camp Read-a-Rama, a day camp for children ages four through eleven that uses children's books as the springboard for all other camp activities.

Derritt Mason is Associate Professor of English at the University of Calgary. He is the author of *The Queer Anxieties of Young Adult Literature and Culture* (2020) and the co-editor, with Kenneth B. Kidd, of *Queer as Camp: Essays on Summer, Style, and Sexuality* (2019).

B. J. McDaniel is the author of the picture book *Hands Up!* (2019; illustrated by Shane W. Evans). She is also a third-year PhD researcher at the University of Cambridge, where her research is focused on readers' responses to the depiction of black children as food in contemporary picture books. To encourage broader representation of children from diverse backgrounds, she organized a conference in Glasgow in August 2019 for REIYL (Researchers Exploring Inclusive Youth Literature), an initiative she cofounded with colleague Joshua Simpson.

Cathryn M. Mercier chairs the Department of Children's Literature and is the graduate program director of the MA in Children's Literature and MFA in Writing for Children in the Gwen Ifill College of Media, Arts, and Humanities at Simmons University. She contributed to *Teaching Young Adult Literature* (2020) and co-authored three biocritical studies of prominent authors. She has served and chaired on many book award committees, including Caldecott, Newbery, Sibert, Boston Globe Horn–Book Award, and the Legacy Award.

William Moebius is Professor Emeritus and former Program Director of Comparative Literature at the University of Massachusetts Amherst. His publications include poetry in *Elegies and Odes* (1969) and elsewhere, translations of Philodemus (*Greek Anthology*, 1973) and of Sophocles's *Oedipus at Colonus* (*Anthology of Greek Tragedy*, 1972), and book chapters in French and English on the picture book.

Philip Nel is University Distinguished Professor of English at Kansas State University. He is the author or co-editor of twelve other books. The most recent are *Was the Cat in the Hat Black? The Hidden Racism of Children's Literature, and the Need for Diverse Books* (2017), four volumes of Crockett Johnson's *Barnaby* (2013, 2014, 2016, 2020; co-edited with Eric Reynolds), and a double biography of Crockett Johnson and Ruth Krauss (2012).

Claudia Nelson recently retired from Texas A&M University, where she was Professor of English and Claudius M. Easley Jr. Faculty Fellow of Liberal Arts. Her most recent book, co-authored with Anne Morey, is *Topologies of the*

Classical World in Children's Fiction: Palimpsests, Maps, and Fractals (2019); she is the author of five previous books and the co-editor of five collections of essays or source documents.

Åse Marie Ommundsen is Professor of Scandinavian Literature at the Faculty of Education and International Studies, Oslo Metropolitan University, and part-time Professor at Nord University. She has published books and articles and given talks on challenging picture books and picture books for adults in Norwegian, Danish, English, French, and Dutch. Recent publications include "Picturebooks for Adults" in *The Routledge Companion to Picturebooks* (2018) and "Competent Children: Childhood in Nordic Children's Literature from 1850 to 1960" in *Nordic Childhoods 1700–1960: From Folk Beliefs to Pippi Longstocking* (2018). In 2013, Ommundsen was awarded the Kari Skjønsberg Award for her research on children's literature.

Emer O'Sullivan is Professor of English Literature at Leuphana Universität Lüneburg and has published widely in German and English on image studies, children's literature, and translation. *Kinderliterarische Komparatistik* (2000) won the IRSCL Award for outstanding research in 2001, and *Comparative Children's Literature* (Routledge 2005) won the Children's Literature Association 2007 Book Award. With Andrea Immel, she co-edited *Imagining Sameness and Difference in Children's Literature* (2017). She is currently working on an updated and expanded edition of *Historical Dictionary of Children's Literature* (forthcoming).

Lissa Paul is Professor at Brock University and has authored or edited seven books and has chapters in another twenty. She is an associate general editor of *The Norton Anthology of Children's Literature* (2005), and her monograph, *The Children's Book Business: Lessons from the Long Eighteenth Century* was the "starter" book for her current work on Eliza Fenwick. Her research is funded by the Social Sciences and Humanities Research Council of Canada, and her new monograph is *Eliza Fenwick: Early Modern Feminist* (2019). Current projects include an edition of Fenwick's letters.

Jacqueline Reid-Walsh is Associate Professor of Curriculum and Instruction and of Women's, Gender, and Sexuality Studies at the Pennsylvania State University. Her work combines archival research with children's literature studies, book studies, juvenilia studies, and girlhood studies. She examines overlooked books in different formats, especially those with movable components. Major publications include her *Interactive Books: Playful Media before Pop-Ups* (2017) and the following, all cowritten with Claudia A. Mitchell: *Girl Culture: An Encyclopedia* (2008), *Seven Going on Seventeen: Tween Studies in the Culture of Girlhood* (2005), and *Researching Children's Popular Culture: The Cultural Spaces of Childhood* (2002).

Mavis Reimer is Dean of Graduate Studies and Professor of English at the University of Winnipeg, where she also directs the Partnership Project, Six Seasons of the *Asiniskaw Īthiniwak*: Reclamation, Regeneration, and Reconciliation. She is co-author, with Perry Nodelman, of the third edition of *The Pleasures of Children's Literature* (2003), editor and co-editor of five collections of scholarly essays, and author and co-author of many scholarly essays on a range of topics in young people's texts and cultures. She was lead editor of the journal *Jeunesse: Young People, Texts, Cultures* between 2009 and 2015.

Kimberley Reynolds is Professor of Children's Literature in the School of English Literature, Language and Linguistics at Newcastle University. In 2013, she received the International Brothers Grimm Award for Research into Children's Literature. She conceived and was the first director of the National Centre for Research in Children's Literature and was involved in founding the UK's Children's Laureate and setting up Seven Stories, the National Centre for Children's Books. She is a past president and honorary fellow of the International Research Society for Children's Literature. Recent book-length publications include *Reading and Rebellion: An Anthology of Radical Writing for Children, 1900–1960* (2018; co-edited with Jane Rosen and Michael Rosen), *Left Out: The Forgotten Tradition of Radical Publishing for Children in Britain, 1910–1949* (2016), and *Children's Literature* in the Oxford University Press series of Very Short Introductions (2012).

Karen Sánchez-Eppler is L. Stanton Williams 1941 Professor of American Studies and English at Amherst College. The author of *Touching Liberty: Abolition, Feminism and the Politics of the Body* (1993) and *Dependent States: The Child's Part in Nineteenth-Century American Culture* (2005), she is currently working on two book projects: *The Unpublished Republic: Manuscript Cultures of the Mid-Nineteenth-Century US* and *In the Archives of Childhood: Playing with the Past* as well as co-editing, with Cristanne Miller, *The Oxford Handbook of Emily Dickinson*. She is one of the founding co-editors of the *Journal of the History of Childhood and Youth* and a past president of C19: The Society of Nineteenth-Century Americanists.

Kevin Shortsleeve is Associate Professor of English at Christopher Newport University, where he teaches courses on children's literature and creative writing. He has published academic studies on Dr. Seuss, Edward Gorey, Walt Disney, literary nonsense, and other subjects. He is also the author of several books for children, including *Thirteen Monsters Who Should Be Avoided* (1998).

Niigaanwewidam James Sinclair is Anishinaabe (St. Peter's / Little Peguis) and Associate Professor at the University of Manitoba. He is an award-winning writer, editor, and activist who won the 2018 Canadian Columnist of the Year at the National Newspaper Awards for his biweekly columns in the *Winnipeg Free Press*. He also won Peace Educator of the Year from Georgetown University's Peace and Justice Studies Association. He is the co-editor of the award-winning *Manitowapow: Aboriginal Writings from the Land of Water* (2011), *Centering Anishinaabeg Studies: Understanding the World through Stories* (2013) and *The Winter We Danced: The Past, the Future and the Idle No More Movement* (2014).

Victoria Ford Smith is Associate Professor of English at the University of Connecticut, where she teaches children's, young adult, and British literature and culture. Her research focuses primarily on child agency and child-produced texts, children's art and visual culture, and literature and culture of the fin de siècle. She is the author of *Between Generations: Intergenerational Collaboration in the Golden Age of Children's Literature* (2017) and articles in *Dickens Studies Annual*, *Children's Literature Association Quarterly*, and *Children's Literature*.

Anna Stemmann is Senior Lecturer for the Field of Children's and Young Adult Literature at University of Bremen. Her publications include *Räume der Adoleszenz: Deutschsprachige Jugendliteratur der Gegenwart in topographischer Perspektive* (2019), "Erzählte Nerdkultur: Selbstreferenzielles Spiel mit dem (populär)kulturellen Archiv" in *Spielarten der Populärkultur: Kinder- und Jugendliteratur und -medien im Feld des Populären* (2019),

and "Märchenspuren in Springfield: *Die Simpsons und das parodistische Spiel mit dem Erzählfundus*" in *Märchen im Medienwechsel. Zur Geschichte und Gegenwart des Märchenfilms* (2017).

Ebony Elizabeth Thomas is Associate Professor in the Literacy, Culture, and International Educational Division at the University of Pennsylvania's Graduate School of Education. A former Detroit Public Schools teacher and National Academy of Education / Spencer Foundation Postdoctoral Fellow, she is an expert on diversity in children's literature, youth media, and fan studies. Thomas is the author of *The Dark Fantastic: Race and the Imagination from Harry Potter to the Hunger Games* (2019) and co-editor of *Reading African American Experiences in the Obama Era: Theory, Advocacy, Activism* (2012).

Joseph T. Thomas Jr. is Professor of English and Comparative Literature at San Diego State University, where he serves as Director of the National Center for the Study of Children's Literature. With Kenneth Kidd, Thomas co-edited *Prizing Children's Literature: The Cultural Politics of Children's Book Awards* (2016). He has published two books, *Poetry's Playground: The Culture of Contemporary American Children's Poetry* (2007) and *Strong Measures* (2007). Thomas has also published and lectured widely on Shel Silverstein and has completed a monograph exploring Silverstein's life and work. This monograph, called *Shel Silverstein, the Devil's Favorite Pet*, rests, unpublishable, on his hard drive.

Eric L. Tribunella is Professor of English at the University of Southern Mississippi, where he teaches children's and young adult literature. He is the author of *Melancholia and Maturation: The Use of Trauma in American Children's Literature* (2010), co-author of *Reading Children's Literature: A Critical Introduction* (2013/2019), editor of

Edward Prime-Stevenson's *Left to Themselves* (2016), and co-editor of *The de Grummond Primer* (2020).

Lynne Vallone is Professor of Childhood Studies at Rutgers University–Camden. Her most recent book is *Big and Small: A Cultural History of Extraordinary Bodies* (2018).

Elisabeth (Lies) Wesseling is Professor in the Department of Literature and Art at Maastricht University, where she is Director of the Centre for Gender and Diversity of the Faculty of Arts and Social Sciences. Her scholarship focuses on the cultural construction of childhood in narrative fiction (children's literature, the novel, film) and science (science-based child rearing advice, developmental psychology, anthropology) from 1850 to 2000.

Boel Westin is Professor Emeritus of Literature at Stockholm University, Department of Culture and Aesthetics, where she was Chair of Children's Literature from 1998 to 2018. Her major publications include *Familjen i dalen. Tove Janssons muminvärld* (1988), *Children's Literature in Sweden* (1991), *Strindberg, sagan och skriften* (1998), *Tove Jansson: Life, Art, Words; The Authorized Biography* (2014), and *Letters from Tove* (2019; co-edited with Helen Svensson). She is Chief Editor of a new history of Swedish children's literature (2021). She is also Chair of the Jury for the Astrid Lindgren Memorial Award.

Karin E. Westman is Associate Professor and Department Head of English at Kansas State University, where she also teaches and conducts research on twentieth- and twenty-first-century British literature, including children's and young adult literatures and women's literature. Her next book will be *Harry Potter in Context: J. K. Rowling's Library*. With Naomi Wood and David Russell, she has served as the co-editor of *Lion and the Unicorn* since 2008.